BIRDS OF ALBERTA

Chris Fisher
John Acorn

The Publisher: Lone Pine Publishing

10145 – 81 Avenue   1808 B Street NW, Suite 140
Edmonton, Alberta   Auburn, WA 98001
Canada T6E 1W9
Website: www.lonepinepublishing.com

Canadian Cataloguing in Publication Data

Fisher, Chris C. (Christopher Charles)
    Birds of Alberta

    Includes bibliographical references and index.
    ISBN 1-55105-173-7

    1. Birds—Alberta—Identification. I. Bird-watching—Alberta. I. Acorn
John Harrison, 1958- II. Title.
    QL685.5.A86F57 1998   598'.097123   C98-910445-1

Senior Editor: Nancy Foulds

Project Editor: Roland Lines

Production Manager: David Dodge

Design and Layout: Rob Weidemann

Cover Design: Rob Weidemann

Cover Illustration: Gary Ross

Illustrations: Gary Ross, Ted Nordhagen, Ewa Pluciennik, Horst Krause

Maps: Pat Marklevitz, Volker Bodegom, Greg Brown, Rob Weidemann

Separations and Film: Elite Lithographers Co., Edmonton, Alberta

Printing: Kromar Printing Ltd., Winnipeg, Manitoba

The publisher gratefully acknowledges the assistance of the Department of Canadian Heritage.

CONTENTS

ACKNOWLEDGEMENTS

The following individuals were of great help to us during the writing of this book, and their contributions are much appreciated: Nancy Baron, Jim and Barb Beck, Jim Butler, Gord Court, Ross Dickson, Jocelyn Hudon, Carole Patterson, Michael Quinn, Isabelle Richardson, Brian Ritchie, Dena Stockburger, Lisa Takats and Terry Thormin. The book owes its final form to discussions with Shane Kennedy, Nancy Foulds and Roland Lines at Lone Pine Publishing. The distribution maps are the work of Pat Marklevitz (with the help of Jack Clements, Jack Park, Brian Ritchie, Richard Thomas and Terry Thormin), and we appreciate greatly his time and effort on this project. Bushnell Sports Optics kindly allowed us to field-test their birding binoculars and scopes. Finally, we are grateful for the superb illustrations by Gary Ross and Ted Nordhagen, and we feel privileged to have their artwork appear alongside our words.

Red-throated Loon
size 65 cm • p. 34

Pacific Loon
size 66 cm • p. 35

Common Loon
size 80 cm • p. 36

Yellow-billed Loon
size 83 cm • p. 37

Pied-billed Grebe
size 34 cm • p. 38

Horned Grebe
size 34 cm • p. 39

Red-necked Grebe
size 50 cm • p. 40

Eared Grebe
size 33 cm • p. 41

Western Grebe
size 56 cm • p. 42

Clark's Grebe
size 55 cm • p. 43

American White Pelican
size 158 cm • p. 44

Double-crested Cormorant
size 74 cm • p. 45

American Bittern
size 64 cm • p. 46

Great Blue Heron
size 132 cm • p. 47

Great Egret
size 99 cm • p. 48

Snowy Egret
size 61 cm • p. 49

Cattle Egret
size 51 cm • p. 50

Black-crowned Night-Heron
size 62 cm • p. 51

White-faced Ibis
size 57 cm • p. 52

Turkey Vulture
size 74 cm • p. 53

Greater White-fronted Goose • size 77 cm • p. 54

Snow Goose
size 78 cm • p. 55

Ross's Goose
size 60 cm • p. 56

Canada Goose
size 89 cm • p. 57

Brant
size 65 cm • p. 58

Trumpeter Swan
size 167 cm • p. 59

Tundra Swan
size 133 cm • p. 60

5

WATERFOWL

Wood Duck
size 46 cm • p. 61

Gadwall
size 51 cm • p. 62

Eurasian Wigeon
size 47 cm • p. 63

American Wigeon
size 52 cm • p. 64

American Black Duck
size 57 cm • p. 65

Mallard
size 61 cm • p. 66

Blue-winged Teal
size 39 cm • p. 67

Cinnamon Teal
size 41 cm • p. 68

Northern Shoveler
size 49 cm • p. 69

Northern Pintail
size 62 cm • p. 70

Green-winged Teal
size 36 cm • p. 71

Canvasback
size 52 cm • p. 72

Redhead
size 51 cm • p. 73

Ring-necked Duck
size 41 cm • p. 74

Greater Scaup
size 45 cm • p. 75

Lesser Scaup
size 42 cm • p. 76

Harlequin Duck
size 42 cm • p. 77

Surf Scoter
size 48 cm • p. 78

White-winged Scoter
size 55 cm • p. 79

Black Scoter
size 48 cm • p. 80

Oldsquaw
size 47 cm • p. 81

Bufflehead
size 36 cm • p. 82

Common Goldeneye
46 cm • p. 83

Barrow's Goldeneye
size 46 cm • p. 84

Hooded Merganser
size 45 cm • p. 85

Red-breasted Merganser
size 57 cm • p. 86

Common Merganser
size 63 cm • p. 87

Ruddy Duck
size 40 cm • p. 88

Osprey
size 60 cm • p. 89

Bald Eagle
size 93 cm • p. 90

Northern Harrier
size 51 cm • p. 91

Sharp-shinned Hawk
size 31 cm • p. 92

Cooper's Hawk
size 44 cm • p. 93

Northern Goshawk
size 59 cm • p. 94

Broad-winged Hawk
size 42 cm • p. 95

Swainson's Hawk
size 52 cm • p. 96

Red-tailed Hawk
size 55 cm • p. 97

Ferruginous Hawk
size 63 cm • p. 98

Rough-legged Hawk
size 55 cm • p. 99

Golden Eagle
size 89 cm • p. 100

American Kestrel
size 20 cm • p. 101

Merlin
size 28 cm • p. 102

Prairie Falcon
size 41 cm • p. 103

Peregrine Falcon
size 44 cm • p. 104

Gyrfalcon
size 57 cm • p. 105

Gray Partridge
size 32 cm • p. 106

Ring-necked Pheasant
size 72 cm • p. 107

Ruffed Grouse
size 43 cm • p. 108

Sage Grouse
size 66 cm • p. 109

Spruce Grouse
size 37 cm • p. 110

GROUSE-LIKE BIRDS

RAILS, COOTS & CRANES

SHOREBIRDS

Blue Grouse
size 49 cm • p. 111

Willow Ptarmigan
size 35 cm • p. 112

White-tailed Ptarmigan
size 34 cm • p. 113

Sharp-tailed Grouse
size 45 cm • p. 114

Wild Turkey
size 109 cm • p. 115

Yellow Rail
size 18 cm • p. 116

Virginia Rail
size 26 cm • p. 117

Sora
size 23 cm • p. 118

American Coot
size 37 cm • p. 119

Sandhill Crane
size 115 cm • p. 120

Whooping Crane
size 140 cm • p. 121

Black-bellied Plover
size 31 cm • p. 122

American Golden-Plover
size 32 cm • p. 123

Semipalmated Plover
size 18 cm • p. 124

Piping Plover
size 19 cm • p. 125

Killdeer
size 26 cm • p. 126

Mountain Plover
size 22 cm • p. 127

Black-necked Stilt
size 37 cm • p. 128

American Avocet
size 45 cm • p. 129

Greater Yellowlegs
size 36 cm • p. 130

Lesser Yellowlegs
size 27 cm • p. 131

Solitary Sandpiper
size 21 cm • p. 132

Willet
size 39 cm • p. 133

Spotted Sandpiper
size 19 cm • p. 134

Upland Sandpiper
size 30 cm • p. 135

Eskimo Curlew
size 33 cm • p. 136

Whimbrel
size 42 cm • p. 137

Long-billed Curlew
size 59 cm • p. 138

Hudsonian Godwit
size 38 cm • p. 139

Marbled Godwit
size 46 cm • p. 140

REFERENCE GUIDE

Ruddy Turnstone
size 24 cm • p. 141

Red Knot
size 27 cm • p. 142

Sanderling
size 20 cm • p. 143

Semipalmated Sandpiper
size 16 cm • p. 144

Western Sandpiper
size 17 cm • p. 145

Least Sandpiper
size 15 cm • p. 146

White-rumped Sandpiper
size 19 cm • p. 147

Baird's Sandpiper
size 19 cm • p. 148

Pectoral Sandpiper
size 23 cm • p. 149

Sharp-tailed Sandpiper
size 22 cm • p. 150

Dunlin
size 21 cm • p. 151

Stilt Sandpiper
size 22 cm • p. 152

Buff-breasted Sandpiper
size 20 cm • p. 153

Ruff/Reeve
size 26 cm • p. 154

Short-billed Dowitcher
size 29 cm • p. 155

Long-billed Dowitcher
size 30 cm • p. 156

Common Snipe
size 28 cm • p. 157

Wilson's Phalarope
size 23 cm • p. 158

Red-necked Phalarope
size 18 cm • p. 159

Red Phalarope
size 21 cm • p. 160

JAEGERS, GULLS & TERNS

Parasitic Jaeger
size 49 cm • p. 161

Long-tailed Jaeger
size 54 cm • p. 162

Franklin's Gull
size 36 cm • p. 163

Bonaparte's Gull
size 33 cm • p. 164

Mew Gull
size 39 cm • p. 165

Ring-billed Gull
size 49 cm • p. 166

California Gull
size 49 cm • p. 167

Herring Gull
size 62 cm • p. 168

Thayer's Gull
size 59 cm • p. 169

9

Glaucous-winged Gull
size 64 cm • p. 170

Glaucous Gull
size 70 cm • p. 171

Sabine's Gull
size 34 cm • p. 172

Caspian Tern
size 53 cm • p. 173

Common Tern
size 37 cm • p. 174

Arctic Tern
size 39 cm • p. 175

Forster's Tern
size 39 cm • p. 176

Black Tern
size 24 cm • p. 177

Rock Dove
size 32 cm • p. 178

Band-tailed Pigeon
size 36 cm • p. 179

Mourning Dove
size 31 cm • p. 180

Black-billed Cuckoo
size 30 cm • p. 181

Eastern Screech-Owl
size 22 cm • p. 182

Great Horned Owl
size 55 cm • p. 183

Snowy Owl
size 60 cm • p. 184

Northern Hawk Owl
size 41 cm • p. 185

Northern Pygmy-Owl
size 18 cm • p. 186

Burrowing Owl
size 22 cm • p. 187

Barred Owl
size 52 cm • p. 188

Great Gray Owl
size 73 cm • p. 189

Long-eared Owl
size 37 cm • p. 190

Short-eared Owl
size 38 cm • p. 191

Boreal Owl
size 27 cm • p. 192

Northern Saw-whet Owl
size 21 cm • p. 193

Common Nighthawk
size 24 cm • p. 194

Common Poorwill
size 21 cm • p. 195

Black Swift
size 18 cm • p. 196

Vaux's Swift
size 13 cm • p. 197

Ruby-throated Hummingbird
size 9 cm • p. 198

Black-chinned Hummingbird
size 8 cm • p. 199

Calliope Hummingbird
size 8 cm • p. 200

Rufous Hummingbird
size 9 cm • p. 201

Belted Kingfisher
size 32 cm • p. 202

Lewis's Woodpecker
size 28 cm • p. 203

Red-headed Woodpecker
size 21 cm • p. 204

Yellow-bellied Sapsucker
size 19 cm • p. 205

Red-naped Sapsucker
size 22 cm • p. 206

Downy Woodpecker
size 17 cm • p. 207

Hairy Woodpecker
size 22 cm • p. 208

Three-toed Woodpecker
size 23 cm • p. 209

Black-backed Woodpecker
size 24 cm • p. 210

Northern Flicker
size 33 cm • p. 211

Pileated Woodpecker
size 45 cm • p. 212

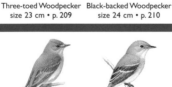

Olive-sided Flycatcher
size 19 cm • p. 214

Western Wood-Pewee
size 14 cm • p. 215

Yellow-bellied Flycatcher
size 14 cm • p. 216

Alder Flycatcher
size 16 cm • p. 217

Willow Flycatcher
size 15 cm • p. 218

Least Flycatcher
size 14 cm • p. 219

Hammond's Flycatcher
size 14 cm • p. 220

Dusky Flycatcher
size 14 cm • p. 221

Cordilleran Flycatcher
size 14 cm • p. 222

Eastern Phoebe
size 18 cm • p. 223

FLYCATCHERS

Say's Phoebe	Great Crested Flycatcher	Western Kingbird	Eastern Kingbird
size 19 cm • p. 224	size 19 cm • p. 225	size 22 cm • p. 226	size 22 cm • p. 227

SHRIKES & VIREOS

Northern Shrike	Loggerhead Shrike	Blue-headed Vireo	Cassin's Vireo	Warbling Vireo
size 25 cm • p. 228	size 23 cm • p. 229	size 14 cm • p. 230	size 14 cm • p. 231	size 14 cm • p. 232

Philadelphia Vireo	Red-eyed Vireo	Gray Jay	Steller's Jay	Blue Jay
size 13 cm • p. 233	size 15 cm • p. 234	size 29 cm • p. 235	size 29 cm • p. 236	size 28 cm • p. 237

JAYS & CROWS

Clark's Nutcracker	Black-billed Magpie	American Crow	Common Raven
size 32 cm • p. 238	size 51 cm • p. 239	size 48 cm • p. 240	size 61 cm • p. 241

LARKS & SWALLOWS

Horned Lark	Purple Martin	Tree Swallow	Violet-green Swallow
size 18 cm • p. 242	size 19 cm • p. 243	size 14 cm • p. 244	size 13 cm • p. 245

Northern Rough-winged Swallow • size 14 cm • p. 246	Bank Swallow size 13 cm • p. 247	Barn Swallow size 18 cm • p. 248	Cliff Swallow size 14 cm • p. 249

Black-capped Chickadee
size 14 cm • p. 250

Mountain Chickadee
size 13 cm • p. 251

Chestnut-backed
Chickadee
size 12 cm • p. 252

Boreal Chickadee
size 14 cm • p. 253

Red-breasted Nuthatch
size 11 cm • p. 254

White-breasted Nuthatch
size 15 cm • p. 255

Brown Creeper
size 13 cm • p. 256

Rock Wren
size 15 cm • p. 257

House Wren
size 12 cm • p. 258

Winter Wren
size 10 cm • p. 259

Sedge Wren
size 11 cm • p. 260

Marsh Wren
size 13 cm • p. 261

American Dipper
size 19 cm • p. 262

Golden-crowned Kinglet
size 10 cm • p. 263

Ruby-crowned Kinglet
size 10 cm • p. 264

Eastern Bluebird
size 18 cm • p. 265

Western Bluebird
size 18 cm • p. 266

Mountain Bluebird
size 18 cm • p. 267

Townsend's Solitaire
size 22 cm • p. 268

Veery
size 18 cm • p. 269

Gray-cheeked Thrush
size 18 cm • p. 270

Swainson's Thrush
size 18 cm • p. 271

Hermit Thrush
size 18 cm • p. 272

American Robin
size 25 cm • p. 273

Varied Thrush
size 24 cm • p. 274

European Starling
size 22 cm • p. 275

Gray Catbird
size 22 cm • p. 276

Northern Mockingbird
size 25 cm • p. 277

Sage Thrasher
size 22 cm • p. 278

Brown Thrasher
size 29 cm • p. 279

American Pipit	Sprague's Pipit	Bohemian Waxwing	Cedar Waxwing
size 17 cm • p. 280	size 17 cm • p. 281	size 20 cm • p. 282	size 18 cm • p. 283

Tennessee Warbler	Orange-crowned Warbler	Nashville Warbler	Yellow Warbler	Chestnut-sided Warbler
size 12 cm • p. 284	size 13 cm • p. 285	size 12 cm • p. 286	size 13 cm • p. 287	size 12 cm • p. 288

Magnolia Warbler	Cape May Warbler	Black-throated Blue Warbler	Yellow-rumped Warbler	Townsend's Warbler
size 13 cm • p. 289	size 13 cm • p. 290	size 13 cm • p. 291	size 14 cm • p. 292	size 13 cm • p. 293

Black-throated Green Warbler	Blackburnian Warbler	Palm Warbler	Bay-breasted Warbler	Blackpoll Warbler
size 13 cm • p. 294	size 13 cm • p. 295	size 14 cm • p. 296	size 14 cm • p. 297	size 14 cm • p. 298

Black-and-white Warbler	American Redstart	Ovenbird	Northern Waterthrush	Connecticut Warbler
size 13 cm • p. 299	size 13 cm • p. 300	size 15 cm • p. 301	size 14 cm • p. 302	size 13 cm • p. 303

Mourning Warbler	MacGillivray's Warbler	Common Yellowthroat	Wilson's Warbler	Canada Warbler
size 13 cm • p. 304	size 14 cm • p. 305	size 13 cm • p. 306	size 12 cm • p. 307	size 14 cm • p. 308

Yellow-breasted Chat
size 19 cm • p. 309

Western Tanager
size 18 cm • p. 310

Spotted Towhee
size 20 cm • p. 311

American Tree Sparrow
size 16 cm • p. 312

Chipping Sparrow
size 14 cm • p. 313

Clay-colored Sparrow
size 14 cm • p. 314

Brewer's Sparrow
size 14 cm • p. 315

Timberline Sparrow
size 14 cm • p. 316

Vesper Sparrow
size 16 cm • p. 317

Lark Sparrow
size 15 cm • p. 318

Lark Bunting
size 18 cm • p. 319

Savannah Sparrow
size 15 cm • p. 320

Baird's Sparrow
size 14 cm • p. 321

Grasshopper Sparrow
size 12 cm • p. 322

Le Conte's Sparrow
size 12 cm • p. 323

Nelson's Sharp-tailed
Sparrow • size 14 cm • p. 324

Fox Sparrow
size 18 cm • p. 325

Song Sparrow
size 16 cm • p. 326

Lincoln's Sparrow
size 15 cm • p. 327

Swamp Sparrow
size 14 cm • p. 328

White-throated Sparrow
size 18 cm • p. 329

Harris's Sparrow
size 19 cm • p. 330

White-crowned Sparrow
size 16 cm • p. 331

Golden-crowned
Sparrow
size 17 cm • p. 332

Dark-eyed Junco
size 15 cm • p. 333

McCown's Longspur
size 15 cm • p. 334

Lapland Longspur
size 16 cm • p. 335

Smith's Longspur
size 16 cm • p. 336

Chestnut-collared
Longspur
size 15 cm • p. 337

Snow Bunting
size 17 cm • p. 338

SPARROWS, GROSBEAKS & BUNTINGS

Northern Cardinal	Rose-breasted Grosbeak	Black-headed Grosbeak	Lazuli Bunting	Indigo Bunting
size 22 cm • p. 339	size 20 cm • p. 340	size 20 cm • p. 341	size 14 cm • p. 342	size 14 cm • p. 343

BLACKBIRDS & ORIOLES

Bobolink	Red-winged Blackbird	Western Meadowlark	Yellow-headed Blackbird	Rusty Blackbird
size 18 cm • p. 344	size 22 cm • p. 345	size 23 cm • p. 346	size 24 cm • p. 347	size 23 cm • p. 348

Brewer's Blackbird	Common Grackle	Brown-headed Cowbird	Baltimore Oriole	Bullock's Oriole
size 23 cm • p. 349	size 31 cm • p. 350	size 18 cm • p. 351	size 19 cm • p. 352	size 20 cm • p. 353

FINCH-LIKE BIRDS

Gray-crowned Rosy-Finch	Pine Grosbeak	Purple Finch	Cassin's Finch	House Finch
size 16 cm • p. 354	size 23 cm • p. 355	size 14 cm • p. 356	size 16 cm • p. 357	size 14 cm • p. 358

Red Crossbill	White-winged Crossbill	Common Redpoll	Hoary Redpoll
size 16 cm • p. 359	size 16 cm • p. 360	size 14 cm • p. 361	size 14 cm • p. 362

Pine Siskin	American Goldfinch	Evening Grosbeak	House Sparrow
size 12 cm • p. 363	size 13 cm • p. 364	size 20 cm • p. 365	size 16 cm • p. 366

INTRODUCTION

BIRDWATCHING IN ALBERTA

Birdwatching has finally become a 'normal' thing to do in Alberta. Whether you pick up the binoculars just a handful of times this year or head out at every opportunity, you will be joining an ever-increasing group of Albertans who find that the pursuit of birds is one of the simplest and most rewarding means of spending time in the natural world. If you stop by any of the 'classic' birding locations in Alberta, such as Beaverhill Lake east of Edmonton or the Inglewood Bird Sanctuary in Calgary, you will no doubt meet kindred souls.

Red-tailed Hawk

Alberta is a good place to watch birds: not only is it geographically diverse, but it is rich with avian life. Habitats in Alberta are traditionally grouped into biophysical regions, broadly classed as mountains, prairies, aspen parkland, boreal forest and Canadian shield, and each region has its own characteristic birdlife. Of course, within each region there is much local variation in birdlife as well as habitat, but at least this system allows a sort of shorthand for referring to broad parts of the province in a biologically meaningful way.

Alberta also has a long tradition of friendly birdwatching. What we mean by this is that Alberta birders, in general, are willing to help beginners, to share their knowledge and to involve novices in their projects. The most conspicuous example of this welcoming attitude is probably the Christmas Bird Count in Edmonton, which has for many years set the world record for the greatest number of participants. Alberta's geographic position might have had a role in shaping our birding personalities: because we get relatively few vagrants and 'important' rarities here, we are less likely to get caught up in the quasi-ornithological prestige associated with being the person to make such a sighting, and we are more likely to take pleasure from the common and expected birds in our area.

BEGINNING TO LEARN THE BIRDS

Birdwatching, or 'birding,' as some people prefer to call it, is challenging, and getting started might be the hardest part. There are almost 400 species of birds to learn if you want to be able to identify everything you can see throughout Alberta—this book will help you get started. The 'standard' North American field guides will also do the trick, but they can be daunting because they cover so many species over such a wide area. By focusing on Alberta, we hope to help you sort out your personal experiences with birds.

The trick to becoming a competent birder is to know, at a glance, what general sort of bird you are looking at, and then to know what the odds of making such a sighting are. To be able to identify any bird at a glance, you will have to spend more than a few hours with binoculars and a field guide. It could conceivably take a lifetime of careful study.

Red-winged Blackbird

After all, there are only a few birders in Alberta who can identify all of our species with confidence. Almost everyone, however, finds they can get plenty of enjoyment from birding without necessarily 'mastering' it.

To an ornithologist (a biologist who studies birds), the species is the fundamental unit of classification, because the members of a species look the most alike, and they naturally interbreed with one another as well. Likewise, to a bird, the species is probably the only 'real' unit of classification—another bird is either a member of the same species, in which case any number of important relationships might develop, or it is not.

Because the concept of species is so important to biologists, it has become important to birders as well. To most birders, a bird has not been identified unless it has been identified 'to species.' Unfortunately, the boundaries between species are not always clear-cut. Birdwatchers are sometimes frustrated when scientists 'lump' formerly separate species together or 'split' a former species into new, separate species. The fuzziness of some species boundaries makes a consensus on such issues unlikely, and the accepted technical definition of a species is continually being debated, and hopefully refined.

To help make sense of the hundreds of bird species in Alberta, scientifically oriented birdwatchers prefer to group them together according to their evolutionary relationships. In order of increasing comprehensiveness, these groupings are the genus, the family and the order, with many subgroupings in between. The birds are then arranged in a 'standard' order that begins with those species that are, in a general sense, most like the evolutionary ancestors of modern birds, and ends with those species that have been most strongly modified by evolutionary change.

To beginners, this evolutionary order might not initially make much sense, but birdwatchers soon come to know that in all books of this sort, the back half will be devoted to the songbirds (the 'passerines,' as they are formally known), while the front half begins with what could informally be called diving birds, wading birds, waterfowl, shorebirds, birds of prey and chicken-like birds, followed by various birds that look more and more like songbirds (everything from hummingbirds and doves to woodpeckers).

There is no simple way to arrange the diversity of birdlife, because the evolution of birds was not a simple process. One thing, however, is certain: many readers will tell us we should have arranged this book alphabetically. Well, apart from placing similar, closely related birds far from one another in the text, such an approach would soon prove impractical. For example, what if you thought you saw a Merlin, and decided to look it up alphabetically? Would you look under 'M' for 'Merlin,' 'H' for 'hawk' or 'F' for 'falcon'? How about 'P' for its former name, 'Pigeon Hawk'? All four would make sense, and none would be as simple as looking in the birds of prey, about a quarter of the way through the text, where they always are in books like this. There is really only one way to begin learning your birds, and that is to bite the bullet, forget the shortcuts, and take pleasure in the task of actually learning the birds.

Merlin

TECHNIQUES OF BIRDWATCHING

Binoculars

As far as birding equipment goes, you will no doubt want to purchase a pair of binoculars. These can cost anywhere from $50 to $1500, and the choices available are many. Most beginners pay less than $200 for their first pair, and many people are initially drawn to compact binoculars, which are small, lightweight and a good way to begin, if you aren't that fussy about pin-sharp details on distant birds.

If you are interested in the best image for your money, there are a few other things you should know. Binoculars come in two basic types: porro-prism (in which there is a distinct, angular bend in the body of the binoculars) and roof-prism (in which the body is straight). Good-quality porro-prism binoculars are less expensive than good-quality roof-prism binoculars: a first-rate pair of porros will cost about $300 to $400; good roof-prism binoculars, which are often waterproof and nitrogen-filled, can cost $800 or more. Expensive binoculars usually have better optics and are more ruggedly built—they generally stand up far better to torture testing.

Mourning Warbler

Binoculars, in general, are characterized by a two-number code. For example, a compact binocular might be an '8 X 21,' while a larger pair might have '7 X 40' stamped on it. In each case, the first number is the magnification of the binocular, while the second number is the diameter, in millimetres, of the front lenses. Seven-power binoculars are the easiest to hand hold and to find birds with; 10-power binoculars give a shakier but more detailed view. Larger lenses gather more light, so a 40-mm or 50-mm lens will perform much better at dusk than a 20-mm or 30-mm lens, at least at the same magnification. For a beginner, an eight-power, porro-prism binocular with front lenses at least 35 mm in diameter would be a good place to start.

Some binoculars have a wider field of view than others, even if the two-number code is identical, which can be a very important factor as well, because many beginners have trouble finding birds in narrow-view binoculars. A good approach is to lock your gaze on the subject and lift the binoculars right up to your eyes. Don't take your eyes off the bird. Alternately, you can search first for an obvious landmark near the bird (a bright flower or a dead branch, for example) and then find the bird from there.

Buff-breasted Sandpiper

One more word of advice: people can become strongly attached to their own pair of binoculars, no matter how inadequate they might be. When you are birding with other folks, if they don't mind, ask them to let you try their binoculars for comparison. Ask them what they like and don't like about them. Be forewarned, however, that as you come to appreciate good optics, your binocular budget is likely to expand. Once you've decided you really like birding, you'll probably want to invest in a pair of good binoculars.

We have been consistently impressed with the quality of Bushnell binoculars, and Bushnell Sports Optics Worldwide offers a wide variety of models, priced for almost any budget, many of which are well-suited for birding. Their top-of-the-line models are sold under the name Bausch & Lomb, and the 10-power Bausch & Lomb Elites are what we use. When you go binocular shopping, you should also consider doing business with a store that specializes in birdwatching, because the sales people there will know from personal experience which models perform best in the field.

Spotting Scopes and Cameras

A spotting scope (a small telescope) and a tripod can be helpful, especially for viewing distant waterfowl and shorebirds. Most spotting scopes are capable of at least 20-power magnification, making them useful for birds out of binocular range. Some scopes will even allow you to take photographs through them, but you should know right now that the challenges of birdwatching pale in comparison to those encountered during bird photography.

If you are sincerely interested in bird photography, we recommend you purchase a 35-mm single-lens reflex camera with at least a 300-mm, telephoto lens and a good, solid tripod. Talk to a knowledgeable camera salesman, and be prepared to spend a lot of money. Your main challenge will be to obtain photos that are not blurred by camera shake or poor optics. A good bird photo can be well worth the trouble and expense.

Barred Owl

Birding by Ear

At some point, you'll probably want to learn bird songs. The technique of birding by ear is gaining popularity, because listening for birds can be more efficient than trying to see them. When experienced birders do breeding-bird surveys each June, they rely mostly on song recognition, rather than sight.

There are numerous tapes and CDs that can help you learn bird songs, and a portable player with headphones will let you quickly compare a live bird with an identified recording. The old-fashioned way to remember bird songs was to make up an English-language version of the song. We've given you some of the classic renderings in the text that follows, such as *who cooks for you? who cooks for you-all?* for the Barred Owl, as well as some renderings in nonsense syllables, such as *chi-chi-churee* for the Snow Bunting. Some of these phrases work better than others, however, especially because birds often add or delete syllables from their calls, and very few birds pronounce consonants in a recognizable fashion.

WATCHING BIRD BEHAVIOUR

It is often said that systematics—the study of the classification, naming and relationships among living things—is the foundation for the rest of biology. In the same sense, once you can confidently identify birds, you can begin to appreciate their behaviour. Some birders find that simply identifying and listing the birds they see gives them satisfaction, but others would rather pursue particular species in detail and learn about their lives.

Eastern Phoebe

The timing of bird migrations is an easy thing to record, as are details of the feeding behaviour, courtship and nesting of birds. Flocking birds can also provide fascinating opportunities to observe social interactions, especially when individual birds can be recognized.

All of these sorts of observations have their equivalents in the science of bird ecology and bird behaviour, which are in turn part of the overall science of ornithology (the study of birds) which is a subfield of zoology (the study of animals) and biology (the study of life). It is important to remember, however, that birding itself is not a science, even though scientists find the observations of birders useful from time to time. Birding, for most people, is recreation. The least likeable birders in any crowd are the ones who think of themselves as amateur scientists and take on a pseudo-professorial air of self-importance. Our advice is to relax and enjoy the birds instead. One of the best ways to watch bird behaviour is to simply look for a bird-rich spot and sit quietly. The edges of forests or wetlands tend to be particularly productive. If you become part of the scenery, the birds will soon resume their activities.

Barrow's Goldeneye

BIRDING BY HABITAT

A bird's habitat is simply the sort of place in which it normally lives. Some birds prefer the bald prairie, others are found in cattail marshes, and still others in the tops of tall trees. If you pay attention to the habitats of birds, you will find that it is not only easier to find a particular species, but also much easier to identify birds, because they are rarely found outside their usual habitat. If you are birding in the mountains, you can afford to ignore most of the shorebirds; if you are out on a boat, don't worry much about the warblers.

CALLING BIRDS CLOSER

'Pishing' and 'squeaking' are common strategies birdwatchers use to call birds in closer. Pishing simply involves making *psh-psh-psh* sounds through pursed lips; squeaking is done by sucking on the back of your hand. There are also bird squeakers on the market that allow you to make attractive sounds without having to master these techniques. The practice of calling birds closer is rapidly losing favour in more crowded birding localities, because some people believe that the birds are spending more time investigating birdwatchers than attending to the details of their own lives, which could lead to all manner of troubles for the birds.

21

BIRD LISTING

You can list your bird sightings as seriously or as casually as you like, or not at all, but lots of people enjoy keeping lists. When you visit a new area, a list becomes a souvenir of your experiences there. Reviewing it, you can remember all sorts of details that made up your trip. Keeping regular accounts of birds in your home area can also become useful data for researchers, and it is interesting to compare the arrival dates and last sightings of hummingbirds and other seasonal visitors, or to note the first sighting of a new visitor to your area. There are bird list programs available for computers, for those who are so inclined, but many naturalists simply keep records in field notebooks. Waterproof books and waterproof pens are a good idea for rainy-day birding, or you might find that a pocket recorder is all you need in the field, with a dry notebook safe back home. Find a notebook that you like, and personalize it with it field sketches, observations, poetry or what-have-you.

Long-tailed Jaeger

BIRDWATCHING ACTIVITIES

Birdwatching Groups

We recommend that you join in on such activities as Christmas bird counts, birding festivals and the meetings of your local birding or natural history club. Meeting other people with the same interests can make birding even more pleasurable, and there is always something to be learned in those sorts of situations. Bird hotlines can provide up-to-date information on the sightings of rarities, which are often easier to re-locate than you might think. In Edmonton call (403) 433-2473; in Calgary call (403) 237-8821.

If you are interested in bird conservation and environmental issues, natural history groups can keep you informed about the situation in your area and what you can do to help. It is also worth noting that the more birders there are in Alberta, the better it will be for us all. Alberta is a mighty big place, and the more eyes we have scanning it, the more likely we will be to spot rarities, as well as to better understand the status and distribution of the expected species.

Bird Conservation

Alberta is a good place to watch birds, especially when compared to the rest of the world. After all, there are still huge areas of more-or-less natural landscape here, and relatively few people, except in a few concentrated areas, to mess it up. In the long term, development for housing, agriculture and forestry are threatening to make things progressively worse rather than better, but the more people there are that take up nature appreciation in the form of birding, the more friends the environment will have.

Birdwatchers have sometimes been accused of flagrantly spending money in the pursuit of seeing birds but not getting actively involved in conservation. We hope this situation is changing. Many bird enthusiasts support groups like Audubon societies, the Nature Trust and the Nature Conservancy, which help birds through such activities as buying and managing tracts of good habitat.

On a local scale, consider landscaping your own property to provide cover and natural foods for birds. The cumulative affects of such 'nature-scaping' can be significant. Remember, too, that for every bird taken by an ornithologist in North America, to be made into a study specimen, some tens of thousands are killed by free-roaming house cats. House cats are called 'house' cats for a reason.

Bird Feeding

Many people set up a backyard birdfeeder to attract birds to their yard, especially in winter. It is possible to attract specific birds to your yard by choosing the appropriate sort of seed or other food. If you have a feeder, keep it stocked through late spring. The weather might look balmy, but before flowers bloom, seeds develop and insects hatch, birds can find springtime tough to survive. When migratory birds return in early spring, resident birds must compete with them, and after a long winter, the pickings are slim. Extra food supplies at this time of year can be especially helpful.

Birdbaths are also a good way to bring birds to your yard, and it is increasingly popular to provide heated birdbaths during sub-zero weather in winter. Be sure to avoid any designs that have exposed metal parts, however, because wet birds can accidentally freeze to them.

In summer, the favourites of the birdfeeding crowd, the hummingbirds, can be attracted to an appropriate location with a feeder that offers artificial nectar (a simple sugar solution of three to four parts water to one part white sugar).

In general, feeding birds is a good thing. Contrary to popular myths, the birds do not become 'dependent' on feeders and therefore forget to behave naturally. There are many good books out about feeding birds and landscaping your yard to provide natural foods and nest sites.

Nest Boxes

Another popular way to attract birds is to set out nest boxes, especially for wrens, chickadees, bluebirds and swallows. Not all birds will use nest boxes: only species that naturally use tree-hole cavities are comfortable in such confined spaces. It is a sad, but true, fact that the two most common bird species at both feeders and boxes—the House Sparrow and the European Starling—are both non-native. For many people, the destruction of these birds (which admittedly do compete with native species) becomes a ruthless personal vendetta. It is puzzling, however, how anyone with an interest in birds can appreciate and enjoy some species while remorselessly killing others, especially when the 'others' are more-or-less distinct from the rest of our birds and are here to stay beyond any possible doubt.

Tree Swallow

ALBERTA'S TOP BIRDING SITES

There are hundreds of areas in our province where you can go for rewarding birdwatching experiences. The following, easily accessible areas were selected to represent a broad range of birds and habitats. 'Can't miss' birds are included in these accounts, as well as rarities, which should never be discounted.

Writing-on-Stone Provincial Park

The spectacular Milk River valley is most accessible at Writing-on-Stone Provincial Park, where a wide variety of habitats support a wealth of birdlife. Say's Phoebes, Cliff Swallows, Common Nighthawks, Rock Wrens and Prairie Falcons nest among the wind-sculpted sandstone, while down in the cottonwood camping area, Spotted Towhees, Brown Thrashers, Mourning Doves, Gray Catbirds, Yellow-breasted Chats, American Goldfinches and occasionally Black-headed Grosbeaks can be seen.

Some of Alberta's most pristine grasslands, where many rare species occur, lie to the east of the park. Loggerhead Shrikes, Long-billed Curlews, Burrowing Owls, Ferruginous Hawks, Sage Grouse and Mountain Plovers can be seen with luck and persistence. More common species include the Western Meadowlark, Upland Sandpiper, Sprague's Pipit, Swainson's Hawk, Golden Eagle, Chestnut-collared Longspur and various grassland sparrows.

NATIONAL PARKS
1 Wood Buffalo NP
2 Elk Island NP
3 Jasper NP
4 Banff NP
5 Waterton Lakes NP

PROVINCIAL PARKS
6 Aspen Beach PP
7 Beauvais Lake PP
8 Big Hill Springs PP
9 Bow Valley PP
10 Brown-Lowery PP
11 Calling Lake PP
12 Chain Lakes PP
13 Cold Lake PP
14 Crimson Lake PP
15 Cross Lake PP
16 Cypress Hills PP
17 Dinosaur PP
18 Dry Island Buffalo Jump PP
19 Fish Creek PP
20 Gooseberry Lake PP
21 Kinbrook Island PP
22 Lesser Slave Lake PP
23 Long Lake PP
24 Midland PP
25 Miquelon Lakes PP
26 Peter Lougheed PP
27 Rochon Sands PP
28 Saskatoon Island PP
29 Sir Winston Churchill PP
30 Taber PP
31 Thunder Lake PP
32 Vermilion PP
33 Wabamun Lake PP
34 William A. Switzer PP
35 Writing-on-Stone PP
36 Wyndham-Carseland PP

OTHER
37 Kananaskis Country
38 Lakeland Provincial Recreation Area

LAKES & RESERVOIRS
1 Beaverhill Lake
2 Big Lake
3 Birch Lake
4 Bittern Lake
5 Brazeau Reservoir
6 Cavan Lake
7 Chappice Lake
8 Chip Lake
9 Coleman Lake
10 Crow Indian Lake
11 Dickson Dam
12 Dowling Lake
13 Eagle Lake
14 Fincastle Lake
15 Frank Lake
16 Ghost Dam
17 Handhills Lake
18 Hastings Lake
19 Kimiwan Lake
20 Kitsim Reservoir
21 Lake Athabasca
22 Langdon Reservoir
23 Lost Lake
24 Margaret Lake
25 Muriel Lake
26 Namaka Lake
27 Pakowki Lake
28 Scope Lake
29 Seebe Dam
30 Slack Slough
31 Stirling Lake
32 Tilley Reservoir
33 Travers Reservoir
34 Verdigris Lake
35 Whitford Lake

OTHER BIRDING SITES
36 Clifford E. Lee Nature Sanctuary
37 Kininvie Marsh
38 Kootenay Plains
39 Porcupine Hills
40 Sheep River Wildlife Sanctuary
41 Wagner Natural Area
42 Wildcat Hills

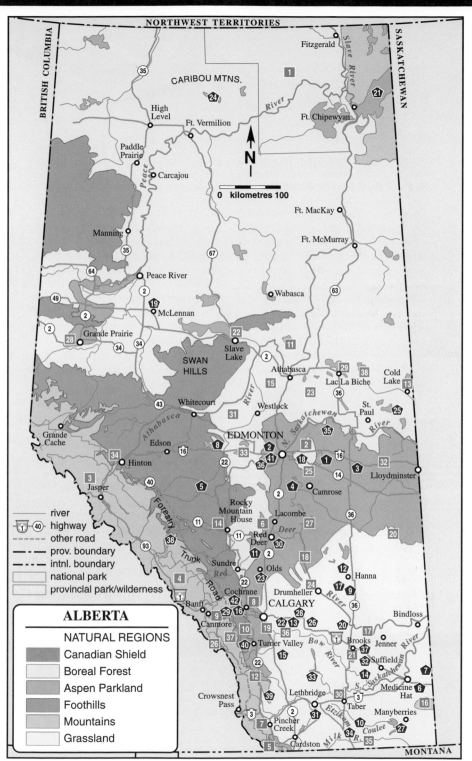

NORTHWEST TERRITORIES

BRITISH COLUMBIA

SASKATCHEWAN

CARIBOU MTNS.

Fitzgerald

Slave River

River

Ft. Chipewyan

High Level

Ft. Vermilion

Paddle Prairie

Carcajou

Peace

N

0 kilometres 100

Ft. MacKay

Manning

Ft. McMurray

Peace River

McLennan

Wabasca

Grande Prairie

SWAN HILLS

Slave Lake

Athabasca

Lac La Biche

Cold Lake

Whitecourt

Westlock

St. Paul

Grande Cache

Edson

EDMONTON

Hinton

Jasper

Rocky Mountain House

Lacombe

Camrose

Lloydminster

Forestry

Red Deer

Red Deer

Sundre

Olds

Hanna

Trunk

Cochrane

Drumheller

Bindloss

Road

Banff

CALGARY

Canmore

Turner Valley

Brooks

Jenner

Bow River

Suffield

Crowsnest Pass

Lethbridge

Medicine Hat

Taber

Manyberries

Pincher Creek

Cardston

MONTANA

ALBERTA

NATURAL REGIONS

- Canadian Shield
- Boreal Forest
- Aspen Parkland
- Foothills
- Mountains
- Grassland

river

highway

other road

prov. boundary

intnl. boundary

national park

provincial park/wilderness

Pakowki Lake

In the heart of the open landscape of southeastern Alberta lies Pakowki Lake, the only large source of water in the region. This lake attracts most of Alberta's species of waterfowl, including such uncommon species as the Cinnamon Teal, along with the Red-winged Blackbird, Yellow-headed Blackbird, American Avocet, Black-necked Stilt and occasionally rarities, such as the Clark's Grebe and the White-faced Ibis.

American Avocet

Cypress Hills Provincial Park

Rising out of the southeastern flatlands, the Cypress Hills are like a displaced Rocky Mountain foothill lost in a sea of grass. There, birds typical of the mountains find themselves isolated in the hills. The 'Aububon's' Yellow-rumped Warbler, 'Oregon' Dark-eyed Junco, MacGillivray's Warbler, Red-naped Sapsucker and Red Crossbill all give a montane character to this area. In addition, the Cypress Hills attract typically northern, boreal forest species, such as the White-crowned Sparrow, Ovenbird, American Redstart, Ruby-crowned Kinglet, Ruffed Grouse and White-winged Scoter. Of course, the grasslands also influence the birdlife in this area, and Mountain Bluebirds, Western Meadowlarks and Swainson's Hawks are regularly seen. In a sense, this park allows birdwatchers to tour our whole avian province in a single day. The Cypress Hills also feature species that are not common anywhere else in Alberta, such as the introduced, but now widespread, Wild Turkey, and the infrequently encountered Poorwill.

Red-headed Woodpecker

Police Point Park, Medicine Hat

Police Point Park boasts an enviable list of exceptional species for the province. From time to time, Eastern Screech-Owls, Red-headed Woodpeckers, Lazuli Buntings and Indigo Buntings have been seen in the area. It is always worth asking at the visitor centre about recent sightings, and the staff at the centre are at the heart of the southeastern Alberta bird-watching scene. Other Alberta first records no doubt await, because this area and the nearby Cypress Hills attract vagrants from the south and from the east. At the time of this writing, a possible sighting of a Pinyon Jay in the Cypress Hills is the most exciting prospect.

Dinosaur Provincial Park

A world heritage site, Dinosaur Provincial Park offers bird-watchers unsurpassed, intimate views of some of the summer species associated with the Red Deer River riparian and badlands communities. In the cottonwood trees around the campground alone, you can sit at your picnic table and see Common Nighthawks, Mourning Doves, Eastern Kingbirds, American Kestrels, American Robins, Veerys, American Goldfinches and Least Flycatchers. For those seeking greater adventure, Spotted Towhees, Brown Thrashers, Gray Catbirds, Yellow-breasted Chats and Baltimore Orioles reside in the riparian areas, while Rock Wrens, Say's Phoebes, Prairie Falcons and Lark Sparrows inhabit drier badlands and sagebrush communities.

Kinbrook Island Provincial Park

Lake Newell, south of Brooks, hosts a wide variety of gulls, ducks and grebes, as well as Double-crested Cormorants and American White Pelicans. Kinbrook Island Provincial Park, on a peninsula in the lake, is one of the best areas in the province to see Western Kingbirds and Yellow-headed Blackbirds, while Lark Buntings, Western Meadowlarks, Sprague's Pipits, Horned Larks, Swainson's Hawks and Ferruginous Hawks can be found in the surrounding open grasslands.

Inglewood Bird Sanctuary, Calgary

Several sanctuaries for both birds and people lie along the Bow River as it winds its way through Calgary. The Inglewood Bird Sanctuary provides year-round opportunities to observe familiar and unusual species. From the Bald Eagles overlooking the river and the thousands of Mallards on the open water through the winter, to the dozens of Canada Geese grazing the lawns through the summer, Inglewood provides naturalists intimate insights into Calgary's avian citizens. Other regular visitors include Common Loons, Hooded Mergansers and various warblers and sparrows. Black-billed Magpies, Black-capped Chickadees, Common Mergansers and Great Horned Owls are among the sanctuary's year-round residents.

More serious birders can look for rarities, such as Thayer's Gulls,

Canada Goose

Sabine's Gulls, jaegers, Yellow-billed Loons, Northern Parulas and Blue-gray Gnatcatchers. Call the Calgary Field Naturalists' bird hotline in for recent reports.

Fish Creek Provincial Park

Fish Creek Provincial Park, in southern Calgary, boasts many of the same species found at the Inglewood Bird Sanctuary, along with a rookery of Great Blue Herons. At the east end of the park, it is common to see Great Horned Owls in winter, along with Bald Eagles along the river. In summer, American White Pelicans are a frequent sight. In the past few years a few Gray Jays have begun to frequent the west end of the park, somewhat outside their usual range.

The Mountain Parks

A trip to our world-famous mountain parks can always be heightened by a birding adventure. White-tailed Ptarmigans, Horned Larks, Gray-crowned Rosy-Finches and Golden Eagle are at home in the alpine zone, while Gray Jays, Common Ravens and Clark's Nutcrackers frequent day-use areas, campgrounds and ski resorts. Along the many trails, look for Mountain Chickadees, Dark-eyed Juncos, Fox Sparrows and brilliant Townsend's Warblers, and listen for the haunting notes of the Varied Thrush.

Some birds sneak into Alberta in the mountains by spilling over the Continental Divide: the ranges of the Steller's Jay, the Chestnut-backed Chickadee and the tiny Calliope Hummingbird rarely exceed the borders of the parks. Along the swift-moving streams and rivers, watch for the delightful American Dipper, and, during winter, vigilant Bald Eagles along the open waters.

Calliope Hummingbird

Each of the parks has its bird specialties. In Banff, a hike along the trail to Johnston Canyon will put you in viewing distance of Black Swift nests. (Ask park naturalists where to look before you go.) In Jasper, the most noteworthy species might be the colourful and endangered Harlequin Duck, which nests along the Maligne River and is in conflict with the rafting industry. Kananaskis Country is best known for the now-famous Golden Eagle migration, which is most accessible from the town of Canmore.

Canmore

The town of Canmore offers much for a visiting birdwatcher. Along the river, many species can be seen both on the water and at feeders in riverside yards. Osprey nesting platforms west of the old railway bridge provide superb opportunities to observe these magnificent fish eagles close at hand, and the open waters of Policeman's Creek, right downtown, are the year-round home of hundreds of Mallards, as well as the occasional Belted Kingfisher.

Slack Slough

Just south of Red Deer, on the east side of Highway 2, lies Slack Slough, a wetland preserve with an elevated viewing platform that is ideal for birdwatching. There, a great variety of waterfowl can be seen from spring through fall, while shorebirds congregate on the low islands during migration. Marsh Wrens, Yellow-headed Blackbirds and Tree Swallows all add to the sense of avian abundance. A trip between Edmonton and Calgary just isn't complete without a stop at 'the slough.'

Aspen Beach

Gull Lake, at Aspen Beach, provides a typical look at a shallow parkland lake and its birdlife. Scan the open water with a scope to look for White-winged Scoters, Common Loons and Western Grebes. Thousands of gulls congregate along the shores, providing challenging opportunities to practise their identification. Shorebirds are also abundant, and they often include uncommon species (although the once numerous Piping Plover no longer breeds there). Many songbirds can be found in the willows back from the lake, including Clay-colored Sparrows, Lincoln's Sparrows and Brown Thrashers.

California Gull

Beaverhill Lake

It is not suitable for swimming, fishing or boating, so at Beaverhill Lake, the recreational opportunities are almost entirely for the birds. A Ramsar site (a wetland of international significance), Beaverhill Lake hosts some of the largest and most concentrated migrations of birds in our province. Highlighted by the annual Snow Goose Festival, thousands of visitors to the lake and surrounding area witness tens of thousands of birds, including Snow, Canada, Ross's and Greater White-fronted geese, Sandhill Cranes, most of Alberta's ducks and almost 40 species of shorebirds. Many of the 267 species recorded in the area are rarities, and the lake always has the potential to produce more unusual sightings. The Beaverhill Bird Observatory and the Francis Point viewing blind provide convenient access to birding sites, but the entire area is worth exploring for its surprising diversity.

Willet

Edmonton's River Valley

The many parks that line the North Saskatchewan River in Edmonton provide excellent opportunities to view a variety of birdlife. The ravines and wooded river valley support resident populations of Black-capped Chickadees, nuthatches, Black-billed Magpies and Pileated Woodpeckers. They are joined by over 20 species of warblers and many other songbirds in migration. During winter Bohemian Waxwings, Merlins, Pine Siskins, redpolls and Pine Grosbeaks can routinely be found along the parks and paths.

The river itself attracts gulls, and glassing a sandbar with binoculars will undoubtedly produce rewarding views of the commonly seen Ring-billed Gull, along with California and Franklin's gulls, and occasionally Herring, Thayer's, Bonaparte's and Glaucous gulls. Common Mergansers are frequently seen throughout the warmer months; Mallards and Common Goldeneyes remain during winter on stretches of open water.

Edmonton's river valley also harbours some uncommon species, such as the Three-toed Woodpecker, Northern Saw-whet Owl, Boreal Owl and Northern Goshawk.

Lakeland Country

Undoubtedly, the Lakeland Recreation Area and the provincial parks of Cold Lake, Sir Winston Churchill and Lesser Slave Lake are the best places in the province to be at the end of May, if you're a birder. The mature trees in these parks come alive with over 20 species of wood warblers, which light up the forests like an arcade game—Blackburnian, Cape May, Canada and Bay-breasted warblers are difficult to find elsewhere in the province. Western Tanagers, Yellow-bellied Sapsuckers and Chipping Sparrows add their colour to the spice of these forested parks, and White-throated Sparrows and Swainson's Thrushes sing their trademark boreal rhythms

Bohemian Waxwing

29

late into the night. There are even some uncommon eastern pioneers, such as the Chestnut-sided Warbler, Nashville Warbler and Great Crested Flycatcher.

On the large lakes, Western Grebes sprint, Red-necked Grebes laugh and Common Loons sing their sobering, heart-stopping courtship ballads. American White Pelicans and Double-crested Cormorants roost or nest in the area, and they can be seen fishing on the waters. The lakes in this area are among the last to freeze up, and in late fall, the typical loons, waterfowl, and gulls are joined by some unusual migrants.

Blackburnian Warbler

Peace Country

Among the fertile farm fields of the Peace Country lie several natural areas that attract a wide variety of birds. Trumpeter Swans might be the area's most charismatic species, and Saskatoon Island Provincial Park provides the best views of this endangered species in the province. Many other species of waterfowl can be seen seasonally in the area, including Snow, White-fronted and Canada geese, and migrant shorebirds and waterfowl stage in large concentrations at Kimiwan Lake. The upland forests in the area host the classic boreal mix, as well as uncommon Alberta breeders, such as the Connecticut Warbler and Gray-cheeked Thrush.

Many migrants that move to and from the West Coast follow the Peace River corridor through Alberta. There are also several rarities, because the Peace River allows an easy, low-elevation ride into the province for West Coast species intent on getting lost.

Wood Buffalo National Park

It is difficult to reach, but in a list of this sort, how can you not include the only place in the world where Whooping Cranes now nest? Of course you can't actually see the nesting Whoopers (they're rightfully off limits to tourists) but the Sandhill Cranes, American White Pelicans, Common Loons, accipiters, Spruce Grouse, warblers, Caspian Terns and Peregrine Falcons won't let you leave disappointed. The Peace-Athabasca delta in the park is a Ramsar site (a wetland of international significance), and it hosts shorebirds and the largest concentration of waterfowl in the province.

Spruce Grouse

ABOUT THE SPECIES ACCOUNTS

This book gives detailed accounts of the 332 bird species that have nested or have been confirmed in Alberta at least 10 times. An additional 56 species, which have less than 10 records from Alberta, are briefly mentioned in an appendix to the species accounts. The order of the birds, and their common and scientific names, follow the American Ornithologists' Union's Check-list of North American Birds (6th edition, and its supplements through July 1997).

As well as discussing the identifying features of the birds, each species account also attempts to bring the birds to life by celebrating their various character traits. We often describe a bird's character in human-related terms, because personifying a bird can help us form a connection with it, but these perceived links between human terms and a birds 'personality' should not be mistaken for actual behaviours: our interpretations do not fully realize the complexities of bird behaviour. Rather, we hope that through a playful delivery, the text will inspire the reader without compromising the wildness of the birds.

Northern Flicker

One of the complications to birdwatching is that many species look different in spring and summer than they do in fall and winter—they have what are generally called breeding and non-breeding plumages—and young birds often look quite different from their parents. This book does not try to describe or illustrate all the different plumages of a species; instead, it focuses on the forms that are most commonly seen in our area. All the illustrations are of adult birds.

ID: It is difficult to describe the features of a bird without being able to visualize it, so this section should be used in combination with the illustrations. Where appropriate, the description is subdivided to highlight the differences between male and female birds, breeding and non-breeding birds and immature and adult birds. The description uses as few technical terms as possible in favour of easily understood terms. Bird's don't really have 'jaw lines,' 'ear patches' or 'chins,' but these and other terms are easily understood by all readers, in spite of their scientific inaccuracy.

Size: The size measurement, an average length of the bird's body from bill to tail, is an approximate measurement of the bird as it is seen in nature. The size is generally given as a range for larger birds, because there is variation between individuals. In addition, wingspans are given for some of the larger birds that are often seen in flight.

Status: A general comment, such as common, uncommon or rare, is usually sufficient to describe the trend in a general context. Specific situations are bound to contrast somewhat as migratory pulses and centres of activity tend to concentrate or disperse birds in some situations.

Habitat: The habitats we have listed describe where each species can most commonly be found. In most cases, it is a fairly generalized description, but if a bird is primarily restricted to a specific habitat, it is described more precisely. Birds can turn up in just about any type of habitat (because of the freedom flight gives them), but in most encounters, they will occur in perfectly logical environments.

RANGE MAP SYMBOLS

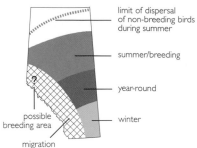

limit of dispersal of non-breeding birds during summer

summer/breeding

year-round

possible breeding area

winter

migration

Nesting: The reproductive strategies used by the different bird species can be very interesting: nest location and structure, clutch size, incubation period and parental duties are among the reproductive aspects that are discussed. Please remember that birdwatching ethics discourage the study of active bird nests. If you disturb a nest, you can drive off the parents during a critical period, and after you have discovered a nest it often becomes exposed to natural predation.

Feeding: Birds are frequently encountered while they are foraging, so a description of their feeding styles and diets can provide valuable identifying characteristics, as well as interesting dietary facts.

Voice: You will hear many birds, particularly songbirds, long before you find them in your binoculars, so a memorable paraphrase of the species's most distinctive sounds can often aid in your identification. These paraphrases are intended to be fun, and they only loosely resemble the call, song or sound produced by the bird. Should one of our paraphases not work for you, make up your own. This rewarding exercise really reinforces the sound in your mind.

Similar Species: Easily confused species are discussed in a brief and concise manner in this section. By concentrating on the most relevant field marks, the subtle differences between species can be reduced to easily identifiable traits. You might find it useful to consult this section when finalizing your identification between a few species; knowing the most relevant field marks will shortcut the identification process.

Best Sites: If you are looking for a particular bird in Alberta, you will have more luck in some places than in others, even within the range shown on the map. We have listed places that, as well as providing a good chance of seeing a species, are easily accessible, which is why so many provincial parks are mentioned.

Western Meadowlark

NON-PASSERINES

Non-passerine birds represent 16 of the 17 orders of birds found in Alberta, but only about 54% of the species. They are grouped together and called 'non-passerines' because, with few exceptions, they are easily distinguished from the passerines, which make up the 17th order and account for nearly half of Alberta's bird species. Being from 16 different orders, however, non-passerines vary considerably in their appearance and habits—they include everything from the 1.5-m-tall Great Blue Heron to the 8-cm-long Calliope Hummingbird.

Mew Gull

Rock Dove

Broad-winged Hawk

Many non-passerines are large, so they are among our most notable birds. Waterfowl, raptors, gulls, shorebirds and woodpeckers are easily identified by most people. Some of the smaller non-passerines, such as doves, swifts and hummingbirds, are frequently thought of as passerines by novice birdwatchers, and they can cause those beginners some identification problems. With a little practice, however, they will become recognizable as non-passerines. By learning to separate the non-passerines from the passerines at a glance, birdwatchers effectively reduce by half the number possible species for an unidentified bird.

Gray Partridge

Whooping Crane

Burrowing Owl

Horned Grebe

RED-THROATED LOON
Gavia stellata

The cool subarctic plateau of the Caribou Mountains stretches the breeding range of Red-throated Loons into northern Alberta. On Margaret Lake, this dainty-bodied loon is a fairly common summer sight. It swims low in the water with its bill held high, as if trying to accentuate its scarlet throat. • The Red-throat is our smallest loon, and it is able to stand upright and to take flight with just a short, quick take-off, which means it can nest on smaller wetlands than its larger relatives. Even so, Red-throats frequently visit large lakes, such as Margaret Lake, to feed. • The Red-throated Loon is supposed to be an excellent meteorologist, becoming very noisy before the onset of foul weather, possibly sensing changes in barometric pressure. • The scientific name *stellata* refers to the star-like, white speckles on this bird's back in its non-breeding plumage.

non-breeding

ID: *Sexes similar:* slim bill, held at an upward angle. *Breeding:* red throat; grey face and neck; black and white stripes from the nape to the back of the head; plain brownish back. *Non-breeding:* back is speckled with white; white face contrasts sharply with dark grey on the crown and the back of the head.

Size: *L* 60–70 cm; *W* 105–111 cm.

Status: locally uncommon during summer; rare in migration.

Habitat: small and large subarctic lakes.

Nesting: on the shorelines of small ponds and wetlands; nest is a mass of aquatic vegetation piled very close to the water's

edge; 2 eggs are incubated by both parents for up to 29 days.

Feeding: dives deeply and captures small fish; occasionally eats aquatic insects and amphibians; might eat aquatic vegetation in early spring.

Voice: Mallard-like *kwuk-kwuk-kwuk-kwuk* in flight; mournful wail during courtship; distraction call is a loud *gayorwork*.

Similar Species: *Common Loon* (p. 36): larger; heavier bill; lacks the white speckling on the back in non-breeding plumage. *Pacific Loon* (p. 35): larger; purple throat and white speckling on the back in breeding plumage; all-dark back in non-breeding plumage.

Best Sites: Margaret Lake; Glenmore Reservoir, Calgary (fall).

PACIFIC LOON
Gavia pacifica

In spring, Pacific Loons shimmer like aluminum on our larger lakes during their stopovers in Alberta. Unfortunately these Arctic breeders move quickly to their summer nesting areas, and there are very few observations of this attractive loon in its breeding plumage. • Spring and fall sightings of the Pacific Loon are equally common, so it appears that this species uses Alberta as a regular travel corridor. The majority of records come from the mountains and the northern half of the province. It is likely, therefore, that birds that winter on the Pacific coast use the low-elevation mountain passes between B.C. and Alberta as they move to and from our province. • There are a couple of breeding records for this species in Alberta, and if nesting does occur regularly, it is likely in the northeast corner of the province or in the Caribou Mountains.

breeding

ID: *Sexes similar. Breeding:* silver-grey crown and nape; black throat is framed by white stripes; white breast; dark back with large, bold, white spots. *Non-breeding:* well-defined light cheek and throat; dark upperparts; dark vent stripe. *In flight:* hunched back; legs trail behind the tail; rapid wingbeats.
Size: *L* 59–73 cm; *W* 103–125 cm.
Status: rare to uncommon migrant in May and October.
Habitat: large, deep lakes.
Nesting: on islands or grassy shorelines of large northern lakes; raised mass of vegetation is used as a nest site; 1 or 2 dark olive eggs with black spots; pair incubates eggs for 28–30 days.

Feeding: dives deeply from the surface for fish and occasionally aquatic invertebrates; dives average 45 seconds; occasionally eats aquatic vegetation.
Voice: calls include a dog-like yelp, a cat-like meow and a raven-like croak.
Similar Species: breeding plumage is distinctive. *Common Loon* (p. 36): larger; lacks the sharp definition between the black and the white on the face and neck and often has a light collar in non-breeding plumage. *Red-throated Loon* (p. 34): carries the bill tilted upward; faint contrast on the face and neck in non-breeding plumage.
Best Sites: Pyramid Lake, Jasper NP; Lake Minnewanka, Banff NP.

35

COMMON LOON
Gavia immer

A classic symbol of northern wilderness, the Common Loon lives in remote, peaceful locales where humanity's impact is easily overlooked. In Alberta, its surreal songs can still be experienced on many of our larger northern lakes. • Loons are well adapted to their aquatic lifestyle: these natural divers have nearly solid bones that give them less buoyancy (most birds have hollow bones), and their feet are placed well back on their bodies for underwater propulsion. • In flight, loons loose some of their grace—with a hunched back, their feet trailing behind the tail and their wings beating continually, they fly quickly and directly from one place to the next. Dignity is regained the instant they descend to the water, however, and land gently on their bellies like miniature float planes. • The word 'loon' might be derived from *lom*, the Scandinavian word for 'clumsy,' referring to this bird's awkwardness on land.

breeding

ID: *Sexes similar. Breeding:* green-black head; stout, thick, black bill; white 'necklace'; white breast and underparts; black-and-white 'checkerboard' upperparts; red eyes.
In flight: long wings beat constantly; hunch-backed appearance; legs trail behind the tail.
Size: *L* 71–89 cm; *W* 120–145 cm.
Status: uncommon to common from May to October.
Habitat: large wetlands and lakes, often those with islands that provide undisturbed shorelines for nesting and with adequate populations of small fish.
Nesting: on a muskrat lodge, small island or projecting shoreline; always very near the water; nest is built from aquatic vegetation; pair shares all parental duties, including nest construction, egg incubation and rearing the young.

Feeding: pursues small fish underwater to depths of 55 m; occasionally eats large, aquatic invertebrates and larval and adult amphibians.
Voice: alarm call is a quavering wail, often called 'loon laughter'; contact call is a long but simple wailing note; intimate calls are soft, short hoots. *Male:* territorial call is an undulating, complex yodel.
Similar Species: *Red-throated Loon* (p. 34): smaller; slender bill; red throat in breeding plumage; white extends from the throat to the chin and ear region in non-breeding plumage. *Pacific Loon* (p. 35): smaller; dusty grey head; most often seen on large lakes in late fall or early spring.
Best Sites: Banff NP; Jasper NP; Lakeland Provincial Recreation Area; large lakes north of Edmonton; Glenmore Reservoir, Calgary (fall).

YELLOW-BILLED LOON
Gavia adamsii

It was the talk of Edmonton in the winter of 1992. A loon had become trapped on the North Saskatchewan River in a stretch of open water that was too small for the bird to take off. After several rescue attempts, the bird was transported to Wabamun Lake. Its identity was only recognized when a visiting birdwatcher from Finland saw a photograph of the loon in a newspaper. • Yellow-billed Loons in non-breeding plumage look extremely similar to Common Loons, and they might be under-reported as a result. • Yellow-bills are the largest loons, and they require long stretches of open water for take-off. • The Yellow-billed Loon nests in the Arctic and northern Europe and Asia. It should be watched for in late fall and winter, when the occasional bird finds itself in the wrong hemisphere as it migrates south from the polar region.

non-breeding

ID: *Sexes similar. Breeding:* pale yellow bill; dark green hood; white collar and breast; large, white spots on the back. *Non-breeding:* yellowish bill; pale brown neck and cheek; more white on the head than in Common Loon.
Size: L 76–89 cm; W 125–140 cm.
Status: rare spring and fall migrant.
Habitat: large lakes and rivers.
Nesting: does not nest in Alberta.

vagrant

Feeding: dives deeply from the surface and captures small fish with its bill; occasionally eats aquatic insects and amphibians; might eat aquatic vegetation in early spring.
Voice: very similar to Common Loon, but it is not vocal while in Alberta.
Similar Species: *Common Loon* (p. 36): lower mandible angles upward less abruptly; upper mandible curves down slightly; nostrils are less feathered.
Best Sites: Cold Lake PP; Inglewood Bird Sanctuary, Calgary; Seebe Dam and Ghost Dam reservoirs.

37

PIED-BILLED GREBE

Podilymbus podiceps

Heard more frequently than seen, the Pied-billed Grebe is the smallest and least colourful of Alberta's grebes. It tends to swim inconspicuously in the shallows of cattail marshes, only occasionally giving voice in an odd chuckle. This sound, which is easy to recognize, might be your only clue that one of these birds is nearby. • Pied-billed Grebes are extremely wary birds, and they are far more common than encounters would lead one to believe. When frightened by an intruder, a Pied-billed Grebe can slowly submerge up to its head, so that only its nostrils and eyes remain above water. • The scientific name *podiceps* means 'rump foot,' in reference to the way the bird's feet are located far back on its body. In flight, the feet extend beyond the tail and help the bird steer.

breeding

ID: *Sexes similar. Breeding:* all-brown body; black ring on the light-coloured bill; bill is flattened side-to-side; black throat; very short tail; white undertail coverts; pale belly; white eye ring; black eyes.
Size: *L* 30–38 cm.
Status: uncommon to common from April to October.
Habitat: ponds, marshes and backwaters with thick emergent vegetation.
Nesting: in thick vegetation along lake edges, ponds and marshes; floating platform nest, made of wet and decaying plants, is anchored to or placed among emergent vegetation;

pair incubates 4 or 5 eggs and raises the striped young together.
Feeding: makes shallow dives and gleans the surface for aquatic invertebrates, small fish, adult and larval amphibians and occasionally aquatic plants.
Voice: loud, whooping call that begins quickly, then slows down: *kuk-kuk-kuk cow cow cow cowp cowp cowp.*
Similar Species: *Eared Grebe* (p. 41): gold ear tufts and chestnut flanks in breeding plumage. *Horned Grebe* (p. 39): gold ear tufts and red neck in breeding plumage. *American Coot* (p. 119): all-black body; often seen on land.
Best Sites: Clifford E. Lee Nature Sanctuary; Kinbrook Island PP.

HORNED GREBE
Podiceps auritus

Cold, mucky wetlands might not seem very inviting, but nothing appeals more to Horned Grebes than a quiet, well-vegetated marsh. Their propensity for these habitats starts early in life, before the birds are born—Horned Grebe eggs often lie in a shallow pool of water on their floating nest. The wet vegetation and tea-coloured water can stain the eggs, improving their camouflage. When an incubating parent is frightened off its nest, it will frequently attempt to cover the eggs with soggy vegetation before leaving them. • Unlike the fully-webbed front toes of most swimming birds, grebes' toes are lobed—the three forward-facing toes have individual flanges that are not connected to the other toes. • This bird's common name and its scientific name, *auritus* (eared), refer to the golden feather tufts that these grebes acquire in breeding plumage.

breeding

ID: *Sexes similar. Breeding:* rufous neck and flanks; black cheek and forehead; golden ear tufts ('horns'); black back; white underparts; red eyes; flat crown. *In flight:* wings beat constantly; hunchbacked appearance; legs trail behind the tail.
Size: L 30–38 cm.
Status: uncommon to common from April to September.
Habitat: never seen on land. *In migration:* wetlands and larger lakes. *Breeding:* shallow, weedy wetlands.
Nesting: usually singly or in groups of 2 or 3 pairs; in thick vegetation along lake edges, ponds, marshes and reservoirs; pair

incubates 4–7 eggs and raises the young together.
Feeding: makes shallow dives and gleans the surface for aquatic insects, crustaceans, mollusks, small fish and adult and larval amphibians.
Voice: loud series of croaks and shrieking notes and a sharp *keark keark* during courtship; usually quiet outside the breeding season.
Similar Species: *Eared Grebe* (p. 41): black neck in breeding plumage. *Pied-billed Grebe* (p. 38): stubbier bill; mostly brown body. *Red-necked Grebe* (p. 40): larger; generally louder; white cheek.
Best Sites: Clifford E. Lee Nature Sanctuary; Kinbrook Island PP.

RED-NECKED GREBE
Podiceps grisegena

As spring evenings settle over Astotin Lake in Elk Island National Park, the enthusiastic laughing calls of courting Red-necked Grebes add a wonderful dimension to the still air as they mix with the songs of robins and the croakings of frogs. Although Red-necked Grebes are not as vocally refined as loons, few can match the verbal vigour of a pair of these birds in peak spring passion. Their wild laughs continue through the nights in late May, in true Alberta 'redneck' fashion.
• All grebes carry their newly hatched young on their backs. The heavily striped young can stay aboard even when the parents dive underwater. • Most of the Red-necked Grebe's breeding range lies in western Canada. • The scientific name *grisegena* means 'grey cheek'—a distinctive field mark of this bird.

breeding

ID: *Sexes similar. Breeding:* reddish neck; whitish cheek; black crown; straight, heavy, yellow bill; black upperparts; light underparts; black eyes. *Non-breeding:* greyish-white throat and cheek.
Size: *L* 43–56 cm.
Status: uncommon to locally common from April to October.
Habitat: *Breeding:* the emergent vegetation zone of lakes and ponds. *In migration:* open, deeper lakes.
Nesting: usually singly; occasionally in loosely scattered colonies; floating platform nest of aquatic vegetation is anchored to submerged plants; eggs are initially white, but often become stained by the wet vegetation.

Feeding: dives and gleans the surface for small fish, aquatic invertebrates and amphibians.
Voice: often-repeated, laugh-like, excited *ah-ooo ah-ooo ah-ooo ah-ah-ah-ah-ah.*
Similar Species: *Horned Grebe* (p. 39): dark cheek. *Eared Grebe* (p. 41): black neck. *Pied-billed Grebe* (p. 38): thicker bill; mostly brown body. *Western Grebe* (p. 42): black upperparts; white underparts. *American Coot* (p. 119): all-black body; often seen on land. *Ducks* (pp. 61–88): all lack the combination of a white cheek and a red neck.
Best Sites: Elk Island NP; Rochon Sands PP; Cold Lake PP; Sir Winston Churchill PP; Vermilion Lakes, Banff NP; Glenmore Reservoir, Calgary (migration).

EARED GREBE
Podiceps nigricollis

Colonies of Eared Grebes fill medium-sized wetlands in Alberta with their minia-ture island nests. The floating platforms cradle pairs of eggs, and when a wave or the wake of a boat hits a colony the nests gently ride the swell. • Like the rest of its clan, the Eared Grebe eats feathers. The feathers often pack the digestive tract, and it is thought that they might protect the stomach lining and intestines from sharp fish bones or parasites, or they might slow the passage of food to give more time for the absorption of nutrients. • Although they are not as dramatic as a pair of Western Grebes, Eared Grebes also dance upon our wetlands during court-ship. • The Eared Grebe is a widely distributed species that occurs in western North America, Europe, Asia, Central Africa and South America. • The scientific name *nigricollis* means 'black neck'—a useful field mark for this species.

breeding

ID: *Sexes similar. Breeding:* black neck, cheek, forehead and back; red flanks; gold ear tufts ('horns'); white underparts; thin, straight bill; red eyes; slightly raised crown. *In flight:* wings beat constantly; hunchbacked appear-ance; legs trail behind the tail.
Size: *L* 30–36 cm.
Status: uncommon to common from April to October.
Habitat: not seen on land. *In migration:* wetlands and larger lakes. *Breeding:* shallow, weedy wetlands.
Nesting: usually colonial; in thick vegetation in lake edges, ponds and marshes; shallow, flimsy,

floating platform nest is made of wet and decaying plants and is anchored to or placed among emergent vegetation; pair incubates the eggs and raises the young.
Feeding: makes shallow dives and gleans the surface for aquatic insects, crustaceans, mollusks, small fish and larval and adult amphibians.
Voice: usually quiet outside the breeding season; mellow *poo-eee-chk* during courtship.
Similar Species: *Horned Grebe* (p. 39): rufous neck. *Pied-billed Grebe* (p. 38): thicker bill; mostly brown body. *Red-necked Grebe* (p. 40): red neck; whitish cheek.
Best Sites: Slack Slough; Kinbrook Island PP.

WESTERN GREBE

Aechmophorus occidentalis

The courtship display of the Western Grebe is one of the most elaborate breeding rituals in the Alberta bird world. These performances can be seen and heard throughout most of May on the province's medium to large wetlands and lakes. During the 'weed dance,' the male and female both raise their torsos gently out of the water, caressing each other with aquatic vegetation held in their long, rapier-like bills. The pair's bond is fully reinforced by the 'rushing' phase, during which the birds glance briefly at one another before exploding into a sprint across the water's surface. Both grebes stand high, feet paddling furiously, with their wings held back and heads and necks rigid, until the race ends with the pair breaking the water's surface in a headfirst dive. • Western Grebes have similar breeding and non-breeding plumages.

ID: *Sexes similar:* long, slender neck; black upperparts from the base of the bill to the tail; white underparts from the chin through the belly; long, thin, yellow bill; white cheek; black on the face extends down to surround the red eyes.

Size: L 51–61 cm.

Status: uncommon from April to October.

Habitat: *Breeding:* large lakes with dense areas of emergent vegetation or thick mats of floating aquatic plants. *In migration:* large, deep lakes.

Nesting: colonial; floating nest is

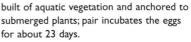

built of aquatic vegetation and anchored to submerged plants; pair incubates the eggs for about 23 days.

Feeding: gleans the water's surface and dives for small fish and aquatic invertebrates.

Voice: high-pitched, frog-like *crreeet-crreeet.*

Similar Species: *Clark's Grebe* (p. 43): eyes are surrounded in white; orange-yellow bill. *Double-crested Cormorant* (p. 45): all-black body. *Common Loon* (p. 36): shorter, stocky neck. *Eared* (p. 41), *Horned* (p. 39) and *Red-necked* (p. 40) *grebes:* much smaller.

Best Sites: Lakeland Provincial Recreation Area; Cold Lake PP; Sir Winston Churchill PP; Crow Indian Lake.

CLARK'S GREBE
Aechmophorus clarkii

If you think you've seen a Western Grebe in Alberta's deep south, look again—Clark's Grebes have been reported on a consistent basis, indicating that a small but reliable number of these birds can breed in our province in favourable years. The Clark's Grebe very closely resembles the more commonly seen Western Grebe, and it is often only with a spotting scope that you can confirm that a particular grebe has 'got a lot of white on its face.' • Ornithologists have yet to work out all the differences between the two species. It was only in 1988 that the Clark's Grebe was elevated to the status of a full species, and physical and behavioural similarities and overlapping ranges make it a challenge to distinguish between Clarks and Westerns. • The Clark's Grebe was named in honour of John Henry Clark, a mathematician, surveyor and bird collector who collected the first scientific specimen near Mexico in 1858.

ID: *Sexes similar:* black upperparts; white underparts; white on the face extends up to surround the red eyes; yellow-orange bill; short tail; long neck.
Size: *L* 52–58 cm.
Status: very rare from April to October.
Habitat: large lakes, marshes and reservoirs with shallow, vegetated margins.
Nesting: often colonial with Western Grebes; nest is a floating mass of vegetation in shallow water; pair incubates 3 or 4 eggs for up to 23 days.
Feeding: surface dives for small fish, aquatic invertebrates and amphibians; often ingests feathers.
Voice: high-pitched, frog-like, prolonged *creeet.*
Similar Species: *Western Grebe* (p. 42): black plumage on the face surrounds the eyes; yellow bill.
Best Sites: Pakowki Lake; Crow Indian Lake; Verdigris Lake.

AMERICAN WHITE PELICAN
Pelecanus erythrorhynchos

Increasingly common in the province, American White Pelicans are often seen skimming low over our larger lakes and prairie rivers, their bellies gliding just over the waves. At other times, these regal birds can be seen high above cities, forests or prairies as they trace rising circles in the warm updrafts. • Groups of foraging pelicans deliberately herd fish into schools, from which the birds dip and scoop the prey with their bills. This communal feeding behaviour reflects the pelicans' highly refined sociability. • To reaffirm a popular myth, the pelican's bill does indeed hold 'more than his belican.' In fact, the pouch can hold up to 12 *l* of water, which must be drained from the sides of the mouth before swallowing the fish. • The scientific name *erythrorhynchos* comes from the Greek words for 'red beak,' although the bill of an American White Pelican in breeding plumage is really orange, not red.

non-breeding

ID: *Sexes similar:* very large, stocky, white bird; long, orange bill and throat pouch; black primary and secondary wing feathers; short tail; naked orange skin patch around the eye. *Breeding:* small, keeled plate develops on the upper mandible; pale yellow crest on the back of the head. *Non-breeding* and *Immature:* white plumage is tinged with brown.
Size: *L* 137–178 cm; *W* 2.8 m.
Status: uncommon to locally common from April to September.
Habitat: *Breeding:* large lakes or rivers.
Nesting: colonial; on bare, low-lying islands; nest scrape is lined with pebbles and debris or is completely unlined; 2 eggs hatch at different times, after approximately 33 days; young are born naked and helpless.
Feeding: surface dips for small fish and amphibians; small groups of pelicans often feed cooperatively by herding fish into large concentrations.
Voice: generally quiet.
Similar Species: *Snow Goose* (p. 55): smaller; much smaller bill. *Tundra Swan* (p. 60) and *Trumpeter Swan* (p. 59): white wing tips; longer, thinner neck.
Best Sites: Sir Winston Churchill PP; Rochon Sands PP; Wyndham-Carseland PP; Kinbrook Island PP; Slave River.

DOUBLE-CRESTED CORMORANT

Phalacrocorax auritus

Double-crested Cormorants are a common sight around many large lakes in Alberta. Whether they are lined up along a gravel bar, perched high on a naked branch or swimming with only their heads breaking the surface, their beauty takes somewhat longer to appreciate than that of many other species. These slick-feathered birds might not appear hygienic and they smell of fish oil, but their mastery of aquatic environments is virtually complete. Double-crested Cormorants lack the ability to waterproof their feathers, which helps them during underwater dives by decreasing their buoyancy, and they are often seen with their wings partially spread, drying their flight feathers. Also aiding the Double-crested Cormorant's aquatic lifestyle are its long, rudder-like tail, its excellent underwater vision and its sealed nostrils. Because these birds cannot breathe through the nose, they can often be identified in flight by their gaping beaks.

breeding

ID: *Sexes similar. Adult:* all-black body; long tail; long neck; thin bill, hooked at the tip; blue eyes. *Breeding:* throat pouch becomes intense orange-yellow; fine, black plumes trail from the eyebrows. *Immature:* brown upperparts; buff throat and breast; yellowish throat patch. *In flight:* rapid wingbeats; kinked neck.

Size: L 66–81 cm; W 132 cm.

Status: uncommon to locally common from April to October.

Habitat: large lakes and large, meandering rivers.

Nesting: colonial; on low-lying islands or precariously high in trees; nest platform is made of

sticks, aquatic vegetation and guano; often nests on islands with pelicans, terns and gulls.

Feeding: long underwater dives of up to 9 m when after small schooling fish or, rarely, amphibians and invertebrates; feeds young by regurgitation.

Voice: generally quiet; occasionally gives piggish grunts or croaks.

Similar Species: *Common Loon* (p. 36): more colourful; shorter neck. *Canada Goose* (p. 57): white cheek; not completely black. *White-winged Scoter* (p. 79) and *Surf Scoter* (p. 78): shorter neck; shorter tail.

Best Sites: Wyndham-Carseland PP; Kinbrook Island PP; Cold Lake PP; Sir Winston Churchill PP; Hastings Lake.

AMERICAN BITTERN
Botaurus lentiginosus

The American Bittern's deep and mysterious booming call is as characteristic of a spring marsh as the sounds of croaking frogs and nighttime showers. Translated into words, it inevitably comes out silly, something like *onk-a-BLONK*, but in person the call makes perfect wetland sense.

• When approached by an intruder, a bittern's first reaction is to freeze—its bill points skyward and its brown vertical streaking blends perfectly with the surroundings. An American Bittern will always face an intruder, and it moves to keep its streaked breast towards the danger, swaying slightly like a cattail in the breeze. Most intruders simply pass by without noticing the bird. An American Bittern will adopt this reed-like position even if it is encountered in an open area. It is apparently unaware that a lack of cover betrays its presence!

ID: *Sexes similar:* brown upperparts; brown streaking from the chin through the breast; straight, stout bill; yellow legs and feet; black outer wings; black streaks from the bill down the neck to the shoulder; short tail.
Size: *L* 59–69 cm; *W* 107 cm.
Status: uncommon from April to October.
Habitat: among tall, dense grasses, bulrushes and cattails in emergent wetlands, lake edges and backwaters.
Nesting: singly; above the waterline in dense vegetation; nest platform is made of grass, sedges and dead reeds; nest often has separate entrance and exit paths.
Feeding: patient stand-and-wait predator; strikes at small fish, amphibians and aquatic invertebrates.

Voice: deep, slow, resonant, repetitive *pomp-er-lunk* or *onk-a-BLONK*; most often heard in the evening or at night.
Similar Species: *Black-crowned Night-Heron* (p. 51): immature lacks the black flight feathers and the black streak from the bill to the shoulder.
Best Site: Beaverhill Lake.

GREAT BLUE HERON
Ardea herodias

The Great Blue Heron is always a memorable sight for Albertans with a passion for the outdoors. Whether they are flushed by a canoe, fishing boat or lakeshore stroll, you can't help but watch as this graceful bird labours into flight and fades from view. • The Great Blue Heron is a patient sentry of the wetlands, where it stands statuesquely surveying the shallow waters for prey. • This heron is often mistaken for a crane, but cranes hold their necks outstretched in flight. • The communal, treetop nests of these birds are sensitive to disturbances. If you discover a colony, it is best to observe the birds' behaviour from a distance. • Anglers occasionally catch a fish with distinctive triangular scars—evidence that it once survived a heron attack. • Great Blue Herons sometimes try to overwinter in our province, but they rarely remain past Christmas.

breeding

ID: *Sexes similar:* large, blue-grey bird; long, curving neck; long, dark legs; blue-grey wing covers and back; straight, yellow bill; chestnut thighs. *Breeding:* colours are more intense; plumes streak from the crown and throat. *In flight:* neck folds back over the shoulders; legs trail behind the body; deep, lazy wingbeats.

Size: L 127–137 cm; W 1.8 m.

Status: common from March to October; a few might overwinter.

Habitat: forages along the edges of rivers, lakes and marshes; also seen in fields and wet meadows.

Nesting: colonial; in a tree; flimsy to elaborate stick and twig platform is added onto, often over years, and can be up to 1.2 m in diameter; pair incubates the eggs for approximately 28 days.

Feeding: patient stand-and-wait predator; strikes at small fish, amphibians, small mammals, aquatic invertebrates and reptiles; occasionally scavenges; occasionally feeds in fields.

Voice: usually quiet away from the nest; occasionally a deep, harsh *frahnk frahnk frahnk* (usually during take-off).

Similar Species: *Black-crowned Night-Heron* (p. 51): much smaller; shorter legs. *Egrets* (pp. 48–50): all are predominantly white. *Sandhill Crane* (p. 120): red cap; flies with its neck outstretched.

Best Sites: Fish Creek PP; Hastings Lake; Carburn Park, Calgary.

GREAT EGRET
Ardea alba

Great Egrets do not regularly breed anywhere near Alberta, but individuals are occasionally spotted in the province during the summer. Almost all of the herons and egrets from the southeastern U.S. disperse widely after breeding, so there are almost as many species on the Alberta checklist as there are in Florida. • The plumes of the Great Egret and the Snowy Egret were widely used to decorate hats in the early 20th century. An ounce of egret feathers cost as much as $32—more than an ounce of gold at that time—and, as a result, egret populations began to disappear. Some of the first conservation legislation in the U.S. was enacted to outlaw the hunting of Great Egrets.

breeding

ID: *Sexes similar:* large, all-white heron; black legs; yellow bill. *Breeding:* white plumes trail from the throat and rump; green patch between the base of the bill and the eyes. *In flight:* head is folded back over the shoulders; legs extend backward.
Size: *L* 94–104 cm; *W* 130 cm.
Status: very rare from May to September.
Habitat: marshes, open riverbanks and lakeshores.

vagrant

Nesting: does not nest in Alberta.
Feeding: patient stand-and-wait predator; occasionally stalks slowly; stabs at almost any small creature it can capture.
Voice: rapid, low-pitched, loud *cuk-cuk-cuk*.
Similar Species: *Snowy Egret* (p. 49): smaller; black bill; yellow feet. *Cattle Egret* (p. 50): smaller; stockier; orange bill and legs.
Best Sites: check local bird hotlines for any recent sightings; Brooks area; Pakowki Lake; Stirling Lake; Glenmore Reservoir, Calgary.

SNOWY EGRET
Egretta thula

The elegant, white plumage and yellow-footed, black legs of the Snowy Egret are rarely seen in Alberta—these birds are vagrants here. Their propensity for post-breeding dispersal is much like that of Great Egrets, but Snowies show up more often in May and June. • Herons and egrets can make use of a variety of feeding techniques, and Snowies use more of these than do our other Alberta species. By poking their bright yellow feet in the muck of shallow wetlands, these birds spook potential prey out of hiding places. In an even more devious hunting strategy, Snowies are known to create shade by extending their wings over open water. When a fish is lured into the shaded spot, it is promptly seized and eaten. Some paleontologists have even suggested that this was the original function of bird wings!

breeding

ID: *Sexes similar. Adult:* snow white plumage; jet-black bill and legs; bright yellow feet. *Breeding:* long plumes on the throat and rump; erect crown; orange-red lore. Immature: similar to adult but with more yellow on the legs. *In flight:* yellow feet are obvious.
Size: L 56–66 cm; W 104 cm.
Status: very rare from May to September.
Habitat: open edges of rivers, lakes and marshes.
Nesting: does not nest in Alberta.

vagrant

Feeding: stirs wetland muck with its feet; stands and waits; occasionally hovers and stabs; eats small fish, amphibians and invertebrates.
Voice: low croaks; bouncy *wulla-wulla-wulla* on breeding grounds.
Similar Species: *Great Egret* (p. 48): larger; yellow bill; black feet. *Cattle Egret* (p. 50): orange-yellow legs and bill.
Best Sites: check local bird hotlines for any recent sightings; Brooks area; Pakowki Lake; Stirling Lake; Glenmore Reservoir, Calgary.

49

CATTLE EGRET
Bubulcus ibis

Over the last century—and without help from humans—the Cattle Egret dispersed from Africa to South America and then North America. The Cattle Egret was first recorded in Alberta in 1964, and although there are no records of it nesting in the province yet, it is being encountered with greater frequency as the decades roll on. • Cattle Egrets are often seen in the company of like-sized gulls while they are in Alberta. Like Franklin's Gulls, these egrets will sometimes follow ploughs, and like Ring-bills they occasionally scavenge at dumps. • Cattle Egrets get their name from their habit of following grazing animals. They catch the insects and other small animals that the ungulates stir up. Unlike other egrets, the diet of this species is made up mostly of invertebrates, and most of their food is terrestrial, not aquatic.

non-breeding

ID: *Sexes similar.* Adult: mostly white; yellow-orange bill and legs. *Breeding:* long plumes on the throat and rump; buff-orange throat, rump, and crown; legs and bill turn orange-red; purple lore. *Immature:* similar to adult, but with black feet.
Size: *L* 48–53 cm; *W* 90–95 cm.
Status: rare from May to September.
Habitat: agricultural fields, ranchlands and marshes.
Nesting: does not nest in Alberta.

vagrant

Feeding: picks grasshoppers, other insects, worms, small vertebrates and spiders from fields; often associated with livestock.
Voice: generally not vocal.
Similar Species: *Great Egret* (p. 48): larger; black legs and feet. *Snowy Egret* (p. 49): black legs; yellow feet. *Gulls* (pp. 163–72): do not stand as erect; grey mantle.
Best Sites: check local bird hotlines for any recent sightings; Brooks area; Pakowki Lake; Stirling Lake.

BLACK-CROWNED NIGHT-HERON
Nycticorax nycticorax

When the setting sun has driven most wetland waders to their nightly roosts, the Black-crowned Night-Herons arrive to haunt these feeding areas and to voice their characteristic squawks. They patrol the shallows for wood frogs and small fish, which they can see in the dim light with their large eyes. • This heron's white 'ponytail' is present for most of the year, but it is most noticeable during the breeding season. • Young night-herons are commonly seen around large cattail marshes in Alberta in fall. Because of their heavy streaking, they are easily confused with American Bitterns. • The Black-crowned Night-Heron is a large-billed bird that can handle sizable prey, and it has even been observed trying to feed on resting flocks of sandpipers. • *Nycticorax*, meaning 'night raven,' refers to this bird's characteristic nighttime call.

breeding

ID: *Sexes similar. Adult:* black cap and back; white cheek and underparts; grey wings; dull yellow legs; stout black bill; large red eyes. *Breeding:* 2 white plumes trail down from the crown. *Immature:* heavily streaked underparts; dull upperparts with light brown spots.
Size: *L* 58–66 cm; *W* 107 cm.
Status: uncommon from April to September.
Habitat: shallow cattail and bulrush marshes, small lakes and slow rivers.
Nesting: colonial; in willows and shrubs; loose nest platform is made of twigs and sticks and lined with finer materials; male gathers the nest material; female constructs the nest.
Feeding: often at dusk; stands motionlessly and waits for prey; stabs for small fish, amphibians, aquatic invertebrates, reptiles, young birds and small mammals.
Voice: deep, guttural *quark* or *wok*, often heard as the bird takes flight.
Similar Species: *Great Blue Heron* (p. 47): much larger; longer legs; back is not black.
Best Sites: Beaverhill Lake; Namaka Lake; Kinbrook Island PP; Kitsim Reservoir.

WHITE-FACED IBIS
Plegadis chihi

If not for Pakowki Lake, the great glorified slough of southern Alberta, it is unlikely that this province could boast of a breeding record for this bird of the Great Plains. It is only in the area of Pakowki, and only on occasion, that White-faced Ibises settle down to nest in Alberta. Most Alberta birdwatchers who have this bird on their lists have seen it elsewhere. • The White-faced Ibis is known for its nomadic behaviour—it searches widely for breeding sites—and its provincial status might change in the future. Wetland restoration projects and periods of high precipitation could encourage more ibises into our province in the years to come. • A trademark of the White-faced Ibis is its heavy, sickle-shaped bill, which it uses so effectively in foraging. *Plegadis* is Greek for 'sickle-shaped.'

breeding

ID: *Sexes similar:* dark chestnut plumage; long, downcurved bill; long, dark legs; white feathers bordering a naked facial patch; greenish lower back and wing covers; dark red eyes. *Breeding:* rich red legs and facial patch. *In flight:* outstretched neck; long, downcurved bill.
Size: L 48–66 cm; W 91 cm.
Status: very rare from May to September.
Habitat: cattail and bulrush marshes, mudflats, brackish wetlands and freshwater marshes.
Nesting: colonial; in bulrushes or other emergent vegetation; deep cup nest is made of coarse materials and lined with fine plant matter; 3 or 4 bluish-green eggs.
Feeding: probes mudflats and gleans the ground for aquatic invertebrates, amphibians and other small vertebrates.
Voice: generally quiet; occasionally gives a series of low, duck-like quacks.
Similar Species: *Long-billed Curlew* (p. 138): light brown overall; daintier bill. *Herons and egrets* (pp. 46–51): all lack the thick, downcurved bill.
Best Sites: Pakowki Lake; Etzikom Coulee; Frank Lake; Stirling Lake.

TURKEY VULTURE
Cathartes aura

Turkey Vultures are unmatched in Alberta at using updrafts and thermals—they tease lift and patrol the skies even when many other soaring birds are grounded. • The head of a Turkey Vulture is naked; as a result, the putrescence they encounter while digging in rotting carcasses is less able to soil their plumage. Vultures eat carrion almost exclusively, and their bills and feet are not as powerful as those of hawks and falcons, which kill live prey. • Vultures are renowned for their ability to regurgitate their meals, which allows parents to transport food to their young and also enables engorged birds to 'lighten up' for a quick take-off. • Recent studies have shown that the American vultures are most closely related to storks, not hawks and falcons. Molecular similarities with storks, and the shared tendency to defecate on their legs to cool down, support this taxonomic reclassification.

ID: *Sexes similar:* very large, all-black bird. *Adult:* small, bare, red head. *Immature:* grey head. *In flight:* tilts side-to-side while soaring; silver-grey flight feathers; black wing linings; wings are held in a shallow V; head is barely visible.
Size: L 66–81 cm; W 173–183 cm.
Status: uncommon from May to September.
Habitat: usually seen flying over open country or shorelines.
Nesting: on a cliff ledge, in a cave crevice or among boulders; no nest material is used; female

lays 2 dull white eggs on bare ground; pair incubates the eggs for up to 41 days.
Feeding: entirely on carrion (mostly mammalian); feeds young by regurgitation; not commonly seen at roadkills.
Voice: generally silent; occasionally produces a hiss or grunt when threatened.
Similar Species: *Golden Eagle* (p. 100) and *Bald Eagle* (p. 90): wings are held flat in profile; do not rock when soaring; larger head.
Best Sites: lower Red Deer River valley; Cold Lake PP; Dry Island Buffalo Jump PP.

53

GREATER WHITE-FRONTED GOOSE

Anser albifrons

Greater White-fronted Geese have been overshadowed by their more flamboyant cousins: Canada Geese are more numerous and more vocal, and Snow Geese appear in spectacular numbers in migrations. Once you come to recognize White-fronts, however, you will wonder how you missed them before. • The Greater White-fronted Geese that migrate through Alberta often travel in flocks of Canada Geese. The slightly smaller White-fronts can best be separated from the Canada Geese by their bright orange feet, which shine like beacons as the birds stand on frozen spring wetlands. • The Greater White-fronted Goose is probably most familiar to hunters, who often call it 'speckle belly.'

ID: *Sexes similar. Adult:* dark brown overall; dark speckling on the belly; orange-pink bill and feet; white around the bill and on the forehead; white hindquarters; black band on the tail. *Immature:* pale belly, without speckles; no white on the face.
Size: *L* 69–84 cm; W 133–155 cm.
Status: uncommon to common in April and from September to October.

Habitat: *In migration:* croplands, fields, open areas and shallow marshes.
Nesting: does not nest in Alberta.
Feeding: dabbles in water and gleans the ground for grass shoots, spouting grain, waste grain and occasionally aquatic invertebrates.
Voice: a high-pitched laugh.
Similar Species: *Canada Goose* (p. 57): white cheek; black neck. *Snow Goose* (p. 55): blue phase has a white head and upper neck.
Best Site: Beaverhill Lake.

SNOW GOOSE
Chen caerulescens

The Snow Goose is to much of Alberta what the Cliff Swallow is to Capistrano. During the last week of April, thousands of people travel to Beaverhill Lake and the town of Tofield for the annual Snow Goose Festival. There, tens of thousands of these Arctic-bound geese pause in farmers' fields to fuel up on the waste grain from the previous year's crops. The birds spread out in the thousands, covering the brown fields with white and thereby earning their name. When the flock takes flight, the black wing tips contrast with the white plumage, and the entire flock can appear dark one moment and white the next as its wheels in the spring skies. • Unlike Canada Geese, which fly in well-formed Vs, migrating Snow Geese usually form unorganized, oscillating, wavy lines.

ID: *Sexes similar. Adult:* white overall; black wing tips; dark pink feet and bill; dark 'grinning patch' on the bill; plumage is occasionally stained rusty by iron in the water. *'Blue Goose':* white head; blue-grey body. *Immature:* grey plumage; dark bill and feet.
Size: *L* 71–84 cm; *W* 140–150 cm.
Status: locally common from March to April and from September to October.
Habitat: shallow wetlands, lakes and fields.

Nesting: does not nest in Alberta.
Feeding: grazes on waste grain and new sprouts; also eats aquatic vegetation, grass and roots.
Voice: loud, nasal, constant *houk-houk* in flight.
Similar Species: *Ross's Goose* (p. 56): smaller; lacks the black 'grin.' *Tundra Swan* (p. 60) and *Trumpeter Swan* (p. 59): larger; white wing tips. *American White Pelican* (p. 44): much larger; larger bill; black in the wings extends much further towards the body.
Best Site: Beaverhill Lake.

ROSS'S GOOSE
Chen rossii

Although it might not fully honour the Ross's Goose to describe it as a miniature version of the Snow Goose, the physical similarities and migratory habits of these two species make it difficult to resist the comparison. Ross's Geese pass through Alberta near the end of the Snow Goose migration, and they tend to get a little lost in the confusing tide of spring migrants. • This goose is most frequently spotted by birdwatchers with spotting scopes, since it might be necessary to scan a large flock of distant Snow Geese to pick out a single Ross's. • Samuel Hearne first described what was to be known as the Ross's Goose in 1770, but it wasn't until 1860 that a specimen was sent to a museum and the species was named. • Bernard Rogan Ross, this bird's namesake, was the Hudson's Bay Company's chief trader, and he spent time investigating the zoology of the boreal forest.

ID: *Sexes similar. Adult:* white overall; black wing tips; dark pink feet and bill; small 'warts' on the base of the bill; plumage is occasionally stained rusty by iron in the water. *Blue phase (very rare):* white head; blue-grey body plumage. *Immature:* grey plumage; dark bill and feet.
Size: L 54–66 cm; W 118–135 cm.

Status: uncommon in March and October.
Habitat: shallow wetlands, lakes and fields.
Nesting: does not nest in Alberta.
Feeding: grazes on waste grain and new sprouts; also eats aquatic vegetation, grass and roots.
Voice: high-pitched, squeaky *luk-luk.*
Similar Species: *Snow Goose* (p. 55): larger; black 'grin.'
Best Site: Beaverhill Lake.

CANADA GOOSE
Branta canadensis

When most Albertans imagine the sight and sound of a wild goose, it is the Canada Goose that comes to mind. The Canada Goose might be Alberta's most recognizable bird, and it can be encountered in a spring field, city park, golf course or wetland. Although the sight of one of these wetland giants can become commonplace by the end of summer, a flock breaking the horizon in early spring foretells the excitement of the coming season. • With big flocks of geese arriving in April, the first downy goslings of the year are normally encountered before mid-May. • The Canada Geese that breed in Alberta are huge, but smaller migrants pass through on their way to and from the Arctic. • The loyalty between pairs of Canada Geese is legendary, but they will often find a new mate once their chosen partner has passed away.

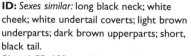

ID: *Sexes similar:* long black neck; white cheek; white undertail coverts; light brown underparts; dark brown upperparts; short, black tail.
Size: *L* 55–122 cm; *W* up to 178 cm.
Status: common from March to October; a few overwinter.
Habitat: lakeshores, riverbanks, ponds, farmlands and city parks.
Nesting: on islands and shorelines; usually on the ground; sometimes on cliffs, in old Osprey nests or on nest

platforms; nest is built with grass and other plant materials and is lined with down.
Feeding: grazes on new sprouts, aquatic vegetation, grass and roots; tips up for roots and tubers.
Voice: loud, familiar *ah-honk.*
Similar Species: *Greater White-fronted Goose* (p. 54): neck is not black; uncommon migrant through Alberta. *Double-crested Cormorant* (p. 45): lacks the white cheek and undertail coverts; generally silent in flight.
Best Sites: Inglewood Bird Sanctuary, Calgary; William Hawrelak Park, Edmonton; Beaverhill Lake (spring); Hanna area (fall).

57

BRANT
Branta bernicla

Every few years, a small number of Brant are seen in Alberta. Normally, this salt-water cousin of the Canada Goose prefers to remain in coastal environments, feasting on eelgrass, but those few birds that find themselves in Alberta must satisfy their hunger with freshwater plants and waste grain. • The few Brant records available suggest that they are more frequently observed in the northern half of the province during fall migrations. • Both light-bellied and dark-bellied forms of this small goose have been recorded in Alberta. The black-bellied Brant, formerly called the 'Black Brant,' is from the West Coast; the light-bellied form is found primarily in the East. • *Branta* is a Latinized form of an Anglo-Saxon word for 'burnt' or 'charred'—a reference to this bird's dark plumage.

'Black Brant'

ID: *Sexes similar. Adult:* black neck, head and breast; dark upperparts; white flecks on the upper neck; white hindquarters; dark feet; black or white belly. *Juvenile:* lacks the white flecks on the neck.
Size: L 59–70 cm; W 110–120 cm.
Status: very rare spring and fall migrant.

vagrant

Habitat: lakeshores and agricultural fields.
Nesting: does not nest in Alberta.
Feeding: grazes on aquatic vegetation and waste grain in Alberta; elsewhere they almost exclusively eat eelgrass.
Voice: deep prolonged *c-r-r-r-uk*, with hissing.
Similar Species: *Canada Goose* (p. 57): white cheek; brown upperparts; much larger.
Best Sites: check local bird hotlines for recent sightings; Coleman Lake (fall).

TRUMPETER SWAN
Cygnus buccinator

The Trumpeter Swan was hunted almost to extinction for its feathers and meat in the early 20th century. A breeding population survived west of Grande Prairie, and families have been transplanted from there to other parts of this species's former range. Lakes in Elk Island National Park now echo with the Trumpeter Swan's bugling notes, and it is hoped that populations will continue to recover. Although their breeding numbers in Alberta are not up to pre-colonial levels, biologists are now growing concerned about overcrowding of Trumpeter Swans on their southern wintering areas. • The Trumpeter is one of Alberta's most charismatic birds, and all Albertans should take pride in the conservation efforts that have allowed this species to recover. • Both 'trumpeter' and *buccinator* refer to this species's loud, bugling voice, which is produced in an extension of the windpipe that runs through the breast bone.

ID: *Sexes similar. Adult:* all-white plumage; large, solid black bill; black feet; all-white wings; neck is held with a kink at the base, when standing or swimming. *Immature:* grey-brown plumage; grey bill.
Size: *L* 150–183 cm; *W* 2.4 m.
Status: locally common from April to October.
Habitat: lakes and large wetlands; very local.
Nesting: often builds a large mound of vegetation on top of muskrat or beaver lodges, and occasionally on shores; female usually incubates 4–6 eggs.

Feeding: tips up, surface gleans and occasionally grazes for vegetation (primarily sago pondweed, duckweed, tubers and roots).
Voice: loud, resonant, bugle-like *koh-hoh*.
Similar Species: *Tundra Swan* (p. 60): smaller; migrant through Alberta; yellow 'teardrop' in front of the eye; softer, more nasal voice. *Snow Goose* (p. 55): smaller; black wing tips; shorter neck.
Best Sites: Saskatoon Island PP; Elk Island NP; Camrose (captive birds); Bow River valley west of Calgary; Mountain View (spring).

TUNDRA SWAN
Cygnus columbianus

Before the last of winter's snows have melted into the fields, Tundra Swans return to our province, bringing joy to all who know their call. These swans pass through our area in large numbers, migrating through rural areas as well as passing overtop even our largest cities. • The snow and ice that they encounter during their passage through Alberta will not be the last on their trip north—Tundra Swans usually reach their breeding grounds in the Arctic before the spring thaw. • Like the Trumpeter Swan, the Tundra Swan's windpipe loops through the bird's sternum, which amplifies its call. The Tundra Swan is called the Whistling Swan in Europe. • The Lewis and Clark exploration team found this bird near the Columbia River, after which its scientific name was later derived.

ID: *Sexes similar. Adult:* white plumage; large, black bill; black feet; all-white wings; yellow 'teardrop' in front of the eye; neck is held straight up. *Immature:* grey-brown plumage; grey bill.
Size: *L* 119–147 cm; *W* 2 m.
Status: common migrant in April and October.
Habitat: *In migration:* shallow areas of lakes and wetlands, agricultural fields and flooded pastures.

Nesting: does not nest in Alberta.
Feeding: tips up, dabbles and surface gleans for aquatic vegetation and aquatic invertebrates; grazes for tubers, roots and waste grain.
Voice: high-pitched, quivering *oo-oo-whoo* is constantly repeated by migrating flocks.
Similar Species: *Trumpeter Swan* (p. 59): larger; breeds in Alberta; loud, bugle-like voice; no yellow on the bill. *Snow Goose* (p. 55): smaller; black wing tips.
Best Sites: Beaverhill Lake; rural farmlands.

WOOD DUCK
Aix sponsa

The release of Wood Ducks at the Inglewood Bird Sanctuary in Calgary has added another dimension of beauty to Alberta's bird fauna. A few pairs of Wood Ducks can now be readily observed swimming proudly in the backwaters of the sanctuary during summer. Wild Wood Ducks, not derived from these introduced ones, offer Alberta birders much more of a challenge—they are uncommonly encountered along wetlands and rivers in the southern half of the province. • Large nest boxes placed high on riverside trees are often intended for these cavity-nesting ducks. • The male Wood Duck is one of the most colourful water birds in North America, and its image routinely adorns books, magazines, postcards and calendars. • The scientific name *sponsa* is Latin for 'promised bride,' suggesting that the male appears formally dressed for a wedding.

ID: *Male:* gaudy; glossy green head; crest is slicked back from the crown; white chin and throat; chestnut breast is spotted with white; white shoulder slash; golden sides; dark back and hindquarters. *Female:* white, 'cleopatra' eye patch; mottled brown breast is streaked with white; brown-grey upperparts; white belly.
Size: L 38–53 cm.
Status: rare to uncommon from April to October.
Habitat: beaver ponds and backwaters with wooded edges.
Nesting: in a hollow or cavity in a tree, up to 9 m high or more; also in artificial nest boxes; usually near water; nest is lined with down from the female's breast.
Feeding: surface gleans and tips up for aquatic vegetation, especially duckweed and aquatic sedges, and grasses; eats more fruits and nuts than other ducks.
Voice: *Male:* ascending *ter-wee-wee.*
Female: squeaky *woo-e-e-k.*
Similar Species: Hooded Merganser (p. 85): white patch on the crest; slim bill. *Harlequin Duck* (p. 77): no crest; blue-grey overall.
Best Site: Inglewood Bird Sanctuary, Calgary.

GADWALL
Anas strepera

Although male Gadwalls lack the striking plumage of most other male ducks, they nevertheless have a dignified appearance. The intricacies of waterfowl plumage—from the bird's overall colour to the structure and shading of individual feathers—is as heightened in Gadwalls as in more showy ducks—it just takes a little more effort to notice. Once you learn its field marks, the Gadwall is surprisingly easy to identify, whether it is on land, on water or in the air. • Ducks in the genus *Anas* (the dabbling ducks) are most often observed tipping up to feed, but the Gadwall's diving habits are more developed than others of this clan. • Gadwalls have recently expanded their range throughout North America.

ID: *General:* black-and-white wing patch (often seen in resting birds); white belly. *Male:* mostly grey; black hindquarters; dark bill. *Female:* mottled brown; brown bill with orange sides.

Size: L 46–56 cm.

Status: common from March to September.

Habitat: shallow wetlands, lake borders and beaver ponds.

Nesting: in tall vegetation, sometimes far from water; nest is well concealed in a scraped hollow, often with grass arching overhead; nest is made of grass and other dry vegetation and lined with down.

Feeding: dabbles and tips up for the leaves, stems, tubers and roots

of water plants; grazes on grass and waste grain during migration; one of the few dabblers to dive routinely for food; also eats aquatic invertebrates, tadpoles and small fish.

Voice: *Male:* simple, singular *quack;* often whistles harshly. *Female:* high *kaak kaaak kak-kak-kak*, in series and oscillating in volume.

Similar Species: *American Wigeon* (p. 64): green speculum; male has a white forehead and a green swipe trailing from each eye; female lacks the black hindquarters. *Mallard* (p. 66), *Northern Pintail* (p. 70) and *other dabbling ducks*: females all generally lack the black hindquarters and the black-and-white wing patch.

Best Sites: almost any shallow wetland; Beaverhill Lake; Frank Lake.

EURASIAN WIGEON
Anas penelope

Every year, a few birdwatchers in Alberta will be scanning a flock of American Wigeons on a temporary spring wetland when a red-headed individual prominently stands out. Eurasian Wigeons might be among the most conspicuous rarities to occur in Alberta, and even beginning birdwatchers have little difficulty in confidently identifying this Asian species—at least the males. • The Eurasian Wigeons in Alberta are probably nothing more than misguided wanderers, following their American cousins on migration. Although they have not been found breeding here, the reliability of sightings each spring has convinced some people that there is a small breeding population in or near Alberta. • North American birds also wander, and American Wigeons have been seen among flocks of Eurasian Wigeons in eastern Russia.

ID: *Male:* rufous head; cream forehead; rosy breast; grey sides; black hindquarters; dark feet; black-tipped, grey bill. *Female:* rufous hints on a predominately brown head and breast; black-tipped, blue bill. *In flight:* large, white wing patch; dusky wing pits.
Size: *L* 42–52 cm.
Status: rare during migration.
Habitat: shallow wetlands, lake edges and ponds.

Nesting: does not nest in Alberta.
Feeding: primarily a vegetarian; dabbles and grazes for grass, leaves and stems; occasionally pirates food from coots.
Voice: high-pitched, 2-toned whistle.
Similar Species: *American Wigeon* (p. 64): white wing pits; male lacks the reddish-brown head.
Best Sites: Beaverhill Lake; Inglewood Bird Sanctuary, Calgary; Frank Lake; Taber area.

AMERICAN WIGEON
Anas americana

The male American Wigeon's characteristic, wheezy laugh seems somewhat misplaced among the wetland orchestra of buzzes, quacks and ticks. Listen carefully, however, and you'll realize where toy makers got the sound for rubber duckies.
• The American Wigeon is generally a vegetarian. Although it frequently dabbles for food, nothing seems to please a wigeon more than the succulent stems and leaves of pond-bottom plants. These plants grow far too deep for a dabbling duck, however, so pirating wigeons often steal from accomplished divers, such as American Coots, Canvasbacks, scaups and Redheads. • American Wigeons are commonly observed grazing on shore, and they are good walkers compared to other ducks. • The male American Wigeon's bright white crown and forehead has led some people, and especially hunters, to call it the 'Baldplate.'

ID: *General:* large, white wing patch; cinnamon breast and flanks; white belly; grey bill with a black tip; green speculum. *Male:* white forehead; green swipe running back from each eye. *Female:* greyish head; brown underparts.
Size: L 46–58 cm.
Status: common from March to October.
Habitat: shallow wetlands, lake edges and ponds.
Nesting: always on dry ground, often far from water; nest is well concealed in tall vegetation and is built with grass,

leaves and down; female incubates the white eggs for 23–25 days.
Feeding: dabbles and tips up for aquatic leaves and the stems of pondweeds; also grazes and uproots young shoots in fields; infrequently eats invertebrates.
Voice: *Male:* nasal, frequently repeated whistle: *whee WHEE wheew. Female:* soft, seldom heard quack.
Similar Species: *Gadwall* (p. 62): lacks the large, white wing patch; male has all-black hindquarters.
Best Sites: almost any shallow wetland; Beaverhill Lake; Frank Lake.

AMERICAN BLACK DUCK
Anas rubripes

Alberta might be the 'duckiest' province in Canada, but the American Black Duck contributes minimally to our fauna. Our province lies well outside the historic breeding range of this species—it is a rare straggler to Alberta from its eastern roots. • Most of the American Black Ducks in Alberta have hybridized somewhat with Mallards, and they tend to be tough-to-identify, dark female Mallard–like birds. • The eastern expansion of the Mallard's range has come at the expense of this dark dabbler—the species boundaries among Mallards and their close relatives are blurred by interbreeding almost everywhere. Habitat loss and the degradation of wetlands in general have further contributed to the decline of the American Black Duck throughout much of its historic breeding range.

ID: *General:* dark brown-black body; light brown head and neck; bright orange feet. *Male:* yellow bill. *Female:* dull green-spotted, black bill. *In flight:* silver-lined wings.
Size: *L* 51–63 cm.
Status: rare during migration.
Habitat: lakes, wetlands, rivers and agricultural areas.
Nesting: does not breed in Alberta.
Feeding: tips up and dabbles in shallows for the seeds and roots of

vagrant

pondweeds; also eats aquatic invertebrates, larval amphibians and fish eggs.
Voice: *Male:* gives a croak. *Female:* loud quack.
Similar Species: *Mallard* (p. 66): lacks the silver-lined underwings; female is lighter overall. *Gadwall* (p. 62): black hindquarters; black-and-white wing patch.
Best Sites: check local bird hotlines for recent sightings.

MALLARD
Anas platyrhynchos

The male Mallard, with his iridescent green head and chestnut breast, is the classic duck of Alberta. Mallards can quite literally be seen every day of the year in our province, as long as there is open water available to them. It is an inspiring scene to watch a small flock of Mallards flying along an open river channel in the depths of winter. • Wild Mallards will freely hybridize with domestic ducks (which were originally derived from Mallards in Europe), and the resulting offspring, often seen in city parks, are a confusing blend of both parents. Mallards will also mate with any other duck that catches their eye. • Male ducks molt after breeding, losing much of their extravagant plumage. This 'eclipse' plumage stage lasts briefly before they molt again into their breeding colours before their fall migration. • Most people think of the Mallard's quack as the classic duck call. • The scientific name *platyrhynchos* is Greek for 'broad, flat bill.'

ID: *General:* dark blue speculum is bordered by white; orange feet. *Male:* glossy green head; yellow bill; chestnut breast; white 'necklace'; grey body plumage; black tail feathers curl upward. *Female:* mottled brown overall; orange bill is splattered with black.
Size: *L* 51–71 cm.
Status: very common from March to November; many overwinter on open water.
Habitat: lakes, wetlands, rivers, springs, city parks and agricultural areas.
Nesting: in tall vegetation or under a bush, often near water; nest is made of grass and other plant material and lined with down; female incubates 7–10 light green to white eggs.
Feeding: tips up and dabbles in the shallows for the seeds of sedges, willows and pondweeds; also eats aquatic invertebrates, larval amphibians and fish eggs.
Voice: *Female:* loud quacks; very vocal. *Male:* deeper quack.
Similar Species: *Northern Shoveler* (p. 69): larger bill; male has a white breast. *American Black Duck* (p. 65): darker than a female Mallard; purple speculum. *Common Merganser* (p. 87): male lacks the chestnut breast and has snowy white underparts.
Best Sites: almost any body of reasonably still, open water.

BLUE-WINGED TEAL
Anas discors

The Blue-winged Teal is a champion of waterfowl migrants. It frequently winters in the southern U.S. and Mexico, so it arrives in Alberta later than most other ducks and leaves earlier, before the onset of winter's cold. • Blue-winged Teals are quick and evasive fliers. Small groups of these ducks can be identified in the air by their twists and turns, which are executed with great precision. • The Green-winged Teal is not the Blue-winged Teal's closest relative. Blue-wings are more closely related to Cinnamon Teals and Northern Shovelers, as a glance at their broad, flat bills will confirm. These three species also have very similar patterns of wing colouration: a pale-blue forewing and a green speculum. • The scientific name *discors* is Latin for 'without harmony,' which might be in reference to this bird's call as it takes flight.

ID: *Male:* blue-grey head; white crescent on the face; black-spotted breast and sides. *Female:* mottled brown overall. *In flight:* blue forewing patch; green speculum.

Size: *L* 36–41 cm.

Status: common from April to September.

Habitat: shallow lake edges and wetlands; prefers areas of short but dense emergent vegetation.

Nesting: primarily on prairie potholes; in grass along shore-lines and in wet meadows, usually very near water; nest is built with grass and considerable

amounts of down; female incubates 8–11 eggs for 24 days.

Feeding: gleans the water surface for sedge and grass seeds, pondweeds, duck-weeds and aquatic invertebrates.

Voice: *Male:* soft *keck-keck-keck. Female:* soft quacks.

Similar Species: *Harlequin Duck* (p. 77): blue-grey overall; white shoulder slash. *Cinnamon Teal* (p. 68) and *Green-winged Teal* (p. 71): lack the white crescent on the cheek. *Northern Shoveler* (p. 69): male has a green head and lacks the spotting on the body.

Best Sites: Beaverhill Lake; Frank Lake.

CINNAMON TEAL

Anas cyanoptera

When the morning sun strikes a spring wetland, male Cinnamon Teals glow upon the water like embers. These handsome ducks are occasionally seen swimming along with their heads partially submerged, skimming aquatic life from the pond's surface. Cinnamon Teals are regular but uncommon breeders in Alberta, and they are spotted only on occasion. • Female Cinnamon Teals have been known to put on a 'broken wing' act to distract predators from their ducklings. • Male Cinnamon Teals, unlike most male ducks, often stay with their mates through most of the incubation period. Males have sometimes even been seen accompanying their mates and her brood. • The scientific name—from *cyano*, 'blue,' and *pteron*, 'wing'—reinforces the similarities of this species to the Blue-winged Teal, with which it has been known to interbreed.

ID: *General:* long, broad bill; blue forewing patch; green speculum. *Male:* rich cinnamon red head, neck and underparts; red eyes. *Female:* mottled brown overall; dark eyes.
Size: L 38–43 cm.
Status: uncommon from April to September.
Habitat: shallow wetlands with extensive emergent vegetation and sedge beds.
Nesting: in tall vegetation, occasionally far from water; builds nest with grass and down in a concealed hollow; female incubates 7–12 eggs for 21–25 days; ducklings fly after 7 weeks.
Feeding: gleans the water's surface for grass and sedge seeds, pondweeds, duckweeds and aquatic invertebrates.
Voice: *Male:* whistled peep. *Female:* rough *karr, karr, karr.*
Similar Species: *Ruddy Duck* (p. 88): male has a white cheek and a blue bill. *Green-winged Teal* (p. 71): grey body; white shoulder slash; green streak trailing from each eye.
Best Sites: Slack Slough; Beaverhill Lake; Frank Lake; Pakowki Lake.

NORTHERN SHOVELER

Anas clypeata

Once you know the field marks of the Northern Shoveler, you will routinely see it along roadways in Alberta. Ditches and flooded fields are just to its liking—the Northern Shoveler prefers to lounge in shallow waters. • The Northern Shoveler's spoon-like bill allows this handsome duck to strain small invertebrates from a pond's mucky bottom. Shovelers eat much smaller organisms than do most other waterfowl, and their intestines are elongated to prolong the digestion of these hard-bodied invertebrates. • Its green head makes the Northern Shoveler easy to confuse with a Mallard, but a closer look at the two reveals many differences, including bill shape. • The scientific name *clypeata* is Latin for 'furnished with a shield'; it refers to the shoveler's massive bill. This species was once placed in its own genus, *Spatula,* the meaning of which needs no explanation.

ID: *General:* large, spatulate bill; blue fore-wing patch; green speculum. *Male:* green head; white breast; chestnut sides. *Female:* mottled brown overall; orange-tinged bill.
Size: *L* 46–51 cm.
Status: common from March to September.
Habitat: shallow marshes, bogs and lakes with muddy bottoms and emergent vegetation, in open and semi-open areas.
Nesting: in a shallow hollow on dry ground, usually within 50 m of water; female builds the nest with dry grass and down and incubates 10–12 eggs for

25 days; ducklings show the distinctive, spoon-like bill after 2 weeks.
Feeding: dabbles in and gleans the water and mud; strains out plant and animal matter, especially aquatic crustaceans, insect larvae and seeds; rarely tips up.
Voice: generally quiet; occasionally a raspy chuckle or quack, most often heard during spring courtship.
Similar Species: *Mallard* (p. 66): blue speculum; lacks the pale blue forewing; male has a chestnut breast and white flanks. *Blue-winged Teal* (p. 67): much slimmer bill; smaller.
Best Sites: Slack Slough; Beaverhill Lake; Frank Lake.

NORTHERN PINTAIL
Anas acuta

Elegant and graceful on the water and in the air, the male Northern Pintail's beauty and style are unsurpassed by most of Alberta's birds. This bird's trademark is its long, tapering tail feathers, which are easily seen in flight and when it dabbles and points its tail skyward. • Migrating Northern Pintails are often seen in flocks of 20 to 40 birds, but some flocks can contain thousands of birds that might settle in a single field. • The Alberta population of pintails has yo-yoed up and down over the last century. According to North American data, this widespread duck appears to be in decline. • Pintails' nests are often more exposed than those of other ducks. • The scientific name *acuta* is Latin for 'pointed'—an obvious reference to this bird's tail feathers.

ID: *General:* long, slender neck; dark glossy bill. *Male:* chocolate brown head; long, tapering tail feathers; white breast; white stripe on the neck; dusty grey body plumage. *Female:* mottled light brown overall. *In flight:* slender and sleek.

Size: *Male:* L 64–76 cm. *Female:* L 51–56 cm.

Status: common from March to October.

Habitat: shallow wetlands, fields and lake edges.

Nesting: in a small depression in vegetation; nest is made of grass, leaves and moss and lined with the female's down;

female incubates 6–9 eggs for up to 24 days.

Feeding: tips up and dabbles in shallows for the seeds of sedges, willows and pondweeds; also eats aquatic invertebrates and larval amphibians; eats waste grain in agricultural areas during migration.

Voice: *Male:* soft, whistling call. *Female:* rough quack.

Similar Species: *Mallard* (p. 66) and *Gadwall* (p. 62): chunkier; lack the tapering tail. *Blue-winged Teal* (p. 67): smaller; green speculum.

Best Sites: Beaverhill Lake; Frank Lake.

GREEN-WINGED TEAL
Anas crecca

Small, tight-flying flocks of Green-winged Teals are among the most speedy and maneuverable of waterfowl. When intruders cause these small ducks to rocket from wetlands, they circle quickly overhead until the threat departs. A predator's best hope of catching a healthy bird is to snatch it from the water. • Green-winged Teals often undergo a partial migration before molting into their post-breeding, 'eclipse' plumage, in which they are flightless (because they do not possess a full set of flight feathers). • Green-winged Teals are much more likely than other teals to overwinter on open water in Alberta. • The scientific name *crecca* is a Latinized imitation of this duck's call.

ID: *General:* small bill; green-and-black speculum. *Male:* chestnut head; green swipe running back from each eye; white shoulder slash; creamy breast is spotted with black; pale grey sides. *Female:* mottled brown overall; light belly.

Size: *L* 30–41 cm.

Status: uncommon to common from April to October.

Habitat: shallow lakes, wetlands, beaver ponds and meandering rivers.

Nesting: well-concealed in tall vegetation; nest is built of grass and leaves and lined with down; female incubates 8 or 9 creamy white eggs.

Feeding: dabbles in the shallows for aquatic invertebrates, larval amphibians, sedge seeds and pondweeds.

Voice: *Male:* crisp whistle. *Female:* soft quack.

Similar Species: *American Wigeon* (p. 64): lacks the white shoulder slash and the chestnut head. *Blue-winged Teal* (p. 67): white crescent on the cheek; blue-grey head; light blue speculum.

Best Sites: Clifford E. Lee Nature Sanctuary; Inglewood Bird Sanctuary, Calgary; Beaverhill Lake; Frank Lake.

CANVASBACK
Aythya valisineria

In profile, the Canvasback casts a noble image—its great sloping bill is an unmistakable field mark. Despite its proud proboscis, this bird is named after its bright white back, which is usually a better field mark at a distance. • Canvasbacks are devoted deep divers, and they seldom stray into areas of wetlands that are too shallow to sustain that activity. Because Canvasbacks prefer the deepest areas of wetlands, you often need binoculars to properly admire the male's wild red eyes, which nicely compliment his rich mahogany head. • The scientific name *valisineria* refers to one of the Canvasback's favourite foods—wild celery *(Vallisneria americana)*. When the species was described by Alexander Wilson, he misspelled the word. According to the rules of nomenclature, such errors must be retained to avoid the confusion that would be caused by multiple spellings.

ID: *General:* head slopes upward from the bill to the forehead. *Male:* canvas white back; chestnut head; black breast and hindquarters; red eyes. *Female:* profile is similar to a male's; brown and grey plumage.
Size: *L* 48–56 cm.
Status: uncommon from April to October.
Habitat: shallow wetlands, lakes and ponds with water plants.
Nesting: basket nest is well concealed in emergent shoreline vegetation, usually suspended over the water; nest is built with reeds and grass and lined with

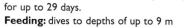

down; female incubates 7–9 olive green eggs for up to 29 days.
Feeding: dives to depths of up to 9 m (usually 3–4 m); feeds on roots, tubers, the basal stems of plants (including pondweeds and wild celery) and bulrush seeds; occasionally eats aquatic invertebrates.
Voice: generally quiet. *Male:* occasional coos and 'growls' during courtship. *Female:* low, soft, 'purring' quack or *kuck*; also 'growls.'
Similar Species: *Redhead* (p. 73): lacks the sloped forehead; male has a grey back and a bluish bill.
Best Sites: Clifford E. Lee Nature Sanctuary; Beaverhill Lake; Frank Lake.

REDHEAD
Aythya americana

In undisturbed pothole lakes, far from city parks, Redheads are fairly common ducks, paddling and dabbling among the crowds of waterfowl. • Although the Redhead is fully equipped with all the attributes of a diving duck, it often feeds on the surface of wetlands like a dabbler. • Female Redheads often nest and brood their young as other ducks do, but they will also become 'brood parasites' at times, by laying their eggs in another duck's nest. • Most birders will tell you to compare the profiles of the Canvasback and Redhead to distinguish between them, but the difference in their back colour is an even more obvious feature. • The scientific name *Aythya* has its origins in the Greek word *aithuia,* meaning 'water bird.'

ID: *General:* blue-grey, black-tipped bill. *Male:* rounded, red head; black breast and hindquarters; grey back and sides. *Female:* dark overall; lighter foreneck and lower face.
Size: *L* 46–56 cm.
Status: uncommon from April to October.
Habitat: large wetlands, lakes and rivers, often near emergent vegetation.
Nesting: deep basket nest is well concealed at the base of emergent vegetation, suspended over water; nest is built with reeds and grass and lined with fine, white down; female occasionally lays eggs in other ducks' nests.
Feeding: dives to depths of 3 m; primarily eats aquatic vegetation, especially pondweeds and duckweeds, and the leaves and stems of plants; occasionally eats aquatic invertebrates.
Voice: generally quiet. *Male:* cat-like meow in courtship. *Female:* rolling *kurr-kurr-kurr; squak* when alarmed.
Similar Species: *Canvasback* (p. 72): clean white back; bill slopes into the forehead. *Lesser Scaup* (p. 76): female has more white at the base of the bill.
Best Sites: Beaverhill Lake; Frank Lake.

RING-NECKED DUCK
Aythya collaris

For anyone who has seen a Ring-necked Duck in the wild, the white ring around the base of the male's bill is obvious, and the expected neck ring is barely visible. You'd think it would have been named the 'Ring-billed Duck,' but the official appellation derives from the scientific name *collaris* (collar) and originated with an ornithologist looking at museum specimens, not a birdwatcher with binoculars.
• The Ring-necked Duck occurs more commonly in the western parts of Alberta, where small, shy groups are often seen swimming at the far end of a beaver pond. Beavers create habitat for many species of animals, and the Ring-necked Duck is not the only species to benefit from their environmental engineering. • Ring-necked Ducks ride high on the surface of wetlands, and they frequently carry their tails clear of the water.

ID: *Male:* dark, angular head with hints of purple; black breast, back and hindquarters; white shoulder slash; grey sides; blue-grey bill with black and white bands at the tip; thin, white ring around the base of the bill. *Female:* dark brown body; light brown head; faint white eye ring.
Size: L 36–46 cm.
Status: uncommon from April to October.
Habitat: wooded ponds, swamps, marshes and sloughs with emergent vegetation; often associated with yellow waterlilies.

Nesting: frequently over water on a hummock or shoreline; bulky nest is made of grass and moss and lined with down; female incubates 8–10 olive tan eggs.
Feeding: dives underwater, mostly for aquatic vegetation, including seeds, tubers and pondweed leaves; also eats aquatic invertebrates.
Voice: seldom heard. *Male:* low-pitched, hissing whistle. *Female:* growling *churr*.
Similar Species: *Lesser Scaup* (p. 76): lacks the white shoulder slash and the black back; uniform-coloured bill with a small black tip. *Redhead* (p. 73): female's head is the same tone as her body.
Best Site: Crimson Lake PP.

GREATER SCAUP
Aythya marila

In the beginning stages of birdwatching, you should probably be content to call every scaup you see in Alberta 'a probable Lesser.' With increased time in the field, however, you will notice that some of these scaups look (often briefly) rounder and more greenish in the head than others, until finally the day arrives when you can undeniably identify a Greater Scaup. • Greater Scaups are known to breed just north of Alberta, and the absence of breeding records in our province does not preclude the possibility that they sometimes breed here also. • Greater Scaups are usually seen on lakes and large wetlands in April and May and then again in September and October.

ID: *General:* rounded or flat-topped head; golden eyes. *Male:* iridescent dark green (often appears black) head; dark breast; white belly and flanks; light grey back; dark hindquarters; blue, black-tipped bill. *Female:* brown overall; well-defined white patch at the base of the bill. *In flight:* white flash through the wing extends well into the primary feathers.
Size: *L* 41–48 cm.
Status: rare in migration.
Habitat: lakes, large marshes and reservoirs, usually far from shore.

Nesting: does not nest in Alberta.
Feeding: deep, underwater dives lasting up to 1 minute; mainly eats aquatic vegetation, crustaceans, mollusks and snails.
Voice: generally quiet in migration; occasionally a collective *scaup.*
Similar Species: *Lesser Scaup* (p. 76): more peaked head with a purple tinge; shorter white wing edge. *Ring-necked Duck* (p. 74): black back; white shoulder slash; white ring around the base of the bill.
Best Sites: Clifford E. Lee Nature Sanctuary; Glenmore Reservoir, Calgary (fall); Frank Lake.

LESSER SCAUP
Aythya affinis

The Lesser Scaup is the Oreo cookie of the Alberta duck clan—it is black at both ends and light in the middle. The readily identifiable males, along with the less striking females, are frequently seen at our city parks, where they are more approachable than in the wild. • Several female scaups might combine their efforts and care for two or more broods of young. Although the young are tended by the females, they feed themselves. • Lesser Scaups, also known as 'Bluebills,' leap up neatly before diving underwater, where they propel themselves with powerful strokes of their feet. • The scientific name *affinis* is Latin for 'adjacent' or 'allied'—a reference to this scaup's close association to other diving ducks. 'Scaup' might refer to a preferred winter food of this duck—shellfish beds are called 'scalps' in Scotland—or it might be a phonetic imitation of one of its calls.

ID: *General:* yellow eyes. *Male:* dark head with hints of purple; black breast and hindquarters; dirty white sides; greyish back; blue-grey bill. *Female:* dark brown overall; well-defined white patch at the base of the bill.
Size: *L* 38–46 cm.
Status: common from April to October.
Habitat: woodland ponds and lake edges with grassy margins.
Nesting: in tall, concealing vegetation, generally close to water; occasionally on islands;

nest hollow is built of grass and lined with down; female incubates 8–10 eggs for about 25 days.
Feeding: dives underwater to depths of about 2 m for aquatic invertebrates, mostly amphipods and insect larvae, and vegetation.
Voice: alarm call is a deep *scaup*. *Male:* soft *whee-oooh* in courtship.
Similar Species: *Greater Scaup* (p. 75): male has a flatter, greenish head and 'cleaner' white sides. *Ring-necked Duck* (p. 74): male has a white shoulder slash and a black back.
Best Sites: Beaverhill Lake; Frank Lake.

HARLEQUIN DUCK
Histrionicus histrionicus

When late spring comes to the Alberta Rockies, gaudy Harlequin Ducks furiously paddle their way around in rushing whitewater streams, stopping from time to time to stand atop an exposed boulder. In June or early July, the males leave the nesting females and travel to the Pacific coast to molt on marine waters. The females keep to the rapids and torrents, raising their families in a pleasantly chaotic setting. • A conflict between river rafters and defenders of the Harlequin Duck has arisen in the Alberta Rockies. The concern lies with the possibility that repeated disturbance to breeding Harlies could affect their nesting success. • In winter, Harlequin Ducks occasionally show up on large rivers far from the mountains. • The Harlequin Duck gets its name from the male's striking plumage— a 'harlequin' is an actor who is colourfully made-up or wears a mask.

ID: *General:* small, rounded duck; blocky head; short bill; raises and lowers its tail while swimming. *Male:* grey-blue body; chestnut sides; white spots and stripes on the head, neck and flanks. *Female:* dusky brown overall; light underparts; 2 or 3 light patches on the head.
Size: *L* 36–48 cm.
Status: locally uncommon from May to September.
Habitat: shallow, fast-flowing mountain streams; prefers undisturbed rivers.
Nesting: under bushes and shrubs or among rocks near streams; shallow nest is lined with grass, plant materials and down; female incubates and rears the young alone.

Feeding: dabbles and dives up to 1.5 m for aquatic invertebrates, mainly caddisfly and stonefly larvae; searches river bottoms, probing rock crevices for invertebrates and fish eggs.
Voice: generally silent outside the breeding season. *Male:* descending trill and squeaky whistles during courtship. *Female:* harsh *ek-ek-ek* or a low croak during courtship.
Similar Species: *Bufflehead* (p. 82): smaller; never found on fast-flowing water; female lacks the white between the eye and the bill. *Surf Scoter* (p. 78) and *White-winged Scoter* (p. 79): females are very similar to female Harlequins. *Other diving ducks:* longer necks; less rounded bodies.
Best Sites: Bow River, upstream from Banff; Maligne River, Jasper NP; Bow Falls, Banff NP; Elbow Falls, Kananaskis Country.

SURF SCOTER
Melanitta perspicillata

When spring storms put whitecaps on Alberta's big lakes, migrating Surf Scoters rest comfortably among the crashing waves. Scoters spend their winters just beyond the breaking surf on both the Atlantic and Pacific coasts, so they are well adapted to life on rough water. • In spring, the Surf Scoter starts passing through Alberta around the middle of May, and it can be seen here for about three weeks. Its return trip in fall is generally more spread out, and birds can be seen in October and November. • There are nesting records for the Surf Scoter in extreme northern Alberta. These breeding areas are difficult to access, however, so the exact extent of the Surf Scoter's breeding population in Alberta remains unknown • The scientific name *Melanitta* means 'black duck'; *perspicillata* is Latin for 'spectacular,' which refers to this bird's colourful bill.

ID: *General:* large, stocky, dark duck; large bill; sloping forehead; all-black wings. *Male:* black overall; white on the forehead and the back of the neck; orange bill and legs; black spot, outlined in white, at the base of the bill. *Female:* brown overall; dark grey bill; light patches on the cheek and ear.
Size: L 43–53 cm.
Status: uncommon from May to November.
Habitat: large, deep lakes.
Nesting: typically in a shallow scrape under bushes or branches, usually very near water; female incubates 5–8 buff-coloured eggs.

Feeding: dives underwater to depths of 9 m; eats the larvae of aquatic insects; occasionally eats aquatic vegetation and mollusks.
Voice: generally quiet; infrequently utters low, harsh croaks. *Male:* occasionally gives a low, clear whistle. *Female:* guttural *krraak krraak.*
Similar Species: *White-winged Scoter* (p. 79): white wing patches; male lacks the white on the forehead and nape. *Black Scoter* (p. 80): male is all black; female has a well-defined, pale cheek.
Best Sites: Cold Lake PP; Elk Island NP; Glenmore Reservoir, Calgary.

WHITE-WINGED SCOTER
Melanitta fusca

As White-winged Scoters race across lakes, their flapping wings reveal their key identifying feature—the white inner-wing patches strike a sharp contrast with the bird's otherwise black plumage. • White-wings are the only scoters that commonly nest across Alberta. They raise their young in everything from prairie potholes to boreal beaver ponds. • Scoters are heavy-bodied ducks, and they require long stretches of open water for take-off. The name 'scoter' is derived from the way these birds scoot across the water's surface, frequently touching cresting waves. Scooting can be a means of travelling quickly from one foraging site to another. • White-winged Scoters are less visible than many other ducks that breed in our province. They can be found in Alberta between late April and mid-November, usually in rafts of various sizes.

ID: *General:* largest scoter; stocky, all-dark duck; large, bulbous bill; sloping forehead; base of the bill is fully feathered. *Male:* black overall; white patch below the eye. *Female:* brown overall; grey-brown bill; light patches on the sides of the head. *In flight:* white wing patches.

Size: L 48–61 cm.

Status: uncommon from May to October.

Habitat: large, deep-water lakes and slow-moving streams.

Nesting: among bushes very near shorelines; in a shallow scrape lined with sticks, leaves,

grass and down, often well concealed by growth; female incubates 9–14 pinkish eggs for up to 28 days.

Feeding: deep, underwater dives lasting up to 1 minute; mainly eats crustaceans; often takes aquatic insects, such as stonefly and caddisfly larvae, and snails.

Voice: courting pair produces guttural and harsh noises, between a *crook* and a *quack*.

Similar Species: *Surf Scoter* (p. 78): no white patches in the wings; male has a white forehead and nape. *Black Scoter* (p. 80): no white patches in the wings.

Best Sites: Elkwater Lake, Cypress Hills PP; Rochon Sands PP; Glenmore Reservoir, Calgary (migration).

BLACK SCOTER

Melanitta nigra

When most birdwatchers have given up on the fall migration and start preparing for the Christmas Bird Count, a small number of Black Scoters race through our province, defying the freeze-up as they pass through in late fall and early winter. • The Black Scoter has been recorded throughout Alberta from May to November on large lakes, but it is the least common of the three scoters in Alberta, and North America in general, and years can pass between reports of this bird in our province. Large flocks of White-winged Scoters and Surf Scoters should be thoroughly checked for this rarely seen bird. • Black Scoters have an especially slender primary feather on each wing that produces a characteristic whistling sound in flight. While swimming, they tend to hold their heads high, or at least level, unlike the other scoters, which tend to look downward.

ID: *General:* dark black plumage; all-black wings. *Male:* black overall; large orange knob on the bill. *Female:* light cheek; dark cap; brown overall; dark grey bill.
Size: L 43–53 cm.
Status: very rare in migration.
Habitat: large, deep-water lakes.
Nesting: does not nest in Alberta.

Feeding: dives underwater; eats aquatic insect larvae; occasionally eats aquatic vegetation and mollusks.
Voice: generally quiet; infrequently an unusual *cour-loo*; wings whistle in flight.
Similar Species: *White-winged Scoter* (p. 79): white wing patches. *Surf Scoter* (p. 78): male has white on the head; female lacks the contrasting pale cheek.
Best Sites: check local bird hotlines for recent sightings; Glenmore Reservoir, Calgary (fall).

OLDSQUAW
Clangula hyemalis

During their spring and fall migrations, these handsome ducks are periodically observed on deep lakes in Alberta. Oldsquaws travel through Alberta between the Arctic and the West Coast, stopping to feed and rest on some of our larger lakes. These elegant ducks tend to stay well offshore, limiting observers to brief glimpses of their long, slender tail feathers. • The breeding and non-breeding plumages of these Arctic-nesting sea ducks are nearly photo-negatives of each other: the spring breeding plumage is mostly dark with white highlights; the winter plumage is mostly white with dark patches. • Oldsquaws are among the noisiest breeders on the tundra, but during migration they pass in silence, cheating Albertans of their distinctive cries. • There is a movement afoot to change this bird's common name, for obvious reasons.

non-breeding

ID: *Breeding male:* dark head with a white eye patch; dark neck and upperparts; white belly; pink bill with a dark base; long, dark central tail feathers. *Non-breeding male:* white head with a dark patch; white neck and belly; dark breast; white patches on the back; pink bill with a dark base; long, dark central tail feathers. *Breeding female:* short tail feathers; grey bill; dark head, throat, wings and back; white underparts. *Non-breeding female:* similar, but generally lighter, especially on the head.
Size: *L* 43–51 cm.

Status: rare during migration.
Habitat: deep lakes, reservoirs and large marshes.
Nesting: does not nest in Alberta.
Feeding: dives underwater for crustaceans and aquatic invertebrates; occasionally eats roots and young shoots.
Voice: courtship call—*owl-owl-owlet*—is rarely heard during the spring migration.
Similar Species: *Northern Pintail* (p. 70): thin white line extending up the base of the neck; grey sides.
Best Sites: Pyramid Lake, Jasper NP; Glenmore Reservoir, Calgary.

BUFFLEHEAD
Bucephala albeola

When the morning mist rises from the calm surface of a woodland pool, the simple black-and-white plumage of a male Bufflehead stands out like a beacon. The white patch on the male's head, which adds to the 'babyface' expression, might serve a role in courtship displays. • The Bufflehead is really a third goldeneye, as similarities in its profile, behaviour and scientific name will attest. • Buffleheads are among the smallest diving ducks in North America. They seem most comfortable occupying the centre of small beaver ponds. • The common name refers to this duck's large head and steep forehead, which are similar in shape to those of a buffalo. The scientific name *Bucephala* also refers to the shape of the head—it means 'ox-headed' in Greek; *albeola* is from the Latin for 'white,' in reference to the male's plumage.

ID: *General:* very small, rounded duck; white speculum in flight; short grey bill; short neck. *Male:* white wedge on the back of the head; head is otherwise dark iridescent green or purple, usually appearing black; dark back; white neck and underparts. *Female:* dark brown head; white, oval ear patch; light brown underparts.
Size: *L* 33–38 cm.
Status: uncommon to common from April to October.
Habitat: open water of lakes, ponds and rivers. *Breeding:* small, wooded ponds and small lakes.
Nesting: often near water; in a tree cavity, usually an abandoned woodpecker nest or a natural cavity; nest chamber can be unlined or filled with a little down; incubates eggs for

28–33 days; ducklings generally remain in the nest for up to 3 days.
Feeding: dives for aquatic invertebrates, mainly water boatmen and mayfly and damselfly larvae, occasionally snails and crustaceans; sometimes eats small fish and pondweeds.
Voice: *Male:* growling call. *Female:* harsh quack.
Similar Species: *Hooded Merganser* (p. 85): white crest is outlined in black. *Harlequin Duck* (p. 77): female has several light spots on the head. *Common Goldeneye* (p. 83) and *Barrow's Goldeneye* (p. 84): males are larger and have a white patch between the eye and the bill. *Other diving ducks:* females are much larger.
Best Sites: Clifford E. Lee Nature Sanctuary; Carburn Park, Calgary.

COMMON GOLDENEYE
Bucephala clangula

The courtship display of the male Common Goldeneye looks for all the world like an avian slapstick routine, although to the bird itself it is probably a serious matter. Beginning in winter, the male performs a number of odd postures and vocalizations, often to rather disinterested females. In one common routine, he arches his puffy, iridescent head backward, until his forehead seems to touch his butt, and then produces a seemingly painful *peent*. • Common Goldeneyes routinely winter on open water throughout Alberta. They provide life and colour in an otherwise frosty landscape, while running the risk of being frozen into the ice while resting and then providing a meal for a Bald Eagle or Common Raven. • Goldeneyes are frequently called 'whistlers,' because the wind whistles through their wings as they fly.

ID: *General:* medium-sized, chunky duck; steep forehead with a peaked head; black wings with large, white patches; golden eyes. *Male:* dark, iridescent green head; round, white cheek patch; dark bill; dark back; white sides and belly. *Female:* chocolate brown head; lighter breast and belly; grey-brown body plumage; dark bill, tipped in yellow in spring/summer.

Size: *L* 41–51 cm.

Status: common from April to October; many overwinter on open water.

Habitat: ponds, lakes and rivers.

Nesting: often close to water, but occasionally quite far from it; cavity nest, up to 18 m high, is lined

with wood chips and down; will use nest boxes; female incubates 6–9 eggs for 28–32 days; ducklings leave the nest after 2–3 days.

Feeding: dives underwater for aquatic insect larvae, crustaceans, tubers and sometimes small fish.

Voice: wings whistle in flight. *Male:* courtship calls are a nasal *peent* and a hoarse *kraaagh*. *Female:* harsh croak.

Similar Species: *Barrow's Goldeneye* (p. 84): male has a large, white, crescent-shaped cheek patch and white spotting high on the back; female has more orange on the bill and a more steeply sloped forehead.

Best Sites: widespread on reasonably deep waters in summer; any open water, often at power plants, in winter; Carburn Park, Calgary (winter).

BARROW'S GOLDENEYE
Bucephala islandica

The Barrow's Goldeneye is one of the most characteristic diving ducks in Alberta's foothills and mountains. It has an amusing foraging style: after making a deep dive for food, the bird pops back up to the surface like a colourful cork. • After becoming familiar with the Common Goldeneye, it is refreshing to see the Barrow's and admire its subtle differences. Although these birds are best seen along the Rockies in Alberta, a few birds stray into the eastern half of the province—some regularly breed in Elk Island National Park. • This species bears the name of Sir John Barrow, secretary to the British Admiralty, who was committed to finding the Northwest Passage. • The scientific name *islandica* refers to Iceland—Barrow's Goldeneyes also breed in Labrador, Greenland and Iceland.

ID: *General:* medium-sized, rounded duck; short bill; steep forehead. *Male:* dark purple head; white crescent on the cheek; white underparts; dark back and wings with white spotting. *Female:* chocolate brown head; orange bill is tipped with black in spring/summer; grey-brown body plumage.
Size: *L* 41–51 cm.
Status: uncommon from April to October.
Habitat: lakes, rivers, ponds and backwaters, usually bordered by deciduous trees; adjacent mixed forests are required for nest sites.
Nesting: in a tree cavity, usually an abandoned woodpecker nest or a natural cavity, up to 15 m

high; down is added to the nest throughout incubation; female incubates 9 or 10 olive green eggs.
Feeding: dives underwater for aquatic nymphs and larvae, especially damselflies and dragonflies; also eats crustaceans and some aquatic plants.
Voice: generally silent. *Male:* 'mewing' call in spring. *Female:* hoarse 'croaks' in spring.
Similar Species: *Common Goldeneye* (p. 83): male has a small, round, white cheek patch and lacks the white spotting on the back; female has a darker bill without the black tip.
Best Sites: Moraine Lake, Banff NP; mountain lakes in Jasper and Waterton Lakes NPs; Carburn Park, Calgary (winter).

HOODED MERGANSER
Lophodytes cucullatus

The male Hooded Merganser might have the most splendid headgear of any Alberta bird. The male raises his crest when he is aroused, whether during courtship or out of agitation. This signal might alert other nearby 'Hoodies' that intruders are present. • Hooded Mergansers are infrequently encountered in Alberta, and they are one of our most sought after ducks from a birdwatcher's perspective. A few birds that winter along the Bow River in Calgary likely offer the easiest opportunity to view these painted-up ducks, although they also winter regularly at the Sundance Power Plant on Wabamun Lake. • The scientific name *Lophodytes* means 'crested diver.' Like other mergansers, it has a slim bill with serrations for holding its slippery aquatic prey.

ID: *General:* slim duck; crested head; thin, pointed bill. *Male:* black head and back; bold white crest is outlined in black; white breast; 2 white shoulder slashes; rusty sides. *Female:* dusky brown body; shaggy, reddish-brown crest. *In flight:* small, white wing patches.
Size: *L* 41–48 cm.
Status: rare to uncommon from April to October; some might over-winter on open water.
Habitat: forested ponds, lakes and rivers.
Nesting: usually in a tree cavity, 4.5–6 m high; rarely on the ground; cavity is lined with leaves, grass and down; female

incubates 10–12 white eggs for 29–33 days.
Feeding: very diverse diet; dives for small fish, caddisfly and dragonfly larvae, snails, amphibians and crayfish.
Voice: low grunts and croaks. *Male:* frog-like *crrrrooo* in courtship display. *Female:* generally quiet; occasionally a harsh *gak* or a croaking *croo-croo-crook*.
Similar Species: *Bufflehead* (p. 82): male lacks the black outline to the crest and the white shoulder slashes. *Other small diving ducks:* females lack the crest.
Best Sites: Inglewood Bird Sanctuary, Calgary; Wabamun Lake PP; Carburn Park, Calgary.

RED-BREASTED MERGANSER
Mergus serrator

Its glossy, slicked-back crest and wild, red eyes give the Red-breasted Merganser a crazed look. Formerly called 'Sawbill' and 'Sea-Robin,' it is probably a good thing that bird names have been standardized—who knows what we'd be calling these punk-haired birds now. • To visit the breeding grounds of the Red-breasted Merganser in Alberta is difficult but rewarding. Red-breasted Mergansers breed on some of Alberta's most remote wilderness lakes. The male performs one of the most unusual courting displays: he lowers the base of his neck underwater and stares about with his blood red eyes. • Red-breasted Mergansers are infrequently encountered on lakes in Alberta during their migration between their coastal wintering grounds and their northern breeding grounds. • The scientific name *serrator* is Latin for 'sawyer'; it refers to this bird's bill.

ID: *General:* large, elongated duck; thin, red, serrated bill; shaggy, slicked-back crest. *Male:* green head; light rusty breast is spotted with black; white collar; grey sides; black-and-white wing covers; red eyes. *Female:* grey-brown overall; reddish head. *In flight:* male has 2 white wing patches separated by 2 narrow, black bars; female has 2 white wing patches.
Size: *L* 48–66 cm.
Status: rare to uncommon from April to November.
Habitat: lakes and large rivers.
Nesting: on the ground near a shoreline, under bushes or branches or in dense grass and sedges; well-concealed nest is

made with plant material and often lined with down; female builds the nest and incubates the eggs.
Feeding: dives underwater for small fish; also eats aquatic invertebrates, fish eggs and crustaceans.
Voice: generally quiet. *Male:* cat-like *yeow* during courtship and feeding. *Female:* harsh *kho-kha.*
Similar Species: *Common Merganser* (p. 87): cleanly defined, white throat; male has a white breast and lacks the crest; female has a chestnut head.
Best Sites: Caribou Mountains; Canadian Shield region in extreme northeastern Alberta; Chip Lake; Glenmore Reservoir, Calgary (migration).

COMMON MERGANSER
Mergus merganser

Straining like a jumbo jet in take-off, the Common Merganser runs along the surface of the water, beating its wings until it gains sufficient speed to become airborne. Once up and away, this great duck flies arrow-straight, low over the water, making broad sweeping turns to follow the meanderings of rivers. • The Common Merganser is the most widespread and abundant merganser in North America. It also occurs in Europe and Asia, where it is called the Goosander. • These ducks are highly social, and they often gather in large groups during migration, when they are easily seen along rivers in our larger cities, without apparent concern for the upcoming winter. • As ice forms, Common Mergansers retreat to the open waters of southern rivers, cooling ponds and springs, which will be the winter homes for some.

ID: *General:* large, elongated body; long, red bill. *Male:* glossy green head without a crest; brilliant orange bill and feet; white body plumage; black spinal stripe. *Female:* rusty head; clean white neck and throat; grey body. *In flight:* shallow wingbeats; body is compressed and arrow-like.
Size: *L* 56–69 cm.
Status: uncommon to common from March to October; some might overwinter on open water.
Habitat: large rivers and deep lakes.
Nesting: often in a tree cavity, 4.5–6 m high; occasionally on the ground, under a bush or log, on a cliff ledge or in a large nest box; usually not far from water; female incubates 8–11 eggs for up to 35 days.

Feeding: dives underwater (up to 9 m) for small fish, usually trout, suckers, perch and minnows; young eat aquatic invertebrates.
Voice: *Male:* harsh *uig-a*, like a guitar twang. *Female:* harsh *karr karr*.
Similar Species: *Red-breasted Merganser* (p. 86): shaggy crest; male has a spotted, red breast; female lacks the cleanly defined, white throat. *Mallard* (p. 66): male has a chestnut breast. *Common Goldeneye* (p. 83): male has a white cheek patch. *Common Loon* (p. 36): white spotting on the back; bill is not orange.
Best Sites: Inglewood Bird Sanctuary, Calgary; North Saskatchewan River, Edmonton; South Saskatchewan River, Medicine Hat.

RUDDY DUCK
Oxyura jamaicensis

Clowns of the wetlands, Ruddy Ducks display energetically on their breeding ponds. With great vigour, the small males pump their bright blue bills, almost touching their breasts. The *plap, plap, plap-plap-plap* of the display increases in speed to its climax: a spasmodic jerk and sputter. • Female Ruddies commonly lay up to 15 eggs—a remarkable feat, considering that their eggs are bigger than those of a Mallard, even though a Mallard is twice the size of a Ruddy Duck. • The Ruddy Duck is the only member of the stiff-tailed duck group found in Alberta. Their large head casts a distinctive profile, which is easily identified even when colours are not obvious. • Ruddy Ducks often seem reluctant to take flight. When they do, like most diving ducks they must patter across the water for quite a distance before they become airborne.

breeding

ID: *General:* small duck; large bill and head; short neck; long, stiff tail feathers (often cocked upward). *Breeding male:* white cheek; chestnut red body; blue bill; black tail and crown. *Female:* brown overall; dark cheek stripe; darker crown and back. *Non-breeding male:* like a female, but with a white cheek.
Size: *L* 38–41 cm.
Status: common from April to September.
Habitat: shallow marshes with dense emergent vegetation (such as cattails or bulrushes) and muddy bottoms.
Nesting: in cattails, bulrushes or other emergent vegetation;

occasionally on a muskrat lodge or a log; basket-like nest is always suspended over water; occasionally uses the abandoned nest of another duck or coot.
Feeding: dives to the bottom of wetlands for the seeds of pondweeds, sedges and bulrushes and for the leafy parts of aquatic plants; also eats a few aquatic invertebrates.
Voice: *Male:* courtship display is *chuck-chuck-chuck-chur-r-r-r. Female:* generally silent.
Similar Species: *Cinnamon Teal* (p. 68): lacks the white cheek and the blue bill. *Diving ducks* (pp. 72–84): females lack the long tail and the dark facial stripe.
Best Sites: Clifford E. Lee Nature Sanctuary; Eagle Lake.

OSPREY
Pandion haliaetus

Throughout the world, in appropriate habitats, the great stick nests of Ospreys rest high atop trees and power poles. Things are no different here in Alberta, where Ospreys patrol over lakes and streams, scanning the water for fish. At the end of a headfirst dive, the bird thrusts its talons forward the instant before striking the water. Rising back into the air and shaking its soggy feathers, the Osprey positions the still-squirming fish to face forward for optimum aerodynamics. • An Osprey's feet are specialized to hold fish: two toes point forward, two point back, and the soles are covered with rough, slime-penetrating scales. Also, Osprey feathers are water resistant, which must be a welcome feature when a large fish briefly pulls an Osprey underwater. • Ospreys are neither hawks nor eagles—taxonomists put them in their own subfamily, with a membership of only one species.

ID: *General:* large raptor; dark brown upperparts; white underparts; dark eye line; light crown. *Male:* all-white throat. *Female:* fine, dark 'necklace.' *In flight:* long wings are held in a shallow M; dark wrist patches; tail is finely banded with black and white.
Size: *L* 56–64 cm; *W* 137–183 cm.
Status: uncommon from April to September.
Habitat: lakes and slow-flowing rivers and streams.
Nesting: on treetops, usually near water; also on specially made platforms, utility poles or transmission towers, 14–27 m high; large stick nest; male feeds the female while she incubates the eggs.

Feeding: dramatic, feet-first dives into the water; fish, averaging 1 kg, make up almost all of the diet.
Voice: series of melodious ascending whistles: *chewk-chewk-chewk*; also an often-heard *kip-kip-kip.*
Similar Species: *Bald Eagle* (p. 90): larger; holds wings flat when soaring; adult has a clean white head and tail, dark underparts and no wrist patches; subadult lacks a well-defined pattern in the plumage.
Best Sites: Wabamun Lake PP; Chip Lake; Brazeau Reservoir; Canmore; Sir Winston Churchill PP; Bow Valley PP; Bow River, Calgary; Waterton Lakes NP.

BALD EAGLE

Haliaeetus leucocephalus

The Bald Eagle is well established in Alberta, but it seems that only a handful of birdwatchers ever see them. On a typical spring or fall outing, or anywhere near open water during winter, you are likely to spot at least one of these birds. Pointing one out to a budding naturalist is one of the most eye-opening things you can do to promote bird appreciation. • Immature Bald Eagles with whitish bellies are among the most frequently misidentified raptors in our area, often mistaken for hawks, Golden Eagles and even ravens. • Bald Eagles are part of the sea eagle group, and they feed mainly on fish, including fish carrion and the stolen prey of Ospreys. Aerial battles between Ospreys and Bald Eagles are among the most spectacular sights a birdwatcher can hope for in Alberta. • The Bald Eagle is not really bald, of course—it is merely white-headed.

ID: *Sexes similar:* very large raptor; broad wings are held flat in flight. *Adult:* white head and tail; dark brown body; yellow beak and feet. *Immature:* 1st-year is brown overall, with a dark bill and some white in the underwings; 2nd-year has a wide, white band at the base of the tail, a light belly and light underwings; 3rd- and 4th-years have light heads, dark eye lines, yellow at the base of the bill, variable white body plumage and paler eyes.
Size: *L* 76–109 cm; *W* 1.7–2.4 m.
Status: uncommon from March to November; some overwinter near open water.
Habitat: large lakes, rivers, cooling ponds and open areas.

Nesting: usually in trees bordering lakes or large rivers; huge stick nest is up to 4.5 m across (largest nest of any North American bird) and is sometimes reused by Ospreys, ravens and Great Horned Owls.
Feeding: waterbirds, small mammals and fish captured at the water's surface; frequently feeds on carrion; pirates fish from Ospreys.
Voice: thin, weak squeal or gull-like cackle: *kleek-kik-kik-kik* or *kah-kah-kah.*
Similar Species: Adult is distinctive. *Golden Eagle* (p. 100): adult is similar to a juvenile Bald Eagle, but with a golden nape, a smaller bill and a shorter neck; immature has a prominent white patch on each wing and at the base of the tail.
Best Sites: *Summer:* Vermilion Lakes, Banff NP. *April:* Wildcat Hills. *Winter:* Wabamun Lake PP; Dickson Dam; open areas of Bow River in Calgary, Canmore and Banff NP; South Saskatchewan River, Medicine Hat.

NORTHERN HARRIER

Circus cyaneus

The Northern Harrier might be the easiest raptor to identify on the wing—no other hawk routinely flies so close to the ground or flashes so white a rump. • Harriers search for food while skimming over the tops of long grasses, relying on sudden surprise attacks to capture their prey. • The courtship flight of the Northern Harrier is a joy to watch. The male performs huge aerial loops in his attempt to impress the female, who remains on the ground. • The scientific name *Circus* refers to this hawk's often erratic flight; 'harrier' refers to its habit of coursing back and forth low over fields. This bird was once known as the Marsh Hawk in North America.

ID: *General:* long wings and tail; white rump; black wing tips. *Male:* grey upperparts; white underparts; indistinct tail bands. *Female:* brownish rather than grey. *Immature:* rich reddish-brown plumage; dark tail bands; streaked breast, sides and flanks.
Size: *L* 41–61 cm; *W* 112–119 cm.
Status: common from March to October.
Habitat: open country, including fields, wet meadows, cattail marshes, croplands and alpine meadows; some migrate at higher elevations in fall.
Nesting: on the ground, often on a slightly raised mound, usually

in grass, cattails or tall vegetation; flat plat-form nest is built of grass, sticks and cat-tails; female incubates 4–6 bluish eggs.
Feeding: hunts in low, coursing flights, often less than 9 m high; eats small mam-mals, birds, amphibians, reptiles and some invertebrates.
Voice: most vocal near the nest and during courtship, but generally quiet; high-pitched *ke-ke-ke-ke-ke-ke* near the nest.
Similar Species: *Rough-legged Hawk* (p. 99): broader wings; wrist patches; fan-like tail. *Red-tailed Hawk* (p. 97): lacks the white rump and the long, narrow tail.
Best Sites: Clifford E. Lee Nature Sanc-tuary; Beaverhill Lake; Slack Slough.

SHARP-SHINNED HAWK

Accipiter striatus

After a successful hunt, the diminutive Sharp-shinned Hawk perches on a 'plucking post' with its prey in its talons. Sharpies prey almost exclusively on birds, so they are experienced feather pluckers. • When delivering food to his nestlings, the male Sharp-shinned Hawk is quite cautious around his mate—she is typically one-third larger than the male and frequently bad tempered. The sexes are such different sizes that they prey on different-sized animals. • Accipiters, named after their genus, are woodland hawks. Their short, rounded wings and long, rudder-like tails give these birds the manueverability to negotiate a maze of tree trunks in pursuit of small birds. • The 'sharp shins' of this hawk serve no purpose in field identification.

Nesting: usually builds a new stick nest each year; nest is normally about 60 cm across; might remodel an abandoned crow nest; female incubates 4 or 5 eggs for up to 35 days; male feeds the female during incubation.

Feeding: pursues small birds through forests; rarely takes small mammals, amphibians and insects.

Voice: silent, except during the breeding season, when an intense and often repeated *kik-kik-kik-kik* can be heard.

ID: *Sexes similar. Adult:* small hawk; short, rounded wings; long, straight tail; blue-grey back; red horizontal bars on the underparts; red eyes. *Immature:* brown overall; brown eyes; vertical, brown streaking on the breast and belly. *In flight:* flap-and-glide flyer; tail is heavily barred and is more-or-less squared off at the tip.

Size: *Male:* L 25–30 cm; W 51–61 cm. *Female:* L 30–36 cm; W 61–71 cm.

Status: uncommon from April to September.

Habitat: dense to semi-open forests; occasionally along rivers; soars on thermals in open areas during migration (especially in fall).

Similar Species: *Cooper's Hawk* (p. 93): usually larger; tail tip is more rounded and has a broader terminal band. *American Kestrel* (p. 101): long, pointed wings; 2 dark 'sideburns'; often seen in open country. *Merlin* (p. 102): pointed wings; rapid wingbeats; lacks the red breast streaks.

Best Sites: Beaverhill Lake; Banff NP; Kananaskis Country (late September).

COOPER'S HAWK
Accipiter cooperii

If songbirds dream, the Cooper's Hawk is sure to be the subject of nightmares. This forest hawk hunts silently, using surprise and speed to its advantage. Bursting from an overhead perch, a Cooper's Hawk will pursue a songbird even through dense forest, eventually grasping its quarry in mid-air and killing it with a talon to the heart. • Now that the persecution of Cooper's Hawks has been almost eliminated, these forest raptors are recolonizing former habitats. In Alberta, Cooper's Hawks are being seen with increasing frequency. • Rural birdfeeders can attract Cooper's and Sharp-shinned hawks—not for the seeds, but for the finches and sparrows that the seeds attract. • This bird bears the name of William Cooper, one of the many hunters who supplied English and American ornithologists with bird specimens for museum collections during the early 19th century.

ID: *Sexes similar. Adult:* short round wings; long tail; squarish head; blue-grey back; reddish horizontal barring on the underparts; red eyes; white, terminal tail band. *Immature:* brown overall; brown eyes; vertical brown streaks on the breast and belly. *In flight:* flap-and-glide flyer; heavily barred, rounded tail.
Size: *Male: L* 38–43 cm; *W* 69–81 cm. *Female: L* 43–48 cm; *W* 81–94 cm.
Status: uncommon from April to September.
Habitat: mixed woodlands, riparian woodlands and suburban areas; usually soars on thermals in open areas during migration.
Nesting: in the crotch of a coniferous or deciduous tree, often among the outer branches; nest is made of sticks and twigs; might reuse an abandoned crow nest; female incubates 4 or 5 bluish eggs for 30–36 days; does not tolerate Sharp-shinned Hawks nesting in the area.

Feeding: pursues prey in flights through forests; eats mostly songbirds, squirrels and chipmunks; often takes its prey to a plucking post prior to eating.
Voice: fast, woodpecker-like *cac-cac-cac-cac.*
Similar Species: *Sharp-shinned Hawk* (p. 92): usually smaller; tail is not as rounded at the tip.
Best Sites: Whitemud Creek ravine, Edmonton; Banff NP; Kananaskis Country (late September).

93

NORTHERN GOSHAWK

Accipiter gentilis

The Northern Goshawk might be the most aggressive and ill-tempered bird in Alberta—it will harass virtually any perceived threat to its nest. It shrieks and swoops at intruders and does not hesitate to rake their backs or heads with its razor-sharp talons. • Goshawks will prey on any animal they can overtake. After chasing and catching their prey in a high-speed aerial sprint, these raptors stab repeatedly at the victim's internal organs with their long talons. • Northern Goshawks require extensive areas of forests in which to hunt and raise their families, and their populations have declined significantly throughout northern Europe and Asia. They are still found in remote areas of Alberta, and they are occasionally even seen within city limits in northern Alberta.

ID: *Sexes similar. Adult:* large size; rounded wings; dark crown; white eyebrow; blue-grey back; finely barred, grey underparts; long, banded tail; red eyes. *Immature:* brown overall; light underparts; pale eyebrow.
Size: *Male:* L 53–58 cm; W 102–109 cm. *Female:* L 58–64 cm; W 109–119 cm.
Status: rare to uncommon year-round.
Habitat: *Breeding:* mature coniferous, deciduous and mixed woodlands. *Non-breeding:* forest edges, parks and farmlands.
Nesting: in deep woods; in a crotch, usually 6–18 m up a deciduous tree; bulky nest is built with sticks and twigs, many still green with leaves; nest is often

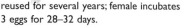

reused for several years; female incubates 3 eggs for 28–32 days.
Feeding: low foraging flights through the forest; feeds primarily on grouse, rabbits, ground squirrels and tree squirrels.
Voice: silent, except during the breeding season, when adults utter a loud, shrill and fast *kak-kak-kak-kak*.
Similar Species: *Cooper's Hawk* (p. 93) and *Sharp-shinned Hawk* (p. 92): smaller; adults have reddish breast bars and no white eyebrow stripe. *Buteo hawks* (pp. 95–99): shorter tails; broader wings. *Gyrfalcon* (p. 105): more pointed wings.
Best Sites: Sir Winston Churchill PP; Edmonton river valley; Banff NP; Kananaskis Country (late September).

BROAD-WINGED HAWK
Buteo platypterus

Unlike its buteo brethren, the Broad-wing does not spend as much time spiralling on rising, warm-air thermals during summer, although it is fully equipped with the basics for soaring. Its breeding-season foraging usually keeps the Broad-winged Hawk in the forest, although you will sometimes see it circling over patches of boreal forest. Migrants, on the other hand, are almost always seen soaring. • While the spectacular migrations of Broad-wings typical of eastern Canada are not seen in Alberta, we hope that our birdwatching friends elsewhere will realize that almost all of the dark-phase Broad-wings in the world nest in Alberta and pass eastward as they head south in fall. • All the soaring hawks (members of the genus *Buteo*) tend to have short tails and broad wings. These features are even more accentuated in the Broad-winged Hawk.

light phase

ID: *Sexes similar. Light-phase adult:* broad, black and white tail bands; generally light underwings with a dark outline; russet barring on the breast; brown upperparts. *Dark-phase adult:* brown wing linings; lighter flight feathers; broadly barred tail; dark brown upperparts. *Immature:* brown streaks on a white breast; buffy and dark brown tail bands.
Size: *L* 36–48 cm; *W* 81–99 cm.
Status: rare to uncommon from May to September.
Habitat: *Breeding:* boreal forests. *In migration:* ridges; also riparian and deciduous forests.
Nesting: usually in a deciduous tree, often near water; occasionally in a coniferous tree; small, bulky stick nest is built in a crotch, 4.5–15 m high; usually builds a new nest each year; occasionally reuses hawk, crow or squirrel nests.

Feeding: swoops from a perch for small animals, especially small mammals, amphibians, insects and young birds.
Voice: high-pitched, whistled *peeeo-wee-ee*; generally silent during migration.
Similar Species: *Other buteos:* lack the broad banding on the tail. *Accipiters* (pp. 92–94): long, narrow tails without the broad banding.
Best Sites: Sir Winston Churchill PP; Chain Lakes, north of Hanna; Elk Island NP; Sheep River Wildlife Sanctuary (fall).

SWAINSON'S HAWK
Buteo swainsoni

While the Red-tailed Hawk can dominate the summer skies over most of the province, the Swainson's Hawk takes centre stage where open country exceeds forests, and especially in grassy areas where Richardson's Ground Squirrels are abundant. • Once you learn to look for relatively pointed wing tips, slightly up-tilted wings and flight feathers that are darker than the wing lining, you will be able to identify these birds as far away as you can see them.
• Twice a year, Swainson's Hawks undertake the longest migration of any Alberta raptor, wintering as far south as the southern tip of South America. Recently, many of our hawks were killed by the incautious use of insecticides in Argentina, reminding us that the conservation of migratory species requires international cooperation. • This hawk bears the name of Englishman William Swainson, an early 19th-century illustrator of natural history.

light phase

dark phase

ID: *Sexes similar:* long wings with pointed tips; narrowly banded tail; dark flight feathers. *Light phase* (more common): dark bib; white belly; white wing linings contrast with the dark flight feathers. *Dark phase:* dark overall; brown wing linings blend with the flight feathers. *In flight:* holds the wings in a shallow V.
Size: *Male: L* 48–51 cm; *W* 132 cm. *Female: L* 51–56 cm; *W* 132 cm.
Status: common from April to September.
Habitat: open fields, grasslands, sagebrush and agricultural areas.

Nesting: often in solitary trees in open fields or on the prairie; builds a large stick nest; often uses the abandoned nests of other raptors, crows, ravens or magpies; uses the same nest repeatedly; female incubates 2 or 3 eggs for about 28–35 days.
Feeding: dives for voles, mice and ground squirrels; also eats snakes, small birds and large insects, such as grasshoppers and crickets.
Voice: typical call, *keeeaar,* is higher pitched than a Red-tail's.
Similar Species: *Red-tailed Hawk* (p. 97): wings held flat in flight; more rounded wing tips. *Other buteos:* flight feathers are lighter than the wing lining. *Golden Eagle* (p. 100): much larger; golden nape; massive bill.
Best Sites: Trans-Canada Highway between Calgary and Saskatchewan; Hwy. 2 between Edmonton and Calgary.

RED-TAILED HAWK
Buteo jamaicensis

Red-tails are the most commonly seen hawks in Alberta, especially in the aspen parkland, and any sizable woodlot will likely host a pair of these birds. • The Red-tailed Hawk's piercing call is as impressive as the profile of an eagle, and the producers of television commercials and movies often cheat by putting the two together. • During their spring courtship, excited Red-tailed Hawks will dive at each other, sometimes locking talons and tumbling through the air together before breaking off to avoid crashing to the ground. • Typical birds are easy to recognize with their brick-red tails, but it takes an experienced eye to identify immature Red-tails, the light-phase 'Krider's Hawk' and the dark-phase 'Harlan's Hawk.'

ID: *Sexes similar. Adult:* some light mottling on the back; typically has a brick red upper tail surface and a dark 'belt.' *Immature:* lacks the red tail; flight feathers are lighter than the wing lining. *In flight:* dark leading edge on the underwing nearest the body; rounded wing tips; holds its wings flat while soaring. *'Harlan's Hawk':* generally dark; dark, mottled tail can have traces of red. *'Krider's Hawk':* very light; nearly white tail; dark leading edge on the underwing.

Size: *Male:* L 46–58 cm; W 117–147 cm. *Female:* L 51–64 cm; W 117–147 cm.

Status: very common from April to October.

Habitat: open country with some trees, roadsides, fields and mixed forests.

Nesting: in woodlands adjacent to fields or shrublands; typically in a deciduous tree; rarely

on cliffs; bulky stick nest is usually added to each year; both parents incubate the eggs; female alone raises the young, which fly at 6¹/₂ weeks.

Feeding: scans for food while perched or soaring; dives to capture prey; occasionally forages by stalking on the ground; eats voles, mice, rabbits, chipmunks, birds, amphibians and reptiles.

Voice: powerful, descending scream: *Keeearrrr!*

Similar Species: *Swainson's Hawk* (p. 96): all-dark back; dark flight feathers; holds its wings in a shallow V; more pointed wing tips. *Ferruginous Hawk* (p. 98): dark legs contrast with the light underparts. *Rough-legged Hawk* (p. 99): white tail base; dark elbow patches on the underwings. *Broad-winged Hawk* (p. 95): broadly banded tail.

Best Sites: Fish Creek PP; Hwy. 2 between Edmonton and Calgary; Elk Island NP.

FERRUGINOUS HAWK
Buteo regalis

Cruising low over the contours of the bald prairie or circling high above the badlands, the Ferruginous Hawk is a bird of Alberta's southeast corner. Its combination of huge size, rich colour and relative rarity make this the favourite buteo of many birdwatchers in the province. • Lately, conservationists have been concerned about this species's numbers in Alberta. It seems that most of the habitat available to these birds is well-populated, and that habitat protection is the key to the species's future. • Ferruginous Hawks typically nest in trees, and on the prairies this might mean that each and every lone cottonwood has either a pair of Swainson's or a pair of Ferruginous hawks in its crown. Artificial nesting platforms erected by conscientious land stewards help reduce this congestion. • A very large, noble bird, this species is well deserving of the scientific name *regalis*.

light phase

ID: *Sexes similar:* largest buteo. *Light-phase adult:* rusty red shoulders and back; light underparts; dark legs; light tail is tipped with rust red. *Dark-phase adult* (less common): dark underparts; white tail; dark wing linings; light flight feathers. *Immature:* very light; might have light-coloured legs.
Size: L 56–69 cm; W 142 cm.
Status: rare to uncommon from April to September.
Habitat: open grasslands, badlands and croplands.
Nesting: usually in a solitary tree, on a cliff or on the ground; large, compact nest is made of sticks, weeds and cow dung and lined with finer materials;

female incubates 2–4 eggs for 32–33 days; male provides the food.
Feeding: dives from high soaring flights; primarily eats ground squirrels, rabbits and hares; also takes snakes and small birds.
Voice: typical, hawk-style *kreeah,* dropping at the end.
Similar Species: *Red-tailed Hawk* (p. 97): underparts are generally darker; dark leading edge on the underwing near the body; usually has a red tail; perched 'Krider's Hawk' is easily confused with an immature Ferruginous. *Swainson's Hawk* (p. 96): dark flight feathers; light wing linings. *Rough-legged Hawk* (p. 99): dark 'elbow' patches.
Best Sites: Hanna; Dinosaur PP; Suffield Military Reserve; Sunnynook-Pollockville; Jenner.

ROUGH-LEGGED HAWK

Buteo lagopus

This Arctic-nesting buteo migrates south through Alberta in October and returns with the Red-tails in late March. It is well adapted to cold climates, and many Rough-legs will overwinter in some parts of Alberta. • Populations of this species cycle with those of northern lemmings. When lemming numbers are high, Rough-legs can produce up to seven young, but in lean years a pair is fortunate to raise a single chick. • The Rough-legged Hawk often 'wind-hovers' to scan the ground below, flapping to maintain a stationary position while facing upwind. • This species is our only buteo with distinctive male and female plumages, which makes it more difficult to identify to species, but more interesting once the identity and gender have been determined. • The Rough-legged Hawk is so called because its feet are fully feathered to the toes; the scientific name *lagopus*, meaning 'hare's foot,' also refers to this feature.

ID: *In flight:* often wind-hovers; light phase has dark 'elbow' patches. *Light-phase female:* black-tipped tail with a broad white base; light head and breast form a 'hood' that contrasts with the dark belly and back. *Light-phase male:* dark tail tip is broader than in the female; less hooded appearance. *Dark-phase adult:* much like 'Harlan's' Red-tailed Hawk, but with a more distinct dark tail tip and light tail base. *Immature:* similar to a light-phase female; light patches in the upperwings.
Size: *L* 48–61 cm; *W* 122–142 cm.
Status: uncommon to common in March and from September to October; uncommon in winter south of Calgary.

Habitat: open grasslands, agricultural fields and meadows.
Nesting: does not nest in Alberta.
Feeding: hovers and soars while searching for prey; primarily eats small rodents; occasionally eats birds, amphibians and large insects.
Voice: alarm call is a cat-like *kee-eer*, usually dropping at the end.
Similar Species: *Other buteos:* rarely hover; adults lack the dark 'elbow' patches and the white tail base. *Northern Harrier* (p. 91): slimmer; longer tail; facial disc.
Best Sites: *Fall:* Sheep River Wildlife Sanctuary. *Winter:* Hwy. 1A between Cochrane and Exshaw; Hwy. 22 between Turner Valley and Cremona.

GOLDEN EAGLE
Aquila chrysaetos

The Golden Eagle is a powerful bird of rugged landscapes. For people who disdain the Bald Eagle's habit of feeding on dead fish, the Golden reigns supreme. (Somehow, word hasn't gotten out that the Golden Eagle is also a habitual carrion feeder.) A few good looks at either species, however, will convince any thoughtful person that their magnificence is incontestable. • In the last few years, naturalists have discovered a mind-boggling migration of thousands of Golden Eagles through a corridor in the Alberta Rockies. They fly high—that is why they were missed for so long—but good binoculars and spotting scopes have allowed eagle watchers to document the phenomenon. Canmore hosts an eagle festival every fall, and the birds are visible from the centre of town. • Golden Eagles and Bald Eagles are not closely related— they share the name 'eagle' because of their huge size.

ID: *Sexes similar. Adult:* huge, dark raptor; golden tint on the neck and head; brown tail is slightly banded with white; yellow feet; dark bill. *Immature:* white tail base and wing patches. *In flight:* broad wings are held flat while soaring; relatively short neck and long tail.
Size: *L* 76–102 cm; *W* 2–2.3 m.
Status: uncommon from March to November; a few overwinter.
Habitat: open and semi-open mountainous areas in the subalpine and alpine; steep canyons and badlands along prairie rivers; occasionally seen at landfills or reservoirs in winter and on migration.
Nesting: usually on a cliff overlooking an area with many small mammals; infrequently in trees; nest is made of sticks,

branches and roots and measures up to 3 m across; often uses the same nest site for many years, and it might become stained white from droppings.
Feeding: swoops on prey from a soaring flight; eats ground squirrels, hares, rabbits, marmots and grouse; often eats carrion; can kill the young of goats, sheep or deer.
Voice: generally quiet; rarely a short bark.
Similar Species: *Bald Eagle* (p. 90): longer neck; shorter tail; immature lacks the distinct white wing and tail patches. *Dark-phase Swainson's Hawk* (p. 96): smaller; more pointed wings are held in a shallow V.
Best Sites: Canmore; Jasper NP; Banff NP; Dinosaur PP; Medicine Hat; Mt. Lorette area, Kananaskis Country (migration).

AMERICAN KESTREL
Falco sparverius

The American Kestrel is the smallest of our five falcons, but it is not merely a miniature version of its relatives. Kestrels are more buoyant in flight, and they are less inclined towards the all-out aerial attacks that have made other falcons such revered predators. • Kestrels typically perch on power lines—a fact that is often the only clue you need to identify them. Also, like the Rough-legged Hawk, the American Kestrel often hunts by wind-hovering. • Some naturalists are worried that the American Kestrel is becoming less common in the parklands, possibly from a lack of nesting sites in old dead trees. • Studies have shown that the Eurasian Kestrel can detect ultraviolet reflections from rodent urine on the ground. It is not known if the American Kestrel has this same ability. • Old field guides refer to this species as the Sparrow Hawk, a name that first referred to a European accipiter.

ID: *General:* small falcon; 2 well-marked moustache stripes. *Male:* rusty back and tail; blue-grey wings; colourful head pattern; lightly spotted underparts. *Female:* rusty back and wings. *In flight:* frequently hovers; long rusty tail; buoyant, indirect flight style.
Size: *L* 19–20 cm; *W* 51–61 cm.
Status: common from April to October.
Habitat: open fields, forests, forest edges, grasslands, roadsides and agricultural areas with hunting perches and nesting trees.

Nesting: in a natural cavity or an abandoned woodpecker cavity (usually a flicker's); occasionally uses an old magpie or crow nest; eggs are incubated for 29–30 days.
Feeding: swoops from a perch (often a power line) or from wind-hovering; mainly eats insects and some small vertebrates.
Voice: loud, often repeated, shrill *killy-killy-killy* when excited; female's voice is lower pitched.
Similar Species: *Merlin* (p. 102): lacks the double facial stripes; does not hover; flight is more powerful and direct. *Sharp-shinned Hawk* (p. 92): short, rounded wings; flap-and-glide flight.
Best Sites: Dinosaur PP; Police Point Park, Medicine Hat.

MERLIN
Falco columbarius

Although it is only slightly larger than a kestrel, the Merlin is another bird alto-gether. Often mistaken for a Peregrine Falcon, the Merlin snatches other birds in mid-air at high speed, in classic falcon fashion. Merlins are frequently seen flying low and fast over trees and houses, hoping to surprise unwary songbirds. • Edmonton has more nesting Merlins (somewhere in the vicinity of 60 pairs) than any other city. In winter, they feed mainly on Bohemian Waxwings, but in summer they switch to House Sparrows. Just when the baby Merlins need food, their parents find a veritable banquet of newly fledged, naïve House Sparrows ripe for the pluck-ing. • The Merlin was formerly known as the Pigeon Hawk, and the scientific name *colum-barius* comes from the Latin for 'pigeon,' which it somewhat resembles in flight. Adult female Merlins can sometimes kill Rock Doves, but the males are too small to take on such a challenge.

ID: *General:* streaked underparts; indis-tinct facial stripes. *Male 'Prairie Merlin':* light blue-grey back and crown. *Female 'Prairie Merlin':* brown back and crown. *'Tundra Merlin':* darker; more heavily marked. *In flight:* rapid wingbeats; long, narrow, band-ed tail; pointed wings.
Size: *L* 25–30 cm; *W* 58–66 cm.
Status: uncommon year-round, mainly in large cities in winter.
Habitat: *Breeding:* mixed and coniferous forests; suburban areas. *In migration:* open fields, grass-lands and lakeshores.
Nesting: in coniferous or deciduous trees, crevices or cliffs; might reuse abandoned raptor, crow, jay or magpie nests; might line the nest with green

vegetation; either parent incubates 4 or 5 eggs for 28–31 days.
Feeding: overtakes smaller birds in flight; also eats large insects and nestlings.
Voice: loud, noisy, cackling cry: *kek-kek-kek-kek-kek* or *ki-ki-ki-ki;* calls in flight or while perched.
Similar Species: *American Kestrel* (p. 101): 2 facial stripes; less powerful flight style. *Peregrine Falcon* (p. 104): larger; well-marked, dark hood and moustache mark. *Prairie Falcon* (p. 103): larger; dark 'wing pits.' *Sharp-shinned Hawk* (p. 92) and *Cooper's Hawk* (p. 93): short, rounded wings; vertical breast streaks. *Rock Dove* (p. 178): broader wings in flight; shorter tail; often glides with its wings held in a V.
Best Sites: well-treed neighbourhoods in Calgary and Edmonton.

PRAIRIE FALCON
Falco mexicanus

Spending time along the big prairie rivers of Alberta wouldn't be the same without the Prairie Falcon. It is the classic falcon of the West, and it is not a familiar bird to eastern birdwatchers. • Prairie Falcons nests on steep sandstone cliffs, and they are often heard high overhead, cackling at the intrusion of people, before they are seen. • Although Prairie Falcons are about the same size as Peregrines, they are more closely related to Gyrfalcons, which shows in both their appearance and hunting styles. A large portion of the Prairie Falcon's diet in Alberta consists of Richardson's Ground Squirrels.
• When young falcons first leave the nest, they have all the equipment for spectacular flight but none of the know-how. One local raptor biologist described it as 'a 16-year-old kid on a Kawasaki Ninja motor bike.'

ID: *Sexes similar:* brown upperparts; light face with dark, narrow moustache stripes; light underparts with brown spotting. *In flight:* black 'wing pits'; pointed wings; long, narrow, banded tail; rapid wingbeats.
Size: *Male: L* 36–38 cm; *W* 94–99 cm. *Female: L* 43–46 cm; *W* 104–109 cm.
Status: uncommon from March to October.
Habitat: *Breeding:* river canyons and valleys. *In migration:* open, treeless country, such as alpine meadows, open fields, grasslands and sagebrush flats.
Nesting: on cliff ledges or crevices; sometimes in trees; rarely in the abandoned nests of other raptors or crows; eggs are laid on bare ground.
Feeding: high-speed aerial attack, often overtaking songbirds

and shorebirds in mid-air; also surprises ground squirrels in low, fast attacks.
Voice: alarm call is a rapid, shrill *kik-kik-kik-kik*.
Similar Species: no other falcon has dark 'wing pits.' *Peregrine Falcon* (p. 104): dark hood; lacks the narrow moustache. *Gyrfalcon* (p. 105): larger. *Merlin* (p. 102): smaller. *Swainson's Hawk* (p. 96): rounded wings in flight; lacks the dark 'wing pits'; immature might have a moustache mark, but is generally heavier and easy to recognize with further scrutiny.
Best Sites: Dinosaur PP; Writing-on-Stone PP; Sheep River Wildlife Sanctuary.

PEREGRINE FALCON
Falco peregrinus

Although Peregrines can be seen with relative ease in Edmonton and Calgary, where birds have been encouraged to nest on high buildings, there is nothing quite like seeing this finely tuned hunter in a natural setting. To watch a Peregrine swoop down on a flock of shorebirds is to witness nature in the raw. • The Peregrine Falcon's awesome speed (it can dive at 360 km/h) and hunting skills were little defense against the pesticide DDT, which was used until the 1970s, and which caused contaminated birds to lay eggs with thin shells. DDT was banned in North America in 1972, but it is still used in parts of Latin America. • In 1997, a radio-tagged Peregrine Falcon took only three days to travel from northern Alberta to its Mexican winter range. • In the 1990s, along the Red Deer River, Alberta saw the return of the first pairs of Peregrines since the early 1960s to nest on natural cliffs.

ID: *Sexes similar. Adult:* blue-grey back; dark, broad moustache; dark hood; light underparts with dark spots. *Immature:* similar patterning as an adult, but brown where the adult is blue-grey; heavier breast streaks; grey (rather than yellow) feet and cere. *In flight:* pointed wings; long, narrow, dark-banded tail.
Size: *Male: L* 38–43 cm; *W* 94–109 cm. *Female: L* 43–48 cm; *W* 109–117 cm.
Status: rare to uncommon from April to October.
Habitat: lakeshores, river valleys, urban areas, alpine meadows, river mouths and open fields; open areas during migration.
Nesting: usually on rocky cliffs or cutbanks; no material is added, but the nest is littered with prey remains, leaves and grass; nest sites are traditionally reused; female (mainly) incubates 3 or 4 eggs for 32–34 days.

Feeding: high-speed, diving swoops; strikes birds in mid-air and guides them to a perch for consumption; pigeons, waterfowl, grebes, shorebirds, jays, flickers, swallows, ptarmigans and larger songbirds are the primary prey.
Voice: loud, harsh, continuous *cack-cack-cack-cack-cack* near the nest site.
Similar Species: *Prairie Falcon* (p. 103): dark 'wing pits'; lacks the dark hood. *Gyrfalcon* (p. 105): lacks the dark hood; seen only in winter in Alberta. *Merlin* (p.102): smaller; lacks the broad moustache stripe.
Best Sites: Craigie Hall at the University of Calgary; east face of the Clinical Sciences Building, Edmonton; Beaverhill Lake.

GYRFALCON
Falco rusticolus

Every year, as the days get shorter and the snow begins to fall, Alberta birdwatchers anxiously await the return of the world's largest falcon. The presence of a handful of Gyrfalcons around open water and grain elevators actually makes some non-Albertans envious of our winters. • The Gyrfalcon is one of the world's most powerful avian hunters. Unlike the Peregrine Falcon, the Gyrfalcon rarely swoops from above with its wings closed—it prefers to outfly its prey, often attacking them from below. When a duck is the unlucky target, its only possible escape might be to plunge into the water headfirst. • The grey Gyrfalcon is the most commonly seen colour phase in Alberta. The white phase—prized by falconers and birders alike—occurs primarily in the eastern Arctic.

grey phase

ID: *Sexes similar:* very large falcon; long tail extends beyond the wing tips when it is perched. *Adult:* usually grey-brown; dark upperparts; lighter, streaked underparts; thin moustache mark; light phase is unmistakable. *Immature:* darker and more heavily patterned than an adult; grey (rather than yellow) feet and cere.

Size: *Male: L* 51–56 cm; *W* 122–130 cm. *Female: L* 56–64 cm; *W* 130–137 cm.

Status: rare from November to March.

Habitat: open and semi-open areas, including marshes, fields and open wetlands, where there are prey concentrations.

Nesting: does not nest in Alberta.

Feeding: strikes prey in mid-air and carries or follows it to the ground; locates prey from an elevated perch, by coursing low over the ground or by soaring; eats mainly birds, especially waterfowl and Rock Doves.

Voice: loud, harsh *kak-kak-kak*.

Similar Species: *Prairie Falcon* (p. 103): dark 'wing pits'; shorter tail. *Peregrine Falcon* (p. 104): contrasting dark hood; shorter tail. *Northern Goshawk* (p. 94): deceptively similar at times; light eyebrow; dark cap; rounded wings in flight.

Best Sites: Calder railway yards and Alberta Grain Terminal, Edmonton; Alberta Grain Terminal, Calgary; south side of Wabamun Lake.

GRAY PARTRIDGE

Perdix perdix

Gray Partridges are perhaps most regularly seen 'gravelling up' along quiet Alberta backroads during the early morning. Like other seed-eating birds, they swallow small stones to help crush the hard seeds they eat. The stones accumulate in the bird's gizzard, a muscular grinding mill in the digestive system. • When flushed, Gray Partridges burst suddenly from cover, flapping furiously and then gliding to a nearby safe haven. During cold weather, Gray Partridges huddle together in a circle with each bird facing outward, always ready to burst into flight. The effect that this eruption can have on one's heartbeat is easy to describe, but impossible to anticipate. • Introduced from Eurasia in the early 1900s, the Gray Partridge is now the most abundant upland gamebird over most of the agricultural areas of Alberta. • Formerly known as Hungarian Partridges, they are still called 'Huns' by many hunters.

ID: *General:* small, rounded bird; short tail; grey breast; mottled brown back; chestnut outer tail feathers and barring on flanks; bare yellowish legs. *Male:* dark brown belly patch; dark chestnut face and throat. *Female:* little or no belly patch; paler face and throat.

Size: L 28–36 cm.

Status: uncommon year-round.

Habitat: grasslands and agricultural fields, especially grain farms.

Nesting: on the ground, in hay-fields or pastures; scratches out a depression and lines the nest with grass; female incubates 15–17 olive-coloured eggs for 21–26 days.

Feeding: at dawn and dusk during summer; throughout the day during winter; gleans the ground for waste agricultural grains and seeds; might also eat leaves and large insects.

Voice: at dawn and dusk; sounds like a rusty gate hinge: *kee-uck;* call is *kuta-kut-kut-kut* when excited.

Similar Species: *Ruffed Grouse* (p. 108): lacks the rusty face and outer tail feathers.

Best Sites: most gravel roads through cropland—watch the roadsides and the ditch.

RING-NECKED PHEASANT
Phasianus colchicus

The spectacular Ring-necked Pheasant was first introduced to Alberta from Eurasia in 1908. Ring-necked Pheasants are now common in Alberta's farmlands, and they are encountered within the limits of many cities. Of our introduced gamebirds, only the Gray Partridge has been more successful. • In winter, pheasants often segregate into small groups of males and larger flocks of females. It is at this time of year that heavy snows and cold can greatly reduce their populations. • Birders hear this bird more often than they see it, and the male's loud *ka-squawk* is unmistakable. Up close, it is truly amazing how many different colours and feather types you can find on this bird. • Although the Ring-necked Pheasant reproduces successfully in Alberta, the provincial population is continually augmented by hatchery releases to support pheasant hunting.

♂

ID: *General:* long tail; large size; unfeathered legs. *Male:* green head; white collar; bronze underparts; naked red face patch. *Female:* mottled brown overall; light underparts.
Size: *Male:* L 76–91 cm. *Female:* L 51–66 cm.
Status: uncommon to common year-round.
Habitat: shrubby grasslands, pastures, ditches, fields and occasionally croplands.
Nesting: on the ground, among grass or sparse vegetation or next to a log or other natural debris; in a slight depression lined with grass and

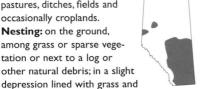

leaves; female incubates 10–12 eggs for up to 25 days.
Feeding: *Summer:* gleans the ground and vegetation for weed seeds and insects. *Winter:* eats mainly buds and seeds.
Voice: loud, raspy, rooster-like *ka-squawk*, mostly by the male.
Similar Species: male is distinctive. *Other grouse:* generally smaller; shorter tails than a female pheasant.
Best Sites: roadsides and hedgerows from Brooks to Dinosaur PP; Edmonton river valley.

RUFFED GROUSE
Bonasa umbellus

When a male Ruffed Grouse is displaying nearby, he makes a sound you feel more than hear—a forest drumbeat that reverberates in your chest. The male struts on a fallen log with his tail fanned and his necked ruffed, as he beats the air with accelerating wing strokes to proclaim his territory. 'Drumming' is primarily restricted to the spring courting season, but Ruffed Grouse also drum for a few weeks in fall. • During winter, the feather bristles on the toes of these birds elongate, providing them with temporary snowshoes. • The Ruffed Grouse is the most common grouse throughout much of Alberta. Many people mistakenly call it a 'partridge' or 'prairie chicken.' • The Ruffed Grouse is named for the black 'ruffs' on the sides of its neck. Displaying males erect these black patches to impress females.

♂

grey phase

ID: *Sexes similar:* small head crest; mottled reddish or grey-brown overall; black shoulder patches; tail is tipped with a dark band. *Female:* incomplete tail band.
Size: L 38–48 cm.
Status: common year-round.
Habitat: mixed and poplar forests.
Nesting: in a shallow depression among leaf litter; often beside logs, boulders and trees; female incubates 9–12 eggs for 23–25 days.

Feeding: gleans the ground and vegetation; eats aspens buds, willow catkins and terrestrial insects.
Voice: *Male:* uses his wings to produce a hollow, drumming courtship sound of accelerating, deep booms, like a lawnmower starting up and stalling. *Female:* clucks and 'hisses' around her chicks.
Similar Species: *Sharp-tailed Grouse* (p. 114): lacks the fan-shaped tail and the black shoulder patches. *Spruce Grouse* (p. 110): lacks the head crest.
Best Sites: Elk Island NP; Sir Winston Churchill PP; Fish Creek PP.

SAGE GROUSE
Centrocercus urophasianus

At dawn, deep in southeastern Alberta, groups of Sage Grouse assemble in early spring at their courtship 'leks.' Males enter the arena, inflate their chests, spread their pointed tail feathers and strut, hoot and boom to intimidate their competitors and attract the attention of females. The most successful males are found at the centre of the lek; immature males and poor strutters are restricted to the periphery. An impressive male can mate with up to 75 percent of the nearby hens. • Alberta Sage Grouse are at the northern limit of the species's range. Our population appears to have declined in the past few decades, and it does not range as far north as it once did. • Organized ecotours are a good way to visit traditional courtship leks in Alberta while minimizing the disturbance to the birds and their habitats.

ID: *Male:* large grouse; black belly and bib; white breast; long, spiked tail. *Female:* black belly; mottled brown plumage.
Size: *Male:* L 69–86 cm.
Female: L 46–61 cm.
Status: rare year-round.
Habitat: sagebrush flats.
Nesting: on the ground, usually under sagebrush; in a depression lined with leaves and grass; female incubates 6–9 eggs for up to 27 days.

Feeding: mostly sagebrush leaves, flowers, buds and insects.
Voice: generally silent, except on breeding grounds. *Male:* gurgles or makes a hollow *plop-plop* sound as he releases air from his air sacs. *Female: quak-quak.*
Similar Species: *Ring-necked Pheasant* (p. 107): female lacks the black belly and has unfeathered legs. *Blue Grouse* (p. 111): fan-shaped tail; lacks the black belly.
Best Sites: Onefour, Manyberries and Wild Horse, south of the Cypress Hills.

SPRUCE GROUSE

Falcipennis canadensis

The Spruce Grouse trusts its camouflaged plumage even in open areas—they are often called 'fool hens'—and daring birds will casually cross logging roads in broad daylight. These grouse are easily approached, but we probably overlook more of them than we notice—setting out to find a Spruce Grouse is nowhere near as easy as bumping into one by accident. • In spring, strutting male Spruce Grouse are seen in open areas along trails and roads. Their deep call is nearly undetectable to the human ear, but a displaying male transforms from his usual dull camouflage to a red-eyebrowed, puff-necked, fan-tailed splendour.
• In Alberta we have two distinct forms of the Spruce Grouse: the 'Franklin's Grouse' in the mountains and the 'Boreal Grouse' in the boreal forest.

'Franklin's Grouse'

ID: *'Boreal Grouse':* chestnut-tipped tail; white-tipped undertail coverts; light belly specks; male is dark grey overall, with a black breast and throat and a red comb over the eye; female is grey or reddish-brown overall and has heavily barred under-parts. *'Franklin's Grouse':* white spots on the uppertail coverts; male has an all-dark tail; female has a white-tipped tail. *Immature:* heavily barred.
Size: *L* 33–41 cm.
Status: uncommon to common year-round.
Habitat: conifer-dominated forest; sometimes disperses into deciduous forests.

Nesting: on the forest floor; in a well-hidden, shallow scrape lined with a few grasses and needles; female incubates 4–7 eggs for up to 21 days.
Feeding: live buds and needles of spruce, pine and fir trees; also eats berries, seeds and a few insects in summer.
Voice: very low, guttural *krrrk krrrk krrrk.*
Similar Species: *Blue Grouse* (p. 111): larger; male lacks the black throat and breast and the chestnut-tipped tail. *Ruffed Grouse* (p. 108): head is crested; dark-tipped tail; lacks the black throat and breast.
Best Sites: Forestry Trunk Road; Wood Buffalo NP; Kananaskis Country.

BLUE GROUSE

Dendragapus obscurus

In dense mountain forests, the deep, owl-like courting notes of the male Blue Grouse carry far across the valleys. Males sometimes begin their breeding calls while patches of snow still remain. • During early summer, hens sometimes hold up traffic as they guide their chicks across mountain roads. • The Blue Grouse makes seasonal migrations, but rather than moving north-south, it moves up and down mountain slopes. During fall and winter it lives near treeline, feeding on berries, buds and conifer needles. • Like the Spruce Grouse, this is a ridiculously trusting bird. Our favourite story involves stopping the car to avoid hitting one, only to have it jump up on the hood and pick bugs off the windshield. Finally, the grouse had to be picked up and moved to the ditch in order to proceed with the day.

ID: *General:* subdued colours; white undertail coverts; unbanded tail; feathered legs. *Male:* grey body; orange comb above the eye; inflated purple throat patches surrounded by white feathers when displaying. *Female:* mottled brownish grey.
Size: *Male: L* 43–48 cm. *Female: L* 46–56 cm.
Status: uncommon year-round.
Habitat: open coniferous forests, shrub meadows and avalanche slopes in mountain valleys.
Nesting: on the ground, often near a fallen log or under a shrub; in a shallow depression lined with dead vegetation, such as leaves, twigs and needles; female incubates 7–10 buff-coloured eggs for 25–28 days.
Feeding: leaves, berries, seeds and flowers; conifer needles and buds in winter; young birds eat grasshoppers and beetles.
Voice: deep, low hoots.
Similar Species: *Spruce Grouse* (p. 110): smaller; male has a black throat and breast. *Ruffed Grouse* (p. 108): smaller; crested head; black shoulder patch; banded tail.
Best Sites: Celestine Fire Road, Jasper NP; Sheep River Wildlife Sanctuary.

WILLOW PTARMIGAN
Lagopus lagopus

To visit the home of the Willow Ptarmigan in Alberta, you must become a mountaineer. A day's hike is often required before you can hope to see this bird. After such an effort, the bird's call, *go-back, go-back, go-back,* seems unwelcoming. • During harsh winters, Willow Ptarmigans have been known to migrate south from the Northwest Territories into the frozen bogs and fields of northernmost Alberta. • Like an avian Snowshoe Hare, this bird turns white in winter and has fluffy feet. *Lagopus* means 'rabbit's foot,' so seeing one should also bring good luck. • This same species is called the Red Grouse in Britain, where it is a famed gamebird on the heathlands, and where it does not change colours with the seasons.

summer

ID: *General:* black outer tail feathers; short, rounded wings; black bill. *Summer male:* chestnut brown head and neck; otherwise mostly white, splashed with brown on the upperparts. *Summer female:* mottled brown overall; white belly, legs and undertail coverts. *Winter:* all white, except for the black eyes, bill, and outer tail, and the red eyebrow.

Size: *L* 33–36 cm.

Status: very rare year-round.

Habitat: open forests and shrub meadows high in the mountains.

Nesting: on alpine tundra; in a

shallow scrape lined with grass and feathers; female incubates 7 eggs for 3 weeks.

Feeding: gleans vegetation and foliage for buds, flowers, leaves and small branches of willows and birch shrubs; occasionally eats insects in summer.

Voice: loud, crackling *go-back go-back go-back.*

Similar Species: *White-tailed Ptarmigan* (p. 113): white tail; never has a reddish head and neck. *Spruce Grouse* (p. 110): female is larger and has no white in the wings.

Best Sites: Tonquin Valley and Signal Mountain, Jasper NP; Fort Chipewyan and Fort McMurray (winter).

WHITE-TAILED PTARMIGAN
Lagopus leucurus

It would be hard to imagine a better-adapted alpine hiker than the White-tailed Ptarmigan. Its plumage perfectly matches the surroundings, regardless of the season, and in winter its feathered feet look like fluffy bedroom slippers, allowing the bird to snowshoe atop the snowdrifts. • This species is the ptarmigan most likely to be encountered in Alberta. The Willow Ptarmigan lives further north, and although a few Rock Ptarmigans have been seen in Alberta, they are very rare indeed. • In severe weather, ptarmigans escape the cold by tunnelling into the snow near willow bushes, where, safe from the howling winds, they nibble on buds. • A brooding female White-tailed Ptarmigan will remain on her nest even if she is closely approached. Nevertheless, this is very stressful to her, and sensitive hikers can make a ptarmigan's tough life somewhat easier by keeping a respectful distance.

♂

summer

ID: *General:* white outer tail feathers; fully feathered feet. *Summer male:* mottled brown overall; white on the wings and belly; red eyebrow during courtship. *Summer female:* mottled brown overall; black barring on the belly. *Winter:* all-white; black eyes and bill; red eyebrow. *Spring and fall:* intermediate plumages.
Size: *L* 31–36 cm.
Status: uncommon year-round.
Habitat: mossy and lichen-covered, rocky areas; willow and alder thickets at or above treeline; might move to lower elevations during winter.

Nesting: on the ground, among rocks in snow-free alpine tundra; in a depression lined with fine grass, leaves and lichens; female incubates 4–8 eggs for 24–26 days; both parents guard their young for up to 2 months.
Feeding: gleans and picks buds, stems, seeds, fruits and flowers from willows and other alpine plants; occasionally eats insects.
Voice: *Male:* high-pitched *ku-kriii kriii*; low *kuk-kuk-kuk.* *Female:* low clucks around her chicks.
Similar Species: *Willow Ptarmigan* (p. 112): lacks the white tail. *Blue Grouse* (p. 111): much larger; lacks the white tail.
Best Sites: The Whistlers, Jasper NP; Skokie Lodge, Banff NP; Ptarmigan Cirque, Kananaskis Country.

SHARP-TAILED GROUSE
Tympanuchus phasianellus

The courtship display of the male Sharp-tailed Grouse has been emulated in the traditional dances of many native cultures on the prairies. Courting Sharp-tails gather at traditional dancing grounds (leks), and with their wings drooping at their sides, their tails pointed skyward and their purple air sacs inflated, the males furiously pummel the ground with their feet. Each male has a small stage that he defends against rival males with both warning calls and kicks.
• Like other grouse, Sharp-tail numbers rise and fall dramatically over the years. However, because of their generalized habitat requirements, Sharp-tailed Grouse occupy a wider variety of places in Alberta than any other grouse. • The Sharp-tailed Grouse is often mistakenly called a 'prairie chicken,' but that name properly belongs to two related species found far to the south. • 'Lek' is derived from the Swedish word for 'play.'

ID: *General:* mottled upperparts; spotted underparts; long central tail feathers; light outer trail feathers. *Male:* purple air sacs on the neck are inflated in display.
Size: L 38–51 cm.
Status: uncommon year-round.
Habitat: open habitats, mostly grasslands, grassy meadows, sagebrush flats and agricultural areas.
Nesting: on the ground; occasionally under shrub; usually close to the lek; in a depression lined with grass and

feathers; female incubates 10–14 eggs for up to 24 days.
Feeding: gleans the ground and vegetation for buds, seeds and flowers; also eats insects and seeds.
Voice: rarely heard; male gives a mournful, cooing *hoo* or *hoo hoo* on the breeding grounds.
Similar Species: *Ruffed Grouse* (p. 108): slight crest; broad-tipped tail. *Ring-necked Pheasant* (p. 107): female has a longer tail, unfeathered legs and less barring on the belly.
Best Sites: Writing-on-Stone PP; Hanna area.

WILD TURKEY
Meleagris gallopavo

The Wild Turkey is a wary bird with refined senses and a highly developed social system. This charismatic bird was introduced into the Cypress Hills in 1962, and its loud, distinctive voice has since become a reliable wake-up call in the park campgrounds. Wild Turkeys were also introduced to the Porcupine Hills, and they have been seen regularly in the foothills near Turner Valley. • Although turkeys prefer to stay on the ground—they can run faster than 30 km/h—they are able to fly short distances, and they roost in trees at night. • The Wild Turkey is the only native North American animal that has been domesticated worldwide. The ancestors of chickens, pigs, cows and sheep all came from Europe, Asia and Africa.

♂

ID: *General:* very large; naked head; dark glossy body plumage; coppery tail, with a light tip; unfeathered legs. *Male:* long central breast tuft; colourful, red-blue head; red wattles. *Female:* blue-grey head; less colourful body.
Size: *Male:* L 122–127 cm. *Female:* L 89–94 cm.
Status: rare to uncommon year-round.
Habitat: mixed woodlands and open forests.
Nesting: on the ground in open woods or at field edges; in a depression lined with grass and leaves; female incubates 10–12 eggs for up to 28 days.
Feeding: forages on the ground for seeds, fruits, bulbs and sedges; also eats insects, especially beetles and grasshoppers, and amphibians.
Voice: wide array of sounds: courting male gives a loud gobble; alarm call is a loud *pert;* gathering call is a cluck; contact call is a loud *keouk-keouk-keouk.*
Similar Species: all other grouse and grouse-like birds are much smaller.
Best Sites: Cypress Hills PP; Porcupine Hills.

YELLOW RAIL
Coturnicops noveboracensis

The Yellow Rail might be the most challenging breeding bird in Alberta to get a good look at. This species is almost always encountered through its distinctive and repetitive call, heard along marsh edges in spring. The call is easily imitated by tapping two small stones together, but birders should resist the temptation to draw calling birds into the open. • Yellow Rails almost always remain undercover in cattails. They are active mainly at night, and although they migrate great distances they are almost never seen in flight. Yellow Rails are encountered most often when they get lost—confused birds are occasionally found in garages, backyards and city parks. • Rails are masters at slipping through tight places with their laterally compressed bodies, and they might get their name from the fact that they look 'as thin as a rail.'

ID: *Sexes similar:* short, pale bill; brown and black stripes on the upperparts; light throat. *In flight:* white trailing edge on the inner wing.

Size: L 17–19 cm.

Status: rare from May to September.

Habitat: sedge marshes.

Nesting: on the ground or low over water, hidden by overhanging plants; shallow cup nest is made of grass or sedges; female

incubates 8–10 eggs for up to 18 days.

Feeding: picks food from the ground and aquatic vegetation; eats mainly snails, aquatic insects, spiders and possibly earthworms; occasionally eats seeds.

Voice: like 2 stones clicking together: *tik, tik, tiktiktik.*

Similar Species: *Sora* (p. 118): lacks the stripes on the back; distinctly different call; breeding birds have a black face and throat.

Best Sites: Beaverhill Lake; Cold Lake–Grand Centre area.

VIRGINIA RAIL
Rallus limicola

The best way to see a Virginia Rail is to sit alongside a wetland marsh, clap your hands three or four times (as if summoning a genie) and wait patiently. At best, this slim bird might reveal itself for an instant, but most often, the bird's voice is all that betrays its presence. • Virginia Rails are scattered through the parklands and prairies of Alberta during the breeding season. They arrive in the province in early May and leave in September. • When pursued by an intruder or predator, a rail will scurry away through dense, protective vegetation, rather than risk a get-away flight. • Rails are very narrow birds that have modified feather tips and flexible vertebrae, all of which allow them to squeeze through the narrow confines of their marshy homes.

ID: *Sexes similar. Adult:* long, downcurved, reddish bill; rusty breast; barred flanks; grey cheek; very short tail. *Immature:* darker overall; light bill; pinkish legs.
Size: *L* 23–28 cm.
Status: rare from May to September.
Habitat: freshwater wetlands, especially cattail and bulrush marshes.
Nesting: concealed in emergent vegetation, usually suspended just over the water; loose basket nest is made of coarse grass, cattail stems or sedges; pair incubates the spotted eggs for up to 20 days.

Feeding: probes into soft substrates for soft-bodied invertebrates, such as earthworms, beetles, snails, spiders, insect larvae and nymphs; gleans vegetation for snails and beetles; also eats pondweeds and seeds.
Voice: call is an often repeated, telegraph-like *tick-tick-tick-tick-queea;* also 'oinks' and croaks.
Similar Species: *Sora* (p. 118): short, yellow bill; black face. *Yellow Rail* (p. 116): short, yellow bill; striped back.
Best Sites: check local bird hotlines for recent sightings.

SORA
Porzana carolina

Halfway between a crazed laugh and a horse's whinny, the call of the Sora puzzles many visitors to cattail marshes. Despite being the most common and widespread rail in North America, the Sora is seldom seen. Patiently standing in a marsh is the best way to spot one, but most birdwatchers are too restless and talkative for that. • The remains of Soras often show up in the nests of Peregrine Falcons. Human birders rarely see Soras, so the fact that Peregrines successfully prey on these birds means the Peregrine's eyesight is all the more impressive. • Soras habitually flick their stubby tails. This odd gesture is thought to be intended for prey animals— while the prey watches the tail, the bill catches it by surprise. • The Sora swims quite well over short distances, even though its feet are not webbed.

breeding

ID: *Sexes similar. Adult:* short, yellow bill; black face and breast; long, greenish legs. *Immature:* brown overall; dark bill; yellow legs.
Size: *L* 20–25 cm.
Status: uncommon to common from May to September.
Habitat: wetlands with abundant emergent cattails, bulrushes, sedges and grasses.
Nesting: usually over water, but occasionally in a wet meadow, under concealing vegetation;

well-built basket nest is made of grass and aquatic vegetation; pair incubates 10–12 eggs for up to 20 days.
Feeding: gleans and probes for seeds, plants, aquatic insects and mollusks.
Voice: alarm call is a sharp *keek*; courtship song begins *or-Ah or-Ah*, descending quickly in a series of *weee-weee-weee* notes.
Similar Species: *Virginia Rail* (p. 117): long, reddish, downcurved bill. *Yellow Rail* (p. 116): streaked back; white wing patches; lacks the black 'mask.'
Best Sites: almost any marsh; Clifford E. Lee Nature Sanctuary.

AMERICAN COOT
Fulica americana

The American Coot looks like a delightful blend of leftover pieces from other birds: it has the bill of a chicken, the feet of a grebe and the body of a duck. With these features, it is not surprising that coots are all-terrain birds that are adept at diving, dabbling, swimming and walking on solid ground. • On rare occasions, a few coots will overwinter on open water in Alberta. • American Coots are constantly squabbling. They can often be seen running across the surface of the water, charging rivals and attempting to intimidate them. • When they first hatch, the orange-headed young are so ugly that they are 'cute as a coot.' • Coots are also colloquially known as 'Mud Hens,' and few non-birders realize that they are not a species of duck.

ID: *Sexes similar. Adult:* dark grey, duck-like bird; pointed, white bill with a black ring near the tip; long green-yellow legs; lobed toes. *Immature:* lighter body; darker bill and legs.
Size: *L* 33–41 cm.
Status: common to very common from May to September; some might overwinter on open water.
Habitat: shallow marshes, ponds and wetlands with open water and emergent vegetation.
Nesting: in emergent vegetation; floating nest, built by the pair, is

usually made of cattails and grass; pair incubates 8–12 eggs for 21–25 days.
Feeding: eats aquatic vegetation, invertebrates, tadpoles and fish; gleans the water surface; sometimes dives.
Voice: calls frequently in summer, day and night: *kuk-kuk-kuk-kuk-kuk;* also grunts.
Similar Species: *Ducks* (pp. 61–88): all lack the chicken-like, white bill and the uniform, black body colour. *Grebes* (pp. 38–43): swim without pumping their heads back and forth; rarely seen on land.
Best Sites: almost any waterbody; Clifford E. Lee Nature Sanctuary; Inglewood Bird Sanctuary, Calgary; Cavan Lake; Slack Slough.

SANDHILL CRANE
Grus canadensis

A deep, resonant rattling announces the approach of a flock of migrating Sandhill Cranes. Those of us who sleep with a partly opened window are usually the first to know they are on migration. As flock after flock glides overhead, notice that they often soar and circle, quite unlike the flocks of geese they can resemble at a distance. As well, notice how far the sound of their call travels, and how it differs from the calls of geese and swans. • Although most cranes are seen during migration, many of them nest in Alberta's foothills and boreal forests, in secluded fens, bogs and marshes. • Cranes mate for life, reinforcing their pair bond each spring with an elaborate courtship dance. It has often been equated with human dancing—a seemingly strange comparison until you see the real thing.

ID: *Sexes similar:* very large, grey bird with a long neck and legs; naked red crown; long, straight bill. *Immature:* patchy reddish brown; lacks the red crown. *In flight:* extends its neck and legs; often glides, soars and circles.

Size: L 102–127 cm; W 1.8–2.1 m.

Status: uncommon from May to October.

Habitat: *In migration:* agricultural fields, mudflats and shorelines. *Breeding:* isolated, open marshes, fens and bogs surrounded by forests or shrubs.

Nesting: on a large mound of aquatic vegetation in the water or along the shoreline; pair incubates 2 olive-splotched eggs for 29–32 days; egg hatching is staggered; young fly at about 50 days.

Feeding: probes and gleans the ground for insects, soft-bodied invertebrates, waste grain, shoots and tubers; frequently eats small vertebrates.

Voice: loud, resonant rattling: *gu-rrroo gu-rrroo gurrroo.*

Similar Species: *Great Blue Heron* (p. 47): flies with its neck folded back over the shoulders; lacks the red forehead patch. *Whooping Crane* (p. 121): rare; all-white plumage with black flight feathers.

Best Sites: *Migration:* Beaverhill Lake; Frank Lake; along Saskatchewan border. *Breeding:* Crimson Lake PP; Wood Buffalo NP.

WHOOPING CRANE
Grus americana

In the 1940s the world population of wild Whooping Cranes dipped to only 15 birds. Since then, one of the most intensive conservation programs in history has managed to increase that number significantly, but a naturally low population growth in this species has so far prevented their numbers from exceeding 200.
• The only breeding area for this species lies in Wood Buffalo National Park, a source of pride for Albertans. It was discovered by University of Alberta zoologist William Fuller in 1954. • Bird-watchers rarely see this species in Alberta, but if you take a trip to the Aransas National Wildlife Refuge in Texas, you can see them up close on their wintering grounds, albeit from the deck of an annoyingly touristy tour boat. • In most respects, the Whooping Crane is a bigger and more flamboyant version of its Sandhill relative.

ID: *Sexes similar. Adult:* tall, very large bird; mostly white; black primary feathers; bare red skin on the forehead and chin; long, pointed bill; black legs. *Immature:* orange-red head and neck. *In flight:* neck and legs are extended.
Size: L 127–152 cm; W 2–2.3 m.
Status: very rare from May to October.
Habitat: *In migration:* wetlands, croplands and fields.
Nesting: in fens, bogs and isolated marshes; large nest is made of heaped vegetation; 2 eggs are incubated for about 30 days; usually only 1 chick survives, if that.
Feeding: picks food from the water or the ground; eats amphibians, small mammals and plant material on the breeding grounds; eats waste grain and some animal material in migration.

Voice: gravelly rattle: *ker-loo ker-lee-loo;* similar to a Sandhill Crane.

Similar Species: *Sandhill Crane* (p. 120): grey, not white and black. *American White Pelican* (p. 44): much shorter legs; secondary feathers are also black. *Snow Goose* (p. 55): much shorter legs and bill; much smaller overall. *Swans* (pp. 59–60): all-white wings.
Best Sites: Wood Buffalo NP (summer); fields along the Saskatchewan border south of Lloydminster (migration); good luck.

BLACK-BELLIED PLOVER
Pluvialis squatarola

In spring migration, the Black-bellied Plover's tuxedo plumage stands out against the still-bleak Alberta soil. These plovers pass through Alberta in large numbers and congregate in open, easily scanned places—they can be identified with confidence in a roadside field, even if you are driving past at 100 km/h. These flocks should not be overlooked, however, since rare migrants often associate with Black-bellied Plovers. • The fall passage of Black-bellied Plovers begins at the end of July with adults in worn-out breeding plumage. It is often not until November that the last of the plain grey immatures have moved through Alberta. • These birds forage with a robin-like run-and-stop technique, frequently pausing to lift their heads for a reassuring scan of their surroundings.
• Unlike other plovers, which have three toes, the Black-belly has a fourth toe high on its ankle, like most sandpipers.

breeding

ID: *Sexes similar:* short, black bill; long, black legs. *Breeding:* black face, breast and belly contrast with the grey-spotted back and the white crown, collar and under-tail coverts. *Non-breeding:* grey-brown upperparts; light under-parts. *In flight:* black wingpits; white tail, white rump.
Size: L 27–34 cm.
Status: uncommon in May and from July to September.

Habitat: ploughed fields, meadows, mudflats and lakeshores.
Nesting: does not nest in Alberta.
Feeding: run-and-stop foraging technique; eats insects, mollusks and crustaceans.
Voice: rich plaintive whistle: *pee-oo-ee.*
Similar Species: *American Golden-Plover* (p. 123): upperparts are golden rather than grey; black undertail coverts; lacks the black wing pits.
Best Sites: Beaverhill Lake; Aspen Beach.

AMERICAN GOLDEN-PLOVER
Pluvialis dominica

A mere 150 years ago, the American Golden-Plover population was among the largest of any bird in the world, but a century ago, market gunners mercilessly culled the great flocks in both spring and fall—a single day's shooting often yielded tens of thousands of birds. Sadly, it is now a challenge to find even a few American Golden-Plovers in Alberta during their May rush to the Arctic. • Even small flocks of this plover fly swiftly, dominating the winds. On occasion, they use thermals to conquer the effects of gravity. • The American Golden-Plover's breeding plumage is a fine example of disruptive colouration. Although the bird is boldly marked, the pattern does a good job of breaking up the image of the bird when it is seen in a wild setting.

breeding

ID: *Sexes similar:* brownish overall; short, black bill; long, black legs. *Breeding:* black face and underparts; white stripe from the shoulder to the forehead; gold-spotted upperparts. *Non-breeding:* speckled with brown. *In flight:* grey wing pits.
Size: L 25–38 cm.
Status: rare to uncommon in May and from September to October.
Habitat: cultivated fields, meadows, mudflats and lakeshores.

Nesting: does not nest in Alberta.
Feeding: run-and-stop foraging technique; picks insects, mollusks and crustaceans.
Voice: soft melodious whistle: *quee, quee-dle.*
Similar Species: *Black-bellied Plover* (p. 122): white undertail coverts; whitish crown; lacks the gold speckling on the upperparts.
Best Sites: Beaverhill Lake; Langdon Reservoir; open fields in the Manning, High Level and Fort Vermilion areas.

123

SEMIPALMATED PLOVER

Charadrius semipalmatus

Small flocks of Semipalmated Plovers touch down on shorelines while passing through Alberta on migration. They begin to arrive in the province by the end of April, passing quickly to their Arctic breeding grounds. The more prolonged fall passage begins in early July, with the last birds filtering out of Alberta by mid-September. July is 'fall' to many shorebirds, especially those that were not successful at breeding in the Arctic. • There are a few nesting records for the Semipalmated Plover in Wood Buffalo National Park, but it is a rare breeder in our province—it is much more common further north. • 'Semipalmated' (and *semi-palmatus*) refers to the slight webbing between the toes of this plover—webbed toes are called 'palmate,' so partly webbed toes are 'semi-palmate.' The webbing is thought to give the bird's feet more surface area when it is walking on soft substrates.

breeding

ID: *Sexes similar. Adult:* dark brown upper-parts; white breast with a single black 'neck-lace'; orange legs; black-tipped, orange bill; black band across the forehead; white patch above the bill and behind the eye. *Immature:* dark legs and bill; brown and white, with little black.
Size: *L* 18 cm.
Status: uncommon to common from April to May and from July to September.
Habitat: sandy beaches, lake-shores, river edges and mudflats.

Nesting: on sand or gravel, often near water; in a depression sparsely lined with vegetation; pair incubates 4 eggs for up to 25 days.
Feeding: run-and-stop feeding, usually on shorelines and beaches; eats crustaceans, worms and insects.
Voice: crisp, high-pitched, 2-part, rising whistle: *tu-wee.*
Similar Species: *Killdeer* (p. 126): larger; 2 black bands across the breast. *Piping Plover* (p. 125): much lighter upperparts.
Best Sites: Beaverhill Lake; Aspen Beach; along lakes on the Saskatchewan border.

PIPING PLOVER
Charadrius melodus

This sand-coloured plover's camouflage has done little to protect it from wetland drainage, increased predation and disturbances by people and cattle, all of which have contributed to its decline in the past few decades. • Young Piping Plovers generally begin walking and leave the nest within about 24 hours of hatching, but they rarely venture more than 150 m from the nest during their first month. These young puffballs match their surroundings perfectly, and they are even tougher to see than the adults. • Researchers have been able to increase the survival of chicks by enclosing the nest with a wire-mesh cage. The wire mesh allows the endangered plovers to pass through to their secure nest site, but it bars access to predatory gulls, foxes and coyotes.

breeding

ID: *General:* pale sandy upperparts; white underparts; orange legs. *Breeding:* black-tipped, orange bill; black forehead band; black 'necklace' (sometimes incomplete, especially in the female). *Non-breeding:* no breast or forehead band; all-black bill.
Size: *L* 18–19 cm.
Status: rare from May to August.
Habitat: sandy beaches and open lakeshores.
Nesting: on bare ground on an open shoreline; in a shallow scrape that might be lined with pebbles; pair incubates 4 eggs for up to 28 days.
Feeding: run-and-stop feeding; eats worms and insects; almost all the food is taken from the ground.
Voice: clear, whistled melody: *peep peep peep-lo.*
Similar Species: *Semipalmated Plover* (p. 124): much darker upperparts. *Killdeer* (p. 126): larger; 2 breast bands; much darker upperparts.
Best Sites: Dowling Lake; Handhills Lake; formerly Beaverhill Lake and Aspen Beach.

KILLDEER
Charadrius vociferus

The Killdeer is often the first shorebird a birdwatcher identifies each and every spring. It has adapted well to urbanization, and it finds golf courses, farms, fields and abandoned industrial areas as much to its liking as shorelines. • If you wander near a nest site, the parents will try to lure you away, crying pitifully and feigning a broken wing. Similar distraction displays are widespread phenomena in birds, but in Alberta, the Killdeer's broken wing act is the best known. • By mid-June, the young have hatched and are scrambling around in a seemingly confused haze. If they become cut off from their parents, they run awkwardly to cover and then crouch down on the ground. • The scientific name *vociferus* aptly describes this vocal bird, but double check all calls in spring—the Killdeer is often imitated by European Starlings.

ID: *Sexes similar. Adult:* long, dark yellow legs; white breast with 2 black bands; brown back; white underparts; brown head; white forehead and eyebrow; black forehead band. *Immature:* downy; 1 breast band.
Size: *L* 23–28 cm.
Status: common to very common from April to October.
Habitat: open ground, fields, lakeshores, sandy beaches, mudflats, gravel streambeds, wet meadows and grasslands.

Nesting: on open ground; in shallow, usually unlined depression; pair incubates 4 eggs for 28 days; occasionally raises 2 broods.
Feeding: run-and-stop feeder; mainly eats insects.
Voice: loud and distinctive *kill-dee kill-dee kill-deer* and variations, including *deer-deer*.
Similar Species: *Semipalmated Plover* (p. 124): smaller; only 1 breast band. *Piping Plover* (p. 125): smaller; lighter upperparts; 1 breast band.
Best Sites: Beaverhill Lake; Aspen Beach; Sir Winston Churchill PP.

MOUNTAIN PLOVER
Charadrius montanus

Don't let the name fool you—this plover prefers to live in vast, open areas far from the Rockies. The Mountain Plover is a bird of dry grasslands, which in Alberta are found only in the southeastern corner of the province. Even there, Mountain Plovers are far from common. Many Alberta birdwatchers have made pilgrimages to find them, only to come away empty. • Like the Upland Sandpiper, the Mountain Plover does little to announce its shorebird heritage—it only rarely approaches shorelines. It is indeed more of a 'grass-piper' than a sandpiper. • After their nesting duties are complete, Mountain Plovers migrate to northern Mexico by way of California, crossing the Rockies and the Coast Ranges twice before settling on their wintering grounds. Mountain Plovers cling to their traditional migratory routes as tightly as any shorebird, and 'lost' individuals are infrequently encountered.

breeding

ID: *Sexes similar:* thin, dark bill; light underparts; sandy upperparts; white forehead; black forecrown; thin black eye line; light legs.
Size: *L* 20–24 cm.
Status: rare from April to September.
Habitat: sparse, dry prairies, heavily grazed pastures and mudflats.
Nesting: near a dry hummock, cactus plant or cow chips; in a

shallow scrape lined with small amounts of grass, cow chips and roots; pair incubates 3 eggs for about 30 days.
Feeding: gleans the ground for insects, especially grasshoppers.
Voice: shrill call note; whistles during spring and summer.
Similar Species: *Upland Sandpiper* (p. 135): longer neck. *Killdeer* (p. 126): 2 breast bands.
Best Sites: Onefour area, in extreme southeastern Alberta.

127

BLACK-NECKED STILT

Himantopus mexicanus

Alberta has recently experienced a modest invasion of Black-necked Stilts, perhaps the most fragile-looking of all North American shorebirds. Breeding pairs have nested here and there in the southern half of the province, and spring migration occasionally produces small flocks of these gangly-legged beauties. These birds always cause a stir on bird hotlines. • Whether in a smelly prairie wetland or an alkaline pond, the stilt's black-tie plumage adds a bit of class to the landscape. It is perhaps fortunate that one of North America's most beautiful birds associates with such bleak and dreary environments. • With proportionally the longest legs of any North American bird, this shorebird truly deserves the name 'stilt.'

♂

ID: *General:* very long, pink-orange legs; dark upperparts; clean white underparts; long, thin, straight bill; small white eyebrow; male is blacker than the female.
Size: *L* 36–38 cm.
Status: rare to uncommon from May to August.
Habitat: *Breeding:* marshy lakes and ponds. *Foraging:* lake edges and exposed mudflats.
Nesting: often colonial; on the ground; in a shallow depression sparsely lined with vegetation;

near alkaline or open shorelines; pair incubates the eggs for about 25 days.
Feeding: picks its prey from the water's surface or from the bottom in saline lakes; primarily eats small flies and other aquatic invertebrates; rarely eats seeds.
Voice: not vocal during migration; loud, sharp *yip-yip-yip-yip* in summer; *kek-kek-kek-kek* in flight.
Similar Species: *American Avocet* (p. 129): upturned bill; no black on the head.
Best Sites: Frank Lake; Pakowki Lake; Kininvie Marsh.

AMERICAN AVOCET
Recurvirostra americana

An American Avocet in breeding plumage is truly an elegant bird. There is something both comical and statuesque about the avocet's combination of an upturned bill and subtle brown and white colours. For many birdwatchers in Alberta, seeing an avocet for the first time is an event worthy of celebration. • During courtship, the female extends her bill forward and lowers her chin until it just clears the water's surface. The male struts around his lovely mate until conditions are just right. After mating, the pair cross their slender bills and walk away in unison, celebrating and reinforcing their bond. • An avocet's upturned bill is just the right shape for skimming food off the surface of shallow waters. • By August, most avocets have lost their peachy hoods and put on their winter greys, which are still worth a second glance.

breeding

ID: *Sexes similar:* long, upturned, black bill; long, pale blue legs; black wings with wide, white patches; white underparts; female's bill is more upturned and shorter than the male's. *Breeding:* peachy-red head, neck and breast. *Non-breeding:* grey head, neck and breast. *In flight:* like a 'winged stick'; long, skinny legs and neck; black-and-white wings.
Size: *L* 43–46 cm.
Status: uncommon from May to September.
Habitat: lakeshores, alkaline wetlands and exposed mud-flats.
Nesting: semi-colonial; along dried mudflats, exposed shore-lines or open areas, always near

water; in a shallow depression sparsely lined with vegetation; pair incubates 4 eggs for up to 29 days.
Feeding: sweeps its bill from side to side along the water's surface; picks up minute crustaceans, aquatic insects and occasionally seeds; male sweeps lower in the water than the female; occasionally swims and 'tips up' like a duck.
Voice: harsh, shrill *plee-eek plee-eek* near the nest.
Similar Species: *Black-necked Stilt* (p. 128): straight bill; mostly black head. *Willet* (p. 133): greyish overall; straight bill.
Best Sites: Beaverhill Lake; Kimiwan Lake; Pakowki Lake; Frank Lake; Tilley Reservoir; Kinbrook Island PP.

GREATER YELLOWLEGS

Tringa melanoleuca

The Greater Yellowlegs is one of the birds that often performs the role of lookout among mixed flocks of migrant shorebirds. At the first sign of danger, these large sandpipers begin calling, bobbing their heads and moving slowly away from the threat. The Greater Yellowlegs usually retreats into deeper water before becoming airborne. • Greater Yellowlegs nest in the northern half of Alberta around bogs and fens. Often, well before your feet begin to sink in the waterlogged ground, a Greater Yellowlegs will begin its high-pitched calls from atop a black spruce or tamarack, alerting you to the upcoming bog. Although it is around these bogs that yellowlegs are generally seen, their nests are tucked off on the perimeter, on a dry ridge. • Distinguishing between the two species of yellowlegs is one of the first major challenges awaiting a beginning birdwatcher in Alberta.

breeding

ID: *Sexes similar:* long, yellow legs; dark, very slightly upturned bill is greyish near its base; bill is longer than the head length. *Breeding:* brown-black back and wing covers; fine, dark streaking on the head, neck and breast; subtle, dark eye line; light lore. *Non-breeding:* grey overall; slight streaks on the head.
Size: *L* 33–38 cm.
Status: uncommon to common from April to October.
Habitat: *In migration:* almost all wetlands, including lake-shores and river shorelines. *Nesting:* bogs, alluvial wetlands, sedge meadows and beaver ponds.
Nesting: in a depression on a dry mound; usually on a ridge near open bogs or natural openings in muskeg; never far from water; well-hidden nest is sparsely lined with leaves, moss and grass; female incubates 4 eggs for 23 days.
Feeding: usually wades in water over its knees; occasionally snatches prey from the water's surface; commonly sweeps its bill from side to side; primarily eats aquatic invertebrates, but will also eat small fish.
Voice: quick, whistled series of *tew-tew-tew-tew-tew*, usually 3–5 notes.
Similar Species: *Lesser Yellowlegs* (p. 131): smaller; shorter bill; call is generally a pair of notes: *tew-tew. Willet* (p. 133): black-and-white wings; heavier bill.
Best Sites: Beaverhill Lake; Slack Slough.

LESSER YELLOWLEGS
Tringa flavipes

Lesser Yellowlegs are among the first shorebirds to arrive in Alberta in spring and the last to leave in fall. They arrive on their northern Alberta nesting grounds in April and don't leave until October. • When disturbed from their forested nesting areas, Lesser Yellowlegs retreat to the tops of spruce trees to scan the surroundings. These treetop perches might seem an odd place for a shorebird, but the yellowlegs and its relatives seem right at home there. • Lesser Yellowlegs and Greater Yellowlegs look very similar, but eventually you will come to recognize them by the look in their eye, subconsciously checking the ratio of bill length to head length, and becoming more sensitive to the slightly upturned, slightly heavier bill of the Greater and the straight, fine bill of the Lesser.

breeding

ID: *Sexes similar:* bright yellow legs; all-dark bill is shorter than the head length; brown-black back and wing covers; fine, dense, dark streaking on the head, neck and breast; subtle, dark eye line; light lore.
Size: *L* 25–28 cm.
Status: common from April to September.
Habitat: *Breeding:* grassy ponds and open forests. *In migration:* shorelines of lakes, rivers and ponds.
Nesting: usually in open muskegs or natural openings in

forests; in a depression on a dry mound; nest is sparsely lined with leaves and grass; pair incubates 4 blotched eggs for 22–23 days.
Feeding: snatches prey from the water's surface; frequently wades in shallow water; primarily eats aquatic invertebrates, but will also take small fish and tadpoles.
Voice: high-pitched *tew-tew*, typically a pair of notes.
Similar Species: *Greater Yellowlegs* (p. 130): larger; slightly longer, upturned bill; call is typically 3–5 notes. *Solitary Sandpiper* (p. 132): white eye ring; greenish legs.
Best Sites: Beaverhill Lake; Slack Slough.

SOLITARY SANDPIPER

Tringa solitaria

The Solitary Sandpiper's nesting strategy remained a mystery until 1903, when a homesteader near Bowden, Alberta, looked into what he thought was a robin's nest, but found a sandpiper instead. The fact that the Solitary Sandpiper nests in trees tells you two things: first, this is no ordinary shorebird; second, it is related to the yellowlegs. Yellowlegs perch atop trees to patrol their breeding sites for danger, but the Solitary Sandpiper is easily distinguished from them by its bold eye ring and olive green legs.
• Shorebirds lay very large eggs and incubate them for comparatively long periods of time. By the time Solitary Sandpiper chicks hatch, they are ready to run out into the world—they have to be, because their mothers coax them down to the ground within hours of birth. For young shorebirds, the hazards of developing in the egg are probably less than the hazards of developing in the nest.

breeding

ID: *Sexes similar:* white eye ring; short green legs; brown-grey, spotted back; white lore; brown-grey head, neck and breast with fine white streaks; dark uppertail feathers with black-and-white barring on the sides.
Size: *L* 19–23 cm.
Status: uncommon from May to September.
Habitat: *Breeding:* heavily forested wetlands. *In migration:* wet meadows, sewage lagoons, muddy ponds, sedge wetlands and beaver ponds.
Nesting: in a spruce tree in a bog or muskeg; will use the

abandoned nest of a thrush, blackbird or other songbird; pair incubates 4 eggs for 23–24 days.
Feeding: stalks shorelines, picking up aquatic invertebrates, such as waterboatmen and damselfly nymphs; also gleans for terrestrial invertebrates; occasionally stirs the water with its foot to spook out prey.
Voice: high, thin *peet-wheet* or *wheet wheet wheet* during summer.
Similar Species: *Yellowlegs* (pp. 130–31): no eye ring; bright yellow legs. *Spotted Sandpiper* (p. 134): incomplete eye ring; spotted breast in breeding plumage; orange, black-tipped bill.
Best Sites: Wagner Natural Area; Crimson Lake PP.

WILLET
Catoptrophorus semipalmatus

This large shorebird of Alberta's southern open areas cuts a rather dull grey figure when it is grounded. The instant it takes flight, however, its striking black-and-white wings flash while it calls its name out loud: *will-will willet, will-willet!* • It is thought that the bright, bold flashes of the Willet's wings can serve as danger warnings to other Willets. They might also intimidate predators during a Willet's dive-bombing defense of its young. Willets are perhaps the most intimidating of the dive bombers in a typical prairie marsh. Their large size, heavy bill, continuous calls and arm's length approaches get the message across: execute a quick and proper retreat. • The scientific name *Catoptrophorus* means 'mirror-bearing,' a reference to its black-and-white wings.

breeding

ID: *Sexes similar:* plump; heavy, straight, black bill; lightly mottled, grey-brown plumage; light throat and belly. *In flight:* black-and-white wing pattern.
Size: *L* 36–41 cm.
Status: uncommon to common from April to August.
Habitat: shores of marshes, wet fields and lakes, but not much water is needed.
Nesting: in open, dry areas and sandy flats, occasionally far from water; in a shallow depression lined with grass and

other vegetation; occasionally builds a cup nest; pair incubates 4 eggs for 22–29 days.
Feeding: feeds by probing muddy areas; also gleans the ground for insects; occasionally eats shoots and seeds.
Voice: loud, rolling *will-will willet, will-willet* on the breeding grounds.
Similar Species: *Marbled Godwit* (p. 140): much longer bill; larger body. *Greater Yellowlegs* (p. 130): long, yellow legs; lacks the bold wing pattern.
Best Sites: Beaverhill Lake; Aspen Beach; Chappice Lake; Brooks area.

SPOTTED SANDPIPER
Actitis macularia

The Spotted Sandpiper is the most commonly encountered sandpiper throughout Alberta. With a stiff-winged, arthritic flight, it bursts unexpectedly from shore, looping out over the water and then back to shore a short distance ahead. One of the easiest ways to identify this bird is through its continuous teetering habits. It is thought that this 'tipsy-teapot' behaviour helps the bird blend into the background water, beside which it frequently perches. • It wasn't until 1972 that the unexpected truths about the Spotted Sandpiper's breeding activities were realized. Like the phalaropes, female Spotted Sandpipers defend territories and leave the males (they might pair with more than one in a season) to tend the nests and eggs. This mating system is called polyandry (from the Greek for 'many men'), and it is found in only about one percent of all bird species. • The scientific name *macularia* is Latin for 'spotted.'

breeding

ID: *Sexes similar:* teeters continuously. *Breeding:* white underparts are heavily spotted with black (more so in the female); yellow-orange legs; yellow-orange, black-tipped bill; white eyebrow. *Non-breeding* and *Juvenile:* pure white breast; brown bill; dull yellow legs.
Size: *L* 18–20 cm.
Status: common from May to September.
Habitat: shorelines, gravel beaches, ponds, rivers, marshes, alluvial wetlands and streams.
Nesting: usually near water; often

under overhanging vegetation, among logs or under bushes; in a shallow depression lined with grass; male almost exclusively incubates and raises the 4 young.
Feeding: picks and gleans along shorelines for terrestrial and aquatic invertebrates; also snatches flying insects from the air.
Voice: sharp, crisp *eat-wheat, eat-wheat, wheat-wheat-wheat-wheat.*
Similar Species: *Baird's Sandpiper* (p. 148): doesn't teeter; lacks the obvious spotting on the underparts. *Other sandpipers:* all lack the spotted breast.
Best Sites: Fish Creek PP; along riverbanks in all major cities in Alberta.

UPLAND SANDPIPER
Bartramia longicauda

For a naturalist travelling through the prairies in May, it is reassuring to see an Upland Sandpiper land on a fencepost and gracefully fold its long wings after its migration from the Argentinean grasslands. For the next several months, the male will maintain a steady vigil over his chosen territory, while his look-alike mate remains concealed nearby. • These uncommon birds react quickly and loudly to the presence of an intruder, but without this behaviour, they would no doubt be much more difficult to find. • *Bartramia* honours William Bartram, a ground-breaking and enthusiastic early-American botanist. An ornithologist in his own right, Bartram's passion for wild things is now immortalized in the scientific name of the Upland Sandpiper.

ID: *Sexes similar:* small head; long, thin neck; mottled upperparts; lightly streaked underparts; dark eyes; light belly and undertail coverts; yellow legs; bill is about the same length as the head width.
Size: *L* 28–32 cm.
Status: uncommon from May to August.
Habitat: hayfields, ungrazed pastures and natural grasslands.
Nesting: in a depression in dense grass or along a marsh; pair incubates 4 eggs for 21–27 days.

Feeding: gleans the ground for insects, especially grasshoppers and beetles.
Voice: courtship song is an airy, whistled *whip-whee-ee you*; alarm call is *quip-ip-ip*.
Similar Species: *Mountain Plover* (p. 127): shorter neck; no breast streaking. *Willet* (p. 133): heavier bill; black-and-white wings in flight. *Buff-breasted Sandpiper* (p. 153): shorter neck; larger head.
Best Sites: Hwy. 36 north of Brooks; roads between Patricia and Empress.

ESKIMO CURLEW
Numenius borealis

The Eskimo Curlew is a bird that birdwatchers now only dream about. Not long ago, however, it was the restaurants of New England that craved this bird—so much so that in a span of 50 years this species went from one of the most abundant to one of the rarest in the world. Like the bison and the Passenger Pigeon, the fate of the Eskimo Curlew teaches that endangered species are not always rare to begin with. Flocks of Eskimo Curlews once led the migratory passage of shorebirds through Alberta, often passing through in the company of golden-plovers. The final nail has not yet been hammered into this bird's coffin, but it has not been seen in Alberta for decades.
• The scattering of farmlands in the Manning, High Level and Fort Vermilion areas might be the best place in North American to search for the Eskimo Curlew. Isolated farmlands in the boreal forest might concentrate the few remaining individuals in late May.

ID: *Sexes similar:* downcurved bill; dark eyebrow; cinnamon brown upperparts; light throat; line of small V-shaped markings on the flanks; light brown underparts; pale eyebrow; dark green legs. *In flight:* cinnamon underwings; unbarred primary feathers.
Size: L 30–35 cm.
Status: possibly extinct.

possibly extinct

Habitat: farmlands, pastures and lakeshores.
Nesting: does not nest in Alberta.
Feeding: picks grasshoppers and worms in fields.
Voice: soft whistled *tee! tee! tee!*
Similar Species: *Whimbrel* (p. 137): larger; darker underparts; dark underwings; barred primaries; longer bill; bluish legs.
Best Sites: none; has not been seen for decades.

WHIMBREL
Numenius phaeopus

In colonial times, the Whimbrel was the rarest of Alberta's curlews; now it is the most abundant throughout North America. It has not directly outcompeted the Long-billed Curlew and the Eskimo Curlew; rather it has avoided the devastation those birds suffered at the hands of the market gunners. Whimbrels are still uncommon in Alberta, however, because they tend to migrate along seacoasts, rather than taking an inland passage through our province. • The airy, soft sound of the word 'whimbrel' derives from one of this bird's calls, which is similar to a hound's whisperings. *Numenius* is from the Greek for 'new moon,' and it refers to the curved shape of the bill.

ID: *Sexes similar:* long, downcurved bill; striped crown; dark eye line; mottled brown body; long legs. *In flight:* dark underwings.
Size: L 38–45 cm.
Status: rare to uncommon in May and August.
Habitat: farmlands, lakeshores and grassy fields.
Nesting: does not nest in Alberta.

Feeding: probes and pecks at invertebrates in mud or vegetation; also eats berries during fall migration.
Voice: usually quiet in migration through Alberta; occasionally a rolling *cur-lee-ou cur-lee-ou.*
Similar Species: *Long-billed Curlew* (p. 138): much larger; larger bill; lacks the stripes on the head and through the eye.
Best Sites: Beaverhill Lake; Fincastle Lake.

137

LONG-BILLED CURLEW
Numenius americanus

In Alberta, the Long-billed Curlew is a mainstay of prairie birdwatching. Male curlews put on spectacular displays over their nesting territory, giving loud ringing calls as they flutter higher and higher, and then gliding down in an undulating flight. • Habitat loss has led to the decline of the Long-billed Curlew in Canada, but the wondrous sight of this large, tawny bird can be had by anyone with the time to drive for a few hours on a prairie road in spring or summer. The future of the Long-billed Curlew concerns conservationists, who point out that our current abundance of rangeland habitats should not be taken for granted. • This bird's long, downcurved bill is a wonderfully dexterous tool for picking up grasshoppers while it keeps a watchful eye above the prairie grass.

ID: *Sexes similar:* very long, downcurved bill (slightly longer in the female); buff-brown underparts; brown upperparts; mottled back; unstriped head; long legs.
Size: L 51–66 cm.
Status: uncommon from April to August.
Habitat: short-grass prairie; occasionally in grainfields and pastures; often near water during migration.
Nesting: usually on dry prairie; in a slight depression sparsely lined with grass and debris; pair incubates 4 eggs for 27–30 days.

Feeding: *In migration:* probes shorelines and mudflats for soft-bodied invertebrates.
Breeding: picks grasshoppers and other invertebrates from the grass and from along sloughs.
Voice: most common call in summer is a loud whistle: *cur-lee cur-lee cur-lee;* also a melodious, rolling *cuurrleeeuuu.*
Similar Species: *Whimbrel* (p. 137): striped head. *Marbled Godwit* (p. 140): slightly upturned, bicoloured bill.
Best Sites: localized on grassy rangelands in the prairies; northeast side of Travers Reservoir.

HUDSONIAN GODWIT
Limosa haemastica

Although Hudsonian Godwits migrate every spring and fall through North America, it is only in spring that they are reliably observed in Alberta. During the fall passage, most of these godwits travel south and east, leaving from the Atlantic coast of Canada and the U.S. and flying non-stop to South America. Still, you can find a few migrants in central Alberta in July—presumably non-breeding birds coming back early from the tundra. • This species breaks the rules for shorebird sexual dimorphism. Male Hudsonian Godwits are more colourful than their mates—a pattern that is common in other types of birds, but rare among the shorebirds.

• Hudsonian Godwits were another victim of the tragic market-hunting activities in the late 19th century. • The *haem-* in *haemastica* is a reference to the blood-coloured breeding plumage of this species (as in 'haemoglobin').

♂

breeding

ID: *General:* long, slightly upturned bull; white rump; black tail; long, black-blue legs. *Breeding:* heavily barred chestnut underparts; dark-brown upperparts; male is more brightly coloured. *Non-breeding:* sandy brown body. *In flight:* black wing pits and wing linings; light flight feathers.
Size: *L* 36–40 cm.
Status: rare from April to May and from July to September.

Habitat: wet fields, marshes and lakeshores.
Nesting: does not nest in Alberta.
Feeding: probes deeply into water or mud; eats insects and other invertebrates; also picks earthworms from ploughed fields.
Voice: sharp, rising *god-WIT!*
Similar Species: *Marbled Godwit* (p. 140): larger; lacks the white rump; lighter in colour.
Best Site: Beaverhill Lake.

MARBLED GODWIT
Limosa fedoa

The Marbled Godwit's bill looks plenty long enough to reach buried prey, but this godwit doesn't seem content with its reach. It is frequently seen with its head submerged beneath the water's surface or with its face pressed right down into a mudflat. These deep probings pay off for this large, comical shorebird, and a godwit looks genuinely pleased with its face covered with mud. • Marbled Godwits are the most common large shorebird throughout the southern half of Alberta. They draw attention to themselves with their loud vocalizations, so vigilant birdwatchers get many opportunities to study this bird throughout the shorebird season.

• The dark tip on a godwit's bill might give the bill extra strength, because the dark pigment, melanin, hardens the structure of both bills and feathers.

breeding

ID: *Sexes similar:* very long, upturned bill with a dark tip and a light reddish base; long neck and legs; buffy-brown plumage; dark mottling on the upperparts. *In flight:* cinnamon wing linings; long, upturned bill.
Size: L 41–51 cm.
Status: common from April to October.
Habitat: muddy shorelines of lakes, reservoirs, wet meadows, moist grasslands and open areas.
Nesting: on short-grass prairie; in a shallow depression sparsely lined with grass; nest site is not well concealed, but

it is vigorously defended by both parents; pair incubates 4 eggs for 21–23 days.
Feeding: probes deeply in soft substrates for worms and insect larvae; picks grasshoppers and beetles from grass; might also eat the tubers and seeds of aquatic vegetation.
Voice: loud, duck-like (2-syllable) squawks: *co-rect co-rect* or *god-wit god-wit.*
Similar Species: *Long-billed Curlew* (p. 138): downcurved bill. *Hudsonian Godwit* (p. 139): very rare migrant; white tail base.
Best Sites: Beaverhill Lake; Aspen Beach; Frank Lake; Brooks-Bassano area.

RUDDY TURNSTONE

Arenaria interpres

In the last two weeks of May, small flocks of boldly patterned Ruddy Turnstones stop off on lakeshores and blacktop fields to mingle and forage among the more populous migrants. Their costume-party faces and black-and-red backs set these birds apart from the average sandpiper—turnstones are our most striking small shorebirds. • If you watch a flock of turnstones for a while, you will see an unusual feeding technique. As the name implies, turnstones flip over small rocks and debris with their bills to expose hidden invertebrates. A turnstone's bill is short, stubby and slightly upturned—ideal for this foraging style. The Ruddy Turnstone is such a highly specialized feeder, that there is a report of a captive 15-day-old chick that refused to eat until its food was tucked under a small rock.

♂

breeding

ID: *Sexes similar:* white belly; black bib; stout, slightly upturned bill; orange-red legs. *Breeding:* ruddy upperparts (female is slightly paler); white face; black collar; grey crown. *Non-breeding:* dark brownish upperparts and face.
Size: L 22–25 cm.
Status: uncommon in May and from August to October.
Habitat: shores of lakes, reservoirs and marshes; also in cultivated fields.
Nesting: does not nest in Alberta.

Feeding: probes under and flips rocks, weeds and shells for food items; also picks, digs and probes for invertebrates from the soil.
Voice: low rattle; also a sharp *cut-a-cut* alarm call.
Similar Species: *Other sandpipers:* all lack the turnstone's bold pattering. *Plovers* (pp. 122–27): equally bold plumage, but in significantly different patterns.
Best Sites: Beaverhill Lake; Aspen Beach; Buffalo Lake.

RED KNOT
Calidris canutus

On the rich, dark fields that surround Beaverhill Lake, small flocks of Red Knots appear during the last few weeks of May. Never abundant in our province, the tubby, red-bellied knots distinguish themselves by colour among the similar-sized plovers and turnstones. • The Red Knot's apparent rarity during fall migration might be a result of its seasonal dress. During the breeding season, Red Knots nest among similarly reddish tundra grasses. In contrast, their drab, non-breeding plumage, which is not red, blends nicely with the uniform greys and browns of open beaches, which they favour during the winter months and in fall migration. • Linnaeus named this bird's genus after King Canute, who, according to some stories, had a great affection for Red Knots, albeit as a main course for supper. The unusual common name can also be traced to the king—Canute was also called 'Knut,' from which we get 'knot.'

breeding

ID: *Sexes similar:* chunky, round-bodied shorebird. *Breeding:* rusty face, breast and underparts; brown, black and chestnut upperparts. *Non-breeding:* pale grey upperparts; white underparts.
Size: L 25–28 cm.
Status: rare to uncommon in May and from July to September.
Habitat: lakeshores, marshes and cultivated fields.

Nesting: does not nest in Alberta.
Feeding: gleans shorelines for insects, crustaceans and mollusks; probes soft substrates, creating a line of small holes in the sand.
Voice: melodious and soft *ker ek* in flight.
Similar Species: *Black-bellied Plover* (p. 122): shorter bill; greyer upperparts in non-breeding plumage. *Other peeps:* all are smaller.
Best Sites: Beaverhill Lake; Frank Lake; Kinbrook Island PP.

SANDERLING
Calidris alba

Famous for chasing the edges of crashing waves on the coastal surf, Sanderlings in Alberta practice on a smaller scale along the shores of our larger lakes. Their dark legs move so quickly that the birds appear to glide over the sand. • The Sanderling is one of the 'peep' sandpipers—a small sandpiper in the genus *Calidris*. Members of this group are notoriously hard to identify in the field. • When resting, Sanderlings tuck one leg up to preserve their body heat. They will often remain resolutely one-legged, hopping ahead of an advancing beach walker, evoking unnecessary sympathy and concern. • This sandpiper is one of the world's most widespread birds. It breeds across the Arctic in Alaska, Canada and Russia, and it spends the winter running up and down sandy shorelines on every continent.

breeding

ID: *Sexes similar:* straight, black bill; black legs. *Breeding:* rufous head, neck and upperparts; white belly. *Non-breeding:* very light overall; dark shoulder patch (often partly hidden).
Size: *L* 18–22 cm.
Status: uncommon to common in May and from July to September.
Habitat: shores of lakes, reservoirs and marshes.
Nesting: does not nest in Alberta.

Feeding: gleans shorelines for insects, crustaceans and mollusks; probes repeatedly, creating a line of small holes in the sand.
Voice: flight call is a sharp *kip*.
Similar Species: *Least Sandpiper* (p. 146): lighter legs. *Semipalmated* (p. 144), *Western* (p. 145) and *Pectoral* (p. 149) *sandpipers:* all lack the reddish breeding plumage and the white winter plumage. *Dunlin* (p. 151): darker; downcurved bill.
Best Sites: Beaverhill Lake; Aspen Beach.

SEMIPALMATED SANDPIPER
Calidris pusilla

Large numbers of Semipalmated Sandpipers visit Alberta's shorelines annually. They peck and probe in mechanized fury, replenishing their body fat for the remainder of their long migrations. Semipalmated Sandpipers migrate almost the entire length of the Americas, and their migratory pit-stops have to provide ample food resources. It is vital that these birds acquire just the right amount of fat—too much slows them down, making them easy targets for fast-flying falcons, but with too little they will run out of energy before they reach the next feeding ground.
• 'Semis' fly in tight flocks, but when the birds land they quickly spread out to forage. • 'Semipalmated' refers to the slight webbing between this bird's front toes. The scientific name *pusilla* means 'small.'

breeding

ID: *Sexes similar:* dark, short, straight bill; dark legs. *Breeding:* mottled upperparts; rufous ear patch; faint streaks on the upper breast and flanks. *Non-breeding:* grey-brown upperparts; white underparts; faint, white eyebrow. *In flight:* narrow, white wing stripe; white rump is split by a black line.
Size: *L* 14–18 cm.
Status: common in May and from July to September.

Habitat: mudflats and the shores of ponds and lakes.
Nesting: does not nest in Alberta.
Feeding: probes soft substrates and gleans for aquatic insects and crustaceans.
Voice: flight call is a harsh *cherk.*
Similar Species: *Least Sandpiper* (p. 146): pale legs. *Dunlin* (p. 151): downcurved bill. *Western Sandpiper* (p. 145): longer, slightly downcurved bill.
Best Sites: Beaverhill Lake; Aspen Beach; Frank Lake.

WESTERN SANDPIPER
Calidris mauri

Migrant Western Sandpipers are infrequently found in Alberta. A sighting in our province is usually the product of a diligent birder—this bird is usually mixed in the wheeling flocks of Semipalmated and Least sandpipers that swirl above our springtime shorelines—and a lost bird—their main migratory corridor and their Arctic breeding grounds lie to the west. • Most field guides tell you to look for a downcurved bill in this species, and on paper this seems like a sensible plan. In the field, however, as angles and lighting change, the bills of peeps can look downcurved one moment, straight the next, and anything in between when double-checked. The only solution to this challenge is to allow oneself to spend a good deal of time getting to know the peeps before announcing a string of 'positive' identifications.

breeding

ID: *Sexes similar:* longish, black, slightly downcurved bill; black legs. *Breeding:* rusty crown, ear and wing patches; V-shaped streaking on the upper breast and flanks; light underparts. *Non-breeding:* grey-brown upperparts; white underparts; white eyebrow. *In flight:* narrow white wing stripe; white rump, split by a black line.
Size: *L* 15–18 cm.
Status: rare to uncommon in May and from July to September.
Habitat: mudflats and the shores of ponds and lakes.

Nesting: does not nest in Alberta.
Feeding: gleans the substrate and probes mud and shallow water; occasionally submerges its head; eats primarily aquatic insects, worms and crustaceans.
Voice: flight call is a high-pitched *cheep*.
Similar Species: *Semipalmated Sandpiper* (p. 144): shorter, straight bill. *Dunlin* (p. 151): black belly, darker breast and wider, white wing stripe in the breeding plumage. *Least Sandpiper* (p. 146): smaller; light-coloured legs.
Best Sites: Beaverhill Lake; Frank Lake.

LEAST SANDPIPER
Calidris minutilla

As both its common and scientific names suggest, the Least Sandpiper is the smallest North American shorebird, although estimating absolute size can be tricky when sandpipers are spread out, running down a beach. • Although light legs are a good field mark for this species, bad lighting or mud can confuse matters. Dark mud can make them look dark, while light mud can make other species's legs look light. • Because Arctic summers are short, shorebirds must optimize their breeding efforts. Least Sandpipers on their way north are already developing massive eggs, and when they nest, the entire clutch might weigh more than half the weight of the female. The young hatch in an advanced state of development, and their first order of business is to prepare for the fall migration south. • Least Sandpipers are most often seen in Alberta in late May.

breeding

ID: *Sexes similar. Adult:* light yellowish legs; ever-so-slightly downcurved, black bill; mottled back; buff-brown breast, head and nape. *Immature:* like an adult, but with a faintly streaked breast.
Size: *L* 13–17 cm.
Status: uncommon to common in May and from July to September.

Habitat: sandy beaches, lakeshores, ditches, sewage lagoons, mudflats and wetland edges.
Nesting: does not nest in Alberta.
Feeding: probes or pecks for insects, crustaceans, mollusks and occasionally seeds.
Voice: high-pitched *kreee.*
Similar Species: *Other peeps:* all have dark legs and are generally larger.
Best Sites: Beaverhill Lake; Aspen Beach; Frank Lake.

WHITE-RUMPED SANDPIPER
Calidris fuscicollis

When a die-hard shorebird watcher is about to go into a peep-induced stupor, one of the birds takes wing and flashes its pure white rump. Oh happy day! There can now be no doubt that a rare White-rumped Sandpiper has been identified. • The white rump on this bird might serve the same signaling purpose as the tail of a White-tailed Deer—it might alert other birds when danger threatens. • When flocks of White-rumps and other sandpipers take to the air, they often defecate in unison. This nervous evacuation might benefit the birds by reducing their weight. • Flocks of White-rumped Sandpipers have been known to collectively rush at a predator and then suddenly scatter in its face. It is thought that these confusion attacks deter the predator's efforts. • The scientific name *fuscicollis* means 'brown neck,' a characteristic that this bird shares with many of its close relatives.

breeding

ID: *Sexes similar:* dark legs; dark bill (about as long as the head width); brown-mottled upperparts. *In flight:* white rump.
Size: L 18–20 cm.
Status: uncommon in May and from August to September.
Habitat: shores of lakes, reservoirs and marshes; also flooded and cultivated fields.

Nesting: does not nest in Alberta.
Feeding: gleans the ground and shorelines for insects, crustaceans and mollusks.
Voice: flight call is a characteristic, squeal-like *tzeet.*
Similar Species: *Other peeps:* all have a dark line through the rump. *Stilt Sandpiper* (p. 152): much longer legs, which trail beyond the tail in flight.
Best Site: Beaverhill Lake.

147

BAIRD'S SANDPIPER
Calidris bairdii

The Baird's Sandpiper is a modest-looking shorebird with extraordinary migratory habits—it flies twice annually between South America and the Arctic, stopping off at mudflats along the way to fuel its muscles. • Like many shorebirds, the Baird's Sandpiper remains on its tundra breeding grounds for a very short period of time. Soon after the chicks hatch, the adult birds flock together and then begin their southern migration, usually in July, abandoning their young in the Arctic. A few weeks after the parents have left, the young flock together in a second wave of southern migrants. • Spencer Fullerton Baird, a director of the Smithsonian Institution, organized several natural history expeditions across North America. Elliott Coues chose to name this bird in Baird's honour.

breeding

ID: *Sexes similar:* black legs and bill; wings extend beyond the tail. *Breeding:* faint, buffy speckling on the breast, face and sides of the neck. *Non-breeding:* scaled look to the upperparts.
Size: *L* 18–19 cm.
Status: uncommon in May and from July to September.
Habitat: sandy beaches, mudflats and wetland edges.
Nesting: does not nest in Alberta.

Feeding: gleans aquatic invertebrates, especially larval flies; also eats beetles and grasshoppers; rarely probes.
Voice: soft, rolling *kriit kriit*.
Similar Species: *Pectoral Sandpiper* (p. 149): sharply delineated, dark breast. *Least Sandpiper* (p. 146): light-coloured legs. *Semipalmated Sandpiper* (p. 144): lacks the buffy face and neck and the 'scaling' on the back.
Best Sites: Beaverhill Lake; Aspen Beach.

PECTORAL SANDPIPER
Calidris melanotos

A neat dividing line between its brown bib and its white underparts makes the Pectoral Sandpiper easy to identify. In fact, it is distinctive enough that few bird-watchers think of it as a 'peep,' despite its membership in the genus *Calidris*.
• Pectoral Sandpipers are fairly common migrants in Alberta, and they have a penchant for feeding in wet, grassy fields. When disturbed, Pectorals stop feeding and crane their necks above the grass to assess the danger. Pectoral Sandpipers often spread out while they feed, only to converge in flight when they are frightened. • Female Pectoral Sandpipers are only two-thirds the size of the males. • The common name 'pectoral' refers to the location of the male's prominent air sacs on the breast. The males inflate these sacs as part of their courtship ritual. The scientific name *melanotos* means 'black back.'

breeding

ID: *Sexes similar:* brown breast streaks contrast with light underparts; slightly down-curved, black bill; longish, yellow legs; dark crown; wing tips extend beyond the tail.
Size: *L* 23 cm (female slightly smaller).
Status: uncommon to common in May and from July to September.

Habitat: along lakeshores, marshes and mudflats.
Nesting: does not nest in Alberta.
Feeding: probes and pecks for small insects (mainly flies, but also beetles and some grasshoppers).
Voice: sharp, short, low *krrick krrick*.
Similar Species: *Other peeps:* all lack the well-defined, dark bib.
Best Sites: Beaverhill Lake; Aspen Beach.

SHARP-TAILED SANDPIPER
Calidris acuminata

For those of you who want a great challenge, we encourage you to study Alberta's 'peeps.' If you want to try for the impossible, search out the Sharp-tailed Sandpiper in the fall migration. This sandpiper, which nests in Siberia, has been seen a number of times in Alberta. It tends to show up in fall, however, when all but the most devout birdwatchers have given up on shorebird identification. • The Sharp-tailed Sandpiper does indeed have sharp tail feathers, but this feature does not easily distinguish it in a shorebird crowd. • The first documented occurrence of this bird in Alberta was in 1975. Because our birdwatching community was alert to it, several more reports occurred in the subsequent years. Report any sightings to Alberta's rare bird committee, so other birders will be made aware of your findings and will possibly substantiate your claim.

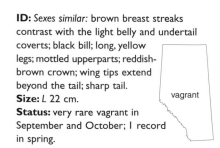

breeding

ID: *Sexes similar:* brown breast streaks contrast with the light belly and undertail coverts; black bill; long, yellow legs; mottled upperparts; reddish-brown crown; wing tips extend beyond the tail; sharp tail.
Size: *L* 22 cm.
Status: very rare vagrant in September and October; I record in spring.

vagrant

Habitat: lakeshores, marshes and mudflats.
Nesting: does not nest in Alberta.
Feeding: probes and pecks the ground, primarily for small insects and other invertebrates.
Voice: 2-toned whistle.
Similar Species: *Pectoral Sandpiper* (p. 149): more heavily marked breast; lacks the white eyebrow and reddish cap.
Best Site: Beaverhill Lake.

DUNLIN
Calidris alpina

Unfortunately, Albertans do not get to witness the immense hypnotic flights of Dunlins seen elsewhere, because these birds pass through our province only in small numbers. Their most popular pit stop in Alberta is Beaverhill Lake, where a few of these red-backed sandpipers mingle close to the water's edge in spring, picking up newly emerged invertebrates. They are fairly distinct in their breeding attire—their black bellies and legs make it look as though the birds have been wading belly-deep in ink. • The Dunlin, like most other shorebirds, nests on the Arctic tundra and winters on the coasts of North America, Europe and Asia. It is among the swiftest of the shorebird migrants—a flock was once observed passing a small plane at 175 km/h. • This species was originally called the 'Dunling' (meaning 'a small brown bird'), but for unknown reasons, the 'g' was dropped.

breeding

ID: *Sexes similar:* downcurved, black bill; black legs. *Breeding:* jet black belly; rusty wings, back and crown; lightly streaked, white breast. *Non-breeding:* grey-brown upperparts; light underparts; light brown streaking on the breast and nape. *In flight:* white wing stripe; white rump is split by a black line.
Size: *L* 19–23 cm.
Status: rare to uncommon in May and from August to October.
Habitat: mudflats and shores of ponds and lakes.

Nesting: does not nest in Alberta.
Feeding: gleans substrates and probes mudflats for aquatic crustaceans, worms, mollusks and insects.
Voice: flight call is a grating *cheezp* or *treezp*.
Similar Species: breeding plumage is distinctive. *Western Sandpiper* (p. 145): smaller; non-breeding plumage is paler overall; bill is less downcurved. *Least Sandpiper* (p. 146): smaller. *Sanderling* (p. 143): paler; usually seen running in the surf.
Best Site: Beaverhill Lake.

STILT SANDPIPER
Calidris himantopus

With the silhouette of a yellowlegs and the foraging behaviour of a dowitcher, the Stilt Sandpiper is often overlooked by birdwatchers. This sandpiper loves water, however, and it often wades breast deep or plunges its head underwater in search of food. • Stilt Sandpipers are the most vegetarian of shorebirds, and one-third of their diet consists of plant matter. A foraging Stilt Sandpiper occasionally sweeps its bill side-to-side through the water, like an avocet. It might also borrow a page from the Wood Stork's foraging book—Stilt Sandpipers have been seen holding their bills submerged for prolonged periods in sand or water, waiting for prey to touch the bill and trigger a strike. • There are several other shorebirds with longer legs than the Stilt Sandpiper, but it is very deserving of the title in comparison to other members of the genus *Calidris*.

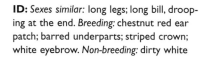

breeding

ID: *Sexes similar:* long legs; long bill, drooping at the end. *Breeding:* chestnut red ear patch; barred underparts; striped crown; white eyebrow. *Non-breeding:* dirty white underparts; dark grey upperparts. *In flight:* legs trail behind the tail.
Size: *L* 20–23 cm.
Status: uncommon in May and from July to September.
Habitat: shores of lakes, reservoirs and marshes.

Nesting: does not nest in Alberta.
Feeding: forages in shallow water, probing deeply; occasionally picks insects from the water's surface or the ground; feeds mostly on invertebrates; also eats seeds, roots and leaves.
Voice: simple, sharp *querp* in flight.
Similar Species: *Yellowlegs* (pp. 130–31): yellow legs; lack the red ear patch.
Best Site: Beaverhill Lake.

BUFF-BREASTED SANDPIPER
Tryngites subruficollis

Shy in behaviour and humble in appearance, the Buff-breasted Sandpiper is a shorebird Albertans never tire of encountering. This species is often discovered in the course of scanning flocks of Black-bellied Plovers or American Golden-Plovers. The Buff-breasted Sandpiper blends beautifully into a spring backdrop of cultivated fields, becoming visible only when it moves. • The courtship activities of this species can be seen during its spring migration, possibly in an attempt to get a head start on the limited nesting time it has on the tundra. Courting male Buff-breasts strut about, lifting their wings high over their heads, like Dracula raising his cape. • In Alberta, Buff-breasted Sandpipers are most commonly observed in the northern half of the province, where they refuel on their way to the Arctic. • 'Buff-breasted' is a far better descriptor than *subruficollis,* which means 'slightly reddish neck.'

breeding

ID: *Sexes similar:* round head; buffy, unpatterned face; large, dark eyes; buff underparts; small spots on the breast; 'scaled' look to the upperparts. *In flight:* white underwings; short tail.
Size: *L* 19–21 cm.
Status: rare to uncommon in May and from August to September.
Habitat: shores of lakes, reservoirs and marshes; also cultivated and flooded fields.
Nesting: does not nest in Alberta.
Feeding: gleans the ground and shorelines for insects, spiders and mollusks; might eat seeds.
Similar Species: *Upland Sandpiper* (p. 135): more boldly streaked on the breast.
Best Sites: Beaverhill Lake; fields near Manning.

RUFF/REEVE
Philomachus pugnax

This Eurasian shorebird appears almost yearly, but in tiny numbers, throughout the province, primarily during its spring migration. They might even be more common than we think—a Finnish birder, who is familiar with the species back home, spotted a flock of seven one May morning at Hastings Lake. • This species is known to have nested in Alaska, but nowhere else in North America. The birds seen in Alberta might be migrants that winter in California. • The male of this species is called a 'Ruff,' while the female is called a 'Reeve.' It is not known whether the male was named for his neck-feather ruffs, or if ruffs were named after the bird. 'Reeve' has even more obscure origins, but some suggest it is linked to the meaning 'observer' or 'bailiff'—the females oversee the tussling courting males, which engage in grouse-like displays on their breeding grounds. The scientific name *pugnax* means 'pugnacious,' which is an appropriate description of the courting males.

breeding

ID: *General:* plump body; small head; yellow-green to red legs; yellow or black bill; brown-grey upperparts. *Breeding male:* black, white or orange neck ruff, usually flattened, but erected during courtship; dark underparts. *Breeding female:* dark blotches on the underparts. *In flight:* thin, white wing stripe; oval, white rump patches; dark line through the rump.
Size: *Male: L* 26–29 cm.
Female: L 22–24 cm.
Status: rare vagrant in April and May.

vagrant

Habitat: marshes and flooded fields.
Nesting: does not nest in Alberta.
Feeding: probes and picks at the surface of mudflats for aquatic invertebrates.
Voice: rarely vocal in Alberta; call is a short *tu-whit.*
Similar Species: *Yellowlegs* (pp. 130–31): slimmer bodies; longer, yellower legs; streaked underparts. *Red Knot* (p. 142): shorter legs; 'cleaner' breast in non-breeding plumage.
Best Sites: Beaverhill Lake; Hastings Lake; Frank Lake.

SHORT-BILLED DOWITCHER
Limnodromus griseus

It is only in comparison to the other dowitcher that anyone would ever think of calling this bird 'short-billed.' In fact, the bill of the Short-billed Dowitcher is only slightly shorter than that of the Long-billed Dowitcher, and it is comparatively longer than that of most other shorebirds. Considering the similarities between the two dowitchers, however, bill length is as good a feature as any to use in distinguishing between them. • Dowitchers and Stilt Sandpipers have shorter wings than most of the other long-distance migrant shorebirds. It is thought that their short wings makes it more practical for these birds to take flight from the shallows in which they feed. • 'Dowitcher' might be from the Iroquois name for this bird, or it might have come from a word meaning 'Dutch.' Either way, it has nothing to do with a dowager—a dignified widow.

non-breeding

ID: *Sexes similar:* straight, long, dark bill; chunky body; white rump. *Breeding:* cinnamon overall; dark upperparts; light barring on the flanks; broad white bands on the tail feathers; occasionally has a white belly. *Non-breeding:* grey upperparts; dirty white underparts; white eyebrow.
Size: *L* 27–30 cm.
Status: uncommon to common from May to October.
Habitat: shores of lakes, reservoirs and marshes.

Nesting: on the ground in a bog, fen or forest clearing; nest is built in a clump of grass or moss; pair incubates 4 light brown eggs for 24–31 days.
Feeding: probes deeply and repeatedly into soft ground for insects, crustaceans and mollusks; sometimes eats seeds.
Voice: flight or alarm call is a mellow *toodu-lu,* occasionally abbreviated to *toodu.*
Similar Species: *Long-billed Dowitcher* (p. 156): migrant in Alberta; heavier barring on the flanks; alarm call is *keek.*
Best Site: Beaverhill Lake.

LONG-BILLED DOWITCHER
Limnodromus scolopaceus

Mudflats and marshes throughout Alberta host these enthusiastic shorebirds during their spring and fall migrations. As a group, dowitchers are easy to recognize—they are plump birds that forage in tight flocks along wet shorelines and 'stitch' up and down into the mudflats like a sewing machine. • Long-billed Dowitchers often migrate with the closely related Short-billed Dowitcher, and the two are almost impossible to tell apart when they are silent. Long-billed Dowitchers do not breed in Alberta, however, unlike their look-alike relatives. • Mixed flocks of shorebirds demonstrate a variety of foraging styles. Some species probe deeply, while others pick at the water's surface or glean the shorelines. It is thought that large numbers of shorebirds can coexist because their different foraging styles reduce competition for the food sources.

breeding

ID: *Sexes similar:* very long, straight, dark bill (longer in the female); very stocky body; short neck. *Breeding:* reddish underparts; lightly barred flanks; dark, mottled upperparts; dark eye line; light eyebrow; long, dark yellow legs; white lower back. *Immature:* grey overall; white belly.
Size: *L* 28–32 cm.
Status: uncommon to common in May and from July to September.
Habitat: along lakeshores, shallow marshes and mudflats.

Nesting: does not nest in Alberta.
Feeding: probes in shallow water and mudflats with an up-down motion; frequently plunges its head underwater; eats worms, larval flies and other soft-bodied invertebrates.
Voice: alarm call is a single, loud *keek*.
Similar Species: *Short-billed Dowitcher* (p. 155): call is *toodu;* faint barring on the flanks; bill is slightly shorter. *Common Snipe* (p. 157): streaked upperparts; longer legs; lacks the white wedge on the lower back.
Best Site: Beaverhill Lake.

COMMON SNIPE
Gallinago gallinago

The eerie, hollow winnowing sound of the Common Snipe is a trademark of Alberta's spring nights, but few people understand its origin. Specialized outer tail feathers vibrate like saxophone reeds as the birds perform shallow, powered dives above the wetlands in which potential mates are waiting and watching. Most of the time, they only 'call' at night, but the occasional bird cannot resist the temptation to perform in daylight. • The Common Snipe is both secretive and well camouflaged, so few people notice it until it flushes suddenly from a nearby grassy tussock. As soon as the snipe takes to the air, it performs a series of quick zigzags—an evasive maneuver designed to confuse predators. Because of this habit, snipes were among the most difficult birds to shoot (in the days when shorebirds were hunted for sport), and skilled sportsmen were known as 'snipers'—a term later adopted by the military.

Nesting: usually in dry grass under vegetation; builds nest with grass and moss; female incubates 4 eggs for about 20 days; both parents raise the young.

Feeding: probes soft substrates for invertebrates, mostly insect larvae and earthworms.

Voice: eerie, accelerating courtship 'song': *woo-woo-woo-woo-woo-woo*; alarm call is a nasal *wheat wheat wheat.*

Similar Species: *Dowitchers* (pp. 155–56): lack the striping on the head; usually seen in flocks. *Godwits* (pp. 139–40): larger; bicoloured bill; longer legs.

Best Sites: most marshy areas; Beaverhill Lake; Aspen Beach.

ID: *Sexes similar:* long, dark bill; short legs; heavily striped head and back; white belly; streaked breast; otherwise mottled brown. *In flight:* quick zig-zags at take-off; shallow dives when courting.

Size: *L* 27–29 cm.

Status: common from April to October; a few might overwinter near open water.

Habitat: cattail and bulrush marshes, sedge meadows, poorly drained floodplains, willow wetlands, bogs and fens.

WILSON'S PHALAROPE
Phalaropus tricolor

The Wilson's Phalarope is the only phalarope that breeds in Alberta, and it is probably the first phalarope a birdwatcher will encounter. • Not only are phalaropes among the most colourful of the shorebirds, they are also among the most unusual. These intriguing birds practise a mating strategy known as polyandry, in which each female mates with several males. The brightly coloured female defends her nest sites from other females and leaves her camouflaged mates to tend the eggs. (It takes a great deal of energy to produce eggs, which is why in most species the female birds to stay with their clutch and protect their investment.) Even John J. Audubon was fooled by the phalarope's breeding habits—he mislabelled the female and male birds in all his phalarope illustrations. • This species bears the name of Alexander Wilson, one of the fathers of North American ornithology.

breeding

ID: *General:* dark, needle-like bill; chestnut throat; black eye line; white eyebrow; light grey underparts; black legs. *Breeding female:* grey cap; very sharp colours. *Breeding male:* dark cap; dull colours.
Size: *L* 22–24 cm.
Status: uncommon to common from May to September.
Habitat: beaver ponds, sedge meadows and cattail marshes. In migration: open water of lakes and reservoirs.
Nesting: near water; well

concealed in a grass-lined depression; male incubates 4 eggs and rears the young.
Feeding: whirls in tight circles while swimming, picking at the stirred-up invertebrates; on land, jabs at food in open areas.
Voice: deep nasal *wu wu wu* on the breeding grounds.
Similar Species: *Red-necked Phalarope* (p. 159): dark head and back; migrant. *Lesser Yellowlegs* (p. 131): yellow legs; streaked underparts.
Best Sites: Beaverhill Lake; Aspen Beach; Cavan Lake; Brooks area.

RED-NECKED PHALAROPE
Phalaropus lobatus

When foraging on the water, phalaropes are easily identified by the way they whirl in circles. This action stirs up the water, which brings planktonic invertebrates into pecking range. • For a few weeks in May, Red-necked Phalaropes are fairly abundant on wetlands in Alberta. Their striking colours make these birds stand out against the shorebird crowd. • The Red-necked Phalaropes that migrate through Alberta in fall have come a long way from their Arctic nesting grounds, but they have still farther to go—most of them winter at sea off western South America, south of the Equator. • Phalaropes have individually webbed toes, like those of grebes and coots. Indeed, 'phalarope' is from the Greek for 'coot's foot.'

breeding

ID: *General:* graceful shape. *Breeding female:* chestnut neck and throat; white chin; dark head; white belly; buff on the wings. *Breeding male:* white eyebrow; less colourful than the female. *Non-breeding:* white underparts; black mask.
Size: *L* 18 cm.
Status: uncommon to common in May and from July to September; rare breeder in northern Alberta.
Habitat: *In migration:* open waterbodies, including ponds, lakes and large sloughs.

Nesting: near water; on a hummock lined with grass and lichens; male incubates the eggs and rears the young.
Feeding: whirls in tight circles in shallow or deep water, picking invertebrates from the water; on land, makes short jabs to pick up food in open areas.
Voice: often noisy in migration; soft *krit krit krit*.
Similar Species: *Wilson's Phalarope* (p. 158): female has a lighter head and back; common Alberta breeder.
Best Sites: Birch Lake; Bittern Lake; Beaverhill Lake.

159

RED PHALAROPE
Phalaropus fulicaria

The Red Phalarope passes through Alberta primarily during the fall migration, when it lacks the distinguishing red plumage that graces it during the breeding season. The nondescript fall wardrobe does little to make it stand out among the much more abundant Red-necked Phalaropes. Still, the Red Phalarope's heavier bill and larger size might be sufficient for a sharp-eyed birder to distinguish between these species in the field. • The Red Phalarope is the least likely of the phalaropes to be seen in Alberta. It is most frequently encountered by Alberta birders who are on mid-winter trips to the coast of southern South America, not in their home province. In other words, it is hardly ever seen in Alberta.

non-breeding

ID: *In flight:* broad white wing stripe; black central tail feathers. *Non-breeding:* blue-grey, unstreaked upperparts; white underparts; black eye patch; black bill.
Breeding female: underparts are broadly red. *Breeding male:* lighter than the female.
Size: L 20–21 cm.
Status: rare migrant from August through November.
Habitat: lakes and large wetlands.

Nesting: does not nest in Alberta.
Feeding: swims in tight circles in deep water, picking at the surface for aquatic invertebrates.
Voice: high-pitched *creep* in flight.
Similar Species: *Red-necked Phalarope* (p. 159): smaller; thinner bill; non-breeding birds have a thinner white wing stripe and a streaked back. *Wilson's Phalarope* (p. 158): non-breeding birds lack the dark mask.
Best Site: Beaverhill Lake.

PARASITIC JAEGER

Stercorarius parasiticus

Although 'jaeger' is a German word for 'hunter,' 'parasitic' more aptly describes this bird's foraging tactics. Swift and relentless, Parasitic Jaegers hound and intimidate gulls, who predictably regurgitate their meal to placate these aerial pirates. Gulls might tolerate having a jaeger roost alongside them, but their neighbour must be most unwelcome. • The Parasitic Jaeger is the most numerous jaeger in the world and likely the most easily seen in Alberta. All jaegers are rare, however, and they are usually seen migrating among gulls. Some of the best places to check for jaegers are landfills. Indeed, the sight of a jaeger might be the only redeeming feature of a trip to the dump. • *Stercorarius* is Latin for 'pertaining to dung'—the result of a confusion among various sorts of naturally putrid material.

light phase breeding

ID: *Sexes similar. Adult:* long, pointed wings; long, pointed central tail feathers; brown upperparts; dark cap; light undersides of wing tips. *Light phase:* white underparts; light collar; light brown neck band. *Dark phase:* brown underparts and collar. *Immature:* barred underparts; central tail feathers extend just past the tail.
Size: *L* 45–52 cm; *W* 85–92 cm.
Status: rare from May to June and from August to September.

Habitat: lakeshores, gravelbars and landfills.
Nesting: does not nest in Alberta.
Feeding: pirates, scavenges and hunts for food; in Alberta, pirates food from gulls and scavenges at landfills.
Voice: generally not vocal in Alberta.
Similar Species: *Long-tailed Jaeger* (p. 162): daintier bird; 2 long tail streamers. *Gulls* (pp. 163–72): all lack the elongated tail feathers.
Best Sites: Beaverhill Lake; various gull-rich landfill sites.

LONG-TAILED JAEGER
Stercorarius longicaudus

The graceful, buoyant flight of the Long-tailed Jaeger is a rare sight in Alberta. Many jaegers undoubtedly pass through Alberta on their way between their coastal wintering grounds and Arctic breeding grounds, but they fly solo, and they stop only briefly at large wetlands, where most Alberta sightings occur. One fine, late-August day at Francis Viewpoint on Beaverhill Lake, we were lucky enough to identify at least two and possibly three Long-tailed Jaegers at a great distance through spotting scopes. • These aerial pirates are easily identified on land or water—they smugly rest with their neat black caps held high and their long tails angled gracefully upward. Jaegers are masters of the air, whether lazily bouncing aloft or engaging in a falcon-like power dive.

light phase breeding

ID: *Sexes similar:* long, twinned tail feathers; dark cap; white throat and belly; yellow collar; grey upperparts; dark flight feathers.
Size: L 51–56 cm; W 70–80 cm.
Status: rare from July to September.
Habitat: lakeshores, gravelbars and landfills.

vagrant

Nesting: does not nest in Alberta.
Feeding: hunts rodents and birds; pirates from gulls; scavenges at landfills.
Voice: generally not vocal in Alberta.
Similar Species: *Parasitic Jaeger* (p. 161): stockier; dark breast band; lacks the long tail streamers. *Gulls* (pp. 163–72): all lack the elongated central tail feathers.
Best Sites: Beaverhill Lake; Frank Lake; Sir Winston Churchill PP.

FRANKLIN'S GULL
Larus pipixcan

The Franklin's Gull is simply not a 'sea gull.' It is affectionately known as the 'Prairie Dove'—it has a dove-like profile and follows tractors across prairie fields the way its cousins follow fishing boats. The Franklin's Gull also scavenges at dumps, but not to the same extent as some other gulls. • On warm summer evenings, you will often see huge numbers of Franklin's Gulls circling overhead. Watch one, and you will see it flutter up to a flying insect, catch it and continue circling. Big emergences of midges and flying ants are usually the source of this excitement. • The scientific name *pipixcan* is from the Aztec for 'Mexico,' where a wintering bird became one of the first specimens of this species to be collected. 'Franklin' refers to Sir John Franklin, the polar explorer.

breeding

ID: *Sexes similar:* grey mantle; white eye ring; black wing tips with white spots; white underparts. *Breeding:* black head; white eye ring; red bill; breast often has a pinkish tinge; red-orange legs. *Non-breeding:* white head; dark patch on the back of the head.
Size: *L* 33–38; *W* 90–95 cm.
Status: common from April to September.
Habitat: agricultural fields, marshlands, meadows, lakes, rivermouths and landfills.
Nesting: colonial; usually in dense emergent vegetation; floating

platform nest is built above water and lined with fine grass and plant down; pair incubates 3 eggs for 25 days.
Feeding: opportunistic; gleans agricultural fields and meadows for insects; catches flying insects in mid-air.
Voice: mewing, shrill *weeeh-ah weeeh-ah* while feeding and in migration.
Similar Species: *Bonaparte's Gull* (p. 164): adult has a black bill and a conspicuous white wedge in the wing tip.
Best Sites: Beaverhill Lake; Aspen Beach; Big Lake.

BONAPARTE'S GULL

Larus philadelphia

For those naturalists who feel disdain for gulls, time spent with the Bonaparte's is a sure cure. These gulls are elegant birds, delicate in both plumage and behaviour, that avoid landfills, preferring to dine on flying insects or from the surface of the water. Their soft, scratchy voices rise excitedly when a flock spies a school of fish and begins plunging into the water in pursuit. • The Bonaparte's Gull nests in trees, in the upper branches of conifers, further distinguishing it from other gulls. • This small gull was not named for the French emperor, but rather for his nephew, zoologist Charles Lucien Bonaparte. The first recorded specimen was a winter bird found near Philadelphia, hence its scientific name.

breeding

ID: *Sexes similar:* black bill; grey mantle; white eye ring; white underparts. *Breeding:* black head; orange legs. *Non-breeding:* white head; dark ear patch. *In flight:* white wedge in wing tip.
Size: *L* 30–36 cm; *W* 80–85 cm.
Status: common from April to October.
Habitat: large lakes, rivers and marshlands.

Nesting: occasionally colonial; in a coniferous tree; re-uses the abandoned stick nests of crows, jays or raptors.
Feeding: dabbles and tips up for aquatic invertebrates, small fish and tadpoles; gleans the ground for terrestrial invertebrates; also captures insects in the air.
Voice: scratchy, soft *eer eer* while feeding.
Similar Species: *Franklin's Gull* (p. 163): adult has a red bill and black wing tips.
Best Sites: Calling Lake PP; Cold Lake PP.

MEW GULL
Larus canus

The Mew Gull is a regular, but often overlooked, bird in our province. Although some breed in remote parts of northeastern Alberta, most sightings of these birds occur during migration. • Most of the Mew Gulls seen in Alberta are first-winter immatures, and telling them from Ring-billed Gulls of the same age takes some practice. Mew Gulls are almost always seen associating with other gulls, so side-by-side comparisons are usually available. Scanning the flocks for an adult bird with an unmarked yellow bill is easy, but scanning for a young bird with the look of a Ring-bill but with a more dove-like profile is more challenging. • This small, dainty, white-headed gull dives for fish more often than our other gulls. It is named for its mewing call.

breeding

ID: *Sexes similar. Adult:* small bill; dark eyes; dove-like profile. *Breeding:* white head and underparts; grey upperparts; all-yellow bill; yellow legs. *Non-breeding:* dark spotting on the head. *Immature:* black-tipped bill; black tail band; well-smudged brown mottling on the head and underparts.

Size: *L* 38–40 cm; *W* 90–105 cm.

Status: rare to uncommon in May and from July to November.

Habitat: shallow wetlands, landfills and rivers.

Nesting: semicolonial; builds a floating nest or nests on the ground,

on a stump or low in a spruce; pair incubates 3 eggs for up to 28 days.

Feeding: forages on the ground or on water; eats insects and small fish; scavenges on carrion and at landfills.

Voice: typical, gull-like *hiyah hiyah hiyak;* distinctive *mee-you mee-you.*

Similar Species: *Ring-billed Gull* (p. 166): heavier bill; immature has less smudged dark spotting on the head and underparts. *Other white-headed gulls:* larger; heavier bill, marked with black and/or red.

Best Sites: Lake Athabasca; Inglewood Bird Sanctuary, Calgary; landfills during migration; check local bird hotlines for sightings.

RING-BILLED GULL
Larus delawarensis

The Ring-billed Gull is the common 'sea gull' in Alberta. Although many appear to be urbanites, they commute daily into the cities. From lakeshores and open fields where they roost, they fly to dumps and city parks. Many a birder in Edmonton has wondered why gulls fly in V-formations to the northwest every night in summer and fall, as though migrating the wrong direction. They are headed out to sleep at Big Lake, near St. Albert. • The fall migration is a prolonged affair, with the last of the birds normally waiting for the first bitter cold snap to chase them from the province, sometime in November. • 'Gull' appears to be derived from a Celtic word describing the wailing cry of these birds. The scientific name *delawarensis* comes from the 'type locality' of this species—the Delaware River.

breeding

ID: *Sexes similar. Adult:* black-ringed, yellow bill; yellowish legs; grey back; yellow eyes; black wing tips; white underparts. *Breeding:* white head. *Non-breeding:* dark spotting on the head. *Immature:* grey back; brown wings and breast; dark-banded tail; dark-tipped bill.
Size: *L* 46–51 cm;
W 115–125 cm.
Status: abundant from March to November.
Habitat: lakes, rivers, landfills, golf courses, fields and parks.
Nesting: colonial; often on open beaches, islands or shorelines; on the ground in a shallow scrape lined with plants, nearby debris, grass and sticks; pair incubates 3–6 eggs for 23–28 days.
Feeding: gleans the ground for arthropods, rodents and earthworms; scavenges; surface-tips for aquatic invertebrates and fish.
Voice: high-pitched *kakakaka-akakaka;* low, laughing *yook-yook-yook.*
Similar Species: *California Gull* (p. 167): larger; darker grey back; dark eyes. *Herring Gull* (p. 168): larger; pink legs; red on the bill. *Mew Gull* (p. 165): smaller; all-yellow bill.
Best Sites: Edmonton; Calgary; any park, landfill or lake.

CALIFORNIA GULL
Larus californicus

It takes a keen eye to recognize a California Gull as it roosts among Ring-bills, but once you learn how, you'll see them all the time. For those people who come to love gull watching, spotting a California Gull might be their first assurance that it is in fact possible to see something other than Ring-bills in your average gang of white-headed gulls. • In 1848 and 1855, Utah's harvests were threatened by swarms of grasshoppers, until large numbers of California Gulls appeared and ate the pests. A monument in Salt Lake City honours this prairie gull, which is now the state bird of Utah, despite its name.
• California Gulls tend to nest communally on low-lying islands. Their simple scrape nests are generally placed no closer than the distance two gulls can bridge with aggressive bill jabs from atop their eggs.

breeding

ID: *Sexes similar. Adult:* yellow bill with red and black spots; yellow-green legs; dark eyes; grey back; black wing tips. *Breeding:* white head; white underparts. *Non-breeding:* dark spotting on the head. *Immature:* mottled brown overall; pinkish legs; pale bill with a black tip.
Size: L 46–51 cm; W 122–137 cm.
Status: uncommon to common from March to November.
Habitat: large lakes, wetlands, farmlands, landfills and parks.
Nesting: colonial; often on open beaches or shorelines; usually on the ground in a shallow scrape lined with plants, grass,

feathers and small sticks; pair incubates 2 or 3 eggs for 23–27 days.
Feeding: gleans the ground for terrestrial invertebrates, especially grasshoppers, earthworms and cutworms; scavenges; surface-tips for aquatic invertebrates.
Voice: high-pitched, nasal *kiarr-kiarr*, most often heard at breeding colonies.
Similar Species: *Ring-billed Gull* (p. 166): adult has light eyes and a black ring around the bill. *Herring Gull* (p. 168): larger; adult has light eyes and pink legs. *Mew Gull* (p. 165): smaller; adult has an all-yellow bill.
Best Sites: Sir Winston Churchill PP; Inglewood Bird Sanctuary, Calgary (migration).

HERRING GULL

Larus argentatus

The Herring Gull isn't just another white-headed gull. It is a bigger bird than the other familiar species, and it has a mean look in its eye, hinting at its predatory habits. Whether it is on a remote northern lake or scrapping with other birds at a landfill, the Herring Gull seems ready for any challenge. It has a stomach for anything digestible, and it can keep up with the best of birds on land, in the water and in the air. • Herring Gulls breed over the northern half of Alberta, and they visit the rest of the province in migration. They are tough birds capable of resisting our cold weather, and they are often seen perched on late spring ice. • Before attaining their full adult plumage and colour, Herring Gulls go through no less than seven changes of brownish plumage. • The scientific name *argentatus* is Latin for 'silvery,' probably in reference to this bird's back or underwing.

breeding

ID: *Sexes similar. Adult:* large; pink legs; yellow bill with a red spot at the tip of the lower mandible; light eyes; light grey back; black wing tips. *Breeding:* white head; white underparts. *Non-breeding:* head and nape are washed with brown. *Immature:* mottled brown.
Size: *L* 58–66 cm; *W* 140–150 cm.
Status: uncommon to common from March to November.
Habitat: *In migration:* large lakes, wetlands, rivers, landfills and public areas.
Nesting: colonial; often nests with gulls, pelicans and cormorants; on the ground on open beaches and islands; in a

shallow scrape lined with plants and sticks; pair incubates 3 eggs for 31–32 days.
Feeding: generalist feeder; surface-tips for aquatic invertebrates and fish; gleans the ground for insects and worms; scavenges dead fish and garbage at landfills; eats other birds' eggs and young.
Voice: loud, bugle-like *kleew-kleew;* alarm call is *kak-kak-kak.*
Similar Species: *California Gull* (p. 167): dark eyes; usually has black on the bill; adult has yellow-green legs. *Ring-billed Gull* (p. 166): adult has yellow legs and a black ring around the bill.
Best Sites: Aspen Beach; Sir Winston Churchill PP; Inglewood Bird Sanctuary, Calgary (migration).

THAYER'S GULL
Larus thayeri

Thayer's Gulls are rare through Alberta, and since most of the birds we see are immatures (the identification of which is beyond the scope of this book), only the most serious birdwatchers pay them much heed. Together with the Herring, Glaucous-winged, Glaucous, Iceland and others, the Thayer's is part of a group of gull species that likely arose from a common ancestor not too far in the past. Hybrids are frequently produced among members of this complex, although such intermediate birds are mercifully uncommon in Alberta. Thayer's were originally considered a subspecies of the Herring Gull, and some ornithologists continue to argue that they do not deserve full species status. • John Eliot Thayer, a Bostonian, provided financial backing for natural history expeditions from Guadeloupe to the Canadian Arctic.

non-breeding

ID: *Sexes similar:* pigeon-like head. *Adult:* dark eyes; dark pink legs; yellow bill with a red spot at the tip of the lower mandible; lighter wing tips than on other white-headed gulls.
Size: *L* 55–62 cm; *W* 133–142 cm.
Status: rare from April to May and from October to November.
Habitat: landfills, large lakes and rivers.

Nesting: does not nest in Alberta.
Feeding: predator, pirate and scavenger; often feeds at landfills and along rivers and lakeshores.
Voice: similar to the Herring Gull: *kak-kak-kak.*
Similar Species: *Herring Gull* (p. 168): light eyes; darker mantle; black wing tips; heavier, longer bill.
Best Sites: Cold Lake PP; Inglewood Bird Sanctuary, Calgary; wherever gulls congregate on migration.

169

GLAUCOUS-WINGED GULL

Larus glaucesens

Because of Alberta's landlocked position, almost all white-headed gulls can be easily identified as one of the 'big three': Ring-billed, California or Herring. Finding a Glaucous-winged Gull is always an oddity, since it is truly a 'sea gull.' This species is frequently encountered throughout the year on the Pacific coast, but even in B.C., it is rarely seen inland. • Glaucous-winged Gulls are large, heavy birds that resemble Glaucous Gulls in some ways and Thayer's Gulls in others. Of these 'not-so-big three,' the Glaucous-winged is by far the least likely to show up in Alberta—it is a vagrant here, with very few birds turning up every few years.

• To make things even more confusing, many of the so-called Glaucous-winged Gulls on the southern B.C. coast are really hybrids with Western Gulls. They look almost exactly like Thayer's Gulls. We do not know if any of these hybrids stray to Alberta.

breeding

ID: *Sexes similar. Adult:* pale grey mantle on the back and wings; grey wing tips; dark eyes; red spot on the lower mandible; heavy yellow bill; pinkish legs. *Immature:* sooty-looking overall.
Size: *L* 60–67 cm; W 130–137 cm.
Status: rare from April to May and from October to November.
Habitat: landfills, rivers and large lakes.

vagrant

Nesting: does not nest in Alberta.
Feeding: predator, pirate and scavenger; feeds at landfills and along lakeshores.
Voice: similar to the Herring Gull: *kak-kak-kak.*
Similar Species: *Herring Gull* (p. 168): darker mantle; black wing tips. *California Gull* (p. 167): darker mantle; black wing tips; dark eyes. *Glaucous Gull* (p. 171): lighter overall.
Best Sites: Grande Prairie region; Inglewood Bird Sanctuary, Calgary.

GLAUCOUS GULL
Larus hyperboreus

In summer, when other gulls squabble over scraps at city landfills, the Glaucous Gull is far away in the Arctic wilderness. This great white gull of the north is as much a part of the Arctic landscape as the Polar Bear, Gyrfalcon and Snowy Owl. • Glaucous Gulls pass through Alberta in small but reliable numbers during their migration to and from the Pacific coast. They are often overlooked, and many a neophyte birdwatcher has been puzzled by the excitement that a white gull can cause. 'Aren't they all white?' is the usual question. • Although the adults are easier to identify, immature Glaucous Gulls are more numerous in Alberta. Fortunately, they are light enough in colour to be more easily recognized than most other immature gulls. • The scientific name *hyperboreus* means 'of the far north.'

non-breeding

ID: *Sexes similar. Adult:* all white, except for pale grey on the back and wings; white wing tips; yellow eyes; red spot on the lower mandible; pinkish legs. *Immature:* always has white wing tips; buff or brown wash on the upperparts.
Size: L 65–75 cm; W 150–165 cm.
Status: rare to uncommon from April to May and from October to December.

Habitat: landfills, rivers and large lakes.
Nesting: does not nest in Alberta.
Feeding: predator, pirate and scavenger; feeds at landfills and scavenges on duck carcasses.
Voice: similar to Herring Gull: *kak-kak-kak.*
Similar Species: *Glaucous-winged Gull* (p. 170): grey wing tips; dark eyes.
Best Sites: Cold Lake PP; Edmonton landfills; Inglewood Bird Sanctuary, Calgary.

SABINE'S GULL
Xema sabini

One reward for persistent birdwatchers in Alberta is to finally see a Sabine's Gull—it is a great-looking bird, and a real rarity. The Sabine's dipping, buoyant flight and shallowly forked tail can best be observed at the end of September, when these birds trickle to the Pacific coast from the Arctic. • The Sabine's Gull is the most tern-like gull in Alberta, and its placement in a separate genus from our other gulls makes good sense. • Sir Edward Sabine was a distinguished military man whose primary interests were astronomy and terrestrial magnetism. He joined an expedition to explore the Arctic Islands, and it was near Cape York that he collected the gull that was to be named in his honour. • *Xema* is a nonsense word invented by a British ornithologist.

breeding

ID: *Sexes similar:* dark slate-grey hood trimmed in black; yellow-tipped, black bill; dark grey mantle; black feet. *In flight:* 3-toned wing, grey at the base, then white, then black at the tip; shallowly forked tail.
Size: *L* 33–35 cm; W 85–90 cm.
Status: rare from May to June and from August to October.
Habitat: lakes and large rivers.

Nesting: does not nest in Alberta.
Feeding: gleans the water surface while swimming or flying; eats mainly insects, fish and crustaceans.
Voice: tern-like *kee-kee*; not frequently heard in migration.
Similar Species: *Bonaparte's Gull* (p. 164) and *Franklin's Gull* (p. 163): lack the boldly patterned wing tips and the forked tail.
Best Sites: Beaverhill Lake; Cold Lake PP; Inglewood Bird Sanctuary, Calgary.

CASPIAN TERN
Sterna caspia

In size and habits, the Caspian Tern bridges the gulf between smaller terns and raucous gulls. It is the largest tern in North America, and its wingbeats are slower and more gull-like than those of its smaller relatives. As well, these big-billed terns are often seen in association with gulls on exposed sandbars or mudflats.
• The Caspian Tern is an exotic element in Alberta's birdlife. Although it breeds in the province, its population is quite small, and sightings of this exciting bird are not regular events. • Caspian Terns are proving to be opportunistic nesters, occupying remote areas primarily in the north but also recently around Taber. They might continue to colonize suitable sites. • This species was first collected on the Caspian Sea in Asia, hence its name.

breeding

ID: *Sexes similar:* black cap; heavy, blood red bill; light grey wing covers; black legs; shallowly forked tail; white underparts; long, frosty, pointed wings.
Size: L 48–58 cm; W 127–140 cm.
Status: rare to uncommon from June to September.
Habitat: *In migration:* shorelines and over large lakes, wetlands and rivers.
Nesting: in a shallow scrape on bare sand, dirt or rocks; nest is sparsely lined with vegetation,

rocks or twigs; pair incubates 1–3 eggs for 20–22 days.
Feeding: hovers over water and plunges headfirst after small fish, tadpoles and aquatic invertebrates; also feeds by swimming and gleaning at the water's surface.
Voice: low, harsh *ca-arr*; loud *kraa-uh*.
Similar Species: *Common Tern* (p. 174) and *Forster's Tern* (p. 176): much smaller; lack the heavy, red bill.
Best Sites: Sir Winston Churchill PP; Scope Lake; Lost Lake; Fincastle Lake; Glenmore Reservoir, Calgary; Lake Athabasca.

COMMON TERN
Sterna hirundo

Cruising over the water, the Common Tern wheels about into a stationary hover, dives headfirst into the water, and then bounces back to the surface with a small fish in its thin bill. • Common Terns patrol the shorelines of lakes and rivers throughout Alberta during the summer months, announcing their presence with shrill cries. Their nesting colonies are loud and noisy, and if an intruder approaches a nest, the parent will dive repeatedly, often defecating quite accurately during the lowest point of the dive. For this and many other reasons, all bird colonies are best avoided. • Terns seem to be effortless fliers, and they are some of the greatest migrants. Recently, a Common Tern banded in Great Britain was recovered in Australia—a record distance for any bird.

breeding

ID: *Sexes similar:* black cap; thin, red, black-tipped bill; light grey wing tips; red legs; white rump; mostly white tail; white underparts. *In flight:* shallowly forked tail; long, pointed wings.
Size: *L* 33–41 cm; *W* 73–77 cm.
Status: common from May to October.
Habitat: large lakes, open wetlands and slow-moving rivers.
Nesting: primarily colonial; usually on a beach or other open area without vegetation; in a small scrape lined sparsely with pebbles, vegetation or shells; pair incubates 3 eggs for up to 27 days.

Feeding: hovers over the water and plunges headfirst after small fish and aquatic invertebrates.
Voice: high-pitched, drawn-out *keee-are,* most commonly heard at colonies, but also in foraging flights.
Similar Species: *Forster's Tern* (p. 176): mostly grey tail; silver-tipped primaries; black mask in non-breeding plumage. *Arctic Tern* (p. 175): rare in migration; all-red bill; deeply forked tail; light primaries. *Caspian Tern* (p. 173): much larger; all-red bill.
Best Sites: Kitsim Reservoir; Kinbrook Island PP; Eagle Lake.

ARCTIC TERN
Sterna paradisaea

The Arctic Tern is among the most enthusiastic of avian migrants, flying from the Arctic to the Antarctic each year—it occurs in Alberta only during spring and fall passages. An Arctic Tern seen in Alberta in May has likely flown in excess of 30,000 km in the previous year. • Because they migrate between the two polar regions, Arctic Terns probably experience more daylight in an average year than any other living thing. • Arctic Terns are fairly vocal during their passage through Alberta, and they are able to scream even when their bill is holding a small fish. They are most easily identified on the ground, when their short legs give them a crouched appearance in comparison to the Common Tern.

breeding

ID: *Sexes similar:* all-orange-red bill; very short, red legs. *Breeding:* black cap and nape; blue-grey mantle; white tail extends to the wing tips; light grey underparts. *Non-breeding:* black band through the eyes and across the nape. *In flight:* deeply forked tail.
Size: *L* 35–42 cm; W 76–80 cm.
Status: rare to uncommon from May to June and from August to September.

Habitat: large lakes and wetlands.
Nesting: colonial; on beaches, islands or tundra; in a shallow, generally unlined scrape; incubates 2 or 3 eggs for up to 22 days.
Feeding: dives into the water from a stationary hover; preys on small fish and aquatic invertebrates.
Voice: harsh, high-pitched *kee kahr!*
Similar Species: *Common Tern* (p. 174): and *Forster's Tern* (p. 176): black-tipped bills.
Best Site: Lake Athabasca.

175

FORSTER'S TERN
Sterna forsteri

One good tern deserves another, which is probably why we have both Common and Forster's terns here in Alberta. The Forster's Tern so closely resembles the Common Tern that the two blend together in most birdwatchers' minds. It usually isn't until they acquire their more distinct fall plumages that birdwatchers begin to note the Forster's presence. Both these birds are quite common in the southern half of Alberta. • Johann Forster, who lived and worked in England, examined tern specimens from the Hudson Bay region, and he was the first to recognize the species that bears his name. Forster was also on board the famous Cook voyage to the south Pacific. On that trip, both his natural history observations and his quarrels with the captain are legendary. • 'Tern' comes from the Old Norse name for these birds, *therna*.

breeding

ID: *Sexes similar. Breeding:* black cap and nape; thin, orange, black-tipped bill; light grey back; red legs; white underparts; white rump; mostly grey tail. *Non-breeding:* lacks the black cap; black mask over the eyes. *In flight:* shallowly forked, grey tail; long, pointed wings.
Size: *L* 36–41 cm; *W* 75–80 cm.
Status: uncommon to common from May to September.
Habitat: *Summer:* cattail marshes and backwaters. *In migration:* lakes.
Nesting: occasionally colonial; in marshes, atop floating vegetation (occasionally on a muskrat lodge or an old grebe's nest); pair incubates the eggs and raises the young.
Feeding: hovers above the water and plunges headfirst after small fish and aquatic invertebrates.
Voice: flight call is a nasal, short *keer keer*; also a grating *tzaap*.
Similar Species: *Common Tern* (p. 174): darker red bill and legs; mostly white tail; dark-tipped primaries; call is longer and drawn out. *Caspian Tern* (p. 173): much larger; all-red bill.
Best Sites: Beaverhill Lake; Kitsim Reservoir; Kinbrook Island PP; Eagle Lake.

BLACK TERN
Chlidonias niger

The dizzying, buoyant flight of the Black Tern is a classic sight above cattail marshes. It dips, dives and swoops, picking insects neatly off the water's surface or catching them in mid-air. Foraging flocks of Black Terns occasionally number in the hundreds, but populations of this bird in Alberta have declined since the 1960s. • Black Terns are agile fliers, but they are not quite agile enough to escape Peregrine Falcons. Prey remains from falcon eiries show that the Black Tern is a common prey item. • Black Terns are frail birds in many ways, but they have dominion over the winds. When they leave Alberta in September, they head off to tropical coasts, to dance over foreign waters until their spring return. • In order to spell this tern's genus name correctly, you must misspell *chelidonias,* the Greek word for 'swallow.'

breeding

ID: *Sexes similar. Breeding:* black head and underparts; grey back, tail and wings; white undertail coverts; black bill; reddish-black legs. *Non-breeding:* white underparts. *In flight:* long, pointed wings; shallowly forked tail.
Size: *L* 23–25 cm; *W* 58–62 cm.
Status: common from May to September.
Habitat: shallow, freshwater cattail marshes, sloughs and lake edges with emergent vegetation.
Nesting: usually colonial; on matted vegetation on the water's surface among emergent vegetation; builds a small platform of loose, dead vegetation; incubates 3 eggs for up to 3 weeks.
Feeding: snatches insects from the air, from tall grass and from the water's surface; also eats small fish.
Voice: greeting call is a shrill, metallic *kik-kik-kik-kik-kik;* typical alarm call is *kreea.*
Similar Species: *Other terns:* all are light in colour, not dark.
Best Sites: Beaverhill Lake; Slack Slough; Kitsim Reservoir; Kinbrook Island PP.

ROCK DOVE
Columba livia

The Rock Dove, or domestic pigeon, is a famous bird. It is popular with animal breeders, a notorious defiler of monuments, a popular scientific subject, a racing animal and a messenger. • In Alberta, these non-migrants seem to concentrate around reliable food sources during winter, such as our province's most notable monuments—grain elevators. Perched out of the wind on a building or bridge, near-frozen Rock Doves look about as miserable as the human pedestrians below. In turn, the doves are a reliable source of food for our winter raptors, such as Merlins and Gyrfalcons. • The Rock Dove was introduced to North America in the 17th century. It was first domesticated from Eurasian birds in about 4500 B.C. as a source of meat.

ID: *Sexes similar:* highly variable in colour (iridescent blue-grey, red, white or tan); usually has a white rump and orange feet; dark-tipped tail. *In flight:* holds its wings in a deep V while gliding.
Size: *L* 31–33 cm.
Status: abundant year-round.
Habitat: urban areas, railway yards, agricultural areas, grain terminals and elevators; high sandstone cliffs provide a more natural habitat for some.

Nesting: on the ledges of barns, cliffs, bridges, buildings and towers; flimsy nest is made of sticks, grass and assorted vegetation; pair incubates 2 eggs for about 18 days.
Feeding: gleans the ground for waste grain, seeds and fruits; occasionally eats insects.
Voice: soft, cooing *coorrr-coorrr-coorrr.*
Similar Species: *Merlin* (p. 102): not as heavy bodied; longer tail; does not hold its wings in a V; wings do not clap on take-off.
Best Sites: any town, city or grain elevator.

BAND-TAILED PIGEON
Columba fasciata

Band-tailed Pigeons, which are extremely scarce throughout Alberta, occur only periodically in our foothills and mountains. Their normal range extends from the western Rockies to the Pacific, but they cross the Continental Divide into our province from time to time. Band-tailed Pigeons are superficially similar to Rock Doves, and they might not be recognized as often as they are seen. • Flocks of Band-tailed Pigeons regularly visit mineral springs throughout their range, attracted by calcium in the water. • This forest-dwelling bird very nearly suffered the same fate as the Passenger Pigeon of eastern North America, which was hunted to extinction before the days of bird conservation.

ID: *Sexes similar:* purple head and breast; white band on the back of the head; grey band on the tail; dark rump; iridescent green nape; yellow, black-tipped bill; greyish wings.
Size: *L* 33–38 cm.
Status: very rare from May to August.
Habitat: agricultural areas, open pine forests and hillsides with fruit-bearing shrubs.

Nesting: does not nest in Alberta.
Feeding: gleans vegetation for nuts and other seeds; frequently eats berries and invertebrates during migration.
Voice: owl-like, deep, hollow *whoo-whoo-whoo*.
Similar Species: *Rock Dove* (p. 178): white rump; dark bill; lacks the grey band on the tail. *Mourning Dove* (p. 180): longer, white-edged tail; lacks the purple head and glossy green nape.
Best Sites: mountain parks; Cochrane.

179

MOURNING DOVE
Zenaida macroura

The soothing coos of the Mourning Dove, filtering through cottonwoods along our prairie rivers, has lulled many a camper into an afternoon siesta. In contrast to its soft vocalizations, when a Mourning Dove bursts into flight its wing tips clap against one another, and its wings can be heard whistling through the air once its typically swift and direct flight is attained. • All members of the pigeon family (including doves), feed 'milk' to their young. It isn't true milk—birds don't have any mammary glands—but a nutritious liquid produced by glands in the bird's crop. The chicks insert their bills down the adult's throat to eat the thick liquid. • The common name of this species reflects its sad song. The scientific name *Zenaida* honours Zénaïde, Princess of Naples, the wife of Charles Lucien Bonaparte (the zoologist-nephew of the French emperor).

ID: *Sexes similar:* olive brown plumage; small head; long, white-trimmed, tapering tail; sleek body; dark, shiny patch below the ear; dull red legs; dark bill; pale rosy underparts.
Size: L 28–33 cm.
Status: uncommon to common from April to October.
Habitat: open woodlands, forest edges, agricultural areas and riparian forests; has benefited from human-induced habitat change.
Nesting: in the fork of a shrub or tree; occasionally on the ground; female builds a fragile, shallow nest from twigs supplied by the male; pair incubates 2 eggs for 14 days.
Feeding: gleans the ground and vegetation for seeds; visits feeders; produces crop milk for its newly hatched young.
Voice: mournful, soft *coooo-coooo-ah coooo-coooo-ah.*
Similar Species: *Black-billed Cuckoo* (p. 181): lighter underparts; darker upperparts; shorter neck. *Rock Dove* (p. 178): stockier; white rump; shorter tail.
Best Sites: Dinosaur PP; Writing-on-Stone PP; Police Point Park, Medicine Hat.

BLACK-BILLED CUCKOO
Coccyzus erythropthalmus

The Black-billed Cuckoo does not sound anything like its famous European relative, nor does it sound quite like any other bird in Alberta. Cuckoos vocalize in loud bursts from a shrubby thicket, repeating deep *ca, coo* and *cow* notes in tangled melodies. They often call on dark, cloudy days, and they are called 'Rain Crows' in some parts of their range. • The infrequently seen Black-billed Cuckoo nests in shrubby areas, within which it gleans much of its food. It is one of the few birds that eats hairy caterpillars, such as tent caterpillars, and it is thought that the Black-billed Cuckoo's population rises and falls in direct relation to caterpillar infestations. • In spite of its seeming reluctance to fly on its breeding grounds, this cuckoo migrates great distances to the tropics for winter.

ID: *Sexes similar:* brown upperparts; white underparts; long, white-spotted undertail; downcurved, dark bill; reddish eye ring.
Size: *L* 30 cm.
Status: rare to uncommon from June to August.
Habitat: densely vegetated woodlands, shrubs and thickets; often in riparian areas.
Nesting: in a shrub or small tree; nest is made of twigs and lined with grass and other vegetation; occasionally lays eggs in other birds' nests; pair normally

incubates 2 or 3 eggs for up to 13 days.
Feeding: gleans hairy caterpillars from leaves, branches and trunks; also eats other insects and berries.
Voice: fast *cu-cu-cu* or *cu-cu-cu-cu-cu*; also a series of *ca, cow* and *coo* notes.
Similar Species: *Mourning Dove* (p. 180): slender neck; peach-coloured underparts. *Yellow-billed Cuckoo* (p. 368): very rare in Alberta; yellow bill; prominent white spots on the undertail; lacks the red eye ring.
Best Sites: Red Deer River valley downstream from Dinosaur PP; check local bird hotlines for recent sightings.

EASTERN SCREECH-OWL
Otus asio

Southeastern Alberta lies at the western fringe of this tiny owl's range. It was only recently that the Eastern Screech-Owl was recognized in the province, with records from Police Point Park in Medicine Hat. Despite the very few records of this bird in Alberta, both the red and grey colour phases have been recorded here. • Despite its small size, the Eastern Screech-Owl is an adaptable hunter. It has a varied diet that ranges from insects, earthworms and fish to birds larger than itself. The Eastern Screech-Owl seems to have a pronounced split personality: by day it is lazy and inactive, frequently remaining in its nesting cavity; at night it is among the most formidable of hunters. • *Otus* and *asio* both generally refer to this owl's 'horns.' The same words are also used, but in reverse order, in the scientific name of the Long-eared Owl (*Asio otus*).

grey phase

ID: *Sexes similar:* short ear tufts; heavy breast streaking; yellow eyes; dark bill; occurs in red and grey colour morphs.
Size: *L* 20–23 cm; *W* 50–55 cm; female slightly larger.
Status: very rare year-round.
Habitat: forests with natural nest cavities.
Nesting: in a natural cavity, abandoned woodpecker hole or artificial nest box; no lining is added; female incubates 4 or 5 eggs for up to 26 days.

Feeding: small mammals, birds and insects, including moths in flight.
Voice: sad, horse-like 'whinny' that rises and then falls.
Similar Species: *Northern Saw-whet Owl* (p. 193): dark facial disc; no ear tufts.
Best Site: Police Point Park, Medicine Hat (ask at the desk about recent sightings).

GREAT HORNED OWL
Bubo virginianus

The Great Horned Owl, our provincial bird, is among the most formidable of Alberta's raptors. It hunts mice, rabbits, grouse and even fish. This common bird has a poorly developed sense of smell, however, which might be why it is the only consistent predator of skunks. • Only the Snowy Owl is as heavy as the Great Horned Owl, although the fluffy feathers of the Great Gray Owl make it look bigger. Great Horned Owls have been known to kill and eat Barred Owls, and to displace Bald Eagles from their nests. • The large eyes of owls are fixed in place, so to look up, down or to the side, they must move their entire heads. Of course, owls have adapted wonderfully to this situation, and they can swivel their necks 180 degrees. • Great Horns are among the most frequently encountered owls. They can easily be recognized by their silhouette on a perch against the nighttime sky.

ID: *Sexes similar:* light grey to dark brown; ear tufts; fine, horizontal breast barring; facial disc has a dark outline; white chin; mottled upperparts.
Size: L 46–64 cm; W 91–152 cm.
Status: common year-round.
Habitat: mixed forests, agricultural areas, shrublands and riparian woodlands.
Nesting: in the abandoned stick nest of another bird; also nests on cliffs; adds little material to the nest; pair incubates the eggs for about 33 days.
Feeding: mostly nocturnal, but also hunts by day in winter; usually swoops from a perch; eats voles, mice, hares, squirrels, skunks, pocket gophers, grebes, geese, grouse and even fish.

Voice: 6 deep hoots during the breeding season: *hoo-hoo-hoo hoo-hoo hooo* or *eat-my-food, I'll-eat you!*
Similar Species: *Long-eared Owl* (p. 190): smaller; thinner, vertical breast streaks; ear tufts are close together. *Eastern Screech-Owl* (p. 182): much smaller; vertical breast streaks. *Great Gray Owl* (p. 189) and *Barred Owl* (p. 188): no ear tufts.
Best Sites: cottonwood forests along prairie rivers; almost any other treed area.

SNOWY OWL
Nyctea scandiaca

When the mercury dips in thermometers and the landscape hardens in winter's grip, Snowy Owls appear atop trees and power poles. Motorists with an eye for these birds can see them in almost any open, flat country—places that remind the owls of their summer tundra homes.
• Feathered to the toes, a Snowy Owl can remain active at cold temperatures, and especially wind chill levels, that send other owls to the woods for shelter.
• As Snowy Owls age, their plumage becomes lighter; old males are the most characteristic in their nearly all-white dress. • Snowy Owls are yearly visitors to Alberta. They can be especially numerous in years when lemming and vole populations are exceedingly low in the Arctic, but some winters they are very hard to find.

♀

ID: *General:* predominantly white; yellow eyes; black bill and talons; no ear tufts. *Adult male:* almost entirely white, with very little dark flecking. *Adult female:* dark barring on the breast and upperparts. *Immature:* heavier barring than an adult female.
Size: *L* 51–69 cm; *W* 137–168 cm; female noticeably larger.
Status: uncommon to common from November to April.
Habitat: open country, croplands and prairies; often perches on fenceposts, buildings and power poles.

Nesting: does not nest in Alberta.
Feeding: swoops from a perch, often punching through the snow to take mice, voles, grouse, hares, weasels and, rarely, songbirds and water birds.
Voice: quiet during winter.
Similar Species: *Great Gray Owl* (p. 189): grey plumage. *Great Horned Owl* (p. 183): ear tufts; some individuals can be almost as light as a Snowy, but most are much browner.
Best Sites: north of the St. Albert airport; west of Medicine Hat; east of Calgary; Olds (February).

NORTHERN HAWK OWL
Surnia ulula

Like the Snowy Owl, the Northern Hawk Owl spends summers in the north and retreats southward during the coldest months to perch alongside roadsides in central Alberta. It is one of Alberta's most sought-after birds, and it appears curious and unfazed by the developed world, allowing us to observe it closely. • The Northern Hawk Owl summers where the days are long, so it is comfortable hunting in daylight. It retains this habit during winter in Alberta, and its long tail and slim body do indeed give it a hawk-like appearance. It flies a bit like a hawk as well. • This species is 'irruptive,' meaning that it is commonly seen in some winters and rarely in others. When a 'hawk owl year' comes around, make the best of it—there might not be a repeat performance for a decade or more.

Nesting: in the abandoned nest of a crow, raven or jay, in an abandoned woodpecker cavity or on a broken-off treetop; adds no lining to the nest; incubates 5–7 eggs for 25–30 days.

Feeding: swoops from a perch; mainly eats voles, mice and birds; also eats insects in summer.

Voice: usually quiet; whistled breeding trill; call is an accipiter-like *kee-kee-kee*.

Similar Species: *Boreal Owl* (p. 192) and *Northern Saw-whet Owl* (p. 193): short tail; vertical breast streaks. *Northern Pygmy-Owl* (p. 186): much smaller; 2 false 'eyes' on the back of the head.

Best Sites: Sundre; north of Crowsnest Pass; High Level; check local bird hotlines for recent sightings.

ID: *Sexes similar:* long tail; no ear tufts; fine horizontal barring on the underparts; light-coloured face is bordered with black; light bill; yellow eyes; white-spotted forehead.

Size: *L* 38–43 cm; *W* 80–90 cm.

Status: rare to uncommon year-round.

Habitat: black-spruce bogs and muskegs, old burns and tree-bordered clearings.

NORTHERN PYGMY-OWL

Glaucidium gnoma

To find a Northern Pygmy-Owl, you can rely either on luck or on chickadees. Small bands of these songbirds delight in mobbing Alberta's smallest owl, and the sound can lead attentive naturalists right up to the pint-sized predator. Two false eyes on the back of the Northern Pygmy-Owl's head help intimidate songbirds during these mobbings. Because the songbirds are less likely to strike a bird that is looking in their direction, the pygmy-owl is able to guard its own back. By imitating this owl's whistled call, birders might themselves be mobbed by chickadees. • The pygmy-owl is small, but fierce, and it regularly catches birds that outweigh it. On such occasions, the owl is often dragged some distance before it kills its prey. • Pygmy-owls occasionally venture into townsites in the mountains and foothills to hunt sparrows and finches at birdfeeders. • The scientific name *gnoma* is Greek for 'knowledge and wisdom'; it comes from the same root as 'gnome,' which is also appropriate.

red phase

ID: *Sexes similar:* long tail; dark breast; false 'eyes' on the nape; light underparts, with dark belly streaks; no ear tufts; dark face; light bill; yellow eyes; white chin; grey and red colour phases.

Size: *L* 18 cm; *W* 38 cm.

Status: rare to uncommon year-round.

Habitat: coniferous, deciduous or mixed forests, often in riparian areas; occasionally in townsites in winter.

Nesting: in an abandoned woodpecker cavity or natural tree hollow; nest is usually

unlined; female incubates 3 or 4 eggs for about 28 days.

Feeding: usually at night; swoops from a perch; eats small rodents, large insects, small birds and amphibians.

Voice: whistled, evenly spaced notes (about 3 every 2 seconds): *kook-kook-kook-kook-kook;* continuous and easily imitated.

Similar Species: *Northern Hawk Owl* (p. 185): much larger; lacks the false 'eyes.' *Northern Saw-whet Owl* (p. 193): short tail; black bill. *Boreal Owl* (p. 192): shorter tail; white face; lacks the false 'eyes.'

Best Sites: foothills near Sundre; check local bird hotlines for recent sightings.

BURROWING OWL
Athene cunicularia

The Burrowing Owl is one of the prairie's most loyal inhabitants, scorning trees in favour of wide open spaces. It is also one of our oddest birds: it nests underground in ground squirrel burrows, and it is seen during the day atop fenceposts or on the dirt mound beside its lair. • The Burrowing Owl is declining in Alberta, and it might be the most threatened bird in our province. Vehicle collisions, the use of agricultural chemicals and the conversion of native grasslands to cropland have all contributed to this bird's decline. Its close association with the Richardson's Ground Squirrel is also a liability, because many Burrowing Owls are mistakenly shot. Operation Burrowing Owl, a campaign to protect the bird and its habitat, has been successful in raising the level of concern among landowners and the general public.

ID: *Sexes similar. Adult:* long legs; rounded head; no ear tufts; yellow bill; short wings; white spotting on the breast; brown upperparts are flecked with white. *Immature:* unspotted, buff-brown breast.
Size: *L* 20–23 cm; *W* 51–61 cm.
Status: rare from April to September.
Habitat: open grasslands and shrublands in treeless prairies.
Nesting: typically colonial; in an abandoned ground squirrel, badger, hare or prairie dog burrow; lengthens the burrow up to 2 m; might add grass, sticks or dried cow dung to the nest site; female incubates 7–9 eggs for up to 30 days.
Feeding: stalks its prey or pounces from flight or from a mound or a fencepost perch; eats mostly ground insects, such as grasshoppers, beetles and crickets; also eats small rodents, birds, amphibians and reptiles.
Voice: call is a harsh *chuk*; gives a rasping, rattlesnake-like warning call when inside its burrow. *Male:* mournful *coo-coo-roo* in courtship.
Similar Species: *Short-eared Owl* (p. 191): heavily streaked breast; short legs; long wings; doesn't nest in burrows.
Best Sites: Brooks area; scan ground squirrel colonies on the prairies.

187

BARRED OWL
Strix varia

The madhouse *who-cooks-for you* of courting Barred Owls is one of the most memorable sounds of Alberta's forests. The escalating laughs, hoots and howls reinforce the bond between pairs. Bold birdwatchers can join in the frenzied activity by imitating the courtship calls, but take care—your voice will be perceived as a threat and might provoke a violent attack from these easily stressed and highly territorial birds. • Barred Owls are easily identified by their voice and by their distinctive dark eyes. They tend to be more vocal during early evening or early morning when the moon is full and the air is calm. Owl watchers can be grateful for this; it means they needn't bother venturing out on cold, dark, rainy nights between midnight and 4:00 a.m. • The Barred Owl has relatively weak talons, and it mainly preys on smaller animals, such as voles.

ID: *Sexes similar:* dark eyes; horizontal streaking around the neck and upper breast; vertical streaking on the belly; light bill; no ear tufts; dark grey-brown-mottled plumage.
Size: L 43–61 cm; W 102–127 cm; female slightly larger.
Status: rare to uncommon year-round.
Habitat: mature coniferous and mixedwood forests, often in riparian areas.
Nesting: in a natural tree cavity, broken-off treetop or abandoned stick nest; adds very little to the nest; female incubates 2 or 3 eggs for up to 33 days.

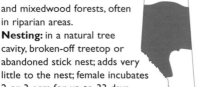

Feeding: nocturnal; swoops from a perch to pounce on its prey; mainly eats mice, voles and squirrels; also eats amphibians and smaller birds.
Voice: most characteristic of all the owls; loud, hooting, rhythmic, laughing call, heard mostly in spring, but also throughout the year: *Who cooks for you? Who cooks for you all?*
Similar Species: *Great Gray Owl* (p. 189) and *Northern Hawk Owl* (p. 185): light-coloured eyes; heavy vertical barring on the underparts. *Great Horned Owl* (p. 183): ear tufts; light-coloured eyes.
Best Sites: Hinton; Rocky Mountain House; check local bird hotlines for recent sightings.

GREAT GRAY OWL
Strix nebulosa

The Great Gray Owl has the most impressive face of any bird. It lets nothing escape its attention—its head swivels smoothly, focusing instantly on sounds and movements. Once a vole is detected, the Great Gray launches from its perch, glides in on fixed wings and often punches through deep snow to acquire its meal.
• This regal and impressive owl is one of the most sought-after birds in Alberta. Many Great Grays are easily approached, so this is also one of our most photographed birds. • Although the magnificent Great Gray Owl is the largest of all North American owls, it is outweighed by as much as 15 percent by the Snowy Owl and the Great Horned Owl. • The Great Gray Owl occurs sporadically in Alberta—it is an irruptive species that can be rare for years before appearing in good numbers. It is most commonly encountered in winter.

ID: *Sexes similar:* grey-brown plumage; large, rounded head; no ear tufts; yellow eyes; well-defined, ringed facial disc; white throat; long tail.

Size: *L* 61–84 cm; *W* 137–152 cm; female larger.

Status: rare to uncommon year-round.

Habitat: forest clearings, roadsides, open meadows.

Nesting: usually near a spruce bog or muskeg; in an abandoned hawk, raven or eagle nest; occasionally nests atop a tall

stump; adds little nest material; female incubates 2–4 eggs for up to 36 days.

Feeding: listens and watches from a perch; then swoops to catch voles, mice, shrews, pocket gophers, squirrels and small hares.

Voice: slow, deep, almost inaudible *hoot hoot.*

Similar Species: *Barred Owl* (p. 188): dark eyes. *Great Horned Owl* (p. 183): ear tufts. *Snowy Owl* (p. 184): mostly white.

Best Sites: High Level; Elk Island NP; Cross Lake PP; Crimson Lake PP; Sundre.

LONG-EARED OWL
Asio otus

Long-eared Owls are widespread across much of Alberta, but they are often overlooked because of their cryptic plumage and reclusive habits. They hunt at night in open areas and return to dense woods to roost during the day. • Long-eared Owls will either inflate or compress their bodies in response to certain situations: to scare off an intruder, the owl expands its air sacs, puffs its feathers and spreads its wings; to hide from an intruder or predator, it compresses itself into a long, thin, vertical form. By slimming down, the owl is trying to blend into the stumps and branches that surround its roost. • The 'ears' referred to in this owl's name are made only of feathers. • All owls, as well as many other birds, such as herons, gulls, crows and hawks, regurgitate 'pellets'—the indigestible parts of their prey compressed into an elongated ball. The feathers, fur and bones that make up the pellets are interesting to analyze, because they reveal what species an owl has recently eaten. Although pellets look disgusting, they are generally quite clean and dry. Owl pellets can be found under frequently used roost sites.

ID: *Sexes similar:* long, relatively close-set 'ear' tufts; slim body; vertical belly markings; light brown facial disc; mottled brown plumage; yellow eyes; white around the bill.
Size: *L* 33–41 cm; *W* 91–119 cm.
Status: rare to uncommon from March to November; a few overwinter.
Habitat: dense, mixed forests and tall shrublands, usually next to open spaces, such as grasslands and meadows.
Nesting: often in an abandoned crow, magpie or hawk nest; occasionally in a natural tree cavity; female incubates 4 or 5 eggs for up to 25–30 days.
Feeding: nocturnal; flies low, pouncing on prey from the air; eats mainly voles and mice, occasionally shrews, pocket-gophers, small rabbits, small birds and amphibians.
Voice: breeding call is a low, soft, ghostly *quoo-quoo*; alarm call is *weck-weck-weck*.
Similar Species: *Great Horned Owl* (p. 183): much larger; 'ear' tufts are farther apart; body is less compressed. *Short-eared Owl* (p. 191): lacks the long 'ear' tufts; nests on the ground.
Best Sites: shortgrass prairie near Medicine Hat; swampy areas in the foothills; check local bird hotlines for recent sightings.

SHORT-EARED OWL
Asio flammeus

The Short-eared Owl flies so characteristically, that after your first encounter with this bird, you will be able to identify it in flight almost 0.5 km away. This owl looks almost headless in flight, and it beats its long wings slowly and deeply, like a big butterfly, as it courses erratically low over meadows and fields. • Short-ears perform an entertaining sky dance over fields in May and June: the birds fly upward and then fall while clapping their wings below their bodies, producing a sound that can be heard at some distance. They do not 'hoot,' because visual displays are more effective for communicating in open environments. • This owl's life revolves around vole populations, leading to nomadic movements in response to prey availability and dramatic fluctuations in its own populations.

ID: *Sexes similar:* yellow eyes, set in black sockets; heavy, vertical streaking on the buffy belly; straw-coloured upperparts; short 'ear' tufts are rarely seen. *In flight:* dark elbow patches; deep wingbeats; long wings.
Size: *L* 33–43 cm; *W* 105–115 cm; female slightly larger.
Status: uncommon to common from March to November; occasionally overwinters.
Habitat: open country, including grasslands, wet meadows and cleared forests.
Nesting: on the ground; in a slight depression sparsely lined with grass; female incubates 4–7 eggs for 26–37 days.

Feeding: forages low over marshes, wet meadows and tall vegetation; pounces from the air; eats mainly voles and other small rodents, as well as insects, small birds and amphibians.
Voice: generally quiet; produces a soft *toot-toot-toot* during the breeding season; also 'barks' like a small dog and 'squeals.'
Similar Species: *Burrowing Owl* (p. 187): much longer legs; shorter tail; shorter wings. *Long-eared Owl* (p. 190): long 'ear' tufts; shorter wings; rarely hunts during the day.
Best Sites: Brooks area; check local bird hotlines for recent sightings.

BOREAL OWL
Aegolius funereus

The Boreal Owl routinely ranks in the top five of the most-desired species to see, according to birdwatcher surveys throughout North America. Alberta is one of the best places in the world to encounter this pint-sized owl, even though few birds are seen each year. Boreal Owls are most often seen in late winter, when they perch conspicuously on bare branches and call regularly during the long nights.
• Because of the Boreal Owl's remote habitat and nocturnal habits, ornithologists have yet to uncover many aspects of its ecology and behaviour. This small owl is known to be very well adapted to snowy forest environments—it is quite capable of locating and catching prey that live beneath the snow. • This approachable owl was named the 'Blind One' by native peoples, because it was easily captured by hand.

ID: *Sexes similar. Adult:* small; rounded head; light face with a dark border; light bill; vertical, rusty streaks on the underparts; white-spotted, brown upperparts; spotted forehead; black eyebrow; short tail. *Immature:* brown underparts; brown face, with white between the eyes.
Size: *L* 23–31 cm; *W* 55–74 cm.
Status: rare to uncommon year-round.
Habitat: mature coniferous and mixed forests, often adjacent to open meadows.
Nesting: in an abandoned woodpecker cavity or natural hollow in a tree; lines the cavity with a few feathers; female incubates 4–6 white eggs for 26–32 days.

Feeding: swoops from a perch for voles, mice, shrews and insects; caches food; might plunge through the snow for its food.
Voice: rapid, accelerating, continuous whistle: *whew-whew-whew-whew-whew-whew*; easily imitated.
Similar Species: *Northern Saw-whet Owl* (p. 193): adult has a dark bill and lacks the heavy forehead spotting and the vertical eyebrow; immature has reddish underparts. *Western Screech-Owl* (p. 368): ear tufts; dark bill; dark face.
Best Sites: Sibbald Creek, Kananaskis Country; check local bird hotlines for recent sightings.

NORTHERN SAW-WHET OWL

Aegolius acadicus

The whistled notes of the Northern Saw-whet Owl are surprisingly common during dark winter nights in Alberta. Heard far more than they are seen, Saw-whets can be encountered in forested areas, including many wooded city parks and ravines. These tiny owls (no taller than this book) are opportunistic hunters—they take whatever they can, whenever they can, and often store what they cannot immediately eat. The stored prey freezes quickly in winter, and it has recently been discovered that the owls 'incubate' the frozen prey to thaw it out.
• 'Owl prowls' during Christmas bird counts concentrate much energy on Saw-whets. These owls can be very numerous in parts of Alberta, but they are not always vocally obliging. • The scientific name *acadicus* is Latin for 'from Acadia' (New Brunswick, Nova Scotia and Maine), the region from which this bird was first collected.

ID: *Sexes similar. Adult:* small; rounded head; light, unbordered face; dark bill; vertical, rusty streaks on the underparts; brown, white-spotted upperparts; streaked forehead; short tail. *Immature:* white patch between the eyes; rich brown upperparts; buff-brown underparts.

Size: *L* 18–23 cm; *W* 43–55 cm.

Status: uncommon to common year-round.

Habitat: pure and mixed coniferous and deciduous forests.

Nesting: in an abandoned woodpecker cavity or natural hollow in a tree; female incubates 5 or 6 white eggs for 27–29 days.

Feeding: swoops from a perch; eats mainly mice and voles, also larger insects, songbirds and shrews, and occasionally amphibians; caches food.

Voice: whistled, evenly spaced notes (about 1 per second): *whew-whew-whew-whew*; continuous and easily imitated.

Similar Species: *Boreal Owl* (p. 192): adult has a light-coloured bill, heavy spotting on the forehead, a dark, vertical eyebrow and a dark border to the facial disc; immature has a brown breast. *Northern Pygmy-Owl* (p. 186): light-coloured bill; proportionately longer tail; eye spots on the nape; lacks the white streaking on the forehead.

Best Sites: Sibbald Creek, Kananaskis Country; Edmonton river valley.

COMMON NIGHTHAWK
Chordeiles minor

Mild-mannered by day, the Common Nighthawk rests on the ground or on a horizontal tree branch, its colour and shape blending perfectly into the texture of the bark. At dusk, however, this bird takes on a new form as a dazzling and erratic flier, catching insects in flight. • Against the deep blue of a prairie sky in the early evening, the white wing patches of these birds are obvious at a great distance. • To many people, the sound of a nighthawk is the sound of summer evenings at their favourite southern Alberta campground. Both male and female nighthawks fly high above the ground, giving forth with their call, a nasal *bjeet;* then, from a great height, the male dives swiftly towards the ground. He thrusts his wings forward at the bottom of the dive, creating a hollow *vroom* sound with the feathers of his wings. There might be no better place in the world to experience nighthawk courtship than atop a hoodoo in the badlands of Alberta.

ID: *Sexes similar:* cryptic, mottled plumage; barred underparts; throat is white in the male, buff in the female. *In flight:* white wrist patches; long, pointed wings; shallowly forked tail; erratic flight.
Size: *L* 22–25 cm.
Status: uncommon to common from May to September.
Habitat: dry coniferous forests, open cottonwood forests, meadows, badlands, larger lakes and grasslands.
Nesting: on bare ground; in a spot chosen by the female; female incubates 2 eggs for about 19 days.
Feeding: catches insects in flight; eats midges, mosquitoes, beetles, flying ants, moths and others.
Voice: frequently repeated, nasal *peent peent;* also makes a deep, hollow *vroom* with its wings.
Similar Species: *Common Poorwill* (p. 195): much less common; lacks the white wrist patches; shorter, rounder wings.
Best Sites: Dinosaur PP; Writing-on-Stone PP; Midland PP; Suffield–Medicine Hat area.

COMMON POORWILL
Phalaenoptilus nuttallii

Few Albertans have heard the telltale evening calls of the Common Poorwill. This secretive nightjar might breed in Alberta, but little evidence exists to prove it. What little is known about our poorwills suggests that they occur in very small numbers, mainly along the southern slopes of the Cypress Hills and in the Milk River canyon. • In 1946, the ornithological community was shocked by the discovery of a Common Poorwill that appeared to be hibernating through winter in a rock crevice. It was cold to the touch and had no detectable breath or heartbeat. As it turns out, poorwills will enter a state of torpor, in which their body temperature drops as low as 6° C, for a few days at a time to survive cold periods. The 1946 discovery was clearly not the first suggestion of this strange habit in poorwills: in 1804, Meriwether Lewis found an unidentified 'goatsucker … to be passing into the dormant state,' and the Hopi named it *Hölchoko*, 'the sleeping one.'

ID: *Sexes similar:* cryptic, light to dark brown plumage; pale throat; finely barred underparts; tail corners are white in the male, buff in the female. *In flight:* rounded wings and tail.
Size: *L* 19–22 cm.
Status: very rare from May to October.
Habitat: dry, open, grassy environments and rocky canyons.
Nesting: typically on bare ground;

pair incubates 2 white eggs for 20–21 days.
Feeding: on the wing; eats mainly moths, beetles and other flying insects.
Voice: frequently heard at dusk and through the night: *poor-will poor-will;* at close range, a hiccup-like sound can be heard at the end of the phrase.
Similar Species: *Common Nighthawk* (p. 194): long, pointed wings; white wrist patches.
Best Sites: Milk River canyon; Cypress Hills PP; sandhills south of Bindloss.

BLACK SWIFT
Cypseloides niger

The fast-flying Black Swift is strongly localized in its mountain breeding range. Only along the steep vertical walls of Johnston Canyon, in Banff National Park, and Maligne Canyon, in Jasper National Park, are small, semi-colonial groups of Black Swifts known to nest in Alberta. Black Swifts have been reported elsewhere in the Alberta Rockies, but so far no one has found any other nesting areas. Additional nest sites could be discovered by investigating remote canyons with similar characteristics to the two known breeding areas. • Black Swifts hunt insects on the wing for much of the day, but as the sun sets over the western peaks, the swifts rocket back to the canyons to spend the night atop their nests. The young grow slowly in the cool, damp canyons, deprived for much of the day of the incubating warmth of their parents. • During pleasant weather, Black Swifts forage high in the air; bad weather brings them closer to the ground.

ID: *Sexes similar:* black overall; slender, sleek body; very small legs. *In flight:* long, tapering wings that angle backward; short, slightly forked tail; rapid wingbeat.
Size: L 18 cm.
Status: locally common from June to September.
Habitat: canyons with streams and waterfalls.
Nesting: semi-colonial; on a canyon ledge, often near a waterfall; nest is made of moss, mud and algae; pair incubates 1 egg for up to 27 days.

Feeding: on the wing; eats flying insects, especially stoneflies, caddisflies and mayflies.
Voice: high-pitched *plik-plik-plik-plik*.
Similar Species: *Swallows* (pp. 243–49): smaller; more colourful; generally lack the boomerang-shaped flight silhouette. *Vaux's Swift* (p. 197): very rare; smaller; lighter colour overall.
Best Sites: Johnston Canyon, Banff NP; Maligne Canyon, Jasper NP.

VAUX'S SWIFT

Chaetura vauxi

The Vaux's Swift is one of the frequent fliers of the bird world, and it is often visible only as a speck in the sky. This high-flying aeronaut feeds, drinks, bathes and even mates on the wing—only incubation and rest keep this bird out of the air. • Vaux's Swifts are primarily found west of the Continental Divide, but in Alberta they have been reported reliably from Waterton Lakes National Park. They have not yet been found breeding in our province, but hollow trees in the region could hold nests of these wide ranging birds. • Swifts cast a characteristic boomerang silhouette in flight. They are shaped much like swallows—they have long, tapering wings, small bills with wide gapes and long, sleek bodies—but these two groups of birds are not closely related. • John Kirk Townsend named this bird after William Sansom Vaux, an eminent mineralogist. Apparently, it is generally considered correct to pronounce 'Vaux' with a hard *x*.

ID: *Sexes similar:* brownish-grey overall; brown upperparts; lighter underparts; very pale throat. *In flight:* squared-off tail; long wings taper backward.
Size: *L* 13 cm.
Status: very rare during summer.
Habitat: forages in forest openings, river valleys and lakeshores; breeds in mature coniferous and deciduous forests.
Nesting: in hollow tree cavity or chimney; nest of sticks, twigs and conifer needles glued to inner wall of cavity with saliva; pair incubates 4 or 5 white eggs for 18–19 days.
Feeding: on the wing, often just above treetops; feeds almost entirely on flying insects, including flies, moths, ants and aphids.

Voice: courtship call is a fast, twittering *chip-chip-chip-cheweet-cheweet.*
Similar Species: *Black Swift* (p. 196): black; much larger. *Bank Swallow* (p. 247): dark breast band on white underparts. *Northern Rough-winged Swallow* (p. 246): dirty white underparts; heavier wings; larger tail.
Best Sites: Waterton Lakes NP.

RUBY-THROATED HUMMINGBIRD

Archilochus colubris

Everyone knows and loves the tiny hummingbirds that buzz into flower beds and visits sugarwater feeders. Ruby-throated Hummingbirds span the ecological gap between birds and bees—they feed on the energy-rich nectar that flowers provide in exchange for pollination. Perhaps it is their size, or their intimate association with flowers, that makes smiles appear whenever people discuss these birds. • The Ruby-throated Hummingbird is the only hummer that is routinely seen outside the mountains in Alberta. • It is interesting to look at this species and admire it as one of nature's engineering marvels. Weighing about as much as a quarter, hummingbirds are capable of speeds of up to 100 km/h. In straight-ahead flight, they beat their wings 75 times a second (slightly less if hovering or reversing), and their migration takes them across the Gulf of Mexico—an incredible, non-stop journey of more than 1030 km.

ID: *General:* tiny; long bill; iridescent green back; light underparts; dark tail. *Male:* ruby red throat; black chin. *Female* and *Immature:* fine streaking on the throat.

Size: *L* 9–9.5 cm.

Status: uncommon from mid-May to August.

Habitat: open aspen forests, parks and gardens.

Nesting: on a horizontal tree limb; tiny, deep cup nest is made of plant down and fibres and held together with spider silk; lichens and leaves are pasted on the exterior walls; female incubates 2 pea-sized eggs for 13–16 days.

Feeding: uses its long bill to probe blooming flowers and special feeders and licks up the nectar and sweetened water; also eats small insects and spiders.

Voice: most noticeable sound is the soft buzzing of the wings in flight; also produces a loud *chick* and other squeaks.

Similar Species: *Rufous Hummingbird* (p. 201): male has red on his flanks and back. *Calliope Hummingbird* (p. 200): much smaller; white-rayed gorget. *Black-chinned Hummingbird* (p. 199): male has a violet throat patch and a large black chin patch.

Best Sites: backyard feeders; Medicine Hat.

BLACK-CHINNED HUMMINGBIRD

Archilochus alexandri

Nestled in the foothills southwest of Calgary lies Turner Valley, the hummingbird capital of Alberta. A variety of hummers have been reported from sugarwater feeders there, including the occasional Black-chinned Hummingbird. This hummingbird is the western counterpart of the Ruby-throated Hummingbird, and its range lies mostly to the south and west of Alberta. During summer, a few of these birds range northward, following the flowers that fill meadows throughout Alberta's mountains and foothills. • Naturalist H.G.L. Reichenbach was obviously deeply influenced by Greek culture—he named several hummingbird genera after Greeks. Archilochus was one of the first Greek poets. The species name *alexandri* is from the name of its discoverer, a doctor who collected specimens in Mexico.

ID: *General:* tiny; long bill; iridescent green back; light underparts; dark tail. *Male:* small violet throat patch; large black chin patch. *Female* and *Immature:* fine streaking on the throat.
Size: L 7.5–9 cm.
Status: rare from June to August.
Habitat: riparian forests and deciduous shrubs.
Nesting: does not nest in Alberta.

Feeding: hovers in the air to probe flowers for nectar; also eats small insects.
Voice: soft, high-pitched, warbling courtship songs; *buzz* and *chip* alarm calls; wings buzz in flight.
Similar Species: *Ruby-throated Hummingbird* (p. 198): male has a red gorget. *Rufous Hummingbird* (p. 201) and *Calliope Hummingbird* (p. 200): females and immatures have more rusty colour in the plumage.
Best Sites: Turner Valley; Kananaskis Country; Crowsnest Pass; Waterton Lakes NP.

CALLIOPE HUMMINGBIRD
Stellula calliope

The male Calliope Hummingbird's sparkling, rose-purple throat rays are unmistakable. As it flits about in the montane forests and foothills, its dainty colours complement the vivid complexion of the landscape. Calliope Hummingbirds dance among flowers, from paintbrushes to columbines, gently probing deep into the blooms for energy-rich nectar. • The Calliope Hummingbird is the smallest North American bird and the smallest long-distance migrant in the bird world. It travels up to 8900 km in a year. Contrary to some popular myths, hummingbirds never hitch rides on the backs of geese or eagles. • Novice birdwatchers often ponder the pronunciation of this bird's name. It is generally accepted as 'ka-LIE-o-pee,' but variations are plentiful—and often amusing.

ID: *General:* iridescent green upperparts; long, narrow bill; short tail. *Male:* light purple streaks run down the throat from the bill; white underparts; light green flanks. *Female:* white underparts; peach-coloured flanks; dark green spots on the throat.
Size: *L* 8 cm.
Status: uncommon from May to August.
Habitat: disturbed areas, avalanche slopes, burns and shrubby meadows.
Nesting: saddled on a branch under an overhanging branch or foliage; tiny cup nest is made of plant down, moss, scales and spider webs; often builds over previously used nests; female incubates 2 eggs for up to 16 days.
Feeding: hover-probes flowers for nectar; also eats small insects.
Voice: high-pitched, chattering *tsew* notes.
Similar Species: *Rufous Hummingbird* (p. 201): longer tail and bill; female often has red spotting on the throat.
Best Sites: Highwood Junction, Kananaskis Country; Turner Valley; Waterton Lakes NP; Bow Valley PP.

RUFOUS HUMMINGBIRD

Selasphorus rufus

The tiny Rufous Hummingbird is a delicate avian jewel, but its beauty hides a relentless mean streak. Sit patiently in a flower-filled meadow or alongside a hummingbird feeder, and you'll soon notice the territoriality and aggressiveness of these birds—they buzz past one another and chase rivals for some distances. Although it must seem like life and death situations to these birds, to our eyes, the scale of the conflicts between these mini-mites is cute. • Hummingbirds have to be 'power smart,' because they are raging metabolic furnaces. The males must defend their feeding territories as insurance policies for their high energy needs. • To attract pollinators (insects and hummingbirds), plants produce colourful flowers with sweet, energy-rich nectar. As hummingbirds visit flowers for the food, they spread pollen from one flower to another, ensuring the plants' survival.

ID: *General:* long, thin, black bill; mostly rufous tail. *Male:* red back, tail and flanks; scaled, scarlet throat; green crown; white breast and belly. *Female:* green back; red-spotted throat; rufous flanks; light underparts.
Size: L 8–9 cm.
Status: common from May to early September.
Habitat: forest edges, meadows and willow shrubs.
Nesting: saddled on a drooping conifer branch; tiny cup nest is made of plant down and spider webs, and is covered with lichens and leaves; female incubates 2 eggs for up to 14 days.
Feeding: hover-probes mostly red flowers for nectar; also eats small insects and sap.
Voice: call is a gentle *chewp chewp*; also makes a fast buzz: *zeee-chuppity-chup.*
Similar Species: *Calliope Hummingbird* (p. 200): smaller; female has less rufous in the tail.
Best Sites: Turner Valley; Highwood Pass, Kananaskis Country; Bow Valley PP; Waterton Lakes NP; Weaslehead Natural Area, Calgary.

BELTED KINGFISHER
Ceryle alcyon

The Belted Kingfisher's distinctive rattle announces that you are in an area of shallow, clear waters filled with small fish. Never far from rivers or lakes, the Belted Kingfisher is generally found perched on a bare branch that extends out over a productive pool. With precise headfirst dives, it can catch fish at depths of up to 60 cm. Kingfishers often hover briefly above the water before diving in. • A breeding pair of kingfishers takes turns excavating the nest burrow. They use their bills to chip away at the soil and then kick loose material out of the tunnel with their feet. Female kingfishers have the traditional female reproductive role for birds, but they are more colourful than their mates. • Alcyon (Halcyone) was the daughter of the wind god in Greek mythology; she and her husband were transformed into kingfishers.

ID: *General:* bluish upperparts; shaggy crest; blue-grey breast band; white collar; long, straight bill; short legs; white underwings; small, white patch near the eye. *Female:* rust-coloured 'belt' (occasionally incomplete). *Male:* no belt.
Size: *L* 28–36 cm.
Status: uncommon to common from April to November; a few overwinter.
Habitat: large rivers, lakes and beaver ponds, adjacent to exposed banks.
Nesting: in a cavity at the end of an earth burrow, often up to 2 m deep, dug by the pair with their bills and claws; pair incubates 6 or 7 eggs for up to 24 days.
Feeding: dives headfirst, either from a perch or from a hover above the water; eats mostly small fish, aquatic invertebrates and tadpoles.
Voice: fast, repetitive rattle, *crrrr-crrrr-crrrr-crrrr*, like a tea cup shaking on a saucer.
Similar Species: *Blue Jay* (p. 237): more intensely blue; smaller bill; behaves in a completely different fashion.
Best Sites: Inglewood Bird Sanctuary, Calgary; river valleys in all our major cities.

LEWIS'S WOODPECKER
Melanerpes lewis

The Lewis's Woodpecker forgoes many traditional woodpecker habits. Rather than clinging to tree trunks and chipping away for grubs, the Lewis's Woodpecker does much of its foraging as fly-catchers do, catching insects on the wing. • In Alberta, Lewis's Woodpeckers have been seen less frequently in recent years. The suppression of forest fires in southwestern Alberta might have hindered recent invasions of these birds from B.C. and Montana. (The Lewis's Woodpecker often forages in recently burned areas, and in open forests in general.) • This woodpecker is named in honour of Meriwether Lewis, one of the co-leaders of the famous Lewis and Clark expedition. Although Lewis was not trained as a naturalist, his diary entries include many concise observations of natural history.

ID: *Sexes similar. Adult:* dark green upperparts; dark red face; light grey breast and collar; pinkish belly; dark undertail coverts; sharp, stout bill. *Immature:* brown head and face; brown breast; lacks the red in the face and the light grey collar.
Size: *L* 28 cm.

Status: very rare from May through the summer.
Habitat: open forests and burned areas.
Nesting: does not nest in Alberta.
Feeding: flycatches for flying invertebrates; probes into cracks and crevices for invertebrates.
Voice: harsh series of *churr-churr-churr-churr-churr* notes.
Similar Species: no other woodpecker is dark green in colour.
Best Sites: Crowsnest Pass; Bow River valley (late May).

203

RED-HEADED WOODPECKER

Melanerpes erythrocephalus

Although its numbers in Alberta might not be significant, the beauty of the Red-headed Woodpecker tips the esthetic scales in its favour. Only a few scattered records give this species its zygodactyl toehold in our province. It is typically a bird of eastern deciduous forests, and in Alberta it is most reliably observed around Medicine Hat and in the Cypress Hills. Birders travelling to Medicine Hat should ask about recent sightings at Police Point Park.

• Alexander Wilson, the 'father' of American ornithology, wrote of the Red-headed Woodpecker: 'His tricoloured plumage, so striking. … A gay and frolicsome disposition, diving and vociferating around the high dead limbs of some large tree, amusing the passenger with their gambols.' • The scientific name *Melanerpes* means 'black creeper'; *erythrocephalus* is Greek for 'blood red–headed.'

ID: *Sexes similar. Adult:* bright red head and throat; black back, wings and tail; white belly, rump and inner wing patches. *Juvenile:* brown head, back, wings and tail; slight brown streaking on the breast.
Size: *L* 19–22 cm.
Status: very rare during summer.
Habitat: open riparian deciduous forests.

vagrant

Nesting: does not nest in Alberta.
Feeding: flycatches aerial insects; hammers dead and decaying wood for grubs; also eats young birds, eggs, corn nuts and berries.
Voice: loud *queer-queer-queer;* occasionally a chattering *kerr-r-ruck.*
Similar Species: adult is distinctive. *Sapsuckers* (pp. 205–6): juveniles have a white patch on each hind wing.
Best Sites: Police Point Park, Medicine Hat; Cypress Hills PP.

YELLOW-BELLIED SAPSUCKER
Sphyrapicus varius

The Yellow-bellied Sapsucker is a common woodland bird throughout much of Alberta. It can be closely approached around its nest sites, which are found almost exclusively in aspen-dominated stands. • Male sapsuckers are easily encountered in woods in May, when they perform characteristic courting rituals. The drumming of sapsuckers differs from that of other Alberta woodpeckers—it has an irregular, Morse code–like rhythm. The cat-like calls of sapsuckers are also distinctive. • Like most woodpeckers, sapsuckers feed their young almost constantly; parents return to the nest with food every 5 to 10 minutes. • The scientific name *varius* refers to the variability of forms that once existed in this species. It is not as variable as it once was, however, because the Red-naped Sapsucker and the Red-breasted Sapsucker, which were once regarded as different forms of the Yellow-bellied Sapsucker, are now considered separate species.

ID: *General:* black bib; red forecrown; black-and-white face, back, wings and tail; yellow wash on the belly. *Male:* red chin. *Female:* whitish chin.
Size: *L* 18–20 cm.
Status: common from early May to September.
Habitat: deciduous and mixed woods.
Nesting: in a cavity; usually in a live birch or aspen with heart-rot; usually lines the cavity with wood chips; pair incubates 5 or 6 eggs for 12–13 days.

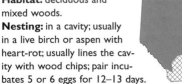

Feeding: hammers trees for insects; creates 'wells' and collects the sap and trapped insects; also flycatches for insects.
Voice: nasal, cat-like meow; territorial/courtship hammering has a Morse code quality and rhythm.
Similar Species: *Red-naped Sapsucker* (p. 206): extremely similar, but it has a small red patch on the back of the head; range is very useful in separating the species.
Best Sites: Cold Lake PP; Elk Island NP; Sir Winston Churchill PP.

RED-NAPED SAPSUCKER
Sphyrapicus nuchalis

Red-naped Sapsuckers arrive in Alberta in May and immediately begin tending to last year's sap taps. Sapsuckers have adopted a variation on the woodpecker theme: they drill lines of parallel 'wells' in tree bark. As the wells fill with sap, they attract insects, and the sapsuckers make their rounds, eating both the trapped bugs and the pooled sap. Sapsuckers don't actually suck sap; they lap it up with a fringed tongue tip that resembles a paintbrush. This deliberate foraging practice has convinced some people that these birds are capable of advance planning. • The Red-naped Sapsucker was formerly considered a subspecies of the Yellow-bellied Sapsucker. Studies in Alberta, where their ranges overlap, show a degree of hybridization, but both species tend to prefer to mate with one of their own kind in most situations.

ID: *General:* red forehead; red patch behind the ear; black-and-white-striped head; black bib; yellow wash on the breast; black-and-white wings and back; white rump; light yellow upper back with fine black streaking. *Male:* red chin and throat. *Female:* white chin; red throat.
Size: *L* 22 cm.

Status: uncommon from late April to September.
Habitat: aspen and birch woodlands and alder shrubs.
Nesting: excavates a cavity in a living aspen or other deciduous tree; occasionally uses the same tree for 2 years, but excavates a new hole; lines the cavity with wood chips; pair incubates 4 or 5 eggs for 13 days.
Feeding: hammers a series of small, square wells in living trees; eats the sap and insects from the wells; frequently flycatches insects.
Voice: call is a cat-like meow; tapping is irregular and Morse code–like.
Similar Species: *Hairy Woodpecker* (p. 208) and *Downy Woodpecker* (p. 207): lack the red forehead and the black bib.
Best Site: Crowsnest Pass.

DOWNY WOODPECKER

Picoides pubescens

Soft taps and hectic staccato calls sound out the activities of the Downy Woodpecker. It is the most common woodpecker throughout most of Alberta and the most likely species to be attracted to backyard feeding stations during the colder months, especially when suet is offered. It is not surprising that the Downy Woodpecker is often the first woodpecker that a novice birdwatcher identifies with confidence. These encounters are not all confusion-free, however, because the Hairy Woodpecker can look remarkably Downy-like at some angles.
• This woodpecker's small bill is amazingly effective at poking into tiny crevices and exposing dormant invertebrates and wood-boring grubs. Like many woodpeckers, it has feathered nostrils to filter out the sawdust it produces by hammering. Woodpeckers also have to cushion their heads from the shock of all that hammering; they have evolved a reinforced, flexible skull, large bill, neck and skull muscles and a brain that is tightly packed in its cranium.

ID: *General:* clear white belly and back; black wings are barred with white; black eye line and crown; short, stubby bill; mostly black tail; white outer tail feathers are spotted with black. *Male:* small red patch on the back of the head. *Female:* no red patch.
Size: *L* 15–18 cm.
Status: common year-round.
Habitat: all wooded environments, including aspen forests and tall deciduous shrubs.
Nesting: pair excavates a cavity in a dying or decaying trunk or limb; excavation lasts more than 2 weeks; lines the cavity with wood chips; incubates 4 or 5 eggs for 11–13 days.

Feeding: forages on trunks and branches; chips and probes for insect eggs, cocoons, larvae and adults; also eats nuts and seeds; attracted to feeders.
Voice: long, unbroken trill: *trrrrrrrrrr*; call is either a sharp *pik* or *ki-ki-ki*.
Similar Species: *Hairy Woodpecker* (p. 208): larger; bill is as long as the head is wide; no spots on the white outer tail feathers.
Best Sites: almost any wooded area.

207

HAIRY WOODPECKER
Picoides villosus

♂

The Hairy Woodpecker is easily confused with its smaller cousin (the Downy), so a second or third look is often required to confirm its identity. Looking like a Downy on steroids, the Hairy Woodpecker is slightly less common and more aloof, but it is certainly a species that will be encountered frequently throughout the life of a birder. • The Hairy Woodpecker does not sing during courtship; instead it drums rhythmically on trees. Its courtship flights are equally unusual —this bird produces loud sounds by beating its wings against its flanks. • The secret to the woodpeckers' wood-boring ways is hidden in their bills. Most woodpeckers have very long tongues, in some cases more than four times the length of the bill. Such a long tongue is made possible by twin structures that wrap around the perimeter of the skull. These structures store the tongue in much the same way that a measuring tape is stored in its case.

ID: *General:* pure white belly; black wings are spotted with white; black cheek and crown; bill is about as long as the head is wide; black tail with white outer tail feathers. *Male:* small red patch on the back of the head. *Female:* no red patch.
Size: *L* 19–24 cm.
Status: uncommon to common year-round.
Habitat: aspen, spruce and mixed forests.
Nesting: pair excavates a nest site in a live or decaying trunk or

limb; excavation lasts more than 2 weeks; lines the cavity with wood chips; pair incubates 4 or 5 eggs for up to 12 days.
Feeding: forages on trunks and branches; chips, hammers and probes bark for insect eggs, cocoons, larvae and adults; also eats nuts, fruit and seeds; attracted to feeders.
Voice: loud, sharp call: *peek peek*; long, unbroken trill: *keek-ik-ik-ik-ik-ik*.
Similar Species: *Downy Woodpecker* (p. 207): smaller; shorter bill; dark spots on the white outer tail feathers.
Best Sites: almost any large woodland.

THREE-TOED WOODPECKER

Picoides tridactylus

Evidence of this woodpecker's foraging activities is seen more commonly than the bird itself in most mature coniferous forests. In its search for insect eggs and invertebrates, the Three-toed Woodpecker flakes off bits of bark from old and dying coniferous trees, exposing the red inner surface of the trunk. After years of serving as forage sites, the trees take on a reddish look and are skirted with bark chips. • Most woodpeckers do not randomly forage for their meals; instead, they often listen for grubs under the bark and in the wood. • The Rocky Mountain race of the Three-toed Woodpecker has a nearly all-white back; Three-toes living in the northern boreal forest have a black-and-white, ladder-like back. • Both the Three-toed Woodpecker and the Black-backed Woodpecker have three toes rather than the usual four.

ID: *General:* black-and-white barring down the centre of the back; white underparts; black barring on the sides; predominantly black head with 2 white stripes; black tail with white outer tail feathers. *Male:* yellow crown. *Female:* black crown with occasional white spotting.
Size: *L* 21–24 cm.
Status: uncommon year-round; irruptive.
Habitat: spruce and fir forests and disturbed areas.
Nesting: excavates a cavity in a dead or dying conifer trunk; excavation can take up to 12 days; pair incubates 4 eggs for up to 2 weeks.

Feeding: gleans under bark flakes for larval and adult wood-boring insects; occasionally eats berries.
Voice: call is a low *pik*; drums in a prolonged series of steady bursts.
Similar Species: *Black-backed Woodpecker* (p. 210): solid black back. *Hairy Woodpecker* (p. 208): clean white back; lacks the barring on the sides.
Best Sites: Lake Louise, Banff NP; Brown-Lowery PP.

BLACK-BACKED WOODPECKER
Picoides arcticus

♂

The Black-backed Wood-pecker frequently chooses to perch and drum on the top of a broken snag during the spring courtship sea-son. The yellow-capped males are so focused on this activity that they are easily approached—a rare pleasure, because these birds, which inhabit remote forested areas that are often difficult to access, are rarely seen even by the most committed naturalist. For the best chance of seeing a Black-backed Woodpecker, enter a recently burned forest (where wood-boring bee-tles thrive), and follow your ears. • This species is irruptive, as is the Three-toed Woodpecker, and during some winters both can be found in good numbers well south of their breeding range, even in places like Medicine Hat, where they forage on coniferous trees in subur-ban gardens. • The scientific name *arcticus* reflects this bird's northern distribution.

ID: *General:* solid black back; white under-parts; black barring on the sides; predomi-nantly black head with a black 'moustache' and a single white line below the eye; 3 toes; black tail with pure white outer tail feathers. *Male:* yellow crown. *Female:* black crown.
Size: *L* 23–25 cm.
Status: rare to uncommon year-round, irruptive.
Habitat: coniferous forests, disturbed areas.
Nesting: excavates a cavity in a dead or dying conifer trunk or limb;

excavation can take up to 12 days; pair incubates 4 eggs for up to 2 weeks.
Feeding: gleans under bark flakes for larval and adult wood-boring insects; occasionally eats berries.
Voice: call is a low *pik*; drums in a pro-longed series of steady bursts.
Similar Species: *Three-toed Woodpecker* (p. 209): white back with black, horizontal barring.
Best Sites: Sir Winston Churchill PP; Whitemud Creek ravine, Edmonton (winter); Brown-Lowery PP; Fish Creek PP (winter).

NORTHERN FLICKER

Colaptes auratus

The Northern Flicker spends much of its time on the ground, feeding on ants and other land insects, and it appears almost robin-like when it hops about in grassy meadows or forest clearings. • Flickers are often seen bathing in dusty depressions (the dust particles absorb oils and bacteria that are harmful to the birds' feathers), or, to clean themselves more thoroughly, they squish ants and then preen themselves with the remains. Ants contain formic acid, which can kill small parasites on the skin and feathers. • There are two forms of the Northern Flicker in Alberta: the 'Yellow-shafted Flicker' nests throughout most of Alberta; the 'Red-shafted Flicker' nests through most of the Rockies and across southern Alberta to the Cypress Hills. There is considerable hybridization between the two forms in the foothills and in the southern prairies, which explains the lumping of these two flicker forms into one species.

'Yellow-shafted Flicker'

'Red-shafted Flicker'

ID: *General:* brown overall; barred back and wings; spotted underparts; black bib; white rump; long bill; grey face; brown crown. *'Yellow-shafted' male:* yellow wing and tail linings; black 'moustache.' *'Red-shafted' male:* red wing and tail linings; red 'moustache.' *Females:* no 'moustache.'
Size: L 33 cm.
Status: common from late March to September.
Habitat: open mixed wood-lands, forest edges, fields and meadows.
Nesting: pair excavates a cavity in a dead or dying deciduous tree; either sex chooses the nest site; excavation

lasts for about 2 weeks; uses nest boxes; lines the cavity with wood chips; pair incubates 5–8 eggs for up to 11 days.
Feeding: forages on the ground for ants and other terrestrial insects; also eats berries and nuts; probes bark; occasionally flycatches.
Voice: loud, laughing, rapid *wick-wick-wick-wick-wick-wick*.
Similar Species: none.
Best Sites: Police Point Park, Medicine Hat; Whitemud Creek ravine, Edmonton; Inglewood Bird Sanctuary, Calgary.

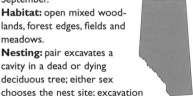

PILEATED WOODPECKER
Dryocopus pileatus

With a laugh and a look that inspired a cartoon character, the Pileated Woodpecker is what most people think a woodpecker ought to be. Its flaming red crest, swooping flight and maniacal call can stop hikers in their tracks. Unfortunately, these magnificent birds are not frequently encountered because they require such extensive areas in which to forage. A pair of breeding Pileated Woodpeckers generally requires more than 40 ha of mature forest to settle. • Telltale foraging cavities are often the only evidence that a Pileated Woodpecker is present in an area. With its powerful bill and stubborn determination, the Pileated Woodpecker chisels out fist-sized, rectangular holes in its unending search for grubs and carpenter ants. • There's no real consensus on whether this bird's name is pronounced 'pie-lee-ay-ted' or 'pill-ee-ay-ted'—it's a matter of preference and good-natured debate ('pee-lee-ay-ted' should not be ruled out either).

♂

ID: *General:* predominantly black; white wing linings; flaming red crest; yellow eyes; stout, dark bill; white stripe running from the bill to the shoulder; white chin. *Male:* red 'moustache'; red crest extends from the forehead. *Female:* no 'moustache'; red crest starts on the crown.
Size: *L* 41–48 cm.
Status: uncommon to common year-round.
Habitat: mature coniferous or mixedwood forests; prefers areas with dead and dying trees.
Nesting: pair excavates a cavity in a dead or dying tree trunk;

excavation can take 3–6 weeks; lines the cavity with wood chips; pair incubates 4 eggs for 15–18 days.
Feeding: often hammers the base of rotting trees, creating fist-sized, rectangular holes; eats carpenter ants, wood-boring beetle larvae, berries and nuts.
Voice: loud, fast, laughing, rolling *yucka-yucka-yucka-yucka* that carries great distances through the woods.
Similar Species: *Other woodpeckers:* much smaller. *American Crow* (p. 240): lacks the white underwings and the flaming red crest.
Best Sites: Whitemud Creek ravine, Edmonton; Fish Creek PP.

PASSERINES

Passerines are also commonly known as songbirds or perching birds. Although these terms are easier to comprehend, they are not as strictly accurate, because some passerines neither sing nor perch, and many non-passerines do sing and perch. In a general sense, however, these terms represent passerines adequately: they are among the best singers, and they are typically seen perched on a branch or wire.

Boreal Chickadee

Northern Rough-winged Swallow

It is believed that passerines, which all belong to the order Passeriformes, make up the most recent evolutionary group of birds. Theirs is the most numerous of all orders, representing about 46% of Alberta's bird species, and nearly three-fifths of all living birds worldwide.

Western Kingbird

Passerines are grouped together based on the sum total of many morphological and molecular similarities, including such things as the number of tail and flight feathers and reproductive characteristics. All passerines share the same foot shape: three toes face forward and one faces backward, and no passerines have webbed toes. Also, all passerines have a tendon that runs along the back side of the bird's knee and tightens when the bird perches, giving it a firm grip.

Tennessee Warbler

Some of our most common and easily identified birds are passerines, such as the Black-billed Magpie, Red-winged Blackbird and House Sparrow, but the passerines also include some of the most challenging and frustrating birds to identify, until their distinct songs and calls are learned.

Philadelphia Vireo

American Robin

213

OLIVE-SIDED FLYCATCHER
Contopus cooperi

The Olive-sided Flycatcher's belly-up-to-the-bar call makes it a favourite with many birders: *Quick-three-beers* it cries, loudly and clearly. In late summer it changes its tune to an equally enthusiastic, but less memorable, *pip-pip-pip*. It's a good thing this feisty little bird has such a distinctive call, because it is often difficult to spot. Look for a big-headed silhouette perched at the tip of a topmost dead limb on a mature conifer. • Flycatchers perch with a distinctive, upright and attentive profile. Their ready-and-waiting stance allows them to quickly launch out when insects fly past. • Flycatchers, phoebes and kingbirds belong to the suborder of perching birds known as the suboscines, which are characterized by their simple calls and drab plumage. • The scientific name *Contopus* means 'short foot.'

ID: *Sexes similar:* dark olive grey 'vest'; light throat and belly; olive brown upperparts; white rump patches; dark bill; no eye ring.
Size: L 19 cm.
Status: uncommon to common from late May to late August.
Habitat: mature spruce-fir and riparian forests and burned over woodlands.
Nesting: high in a conifer, usually on a horizontal branch far from the trunk; nest is made with twigs and plant fibres and bound with spider silk; female incubates 3 eggs for 14 days.
Feeding: flycatches insects from a perch.
Voice: *Male:* chipper and lively *quick-three-beers*, with the 2nd note highest in pitch; descending *pip-pip-pip* when excited.
Similar Species: *Western Wood-Pewee* (p. 215): smaller; lacks the white rump patches.
Best Sites: near treeline in Kananaskis Country.

WESTERN WOOD-PEWEE
Contopus sordidulus

Following this bird's characteristic, down-slurred call leads to the middle level of the forest, where the Western Wood-Pewee sings persistently throughout the day. When it's not singing, it launches itself in long, looping foraging ventures. Western Wood-Pewees are not as faithful to their perches as many other flycatchers; after launching out after an insect, they sometimes alight upon a different perch from the one they left. • The nest of the Western Wood-Pewee is well camouflaged by both its shape and colour—the completed structure resembles little more than a bump on a horizontal limb. As if this concealing masterpiece didn't provide enough protection, these small flycatchers vigorously defend their nests by chasing and vocalizing against hawks, jays and chipmunks. • The scientific name *sordidulus* refers to this bird's dirty, dusky colour.

Habitat: open woodlands and deciduous, ponderosa pine and riparian forests.
Nesting: on a horizontal tree limb; small cup nest is made with plant fibres and bound with spider silk; female incubates 3 eggs for 12–13 days.
Feeding: flycatches insects.
Voice: plaintive whistle, *peeeyou*, that drops off at the end; song is *fee-rrr-eet.*
Similar Species: *Olive-sided Flycatcher* (p. 214): white rump patches; larger. *Dusky* (p. 221), *Hammond's* (p. 220) and *Least* (p. 219) *flycatchers:* white eye rings. *Willow Flycatcher* (p. 218): darker lower mandible; browner upperparts; lighter underparts.
Best Sites: Elk Island NP; Inglewood Bird Sanctuary, Calgary.

ID: *Sexes similar:* dark olive brown upperparts; light underparts; 2 faint white wing bars; no eye ring; light-coloured lower mandible; light undertail coverts; light-coloured throat.
Size: *L* 13–15 cm.
Status: common from May to September.

215

YELLOW-BELLIED FLYCATCHER
Empidonax flaviventris

The confusing collection of empidonax flycatchers are the bane of mosquitoes—and the bane of birdwatchers, too. The Yellow-bellied Flycatcher is the most elusive and secretive of this confusing clan—it does not habitually perch in the open—but it does its best to distinguish itself from the other 'empids' by nesting on the ground and offering a simple *choo-wheep* call. Unfortunately the Yellow-bellied Flycatcher usually doesn't sing until the end of June. • Alberta offers a fine challenge to the birdwatcher: our province boasts an inordinately large assemblage of virtually indistinguishable flycatchers. Their confusing plumage should not deter novice birders; just remember that the best way to learn them is to actually become a bird *watcher*, and not to expect instant identifications.

ID: *Sexes similar:* olive green upperparts; 2 whitish wing bars; eye ring; white throat; yellow underparts; pale olive breast.

Size: *L* 13–15 cm.

Status: locally common from May to August.

Habitat: shady coniferous and mixedwood forests, bogs and fens.

Nesting: small cup nest is built in a fork in a small shrub; female incubates 3 or 4 eggs for 13 days.

Feeding: flycatches for insects; also gleans vegetation for larval and adult invertebrates.

Voice: *Male:* chipper *pe-wheep*; short *killik*.

Similar Species: *Western Wood-Pewee* (p. 215): olive grey upperparts; darker lower mandible. *Least* (p. 219), *Alder* (p. 217) and *Dusky* (p. 221) *flycatchers:* browner upperparts; less yellow underparts.

Best Site: Long Lake PP.

ALDER FLYCATCHER
Empidonax alnorum

The Alder Flycatcher is virtually indistinguishable from the other empidonax flycatchers until it opens its small beak: with a hearty *free beer,* its identity is revealed. Once this aggressive bird has been spotted, its feisty behaviour can be observed without distraction as it drives away rivals and pursues flying insects.
• This non-descript bird is well named, because it is often found in alder and willow shrubs—a fact that can help in its identification.
• Voice recognition is very important to many species of birds, and Alder Flycatchers instinctively know the simple phrase of their species (many birds have to learn their songs and calls). Even if a young Alder is isolated from the sounds of other Alder Flycatchers, it can produce a perfectly accept-able *free beer* call when it matures. • The Willow Flycatcher is a close relative of the Alder, and these two species were once grouped together as a single species—the Traill's Flycatcher.

ID: *Sexes similar:* greenish-brown upperparts; slight eye ring; 2 white wing bars; orange lower mandible; longish tail; yellow-green underparts.
Size: L 15–17 cm.
Status: common from May to August.
Habitat: edges of wet areas in willows and birch thickets, muskeg edges and streamside vegetation.
Nesting: in a fork in low bush or shrub; small cup nest is loosely

woven of grass and other plant materials; female incubates 3 or 4 eggs for 12–13 days.
Feeding: flycatches from a perch for beetles, bees, wasps and other flying insects; also takes berries and occasionally seeds.
Voice: snappy *free beer!*
Similar Species: *Western Wood-Pewee* (p. 215) and *Willow Flycatcher* (p. 218): inconspicuous eye rings. *Least* (p. 219), *Cordilleran* (p. 222), *Dusky* (p. 221) and *Hammond's* (p. 220) *flycatchers:* generally look the same; habitat, range and voice are good distinguishing characteristics.
Best Sites: Wagner Natural Area; Sibbald Creek Trail, Kananaskis Country.

217

WILLOW FLYCATCHER

Empidonax traillii

Southern spring winds carry the first Willow Flycatchers into Alberta's forests in mid-May. The date of their arrival is often easily recognized, because these small birds announce their presence with a simple, sneezy *fitz-bew* song. From swaying willow perches, Willow Flycatchers sing and survey their chosen territories. • On its nesting grounds, the Willow Flycatcher is an inconspicuous bird that prefers to remain out of sight. Only when an avian intruder violates this small bird's territory does the resident Willow Flycatcher aggressively reveal itself. It will drive away all other birds and fight furiously with rival males. • Thomas Stewart Traill was an Englishman who helped John J. Audubon find a British publisher for his book *Ornithological Biography*.

ID: *Sexes similar:* olive brown upperparts; 2 whitish wing bars; no eye ring; white throat; yellowish belly; pale olive breast.
Size: *L* 15 cm.
Status: locally common from May to August.
Habitat: willow and dwarf-birch thickets.
Nesting: small cup nest is built in a fork in a small shrub; female incubates 3 or 4 eggs for 13 days.

Feeding: flycatches for insects; also gleans vegetation for invertebrates.
Voice: *Male:* quick, sneezy *fitz-bew* that drops off at the end; up to 30 calls a minute.
Similar Species: *Western Wood-Pewee* (p. 215): olive grey upperparts; darker lower mandible. *Cordilleran* (p. 222), *Least* (p. 219), *Hammond's* (p. 220) and *Dusky* (p. 221) *flycatchers*: light-coloured eye rings.
Best Sites: Bow Valley PP; Sibbald Creek Trail, Kananaskis Country.

LEAST FLYCATCHER

Empidonax minimus

The Least Flycatcher is one of the boldest and most pugnacious songbirds in the aspen forests of Alberta. During the nesting season, it is noisy and conspicuous, cheerily calling out its simple, diagnostic two-part call throughout much of the day. Even though it is not as glamorous as other aspen residents, the Least Flycatcher is conspicuous, and you should see one whenever you visit an aspen stand in June. • Fighting male Least Flycatchers are pint-sized fluffs of terror. The victor wins the right to select and chase a female for considerable distances in the hope of mating with her. The courtship might not be romantic, but afterwards, the males do their best to defend their mates. • Female Least Flycatchers are extremely persistent incubators— a toppled tree was once found with a female still on the nest.

ID: *Sexes similar:* olive brown upperparts; 2 white wing bars; light-coloured eye ring; long, narrow tail; dark bill; light throat; dark tail.

Size: L 13–15 cm.

Status: common from May to August.

Habitat: aspen forests and alder and willow thickets.

Nesting: on a horizontal branch in a small tree or shrub; female builds the small cup nest with plant fibres and bark and lines it with grass, plant down and feathers; female incubates 4 eggs for up to 15 days.

Feeding: flycatches insects and gleans the foliage of trees and shrubs for insects; also eats fruit and seeds.

Voice: constantly repeated, whistled *che-bec che-bec* or *Quebec Quebec.*

Similar Species: *Willow Flycatcher* (p. 218): no eye ring. *Hammond's Flycatcher* (p. 220): darker underparts and throat. *Dusky Flycatcher* (p. 221): outer tail feathers have whitish edges. *Cordilleran Flycatcher* (p. 222): yellow throat.

Best Site: Elk Island NP.

HAMMOND'S FLYCATCHER

Empidonax hammondii

From coulee bottoms on the grasslands to the summits of Alberta's peaks, different empidonax flycatchers associate with different habitat zones. The Hammond's Flycatcher occupies the penthouse—it lives at higher elevations than other empidonax flycatchers, commonly nesting at up to 3000 m in the Rockies. It tends to prefer conifer stands that are greater than 8 ha in size and at least 80 years of age. If logging or other development projects make such areas harder to come by, this species might become increasingly dependent on our national parks for habitat preservation. • William Hammond, after whom this bird is named, was an army surgeon who sent animal specimens from western North America to the Smithsonian Institution in Washington, D.C.

ID: *Sexes similar:* olive brown upperparts; 2 white wing bars; distinct, light eye ring; grey face; dark lower mandible; light grey throat; dark tail with grey outer edge.
Size: L 14 cm.
Status: uncommon from May to August.
Habitat: coniferous forests, especially stands of mature spruce-fir.
Nesting: on a limb in a coniferous tree; small cup nest is made with plant fibres, leaves and grass and lined with feathers

and grass; female incubates 3 or 4 eggs for up to 15 days.
Feeding: flycatches and hover-gleans vegetation for insects.
Voice: *Male:* quick, whistled *tse-beek, seweep sup seep* or *peek.*
Similar Species: *Willow Flycatcher* (p. 218): no eye ring. *Least Flycatcher* (p. 219): light lower mandible; call is *che-bec. Cordilleran Flycatcher* (p. 222): yellow underparts. *Dusky Flycatcher* (p. 221): practically indistinguishable in the field, except for its deciduous forest habitat.
Best Site: Banff NP.

DUSKY FLYCATCHER
Empidonax oberholseri

Late spring storms can be disastrous for entire populations of Dusky Flycatchers. Snow and freezing rain in May and June can kill nearly all the Dusky Flycatchers in the affected region. Fortunately, such weather is normally a localized event; the following year, other Dusky Flycatchers return to fill the void created by the unseasonable storms. • The male Dusky Flycatcher stays around the nest after the eggs are laid to help the female raise the young birds. • The Dusky Flycatcher is a classic western species, but its range extends eastward into an isolated pocket in the Cypress Hills. • The scientific name *ober-holseri* honours Dr. Harry Oberholser, one of the finest 20th-century ornithologists. He worked for the U.S. Fish and Wildlife Service and the Cleveland Natural History Museum.

ID: *Sexes similar:* olive brown upperparts; 2 faint, white wing bars; light-coloured eye ring; dark bill with orange at the base of the lower mandible; white throat; long, dark tail trimmed with white.

Size: *L* 13–15 cm.

Status: uncommon from May to August

Habitat: deciduous forests, willow thickets, mixed coniferous forests and avalanche slopes.

Nesting: in the crotch of a small shrub; small cup nest is made of weeds, plant fibres, feathers, grass and fur; female incubates 3 or 4 eggs for 15–16 days.

Feeding: flycatches for aerial insects; also gleans and hover-gleans leaves, limbs and bark for larval and adult insects.

Voice: *Male:* quick, whistled *tse-beek preet*, rising at the end.

Similar Species: *Willow Flycatcher* (p. 218): no eye ring. *Least Flycatcher* (p. 219): light-coloured lower mandible; call is *che-bec*. *Cordilleran Flycatcher* (p. 222): yellow underparts. *Hammond's Flycatcher* (p. 220): looks practically the same; occurs in mature spruce-fir forest habitats; call is *tse-beek*.

Best Sites: Beauvais Lake PP; Cypress Hills PP; William A. Switzer PP; Jasper NP; Banff NP; Stoney Trail, Kananaskis Country.

CORDILLERAN FLYCATCHER
Empidonax occidentalis

After launching from an exposed perch, a Cordilleran Flycatcher demonstrates the foraging technique characteristic of its family—it snaps up a flying insect in mid-air and then loops back to the same perch it vacated moments earlier. • The Cordilleran Flycatcher arrives in Alberta's Rocky Mountains in May and begins nesting in the latter part of June. • 'Hawking' and 'sallying' are other words used interchangeably with 'flycatching.' • The Cordilleran Flycatcher and the Pacific-slope Flycatcher were formerly lumped together in one species, called the Western Flycatcher. Although they are now regarded as distinct species, their similar field characteristics and vocalizations remain a troubling issue that perpetuates their uncertain status. Although the Cordilleran Flycatcher is generally thought to be the type found in Alberta, some people believe, based on vocalizations, that both Pacific-slope and Cordilleran flycatchers occur here. • The scientific name *occidentalis* is Latin for 'western.'

ID: *Sexes similar:* olive green upperparts; 2 white wing bars; yellowish throat; light-coloured eye ring; orange lower mandible.
Size: *L* 14 cm.
Status: rare from May to September.
Habitat: coniferous and riparian woodlands or shady deciduous forests, often near seepages and springs.
Nesting: in a cavity in a small tree, bank, bridge or cliff face; lines the cavity with moss, lichens, plant fibres, bark, fur and feathers; female incubates 3 or 4 eggs for 15 days.

Feeding: flycatches for insects.
Voice: *Male:* call is a chipper whistle: *swee-deet.*
Similar Species: *Willow Flycatcher* (p. 218) and *Western Wood-Pewee* (p. 215): no eye rings. *Least* (p. 219), *Hammond's* (p. 220) and *Dusky* (p. 221) *flycatchers:* lack the almond-shaped eye ring and the completely orange lower mandible; songs are very useful in field identification.
Best Sites: Bow River valley and High-wood River valley along the eastern slopes of the Rockies.

EASTERN PHOEBE
Sayornis phoebe

Although many birds pump their tails while perched, few Alberta species can match the zest and frequency of the Eastern Phoebe's tail wag. • The Eastern Phoebe's nest building and territorial defence is normally well underway by the time most other songbirds arrive in Alberta in mid-May. Eastern Phoebes might reuse nest sites for many years, or they might choose a new location. Whatever the case, the nest is always protected from spring rains by some kind of roof.

Eastern Phoebes frequently build their mud nests on buildings, so their courting and territorial behaviours are easily enjoyed by their human landlords. • Too often, people unnecessarily remove phoebes' mud nests from outbuildings. Because of this bird's insectivorous diet, it can be effective at controlling pests. Mind you, an old nest can harbour enough mites to cause a household problem after the birds leave for the winter.

ID: *Sexes similar:* grey-brown upperparts; light underparts; no eye ring; no obvious wing bars; all-black bill; faint yellow-green belly; dark legs; frequently flicks its tail.
Size: *L* 17–18 cm.
Status: common from April to August.
Habitat: forest edges and clearings, near lakes or rivers.
Nesting: under the ledge of a building, picnic shelter, culvert, bridge, cliff or well; cup-shaped, mud nest is lined with moss, grass, fur and feathers; female incubates 4 or 5 eggs for 16 days.

Feeding: flycatches flying beetles, flies, wasps, grasshoppers, mayflies and other insects; occasionally plucks aquatic invertebrates and small fish from the water's surface.
Voice: hearty, snappy *fee-bee*, delivered frequently; call is a sharp *chip*.
Similar Species: *Western Wood-Pewee* (p. 215): smaller; greyish underparts. *Olive-sided Flycatcher* (p. 214): dark vest. *Empidonax flycatchers* (pp. 216–22): most have an eye ring and wing bars. *Say's Phoebe* (p. 224): larger; apricot belly.
Best Sites: Fish Creek PP; Cold Lake PP.

SAY'S PHOEBE

Sayornis saya

The Say's Phoebe is a flycatcher that is partial to rocky environments in Alberta, although it is often seen in moist parkland clearings as well. It often nests under a ledge, shielded from harsh weather, and it frequently reuses nesting sites from year to year. The Say's Phoebe is remarkably tolerant of arid conditions; it is capable of extracting all the water it requires from the insects it eats. • This large, handsome flycatcher, with its soft brown plumage and apricot belly, has a subtle beauty, but its habit of flicking its tail while perched might be its most diagnostic trait. • This species is the only bird whose genus and species names are derived from the same person, Thomas Say, a versatile naturalist whose primary contributions were in the field of entomology.

ID: *Sexes similar:* apricot belly and undertail coverts; dark tail; brown-grey breast and upperparts; dark head; no eye ring; very faint wing bars.

Size: *L* 19 cm.

Status: uncommon from May to early September.

Habitat: open areas and shrublands, often near cliffs or building.

Nesting: in a cavity on a cliff face, on a beam or under a bridge, eave or other structure; nest is made with grass, moss and fur; female incubates 4 or 5 eggs for up to 17 days.

Feeding: flycatches for aerial insects; also gleans buildings and vegetation for insects.

Voice: call is a softly whistled *pee-ter* or *pee-ur;* song is *pitseedar.*

Similar Species: *Other flycatchers:* all lack the apricot belly.

Best Sites: Dinosaur PP; Writing-on-Stone PP.

GREAT CRESTED FLYCATCHER
Myiarchus crinitus

More typical of eastern North America, the Great Crested Flycatcher only occurs regularly at a few spots in Alberta. Despite its irregular occurrence in our province, few species are as typical of the parkland natural region, and there are several well-documented incidents of breeding. • The Great Crested Flycatcher's nesting habits are unusual for a flycatcher. It is a cavity nester, and it will even use nest boxes intended for bluebirds. Elsewhere in North America, the Great Crested Flycatcher has been known to have unusual tastes in decor: it occasionally lays a shed snakeskin as a door mat for its nest entrance. The purpose of this uncommon, but noteworthy, practice is not fully understood. These versatile birds have been known to substitute plastic wrap for genuine reptilian skin.

ID: *Sexes similar:* yellow belly; grey throat; chestnut tail linings; dark olive brown upperparts; small crest; black, heavy bill.
Size: *L* 18–20 cm.
Status: rare to uncommon from mid-May to September.
Habitat: deciduous and mixedwood forests, near clearings or edges; occasionally in more open sites.
Nesting: in a cavity or nest box, often lined with grasses, bark strips and feathers; infrequently hangs a shed snakeskin or plastic wrap from the hole; female incubates 5 eggs for 13–15 days.
Feeding: often in the upper branches of deciduous trees, where it flycatches for aerial insects; might also glean caterpillars and occasionally fruit.
Voice: loud, whistled *wheep.*
Similar Species: *Yellow-bellied Flycatcher* (p. 216) and *other flycatchers:* smaller; lack the chestnut tail linings.
Best Sites: Cold Lake PP; Muriel Lake; Vermilion PP.

225

WESTERN KINGBIRD
Tyrannus verticalis

The tumbling aerial courtship display of the Western Kingbird makes for an entertaining spring scene. Twisting and turning all the way, the male flies about 20 m up into the air, stalls, and then tumbles, flips and twists as he falls towards the ground. • Western Kingbirds are commonly seen surveying for prey from fenceposts, barbed wire and power lines. Once a kingbird spots an insect, it might chase its prey for up to 15 m before a capture is made. If you have ever chased these same species with an insect net, you know the kingbird does very well indeed. • Throughout much of Alberta, the Western Kingbird is not as common as its eastern counterpart. Where numbers of this bird do occur, it is prized by Alberta's naturalist community. • The scientific name *verticalis* refers to this bird's hidden, red crown patch, which is flared in courtship displays and in combat with rivals.

ID: *Sexes similar:* grey head and breast; yellow belly and undertail coverts; dark brown tail; white outer tail feathers; white chin; black bill; ashy grey upperparts; dark grey mask; thin, orange-red crown.
Size: *L* 20–23 cm.
Status: locally common from May to September.
Habitat: open areas and willow and cottonwood stands in agricultural, open and riparian areas.
Nesting: near the trunk of deciduous tree; frequently on human structures, such as barns, towers and power pole crossbeams; cup nest is lined with fur, twigs, roots and feathers; female incubates 4 or 5 eggs for 14 days.

Feeding: flycatches aerial insects, such as bees, wasps, butterflies and moths; occasionally eats berries.
Voice: chatty, twittering *whit-ker-whit*; also *pkit-pkit-pkeetle-dot.*
Similar Species: *Eastern Kingbird* (p. 227): black upperparts; white underparts.
Best Sites: Kinbrook Island PP; Dinosaur PP.

EASTERN KINGBIRD

Tyrannus tyrannus

When you think of a tyrant animal, images of a large carnivorous dinosaur are much more likely to come to mind than a little bird. True as that might be, no one familiar with the pugnacity of the Eastern Kingbird is likely to refute its scientific name, *Tyrannus tyrannus*. This kingbird is a brawler, and it will fearlessly attack crows, hawks and even humans that pass through its territory. Intruders are often vigorously pursued, pecked and plucked for some distance, until the kingbird is satisfied that there is no further threat.
• The butterfly-like courtship flight of the Eastern King-
bird, characterized by short, quivering wingbeats,
belies the gentle side of this species's personality.
• Eastern Kingbirds rarely walk or hop on the
ground. They prefer to fly, even for very short
distances. • The red crown, for which kingbirds are named, is rarely seen outside the
courtship season.

ID: *Sexes similar:* black upperparts; white underparts; white-tipped tail; black bill; small crest; thin orange-red crown; no eye ring; black legs.
Size: *L* 22 cm.
Status: locally common from May to August.
Habitat: open areas with willow and birch shrubs, agricultural areas and riparian regions.
Nesting: on a horizontal limb; also in cavities and human-made structures; pair builds the cup nest with plant fibres, grass, roots, feathers and fur; female incubates 3 or 4 eggs for up to 14 days.
Feeding: flycatches aerial insects; infrequently eats berries.
Voice: call is a quick, loud, chattering *kit-kit-kitter-kitter;* also a buzzy *dzee-dzee-dzee.*
Similar Species: *Tree Swallow* (p. 244): lacks the black back and the white-tipped tail; more streamlined.
Best Sites: Dinosaur PP; Writing-on-Stone PP; Kinbrook Island PP.

NORTHERN SHRIKE
Lanius excubitor

This predatory songbird is the winter replacement for the Loggerhead Shrike in Alberta. Although most of the Northerns we see are migrants, a few breed in Alberta's far north, and a greater number can be found all winter in the southern half of our province. The fact that the Northern Shrike is a winter species, while the Loggerhead Shrike is here in summer, makes distinguishing between these similar birds less onerous for the average birder. • The Northern Shrike looks a little like a grey robin with the bill of a small hawk, and it can kill and eat small birds and rodents. When this shrike strikes, it seizes its prey with its feet and pecks at the animal with its hooked-bill until it succumbs. • The Northern Shrike's macabre habit of impaling its kills on thorns and barbs has earned it the names 'butcher bird' and 'nine-killer.' *Lanius* is Latin for 'butcher,' and *excubitor* is Latin for 'watchman' or 'sentinel'—'watchful butcher' is an appropriate description of the Northern Shrike's foraging behaviour.

ID: *Sexes similar. Adult:* black tail and wings; pale grey upperparts; finely barred, light underparts; black mask does not extend above the hooked bill. *Immature:* faint mask; light brown upperparts. *In flight:* white wing patches; white-edged tail.
Size: *L* 25 cm.
Status: rare to uncommon from October to April; mostly migratory; rare in northern Alberta in summer.
Habitat: shrublands, grasslands and roadsides.
Nesting: on the taiga; in spruce, willows or shrubs; loose, bulky nest is made with sticks, bark and moss.
Feeding: swoops down on prey from a perch or chases prey through the air; regularly eats small birds, shrews and rodents; commonly takes insects if they are available.
Voice: usually silent; infrequently calls a grating *shek shek* during migration.
Similar Species: *Loggerhead Shrike* (p. 229): summer resident; adult's black mask extends above the bill; juvenile has brownish-grey, barred upperparts.
Best Sites: Wabamun Lake PP (winter); Beaverhill Lake (migration).

LOGGERHEAD SHRIKE

Lanius ludovicianus

Like a regular songbird, the Loggerhead Shrike sings to establish its territory and attract a mate, but it also displays its prey impaled on thorns and barbed wire. These trophies demonstrate a male's hunting competence to female shrikes. (They might also serve as a means of storing excess food items during times of plenty.) In spring, you can often see dead birds, small mammals, insects and reptiles skewered out in the sun—it's reminiscent of the way some people used to display the carcasses of hawks and coyotes. • Although a drive through southern Alberta ranchland can easily turn up a dozen Loggerhead Shrikes, conservationists are concerned about this species's future. Loggerhead Shrikes are thought to be doing poorly on their winter ranges and where prairie habitat is replaced by cropland. • The Loggerhead Shrike has very acute vision and an uncanny memory for the location of its food stores. • This bird is called 'loggerhead' because of its proportionally large head.

ID: *Sexes similar. Adult:* black tail and wings; grey crown and back; white underparts; barred flanks; black mask extends above the hooked bill. *In flight:* white wing patches; white-edged tail. *Juvenile:* brownish-grey, barred upperparts.

Size: *L* 23 cm.

Status: uncommon from April to early October.

Habitat: open areas with shrublands and grasslands.

Nesting: in a low crotch in a shrub or small tree; bulky cup nest is made with twigs and grass and lined with fine materials; female incubates 5 or 6 eggs for 15–17 days.

Feeding: swoops down on prey from a perch or attacks in pursuit; regularly eats small birds, rodents and shrews; will commonly take insects if they are available; also eats carrion.

Voice: *Male:* bouncy hiccup, *hugh-ee hugh-ee*, during summer; infrequently a harsh *shack-shack*.

Similar Species: *Northern Shrike* (p. 228): winter resident; adult is larger and has finely barred underparts; immature has a faint mask and brown-grey, unbarred upperparts. *Northern Mockingbird* (p. 277): quite rare; lacks the black mask; generally more sleek and slim.

Best Sites: ranchland in southeastern Alberta; Jenner to Bindloss area.

229

BLUE-HEADED VIREO

Vireo solitarius

From the canopies of mature deciduous and mixedwood forests, the deliberate notes of the Blue-headed Vireo penetrate through the dense foliage. The distinctive 'spectacles' that frame this bird's eyes provide a good field mark, and they are among the boldest of eye rings belonging to our songbirds. • During courtship, male Blue-headed Vireos fluff out their yellowish flanks and bob ceremoniously to their prospective mates. Once mating and egg laying are complete, the elusive character of these birds is transformed, and a menacing and protective parent emerges—these vireos aggressively defend their nests against all threats. Even so, Brown-headed Cowbirds manage to find temporarily vacated vireo nests in which to lay their eggs. As human development continues to carve through northern Alberta, cowbirds might pose an increasing threat to their Blue-headed hosts.

ID: *Sexes similar:* white 'spectacles'; 2 white wing bars; blue-grey head; green upperparts white underparts; yellow flanks; dark tail; stout bill; dark legs.

Size: *L* 14 cm.

Status: uncommon to common from May to mid-September.

Habitat: coniferous forests mixed with deciduous trees, frequently with dense understorey shrubs.

Nesting: in a horizontal fork in a coniferous tree; hanging, basket-like cup nest is made of

grass, roots, plant down, spider silk and cocoons; pair incubates 4 eggs for 14 days.

Feeding: gleans foliage for invertebrates; occasionally hover-gleans to pluck insects from vegetation.

Voice: *Male:* slow, purposeful, robin-like notes: *look up … see me … here I am.*

Similar Species: *Cassin's Vireo* (p. 231): greenish head. *Warbling Vireo* (p. 232), *Red-eyed Vireo* (p. 234) and *Tennessee Warbler* (p. 284): all lack the white 'spectacles.'

Best Sites: Cold Lake PP; Sir Winston Churchill PP.

CASSIN'S VIREO
Vireo cassinii

Southwestern Alberta must appear welcoming to birds: so many of our rarest species enter the province through mountain passes in this region. The Cassin's Vireo is no exception, and this West Coast bird rarely ventures far enough east to lose sight of the mountains. • Recently, the American Ornithologists' Union gave its support to the notion that what was once called the Solitary Vireo actually constitutes three species, as was suggested by molecular systematics and behavioural studies. The other two species are the Blue-headed Vireo and the Plumbeous Vireo. Despite what birders might think about so-called 'fashions,' in which some systematists prefer to lump species together while others are prone to splitting, the goal of all serious reclassifications is to reflect the reality of species in nature. • John Cassin was one of the world's greatest bird taxonomists, and it is appropriate that five birds have been named in his honour.

ID: *Sexes similar:* white 'spectacles'; 2 white wing bars; green head and upperparts; white underparts; green flanks; dark tail; stout bill; dark legs.
Size: *L* 14 cm.
Status: rare to uncommon from May to mid-September.
Habitat: coniferous forests mixed with deciduous trees, frequently with dense understorey shrubs.
Nesting: in a horizontal fork in a coniferous tree; hanging, basket-like

cup nest is made of grass, roots, plant down, spider silk and cocoons; pair incubates 4 eggs for 14 days.
Feeding: gleans foliage for invertebrates; occasionally hover-gleans to pluck insects from vegetation.
Voice: *Male:* slow, purposeful, robin-like notes: *vreeip? vreeip!*
Similar Species: *Blue-headed Vireo* (p. 230) blue head. *Warbling Vireo* (p. 232), *Red-eyed Vireo* (p. 234) and *Tennessee Warbler* (p. 284): all lack the white 'spectacles.'
Best Site: Waterton Lakes NP.

231

WARBLING VIREO
Vireo gilvus

When the first Warbling Vireo of the year is heard in Alberta, usually before the end of May, its wondrous voice often initially confuses even experienced listeners. Warbling Vireos are often inadvertently overlooked, because they are among the dullest looking and most nondescript of our forest birds. Lacking any splashy field marks, they are exceedingly difficult to spot, unless a bird suddenly moves from one leaf-hidden stage to another. The Warbling Vireo ranks high among Alberta's songsters, however, and its often-repeated song, with its oscillating quality, delights anyone listening. The phrases finish on an upbeat, as if asking a question of the woods. It often takes a bit of neck-craning searching to find the bird itself, however, and once it is in view its song is often forgotten while searching for a visual clue to its identity. • There are two subspecies of Warbling Vireo represented in Alberta—they might be classified into separate species when their status is better understood—but they are almost impossible to tell apart in the field.

ID: *Sexes similar:* white eyebrow; no wing bars; olive-grey upperparts; greenish flanks; light underparts; grey crown.
Size: *L* 14 cm.
Status: uncommon to common from mid-May to early September.
Habitat: open deciduous forests.
Nesting: in a horizontal fork in a deciduous tree or shrub; hanging, basket-like cup nest is made of grass, roots, plant down, spider silk and a few feathers; pair incubates 4 eggs for 12 days.

Feeding: gleans foliage for invertebrates; occasionally hovers and plucks insects from vegetation.
Voice: *Female:* occasionally sings from the nest. *Male:* musical warble: *I love you I love you Ma'am* or *iggly wiggly iggly piggly iggly eeek.*
Similar Species: *Red-eyed Vireo* (p. 234): black eye line extends to the bill; blue-grey crown. *Tennessee Warbler* (p. 284): grey head; olive back. *Orange-crowned Warbler* (p. 285): smaller; darker underparts.
Best Site: Inglewood Bird Sanctuary, Calgary.

PHILADELPHIA VIREO
Vireo philadelphicus

While many similar-looking birds sound quite different, the Philadelphia Vireo and Red-eyed Vireo are two species that sound very similar but are easy to tell apart once you get them in the binoculars. Most forest songbirds are initially identified by voice, however, so the Philadelphia Vireo is often neglected because its song is nearly identical to the more abundant Red-eyed Vireo. Like most other vireos, Phillies are difficult to observe; they seem to prefer to perch and sing near the tops of exceptionally leafy trees. • This bird bears the name of the city in which the first scientific specimen was collected. Philadelphia was the centre of America's scientific community in the early 1800s; much of the study of birds and other natural sciences originated in Pennsylvania.

ID: *Sexes similar:* white eyebrow; yellow breast and flanks; greyish head; dark eye line extends forward to the bill; dark olive green upperparts; white belly; thick bill.
Size: *L* 13 cm.
Status: uncommon from mid-May to mid-September.
Habitat: willow stands in deciduous forests.
Nesting: high up in a deciduous tree or shrub; basket-like cup nest hangs from a horizontal fork and is made of grass, roots, plant down and spider silk; pair incubates 4 eggs for up to 13 days.

Feeding: gleans foliage and other vegetation for invertebrates; frequently hovers to search for food in foliage.
Voice: *Male:* song is a continuous, robin-like run of phrases: *Look-up way-up Tree-top see-me Here-I-am*; perhaps a little higher-pitched than a Red-eyed Vireo.
Similar Species: *Red-eyed Vireo* (p. 234): black-bordered, blue-grey cap; lacks the yellow wash on the belly; song is slightly lower pitched. *Warbling Vireo* (p. 232): dusky eye line; lacks the yellow wash on the belly. *Tennessee Warbler* (p. 284): well-defined, grey cap; greenish back.
Best Sites: foothills west of Calgary.

RED-EYED VIREO

Vireo olivaceus

The Red-eyed Vireo is the undisputed champion of vocal endurance in Alberta. In spring and early summer, males sing continuously through the day until long after most songbirds have chosen to curtail their melodies—usually five or six hours after sunrise. One patient ornithologist estimated that this vigorous vireo sings its phrases up to 21,000 times a day. Red-eyes sound a lot like American Robins, and beginning birdwatchers are often delighted to discover this nifty bird, hiding behind a 'familiar' song, right in front of their eyes.

• Red-eyed Vireos adopt a particular stance when they hop up and along branches. They tend to be more hunched over that other songbirds, like a gargoyle, and they hop with their bodies diagonal to their direction of travel.

• For a songbird to have red eyes is quite uncommon. Red eyes tend to be more prevalent in non-passerines, such as accipiters, grebes and some herons. There is no firm agreement about the reason for this vireo's eye colour. • Red-eyed Vireos are frequently parasitized by Brown-headed Cowbirds.

ID: *Sexes similar:* white eyebrow; black eye line; black-bordered, blue-grey crown; olive green upperparts; olive cheek; light underparts; no wing bars; red eyes (seen only at close range).

Size: *L* 15 cm.

Status: common from mid-May to mid-September.

Habitat: deciduous forests with semi-open canopies and shrublands.

Nesting: in a horizontal fork in a deciduous tree or shrub; hanging, basket-like cup nest is made of grass, roots, spider silk and cocoons; female incubates 4 eggs for 11–14 days.

Feeding: gleans foliage for insects, especially caterpillars; also eats berries.

Voice: call is a cat-like meow. *Male:* song is a continuous, robin-like run of phrases, with distinct pauses in-between: *Look-up way-up tree-top see-me Here-I-am.*

Similar Species: *Philadelphia Vireo* (p. 233): yellow belly; lacks the black border to the blue-grey cap. *Warbling Vireo* (p. 232): dusky eye line does not extend to the bill.

Best Site: Edmonton river valley.

GRAY JAY

Perisoreus canadensis

There is no other bird in Alberta that can equal the Gray Jay for boldness. Small family groups glide slowly and unexpectedly out of conifer forests, attracted by any foreign sound or potential feeding opportunity. They are well known to anyone who camps or picnics in the mountains or the boreal forest. These 'Camp Robbers,' 'Whiskey Jacks' or whatever else they are affectionately called locally, quickly welcome themselves to any passers by.

• Gray Jays lay their eggs and begin incubation as early as late February. Their nests are well insulated to conserve heat, and nesting early means the jays will be feeding their quickly growing nestlings when the forests are full of food in spring. • Gray Jays often store food. They have specialized salivary glands that they use to coat the food with a sticky mucous, which helps preserve the food. • 'Whiskey Jack' is derived from the Algonquin name for this bird, *wiskedjack*.

ID: *Sexes similar. Adult:* fluffy, pale grey plumage; long tail; light forehead; darker on the back of the head; dark grey upperparts; light grey underparts; white cheek; dark bill. *Immature:* dark sooty grey overall.

Size: *L* 29 cm.

Status: locally common year-round.

Habitat: dense and open coniferous and mixed forests, townsites, scenic overlooks and campgrounds.

Nesting: in the crotch of a conifer tree; bulky, well-insulated nest is made with plant fibres, roots, moss, twigs, feathers and fur;

female incubates 3 or 4 eggs for 17 days.

Feeding: searches the ground and vegetation for insects, fruit, songbird eggs and nestlings, carrion and berries; stores food items.

Voice: complex vocal repertoire; soft, whistled *quee-oo*; chuckled *cla-cla-cla*; also imitates other birds.

Similar Species: *Clark's Nutcracker* (p. 238): adult has a heavy black bill and a black-and-white tail and wings. *Northern Shrike* (p. 228): black mask; black-and-white wings and tail.

Best Sites: Waterton Lakes NP; Kananaskis Country; Banff NP; Jasper NP.

STELLER'S JAY

Cyanocitta stelleri

The Steller's Jay is the classic crested jay of areas west of the Continental Divide, where Blue Jays never venture, and it is the provincial bird of B.C. In Alberta, Stellers are spotted most often in the Rockies, but their only stronghold appears to be Waterton Lakes National Park. During the coldest months, these remarkably beautiful birds drop down into the townsite to feed greedily and clumsily on hanging and platform feeders. They tend not to stay in town in summer; instead they retreat to Cameron Lake and other higher-elevation sites. Wintering Steller's Jays have been seen at all the other mountain towns in Alberta, and they occasionally wander east out onto the prairies as well. • Steller's Jays are bold, and like all corvids they will not hesitate to steal food scraps from inattentive picnickers. • George Wilhelm Steller, the first European naturalist to visit Alaska, collected the 'type' specimen of this species.

ID: *Sexes similar:* glossy blue plumage; black head and nape; large, black crest; white streaks on the forehead and chin; wings and tail are accentuated by dark blue.
Size: *L* 29 cm.
Status: locally uncommon year-round.
Habitat: coniferous and mixed forests, campgrounds, picnic areas and townsites.
Nesting: in the crotch of a conifer tree; bulky stick and twig nest is lined with mud, grass and conifer needles; female incubates 4 eggs for 16 days.
Feeding: searches the ground and vegetation for insects, small vertebrates and various other food items; forages in treetops for nuts, berries and other birds' eggs; visits bird feeders during winter.
Voice: harsh, noisy *shack-shack-shack*, along with a variety of other calls.
Similar Species: *Blue Jay* (p. 237): white underparts; black 'necklace'; white wing bar.
Best Site: Waterton Lakes NP.

BLUE JAY
Cyanocitta cristata

The Blue Jay embodies all the aggressive virtues of the corvid family: it is beautiful, resourceful and vocally diverse, but at times it can become almost too loud and mischievous. Only the Black-billed Magpie is louder, and interactions between these two species can be amusing. We have watched jays hide peanuts under leaves, only to have them stolen and re-buried by magpies, reclaimed by the jays, and so on. • With its loud call, blue-and-white plumage and large crest, the Blue Jay is familiar to anyone with sunflower seeds or peanuts at their birdfeeder. • The Blue Jay has been able to expand its range westward over the years, partly as a result of the spread of human development. Feeders and landfills enable wintering birds to cope with harsh winters, and forest fragmentation has invited the jays deeper into the once impenetrable forests. Canmore, in particular, has seen a tremendous increase in Blue Jay numbers in recent years. • If you have several Blue Jays visiting your yard, you can try to recognize individual birds by their characteristic head patterns.

ID: *Sexes similar:* blue crest; black 'necklace'; blue upperparts; white underparts; white flecking on the wings; white wing bar; black bill.
Size: *L* 28 cm.
Status: common year-round.
Habitat: mixed deciduous forests, agricultural areas and townsites.

Nesting: in the crotch of a tree or tall shrub; pair builds a bulky stick nest and incubates 4 or 5 eggs for 18 days.
Feeding: forages on the ground and among vegetation for nuts, berries, eggs, nestlings and birdseed; also eats insects and carrion.
Voice: noisy, screaming *jay-jay-jay;* nasal *too-wheedle too-wheeled,* like the horn of a Model-T Ford; also imitates other sounds.
Similar Species: *Steller's Jay* (p. 236): dark hood; dark underparts.
Best Sites: cities and towns, particularly Edmonton and Red Deer.

237

CLARK'S NUTCRACKER

Nucifraga columbiana

The Clark's Nutcracker is reason alone to travel to Alberta's mountains. More than any other songbird, it provides the perfect complement to the snow-capped peaks of the Rockies. These birds have loud, dominant personalities, and they make themselves known at many viewpoints and picnic areas in our mountain parks. Their aggression is really misunderstood curiosity fed by the unhealthy food offerings of tourists. When nutcrackers see you coming from a lookout perch, they swoop down boldly to take advantage of their human visitors. • Nutcrackers store most of the food they collect during the summer. In winter, they have an amazing ability to retrieve a good proportion of the thousands of items they buried up to nine months previously. • When Captain William Clark first collected this bird, its large, straight bill misled the famous western explorer into believing it was a woodpecker. • Despite its name, this bird actually 'cracks' more conifer cones than nuts.

ID: *Sexes similar:* light grey head, back and underparts; large, black bill; black wings with flashy, white inner wing patches. *In flight:* black central tail feathers; white outer tail feathers.
Size: L 30–33 cm.
Status: uncommon to common year-round.
Habitat: open coniferous and mixed forests, scenic overlooks, krummholz forests and townsites; moves to lower elevations in winter.

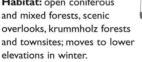

Nesting: on a horizontal limb; twig and stick platform nest is lined with grass and strips of bark; pair incubates 2–4 eggs for 16–22 days, starting in March.
Feeding: forages on the ground and among trees for pinecones; hammers the cones with its bill; also eats insects; stores food for winter.
Voice: loud, harsh, squawking *kra-a-a-a-a.*
Similar Species: *Gray Jay* (p. 235): grey wings and tail.
Best Sites: Lake Louise and Peyto Lake, Banff NP; Mt. Edith Cavell, Jasper NP.

BLACK-BILLED MAGPIE
Pica pica

The saying 'familiarity breeds contempt' is well illustrated by the Black-billed Magpie in Alberta. Truly among North America's most beautiful birds, magpies are too often discredited because of their raucous and aggressive demeanor. Most Albertans are jaded by the omnipresence of magpies, but eastern visitors to our province are often captivated by their beauty and approachability. • The Black-billed Magpie is one of the most exceptional architects among our birds. The elaborate domed nest that it constructs can be found in a spruce or deciduous tree or on an iron bridge. Constructed of sticks and held together with mud, the domed compartment conceals and protects the eggs and young from harsh weather and predators. The nests are so well constructed that abandoned sites remain in trees for years, often serving as nest sites for non-builders, such as owls. • For those who think magpies should be destroyed because 'they kill songbirds,' we refer you to the many dozens of common songbirds treated in this book, and the fact that the magpie has failed to eliminate even one species among them.

ID: *Sexes similar:* long, black tail; black head, breast and back; rounded, black-and-white wings; black undertail coverts; black bill; white belly.
Size: *L* 46–56 cm.
Status: very common year-round.
Habitat: open forests, agricultural areas, riparian thickets, townsites and campgrounds.

Nesting: in a tree or tall shrub; domed stick and twig nest is often held together with mud; female incubates 5–8 eggs for up to 24 days.
Feeding: forages on the ground for insects, carrion and garbage; picks insects and ticks off large ungulates.
Voice: loud, nasal, frequently repeated *ueh-ueh-ueh*; also many other vocalizations.
Similar Species: none.
Best Sites: cities and towns; mountain parks.

AMERICAN CROW
Corvus brachyrhynchos

American Crows are wary and intelligent birds that have flourished in spite of considerable efforts, over many generations, to reduce their numbers. Crows are not ecological specialists, and part of their strength lies in their generalized habits, which allow these highly adaptable birds to do well in a variety of environments. • In most parts of North America, crows remain year-round, but most birds recognize the perils of an Alberta winter and migrate southward from the province by the end of November. • In fall, when their reproductive duties are completed, American Crows group together in flocks of thousands. These thrilling aggregations (known as 'murders') are merely get-togethers in preparation for evening roosts and preambles for the fall exodus. • The scientific name, *Corvus brachyrhynchos*, despite sounding cumbersome, is Latin for 'raven with the small nose.'

ID: *Sexes similar:* all-black body; fan-shaped tail; black bill and legs; slim, sleek head and throat; thin bill.

Size: *L* 43–53 cm; *W* 94 cm.

Status: very common from mid-March to October; a few remain throughout winter.

Habitat: urban areas, agricultural fields and shrublands.

Nesting: in coniferous or deciduous trees and on power poles; large stick and branch nest is lined with fur and soft plant materials; female incubates 4–6 eggs for up to 18 days.

Feeding: very opportunistic; feeds on carrion, small vertebrates, other birds' eggs and nestlings, berries, seeds, invertebrates and human garbage.

Voice: distinctive, far-carrying, repetitive *caw-caw-caw.*

Similar Species: *Common Raven* (p. 241): larger; wedge-shaped tail; shaggy throat.

Best Sites: cities and towns, particularly at the University of Calgary in September and early October.

COMMON RAVEN

Corvus corax

Whether stealing food from a flock of gulls, harassing a Bald Eagle in mid-air, dining from a roadside carcass or confidently strutting among campers at a park, the raven is worthy of its reputation as a clever bird. It might well be the smartest bird in Alberta. Glorified in cultures worldwide, the Common Raven does not act by instinct alone. Whether tumbling aerobatically through the air, delivering complex vocalizations or sliding playfully down a snowbank on its back, this raucous bird demonstrates behaviours that many people think of as exclusively human.
• Their deep, hoarse *quork*, with a multitude of variations, demonstrates a complexity in language and behaviour that is only now revealing its secrets to patient ornithologists. • Few birds naturally occupy as large a natural range as the raven, but Alberta's mountain parks and northern communities remain some of the most reliable places in which to experience their habits. In recent years, they have become more common in the parkland region as well.

ID: *Sexes similar:* all-black plumage; heavy, black bill; wedge-shaped tail; shaggy throat; rounded wings.
Size: *L* 61 cm; *W* 127 cm.
Status: uncommon to common year-round.
Habitat: grasslands, shrublands, townsites, campgrounds and landfills.
Nesting: on power poles, steep cliffs and tall conifer trees; large stick and branch nest is lined with fur and soft plant materials; female incubates 4–6 eggs for 18–21 days.

Feeding: very opportunistic; feeds on carrion, small vertebrates, other birds' eggs and nestlings, berries, invertebrates and hoofed mammal afterbirth.
Voice: deep, guttural, far-carrying, repetitive *craww-craww* or *quork quork*; also many other vocalizations.
Similar Species: *American Crow* (p. 240): smaller; rounded tail; slim throat; slimmer bill; call is a higher-pitched *caw*.
Best Sites: Banff; Canmore; Jasper; Fort McMurray; Turner Valley area.

HORNED LARK

Eremophila alpestris

Horned Larks are easy to see but tough to identify when they fly dangerously close to the front of your car on gravel roads in the prairies. They usually change course an instant before a fatal collision, briefly showing their distinct black tail feathers. Their first instinct when threatened is to outrun their pursuer on the ground. Cars can easily overtake them, however, so they take to the air when their first attempt to flee fails. • Late winter is also a good time to observe these open country specialists as they congregate in huge flocks on farm fields, often in the company of Snow Buntings. Most of these birds are destined to migrate north with the first hints of warmth. Horned Larks are among the earliest of our courting birds, and their high, melodic voices show why larks are such well-respected birds. • Despite this bird's widespread choice of habitat, its scientific name, which means 'lark of the mountains,' refers only to its alpine haunts.

♂

ID: *Male:* small black 'horns' (often not raised); black line running under the eye from the bill to the cheek; light yellow to white face; dull brown upperparts; black breast band; dark tail with white outer tail feathers; light throat. *Female:* less distinctive head patterning; duller plumage overall.
Size: *L* 18 cm.
Status: common from February to November; a few winter in southern Alberta.
Habitat: open areas, including alpine tundra, fields and roadways.

Nesting: on the ground; in a shallow scrape lined with grass, plant fibres and roots; female chooses the nest site and incubates 3 or 4 eggs for up to 12 days.
Feeding: gleans the ground for seeds; occasionally feeds its young insects during the breeding season.
Voice: tinkling *tsee-titi,* given in flight.
Similar Species: *Open-country sparrows* (pp. 309–16) and *longspurs* (pp. 334–37): all lack the facial pattern and the black outer tail feathers.
Best Sites: gravel roads near Lethbridge, Taber and Medicine Hat.

PURPLE MARTIN
Progne subis

If only Purple Martins were as common as their apartment-style houses! House Sparrows and European Starlings are often blamed for the failure of a Purple Martin house to attract birds, but they might not be the problem. For best results, place the house high on a pole in the middle of a large, open area near water and paint it white, so that the birds do not overheat. A Purple Martin colony can provide an endlessly entertaining summer spectacle: the adults spiral around the house, and the young perch clumsily at the opening of their apartment cavity.
• When young martins leave their nests, they usually spend some time on the ground before mastering flight. During that time, the parents are prone to diving and screaming at people, and the effect can be hair raising in the extreme. • The scientific name of our largest swallow, *Progne,* refers to the Pandion's daughter, who changed herself into a swallow in Greek mythology.

ID: *General:* dark blue, glossy body; slightly forked tail; pointed wings; small bill. *Male:* dark underparts. *Female:* grey underparts.
Size: *L* 18–20 cm.
Status: uncommon from May to August
Habitat: *Nesting:* near semi-open forests, often near water. *In migration:* over rivers, reservoirs and agricultural areas.
Nesting: communal; usually in a human-made, apartment-style birdhouse, rarely in tree cavities or other natural cavities; nest materials include feathers,

grass, mud and vegetation; female incubates 4 or 5 eggs for 15–16 days.
Feeding: mostly in flight; usually eats flies, ants, bugs, dragonflies and mosquitoes; might also walk on the ground, eating insects and rarely berries.
Voice: rich, fluty, robin-like *pew-pew,* often heard in flight.
Similar Species: *European Starling* (p. 275): longer bill; lacks the forked tail. *Barn Swallow* (p. 248): deeply forked tail; creamy brown underparts.
Best Sites: individual martin houses in appropriate locations.

TREE SWALLOW
Tachycineta bicolor

Tree Swallows, our most common summer swallows, typically perch beside their fencepost nest boxes. When conditions are favourable, these busy birds are known to return to their nest site and feed their young 10 to 20 times an hour, which provides observers with plenty of opportunity to watch and photograph the birds. They are among the most proficient of Alberta insect eaters, gracefully catching even the most elusive flying insects in mid-air. • When Tree Swallows leave their nests to forage, they frequently cover their eggs with feathers from the nest. These swallows are so enticed by feathers that nest-building parents will sometimes swoop down to get feathers tossed in the breeze. • In the bright spring sunshine, the back of the Tree Swallow appears blue; prior to the fall migration the back appears to be green. • The scientific name *bicolor* is Latin for 'two colours,' in reference to the contrast between this bird's dark upperparts and white underparts.

ID: *Sexes similar. Adult:* iridescent blue-green head and upperparts; white underparts; no white on the cheek; dark rump; small bill; long, pointed wings; shallowly forked tail. *Female:* slightly duller. *Immature:* brown above; white below.
Size: *L* 14 cm.
Status: common from mid-April to August.
Habitat: open areas, such as beaver ponds, marshes, fields, townsites and open woodlands.
Nesting: in a tree cavity or nest box; nest is made of weeds, grass and feathers; female incubates 4–6 eggs for up to 19 days.
Feeding: catches flies, beetles and ants on the wing; also takes stoneflies, mayflies and caddisflies over water.
Voice: alarm call is a metallic, buzzy *klweet.*
Similar Species: *Violet-green Swallow* (p. 245): white cheek; white rump patches. *Bank Swallow* (p. 247): brown upperparts. *Northern Rough-winged Swallow* (p. 246): light brown smudge on the upper breast.
Best Sites: individual nest boxes in appropriate locations.

VIOLET-GREEN SWALLOW
Tachycineta thalassina

Because of its affinity for cliffs and rocky places, the range of the Violet-Green Swallow in Alberta includes both the mountains and the badlands, along with a few big cliffs along the valleys of the prairie rivers. Within these superficially dissimilar areas, Violet-greens can routinely be seen darting above cliffs and rivers in the leisurely pursuit of flying insect prey. • At first sight, Violet-greens look an awful lot like Tree Swallows, which is to be expected, given their close relationship. • Swallows occasionally eat mineral-rich soil, egg shells and exposed shellfish fragments, possibly to recoup the minerals lost during egg laying. In this way, 80-million-year-old clam beds are slowly being recycled and incorporated into the living tissues of these birds. • Swallows are swift and graceful flyers, routinely travelling at speeds of 50 km/h. • The scientific name *thalassina* is Latin for 'sea green,' a tribute to this bird's body colour.

ID: *Sexes similar:* iridescent blue-green plumage; white underparts; white on the cheek; white rump patches; small bill; long, pointed wings; shallowly forked tail; small feet. *Female:* duller and more bronze than the male.

Size: *L* 13 cm.

Status: uncommon from late April to August.

Habitat: open environments, including beaver ponds, marshes, townsites and mixed woodlands.

Nesting: in a tree cavity, rock crevice or nest box; nest is made of weeds, grass and feathers; female incubates 4–6 eggs for up to 15 days.

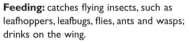

Feeding: catches flying insects, such as leafhoppers, leafbugs, flies, ants and wasps; drinks on the wing.

Voice: buzzy, trilling *tweet tweet*; harsh *chip-chip*.

Similar Species: *Tree Swallow* (p. 244): lacks the white cheek and the white rump patches. *Bank Swallow* (p. 247) and *Northern Rough-winged Swallow* (p. 246): brown upperparts; lack the white cheek.

Best Sites: Milk River valley; Bow Valley PP; Banff NP.

NORTHERN ROUGH-WINGED SWALLOW

Stelgidopteryx serripennis

Northern Rough-winged Swallows are almost the same colour as the sandy banks in which they live. These loners nest in burrows along rivers and streams, enjoying their own private piece of waterfront. They don't mind joining a crowd when foraging, however, and they often appear in mixed flocks of swallows 'hawking' insects over a river or lake. • An early 20th-century ornithologist once caught a Northern Rough-winged Swallow and released it 50 km from its nest. He immediately drove back to where he had captured the bird, only to find it feeding its nestlings. • Unlike other Alberta swallows, male Northern Rough-wings have curved barbs along the outer edge of their primary wing feathers. The purpose of this saw-toothed edge remains a mystery to ornithologists. The ornithologist who initially named this bird must have been very impressed with its wings: *Stelgidopteryx* (scaper wing) and *serripennis* (saw feather) refer to this unusual characteristic.

ID: *Sexes similar:* brown upperparts; light brownish-grey underparts; small bill; dark cheek; dark rump. *In flight:* long, pointed wings; notched tail.
Size: L 14 cm.
Status: uncommon to common from late April to August.
Habitat: open areas, such as rivers, lakes and marshy areas.
Nesting: occasionally in small colonies; at the end of a burrow lined with leaves and dry grass; sometimes reuses kingfisher burrows, rodent burrows and other land crevices.
Feeding: catches flying insects on the wing; occasionally eats insects from the ground; drinks on the wing.
Voice: generally quiet; occasionally a quick, short, squeaky *brrrtt.*
Similar Species: *Bank Swallow* (p. 247): dark breast band. *Tree Swallow* (p. 244): female has green upperparts and a clean white breast. *Violet-green Swallow* (p. 245): female has green upperparts, a white cheek, white rump patches and a white breast.
Best Sites: Whitemud Creek ravine, Edmonton; Inglewood Bird Sanctuary, Calgary.

BANK SWALLOW
Riparia riparia

A colony of Bank Swallows can be a constant flurry of activity as the birds pop in and out of their earthen burrows between foraging or other dutiful flights. These small birds diligently excavate their own burrows, first with their small bills and later with their feet. Incredibly, Bank Swallows have been known to excavate burrows 1.5 m long, but the typical length is a mere 60–90 cm. • In medieval Europe, it was thought that swallows spent winter in the mud at the bottom of swamps, since they were not seen during that season. That belief is untrue, but it might have been started by the existence of a ground-nesting swallow. • *Riparia* is from the Latin for 'riverbank,' which is a common nesting site for this bird. If you approach a colony by canoe, the birds will burst from their burrows in the hundreds and circle nervously until the river carries you safely away. • When you are trying to identify this swallow, there is a simple rule to remember: bankers wear vests and so do Bank Swallows. • In Europe, the Bank Swallow is known as the Sand Martin. ('Martin' is just a name for a large swallow, the way 'eagle' refers to a large hawk.)

ID: *Sexes similar:* brown upperparts; light underparts; brown breast band; long, pointed wings; shallowly forked tail; white throat; dark cheek; small legs.
Size: *L* 13 cm.
Status: uncommon to common from May to August.
Habitat: steep banks, lakeshores and open areas.
Nesting: colonial; in a burrow in a steep earthen bank; pair excavates the cavity and incubates 4 or 5 white eggs for up to 16 days.

Feeding: catches flying insects; drinks on the wing.
Voice: twittering chatter: *speed-zeet speed-zeet.*
Similar Species: *Northern Rough-winged Swallow* (p. 246): lacks the dark breast band. *Violet-green Swallow* (p. 245): green upperparts; white cheek and rump patches; lacks the dark breast band. *Tree Swallow* (p. 244): lacks the dark breast band; greenish upperparts.
Best Sites: Laurier Park, Edmonton; Inglewood Bird Sanctuary, Calgary.

BARN SWALLOW

Hirundo rustica

Although Barn Swallows do not occur in mass colonies, they are the most familiar swallow to most Albertans because they usually build their nests on human structures. In the eaves of barns or picnic shelters, or in any other structure that provides protection from the rain, this swallow's cup-shaped mud nest is nestled up high away from terrestrial predators. Because of this close human association, it is not uncommon for a nervous parent bird to dive repeatedly at 'intruders,' forcibly encouraging them to retreat. • Unfortunately, not everyone appreciates the craftsmanship of the mud nests, and many Barn Swallow families have been unceremoniously scraped off a building just as the nesting season has begun. These graceful birds are natural pest controllers, and, in our opinion, a Barn Swallow nest full of hungry babies is a much finer sight than a half circle of dried mud on the wall from which such a nest has been scraped. • 'Swallow tail' is a term used to describe something that is deeply forked. In Alberta, the Barn Swallow is the only swallow that displays this feature.

ID: *Sexes similar:* long, deeply forked tail; rust-coloured throat and forehead; blue-black upperparts; rust- to buff-coloured underparts; long, pointed wings.
Size: *L* 18 cm.
Status: common from May to August.
Habitat: near rivers, lakes, marshes, bridges, culverts and other structures in open country and cities.
Nesting: on a wall, under a roof, on a bridge, in a culvert or in a cave; cup nest is made of mud; pair incubates 4–7 eggs for 12–17 days.
Feeding: catches flying insects on the wing.
Voice: constantly buzzy, electric chatter: *zip-zip-zip;* also *kvick-kvick.*
Similar Species: *Cliff Swallow* (p. 249): squared-off tail; light-coloured rump and underparts.
Best Sites: just about any farm building or picnic shelter that is not frequently disturbed.

CLIFF SWALLOW
Petrochelidon pyrrhonota

If the Cliff Swallow were to be renamed in the 20th century, it would probably be called the 'Bridge Swallow,' because almost every river bridge in Alberta seems to have a colony under it. Clouds of Cliff Swallows will sometimes whip up on either side of the roadway, especially when the colony is in the process of nest building. If you stop to inspect the underside of a bridge, you might see hundreds of gourd-shaped nests stuck to the pillars and structural beams. Cliff Swallows are always ready to take flight, and an intrusion seems to produce many more birds than the nest colony could possibly house.
• Master mud masons, Cliff Swallows roll mud into balls with their bills and press the pellets together to form their characteristic nests within several days. Brooding parents peer out the circular neck of the nest, with their gleaming eyes watching the world go by. • During years of high run off and prolonged rains, floods can wipe out entire nesting colonies of Cliff Swallows.
• The Cliff Swallow is the species that predictably returns each spring to the Capistrano mission in California.

ID: *Sexes similar:* square tail; buffy rump; blue-grey head and wings; cream-coloured forehead; rusty cheek, nape and throat; buffy breast; white belly; spotted undertail coverts.
Size: *L* 14 cm.
Status: locally common from May to August.
Habitat: steep banks, cliffs, bridges and buildings near watercourses; forages over water, fields and marshes.
Nesting: colonial; under bridges and on cliffs and buildings; builds a

gourd-shaped mud nest with a small opening near the bottom; pair incubates 4 or 5 eggs for up to 16 days.
Feeding: catches flying insects on the wing; occasionally eats berries; drinks on the wing.
Voice: twittering chatter: *churrr-churrr,* also an alarm call: *nyew.*
Similar Species: *Barn Swallow* (p. 248): deeply forked tail; dark rump; rust-coloured underparts.
Best Sites: Dinosaur PP; Wyndham-Carseland PP; Chateau Lake Louise, Banff NP; Blindman River bridge on Hwy. 2.

BLACK-CAPPED CHICKADEE

Poecile atricapillus

Flocks of Alberta's most lovable bird flit from tree to tree, scouring branches and shrivelled leaves for insects. In fall, they are joined by warblers and vireos, and in winter they sometimes associate with nuthatches. Spring finds them paired off raising families, and the newly fledged young forage with the parents in summer.
• Black-capped Chickadees commonly visit backyard feeders during winter, and they are easily enticed to an outstretched hand that offers a sunflower seed. • Most songbirds, including Black-capped Chickadees, have both songs and calls. The chickadee's *pee-oo-oo* song is delivered primarily during courtship, to attract mates and to defend territories. The *chick-a-dee-dee-dee* call, which can be heard year-round, is used to keep flocks together and to maintain contact among the birds.
• The scientific name *atricapillus* is Latin for 'black crown.'

ID: *Sexes similar:* black cap and bib; white cheek; grey back and wings; white under-parts; light buff sides; dark legs.
Size: L 13–15 cm.
Status: common to very common year-round.
Habitat: aspen forests, riparian woodlands, urban areas, backyard feeders, willow groves and mixed forests.
Nesting: in a natural cavity or an abandoned woodpecker nest; can excavate a cavity in soft, rotting wood; lines the nest with fur, feathers, moss, grass and

cocoons; female incubates 6–8 eggs for up to 13 days.
Feeding: gleans vegetation, branches and the ground for small insects and spiders; visits backyard feeders; also eats conifer seeds and invertebrate eggs.
Voice: call is a chipper, whistled *chick-a-dee-dee-dee*; song is a simple, whistled *swee-tee* or *pee-oo-oo.*
Similar Species: *Mountain Chickadee* (p. 251): white eyebrow; black eye line. *Boreal Chickadee* (p. 253): grey-brown cap and flanks. *Chestnut-backed Chickadee* (p. 252): rusty back and flanks; dark brown cap.
Best Sites: backyard feeders; Edmonton.

MOUNTAIN CHICKADEE
Poecile gambeli

The Mountain Chickadee breeds at higher elevations than our other chickadees, and it occurs most commonly, and appropriately, in the mountains. In winter, these year-round residents sometimes forage right up to the timberline. It is more common, however, for them to move down into the montane forests for winter. • Townsites in the mountains offer excellent viewing opportunities in winter, especially at feeders—scan the flocks of chickadees and you will often find Mountain, Black-capped and Boreal chickadees foraging together. • When intruders approach the nest of a chickadee, both parents flutter their wings and hiss loudly at the perceived threat. Chickadee nests are attractive to insects, and bumblebees have been known to invade a chickadee cavity and chase the small bird from its nest. • The scientific name *gambeli* honors William Gambel, a 19th-century ornithologist who died of typhoid fever in the Sierra Nevada at the age of 28.

ID: *Sexes similar:* white eyebrow through the black cap; white cheek; black bib; grey upperparts and tail; light grey underparts.
Size: *L* 13 cm.
Status: uncommon year-round.
Habitat: coniferous forests, especially old-growth spruce-fir forests, and occasionally shrubby areas, aspen forests and urban areas.
Nesting: in a natural cavity or abandoned woodpecker nest; can excavate a cavity in soft, rotting wood; lines the nest with fur, feathers, moss or grass; incubates 5–9 eggs for up to 14 days.
Feeding: gleans vegetation, branches and the ground for insects and spiders; visits feeders; also eats conifer seeds and invertebrate eggs.
Voice: song is a sweet, clear, whistled *fee-bee-bay*; call is chick *a-dee a-dee a-dee*.
Similar Species: *Black-capped Chickadee* (p. 250): lacks the white eyebrow. *Boreal Chickadee* (p. 253): grey-brown cap and flanks. *Chestnut-backed Chickadee* (p. 252): rusty back and flanks; dark brown cap.
Best Sites: Waterton Lakes NP; Banff NP; Jasper NP; Canmore; Bow Valley PP.

CHESTNUT-BACKED CHICKADEE
Poecile rufescens

The Chestnut-backed Chickadee is typically a bird of the West Coast, but it extends its range into a narrow region of the Rocky Mountains, following the cool, moist cedar and fir forests eastward from the coast. Every year, a few of these rusty birds wander into the Waterton Lakes area. They have been seen regularly in the park ever since 1939. The rest of Alberta doesn't seem to suit them, however, and there are few records of this species occurring regularly in our province outside Waterton. To date, no evidence of breeding has turned up in Alberta.
• With its dark brown cap and rusty back and flanks, the Chestnut-backed Chickadee is the most colourful member of its family. • 'Chickadee' is an onomatopoeic derivation of these birds' calls. The scientific name *rufescens* is from the Latin for 'to become reddish.'

ID: *Sexes similar:* dark brown cap; black bib; rusty back and flanks; white cheek; light underparts; grey wings and tail.
Size: *L* 12 cm.
Status: locally rare year-round.
Habitat: moist coniferous forests.
Nesting: does not nest in Alberta.

Feeding: gleans vegetation, branches and the ground for small insects and spiders; also eats conifer seeds.
Voice: rapid, whistled *tsick-a-dee-dee*.
Similar Species: *Mountain Chickadee* (p. 251): white eyebrow; black eye line. *Black-capped Chickadee* (p. 250): black cap; grey back; buffy flanks. *Boreal Chickadee* (p. 253): grey-brown cap and flanks.
Best Site: Waterton Lakes NP.

BOREAL CHICKADEE
Poecile hudsonicus

Alberta is well blessed with chickadees, in terms of both species and individuals. Birdwatchers generally love these energetic little 'tits,' and the Boreal Chickadee is especially sought-out as the northern representative of this endearing troupe. Softer-spoken and more introverted than the Black-cap, the Boreal slips into the great forest communities in the northern parts of our province. • Chickadees burn so much energy that they must replenish their stores daily to survive the winter—they have insufficient fat reserves to survive a prolonged stretch of cold weather. Chickadees store food for winter in holes and bark crevices. • During cold winter nights, all chickadees enter into a state of torpor, in which the bird's metabolism slows so that it uses less energy. • The scientific name *hudsonicus* refers to the northern (Hudsonian) region of Canada.

ID: *Sexes similar:* grey-brown cap; black bib; grey-brown flanks; light grey underparts; light brownish back; white cheek patch.
Size: *L* 13–14 cm.
Status: uncommon to common year-round.
Habitat: mature and young spruce and fir forests.
Nesting: excavates a cavity in soft, rotting wood or uses a natural cavity or abandoned woodpecker nest in a conifer tree; female lines the nest with fur, feathers, moss and grass; female

incubates 5–8 eggs for around 15 days.
Feeding: gleans vegetation, branches and infrequently the ground for small tree-infesting insects (including their pupae and eggs) and spiders; also eats conifer seeds.
Voice: soft, nasal, whistled *scick-a day day day.*
Similar Species: *Black-capped Chickadee* (p. 250): black cap; buffy flanks. *Mountain Chickadee* (p. 251): white eyebrow; black eye line.
Best Sites: Canmore; Bow Valley PP; Sir Winston Churchill PP.

RED-BREASTED NUTHATCH
Sitta canadensis

The nasal *yank-yank-yank* call of the Red-breasted Nuthatch is a very familiar sound throughout the forested regions of Alberta. The distinctiveness of this bird's voice and its willingness to join mixed flocks of warblers, chickadees and kinglets makes it a common sight. • The Red-breasted Nuthatch smears the entrance of its nesting cavity with sap. This sticky doormat could inhibit ants and other insects from entering the nest chamber—some of these small creatures can be a serious threat to nesting success. • Red-breasted Nuthatches visit their neighbourhood birdfeeder 'cafeteria' with great regularity, but they dart in like missiles, never lingering longer than it takes to grab a seed and dash off again to eat it or stash it in seclusion. • The scientific name *canadensis* means 'of Canada.' (Species named after places usually have scientific names that end with *-ensis;* species named after men end with *-i;* species named after women end with *-ae*).

ID: *General:* rusty underparts; grey-blue upperparts; white eyebrow; black eye line; black cap; straight bill; short tail; white cheek. *Male:* deeper rust on the breast; black crown. *Female:* light red wash on the breast; grey crown.
Size: *L* 11 cm.
Status: common year-round.
Habitat: spruce-fir and pine forests.
Nesting: excavates a cavity or uses an abandoned woodpecker nest; usually smears the entrance with sap; nest is made of

bark shreds, grass and fur; female incubates 5 or 6 eggs for 12 days.
Feeding: forages down trees while probing under loose bark for larval and adult invertebrates; eats many pine and spruce seeds during winter; visits feeders.
Voice: slow, continually repeated, nasal *yank-yank-yank.*
Similar Species: *White-breasted Nuthatch* (p. 255): lacks the black eye line and the red underparts. *Mountain Chickadee* (p. 251): black bib; lacks the red breast.
Best Sites: backyard feeders; Edmonton river valley.

WHITE-BREASTED NUTHATCH

Sitta carolinensis

The White-breasted Nuthatch carries a built-in surprise: it looks like a normal songbird, but then it begins to forage on tree trunks upside down! To nuthatches, this gravity-defying act is as natural as flying and laying eggs. • White-breasted Nuthatches frequently visit backyard feeders throughout much of Alberta. In the parkland and southern boreal forest they are a reliable sight, but places in southern Alberta, such as Medicine Hat, can go many winters without having a good 'invasion' of White-breasts. • Unlike woodpeckers and creepers, a nuthatch does not use its tail to brace itself against a tree trunk—nuthatches clasp the trunk through foot power alone. • The scientific name *carolinensis* means 'of the Carolinas'—an indication of this bird's more southern breeding distribution than its Red-breasted cousin.

♂

ID: *Sexes similar:* white underparts; white face; grey-blue back; rusty undertail coverts; short tail; straight bill; short legs. *Male:* black cap. *Female:* dark grey cap.
Size: *L* 15 cm.
Status: common year-round.
Habitat: aspen and mixed-wood forests and backyards.
Nesting: in a natural cavity or an abandoned woodpecker nest in a large deciduous tree; lines the cavity with bark, grass, fur

and feathers; female incubates 5–8 eggs for up to 14 days.
Feeding: forages down trees headfirst in search of larval and adult invertebrates; also eats many nuts and seeds; regularly visits feeders.
Voice: frequently repeated *yarnk-yarnk-yarnk.*
Similar Species: *Red-breasted Nuthatch* (p. 254): black eye line; rusty underparts. *Chickadees* (pp. 250–53): all have a black bib.
Best Sites: backyard feeders; Edmonton river valley.

BROWN CREEPER
Certhia americana

Creepers are downright hard to find. Embracing old-growth mixed and coniferous forests, they often go unnoticed until part of a tree trunk suddenly takes the shape of a bird. Intent on its feeding, the creeper spirals up large trees trunks, myopically plucking hidden invertebrate morsels from bark fissures with its tweezer-like bill. When it reaches the upper branches, the creeper takes a short flight down to the base of a neighbouring tree to begin another grooming ascent. When Brown Creepers are frightened, they freeze and flatten against tree trunks, becoming even tougher to see. • The thin whistle of a Brown Creeper is so high-pitched that it is beyond the hearing of some birders. Even if you can hear the creeper's call, it can be hard to tell it from a Golden-crowned Kinglet's or even a Bohemian Waxwing's. • There are many species of creepers in Europe and Asia, but the Brown Creeper is the only one found in North America.

Nesting: under loose bark; nest is made with grass and conifer needles woven together with spider silk; female incubates 5 or 6 eggs for 15–17 days.

Feeding: hops up trunks and large limbs, probing loose bark for adult and larval invertebrates.

Voice: faint, high-pitched *trees-trees-trees see the trees.*

Similar Species: *Nuthatches* (pp. 254–55): grey-blue back. *Black-and-white Warbler* (p. 299): black-and-white plumage; shorter tail. *Woodpeckers* (pp. 203–12): all lack the brown back streaking and have a straight bill.

Best Sites: Whitemud Creek ravine, Edmonton; Cave and Basin Trail and Fenland Trail, Banff NP.

ID: *Sexes similar:* brown back is heavily streaked with greyish white; white eyebrow; white underparts; down-curved bill; long, pointed tail feathers; rusty rump.

Size: *L* 13 cm.

Status: uncommon year-round.

Habitat: mainly coniferous forests, such as spruce, fir and pine.

ROCK WREN
Salpinctes obsoletus

If you are out in the bentonite clay and sandstone cliffs of Alberta's badlands, watch for a stone-like bird sitting high on a hill, singing loudly. The Rock Wren, a small grey bird, chooses this stark and barren landscape in which to nest. It moves secretly, helped by the convoluted topography that makes the badlands such an easy place to hide. • The Rock Wren is well suited to its chosen home: it has a rather flattened body that allows it to compress itself and squeeze into crevices and cracks to avoid the midday heat. • Rock Wrens display the unusual habit of 'paving' a walkway to their nests. They sometimes adorn their gravel welcome mat with up to 1500 carefully placed stones and pebbles, although typically only a few are used. • It is during the cooler hours of the day, around dawn and dusk, that these birds are most easily seen and heard, their songs echoing through the eroded landscape.

ID: *Sexes similar:* grey-brown upperparts; light underparts; white throat; finely streaked, white breast; rusty brown rump and tail; downcurved bill; tail is trimmed with buff-coloured tips.
Size: *L* 15 cm.
Status: locally uncommon from May to August.
Habitat: rocks and cliffs.
Nesting: in a small crevice or hole in a cliff; places small stones at the opening; nest is made of grass and rootlets and

lined with a variety of items; incubates 5 or 6 eggs for up to 14 days.
Feeding: forages on the ground and picks up insects and spiders from around and under rocks.
Voice: harsh *tra-lee tra-lee tra-lee*; long, drawn out, melodious *keree keree keree*, *chair chair chair, deedle deedle deedle, tur tur tur, keree keree trrrrrr.*
Similar Species: *House Wren* (p. 258): brown upperparts; shorter bill.
Best Sites: Dinosaur PP; Writing-on-Stone PP; Grassi Lakes, above Canmore.

HOUSE WREN
Troglodytes aedon

The House Wren's cheery song and energetic demeanor make it a welcome addition to any neighbourhood. A family of wrens in a classic wren box can brighten a backyard, but they do become a nuisance when they fill all boxes but their own with tightly packed twigs. Like so many other examples of 'bad manners' in birds, this tendency is best accepted rather than despised. • There is at least one pair of nesting House Wrens in many older communities in Alberta. In towns, however, they are generally overshadowed by House Sparrows, so a country visit gives a better chance to appreciate this joyful bundle of birdlife. • In Greek mythology, Zeus transformed Aedon, the queen of Thebes, into a nightingale. The wonderfully bubbling call of the House Wren is somewhat similar to a nightingale's.

ID: *Sexes similar:* unstreaked, brown upperparts; faint eyebrow; short 'cocked up' tail is finely barred with black; faint eye ring; throat is lighter than the underparts.
Size: *L* 12 cm.
Status: uncommon to common from May to early September.
Habitat: aspen forests, shrublands and dense understorey vegetation.
Nesting: typically at low elevations; often in a natural cavity or abandoned woodpecker nest; also in bird boxes; nest is made with sticks and grass and lined with feathers, fur and other soft materials; incubates 6–8 eggs for up to 19 days.
Feeding: gleans the ground and vegetation for insects, especially beetles, caterpillars, grasshoppers and spiders.
Voice: smooth, running, bubbly warble—*tsi-tsi-tsi-tsi oodle-oodle-oodle-oodle*—that lasts about 2–3 seconds.
Similar Species: *Winter Wren* (p. 259): shorter tail; darker overall; dark barring on the flanks.
Best Sites: older communities throughout Alberta.

WINTER WREN
Troglodytes troglodytes

Winter Wrens boldly announce their claim to a patch of spruce-fir woodland, where they often make their homes in the upturned roots of fallen trees. The song of the Winter Wren is distinguished by its melodious, bubbly tone and its uninterrupted length. No other singer in Alberta can sustain their song for up to 10 music-packed seconds. • When it is not singing, the Winter Wren can be observed skulking beneath the forest understorey, probing the nooks and crannies for food. While the female incubates the eggs and raises the young, the male helps out by bringing food, but he sleeps elsewhere in his own nest. • *Troglodytes* is Greek for 'creeping in holes' or 'cave dweller.' This bird's common name might refer to the fact that they winter regularly in the northern U.S. and coastal B.C. Only a few records exist of Winter Wrens braving Alberta's harsh winters.

ID: *Sexes similar:* very short, 'cocked up' tail; dark brown upperparts; light brown underparts; fine, light eyebrow; dark barring on the flanks.

Size: *L* 10 cm.

Status: uncommon from mid-April to August.

Habitat: spruce and fir forests with dense understoreys; often near water.

Nesting: in an abandoned woodpecker cavity, in a natural hole, under bark or under upturned tree roots; bulky nest is

made with twigs, moss, grass and fur; male frequently builds up to 4 'dummy' nests prior to egg-laying; female incubates 6 or 7 eggs for up to 16 days.

Feeding: forages on the ground and on trees for beetles, wood borers and other invertebrates.

Voice: *Male:* song is a tumbling warble of quick notes, often more than 8 seconds long.

Similar Species: *House Wren* (p. 258): tail is longer than the leg; less barring on the flanks.

Best Sites: Sir Winston Churchill PP; Johnston Canyon and Lake Louise, Banff NP.

SEDGE WREN

Cistothorus platensis

Like most other wrens, the Sedge Wren is secretive and difficult to observe, and this bird is the least familiar of all our Alberta wrens. Its haunts include sedge meadows and long grasses, although a meadow populated with these birds one summer can be strangely empty the following year. • Once the male Sedge Wrens arrive on their territories, they set out on a construction frenzy. The energetic males might build several incomplete nests throughout their territory before the females arrive. The females are toured around to choose a nest, which is then soon completed by the male in preparation for egg-laying. The 'dummy' nests scattered around the territory are not wasted: they often serve as dormitories for young and adult birds late in the season. • The Sedge Wren used to be called the Short-billed Marsh Wren. The scientific name *platensis* refers to the Rio de la Plata in Argentina.

ID: *Sexes similar:* short, narrow tail (often cocked up); faint, light eyebrow; slightly streaked crown; faint stripes on the back; barring on the wing coverts; dirty white underparts; buff-orange flanks.

Size: L 10–11.5 cm.

Status: rare from May to August.

Habitat: sedge meadows and grassy fields.

Nesting: usually less than 1 m from the ground; well-built globe is woven from sedge and grass leaves and has a side entrance; female incubates 4–8 eggs for up to 14 days.

Feeding: forages low in dense vegetation, where it picks and probes for adult and larval insects and spiders; occasionally catches flying insects.

Voice: rattling trill: *chap-chap-chap-chap, chap, chap p-p-r-r-r-r.*

Similar Species: *Marsh Wren* (p. 261): broad, obvious white eyebrow; heavily streaked back; unstreaked crown.

Best Sites: Beaverhill Lake area; check with local birders for recent sightings.

MARSH WREN
Cistothorus palustris

The energetic and reclusive Marsh Wren is almost always associated with cattail marshes or dense, wet meadows. Although it prefers to stay hidden in the deep vegetation, its distinctive, old-fashioned sewing machine song is one of the characteristic voices of our wetlands. Patient observers might be rewarded with a brief glimpse of a Marsh Wren perching atop a cattail reed as it quickly evaluates its territory. • Marsh Wrens occasionally destroy the nests and eggs of other Marsh Wrens and blackbirds. Red-winged Blackbirds, in turn, occasionally destroy the nest and eggs of Marsh Wrens. • Like other wrens, male Marsh Wrens are feverish nest builders—they might build up to 20 nests, which later serve as decoys or dummy nests for their would be enemies. Although a female might be attracted by a male's construction talents, she only lays her eggs in a nest of her own building. • The scientific name *palustris* is Latin for 'marsh.'

ID: *Sexes similar:* white chin; lighter brown upperparts; black triangle on the upper back, streaked with white; white eyebrow; unstreaked, brown crown; long, thin, down-curved bill.
Size: L 13 cm.
Status: uncommon to common from late April to October.
Habitat: cattail and bulrush marshes.
Nesting: in cattail marshes; globe-like nest is woven with cattails, bulrushes, weeds and grass and lined with cattail down; female incubates 4–6 eggs for 12–16 days.

Feeding: gleans vegetation and flycatches for adult aquatic invertebrates, especially dragonflies and damselflies; occasionally eats other birds' eggs.
Voice: *Male:* rapid series of *zig-zig-zig-zig*, like an old sewing machine.
Similar Species: *Sedge Wren* (p. 260): streaked crown; buff underparts. *House Wren* (p. 258): faint eyebrow; lacks the white streaking on the back.
Best Sites: Slack Slough; Beaverhill Lake.

AMERICAN DIPPER
Cinclus mexicanus

The American Dipper is an unusual songbird: along fast-flowing mountain waters, it stands on a streamside rock, doing deep knee bends; then it zips upstream and dives into the water, disappearing momentarily below the surface as it hunts for insects while walking underwater. The dipper's stout body, strong claws and thick feathers enable it to survive these frigid forays. • The American Dipper's loud, ringing song, which it sings even in the depth of winter, can be heard above the roar of rivers and the babbling of brooks. It is wren-like, a clue to their related-ness. • John Muir wrote: 'Find a fall, or cascade, or rushing rapid ... and there you will find the complementary Ouzel, flitting about in the spray, diving in foaming eddies, whirling like a leaf among beaten foam-bells; ever vigorous and enthusiastic, yet self-contained, and neither seeking nor shunning your company.' ('Water Ouzel' is an old name for the American Dipper.)

ID: *Sexes similar. Adult:* slate grey plumage; head and neck are darker than the body; short tail; short neck; pinkish legs; straight, black bill; stout body. *Immature:* lighter bill; light underparts.
Size: L 19 cm.
Status: uncommon to common year-round.
Habitat: *Summer:* fast-flowing creek, stream and river edges. *Winter:* open water, often at lower elevations.
Nesting: under a rock ledge,

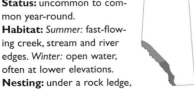

overhang, uprooted tree or bridge; bulky globe nest is made of moss and grass; nest entrance faces the water; female incubates 4 or 5 eggs for up to 17 days.
Feeding: wades or flies through the water or plunges below the surface for aquatic larval insects, fish fry and eggs.
Voice: vocal throughout the year; song is clear and melodious; alarm call is a harsh *tzeet.*
Similar Species: none.
Best Sites: all mountain streams; Johnston Canyon, Banff NP; Canmore (winter).

GOLDEN-CROWNED KINGLET

Regulus satrapa

Kinglets often flock together to forage. They use branches as swings and trapezes, flashing their regal crowns and constantly flicking their tiny wings. It is remarkable that a tiny insect-eating bird can survive our winters, and in that respect they are even more amazing than chickadees. • Golden-crowned Kinglets are among the regular participants in bird waves that work through coniferous forests. Although they often forage high in the trees, their behaviour and indifference to humans normally makes them easy to observe. Their ever-present, high-pitched voices are faint and are often lost in the slightest woodland breeze, but Golden-crowned Kinglets are continually on the move, so once they are heard, they can be spotted darting across open areas in the canopy. • *Regulus* is derived from the Latin word for 'king.'

ID: *General:* olive back; darker wings and tail; light underparts; dark cheek; 2 white wing bars; black eye line; white eyebrow; black border to the crown. *Male:* reddish-orange crown. *Female:* yellow crown.
Size: *L* 10 cm.
Status: uncommon to common from late March to October; rare in winter.
Habitat: mixed and pure forests of spruce, pine and fir.
Nesting: usually in a spruce tree;

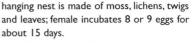

hanging nest is made of moss, lichens, twigs and leaves; female incubates 8 or 9 eggs for about 15 days.
Feeding: gleans and hovers for insects, some berries and occasionally sap.
Voice: faint, high-pitched, accelerating *tsee-tsee-tsee-tsee, why do you shilly-shally?*
Similar Species: *Ruby-crowned Kinglet* (p. 264): eye ring; lacks the black border to the crown.
Best Sites: Jasper NP; Fenland Trail and Cave and Basin Trail, Banff NP.

263

RUBY-CROWNED KINGLET

Regulus calendula

The loud, long, rolling song of the Ruby-crowned Kinglet echoes through Alberta's coniferous forests in May and June. It is one of the most frequently heard birds in forested areas, and it is not uncommon to hear the song of this bird, the wind in the branches and not much else. • The male holds his small ruby crown erect during courtship to impress prospective mates. Throughout most of the year, however, the crown remains hidden among the dull feathers on top of the bird's head, invisible even to binoculars.

• Mass movements of kinglets can make it difficult to sort these birds from the superficially similar wood warblers and vireos.

• As a beginner, John referred to this species as the 'in-the-mood bird,' because he was unable to get a look at anything other than its underside, and the main part of its song sounded much like the famous Benny Goodman tune.

ID: *General:* olive green upperparts; dark wings and tail; 2 strong, white wing bars; incomplete eye ring; light underparts; short tail; flicks its wings. *Male:* small red crown (usually not seen). *Female:* no crown.
Size: L 10 cm.
Status: common from late April to late October.
Habitat: lodgepole pine, fir and black spruce forests.
Nesting: usually in a spruce tree; hanging nest is made of moss, lichens, twigs and leaves; female incubates 7–9 eggs for up to 16 days.

Feeding: gleans and hovers for insects and spiders; infrequently eats seeds and berries.
Voice: song is an accelerating and rising *tea-tea-tea-tew-tew-tew look-at-Me, look-at-Me, look-at-Me* or *Mister-WHAT cha-call-EM what-you-DO ...*
Similar Species: *Golden-crowned Kinglet* (p. 263): dark cheek; black border to the crown; male has an orange crown; female has a yellow crown. *Orange-crowned Warbler* (p. 285): no eye ring or wing bars.
Best Sites: almost all coniferous forests; Vermilion Lakes area, Banff NP.

EASTERN BLUEBIRD

Sialia sialis

Bluebirds are perhaps the most loved birds across North America. Numerous books, poems and songs have been composed to reflect our fascination with these beauties. Eastern Bluebirds are by no means as common as Mountain Bluebirds in Alberta, but this species is occasionally seen between the Cypress Hills and Cold Lake along our eastern border. A few pairs have nested in our province, in bluebird boxes. • The bluebird trails that run along the fenceposts of Alberta's highways have become a wildlife success story whose intrinsic rewards have motivated several generations of Albertans. The erection of new boxes continues to be a valuable process, combined with the essential maintenance of existing nesting cavities. Bluebird boxes are easy to make, and Alberta's long winters provide excellent opportunities to spend time in the woodshop and produce birdhouses. If proper directions are not followed, however, the houses intended for bluebirds will be used to propagate a new generation of bluebird competitors.

♂

ID: *General:* chestnut red breast to chin; light grey belly and undertail coverts; dark bill and legs. *Male:* deep blue head, back and wings; chestnut red flanks. *Female:* light eye ring; grey-brown head and back; blue wings and tail.
Size: *L* 18 cm.
Status: very rare, probably from March to September.
Habitat: open forests and low-elevation grasslands.
Nesting: in an abandoned woodpecker cavity, natural cavity or nest box; nest is built of stems

and twigs; female incubates 4 or 5 eggs for 12–16 days.
Feeding: swoops from a perch and pursues flying insects; also forages on the ground for invertebrates.
Voice: song is a rich, warbling *turr, turr-lee, turr-lee;* call is a chittering *pew.*
Similar Species: *Mountain Bluebird* (p. 267): lacks the red underparts. *Lazuli Bunting* (p. 342): white belly; conical bill; darker upperparts; white wing bars.
Best Sites: check local bird hotlines for any recent sightings.

265

WESTERN BLUEBIRD
Sialia mexicana

The male Western Bluebird wears the colours of the sky on his back and the setting sun on his breast. Unfortunately, this beauty is the rarest of the three bluebirds known in Alberta. There appear to be just a few breeding records of this species in the foothills region, where birds from west of the Rockies settled where they found appropriate habitat. The Western Bluebird has only recently been confirmed as a breeder in Alberta, and very little information exists about its status in the province. Elsewhere, Western Bluebirds normally raise two broods a year.

• Like all blue birds, the feathers of these birds are not actually pigmented blue. The blue colour is a result of the feather's microscopic structure: shiny blues that change hue and intensity with the angle of view are produced by iridescence (like soap bubbles); dull blues come from 'Tyndall scatter,' the same process that produces the blue of the sky.

ID: *General:* chestnut red breast; light grey belly and undertail coverts; dark bill and legs; some chestnut on the back. *Male:* deep blue head, back, wings and chin; chestnut red flanks. *Female:* light eye ring; grey-brown head and back; blue wings and tail.
Size: *L* 18 cm.
Status: very rare, probably from March to September.
Habitat: open forests and low-elevation grasslands.
Nesting: in an abandoned woodpecker cavity, natural cavity or nest box; nest is built of stems, conifer needles and

twigs; female incubates 4–6 eggs for up to 17 days.
Feeding: swoops from a perch and pursues flying insects; also forages on the ground for invertebrates.
Voice: song is a harsh *cheer cheerful charmer;* call is a soft *few* or a harsh *chuck.*
Similar Species: *Mountain Bluebird* (p. 267): lacks the red underparts. *Lazuli Bunting* (p. 342): white belly; conical bill; darker upperparts; white wing bars. *Townsend's Solitaire* (p. 268): never has a reddish breast; buffy patches in the wings and tail.
Best Sites: Turner Valley area; Kootenay Plains, west of Rocky Mountain House.

MOUNTAIN BLUEBIRD
Sialia currucoides

The male Mountain Bluebird is like a piece of spring sky come to life. Just as the last snowbanks melt into the ground, Mountain Bluebirds wing their way into Alberta, spawning Spring Azure butterflies wherever their feather tips flake off—or so we might like to believe. • Bluebirding in Alberta is now better than it has been in quite some time, and it is quite easy to observe roadside pairs throughout much of the province. • The spring and fall migrations of the Mountain Bluebird routinely consist of small groups of birds, but on occasion, Mountain Bluebirds migrate in flocks numbering more than 100. • Natural nest sites, such as woodpecker cavities or holes in badland sandstone, are in high demand, and aggressive starlings often usurp bluebirds from these locations. As a result, bluebirds now turn to the artificial nest boxes that have been established in many rural areas in Alberta.

ID: *General:* black eyes, bill and legs. *Male:* sky blue body; upperparts are darker than the underparts. *Female:* sky blue wings, tail and rump; blue-grey back and head; grey underparts.

Size: *L* 18 cm.

Status: uncommon to common from mid-March to mid-September.

Habitat: open forests, forests edges, burned forests, agricultural areas and grasslands.

Nesting: in an abandoned woodpecker cavity, natural cavity or nest box; nest is built of plant stems, grass, conifer needles and twigs and frequently

lined with a few feathers; female incubates 5 or 6 pale blue eggs for 13 days.

Feeding: swoops from a perch for flying and terrestrial insects; also forages on the ground for a variety of invertebrates, such as beetles, ants and bugs.

Voice: call is a low *turr turr*. *Male:* song is a short warble of *chur* notes.

Similar Species: *Blue Jay* (p. 237): prominent crest. *Townsend's Solitaire* (p. 268): peach-coloured patches in the wings and tail; white outer tail feathers.

Best Sites: Cochrane area; Hwy. 22 south of Longview; Hwy. 14 east of Edmonton; Dinosaur PP.

267

TOWNSEND'S SOLITAIRE
Myadestes townsendi

This slim thrush is frequently observed in the mountains, perched slightly hunched on an exposed limb, surveying the area for food. It flutters out to catch insects in mid-air or follows them to the ground and grasps them with a soft pounce. In flight, the warm, peachy wing linings of this western speciality shine like sunlight through a bedroom window. • Like our other thrush allies, solitaires are early migrants through Alberta. In April and May, Townsend's Solitaires can be spotted not just in the mountains, but in patches of forests in Alberta's grass-lands and parkland areas. • The Townsend's Solitaire is a mountain species throughout most of its range; in Alberta, it has also been known to nest in the Cypress Hills. In winter, it sometimes appears as far east as Edmonton. • During the sum-mer months, solitaires are rarely seen in groups—this solitary tendency is represented in their name.

ID: *Sexes similar. Adult:* grey body; darker wings and tail; peach-coloured wing patches (very evident in flight); white eye ring; white outer tail feathers; long tail. *Immature:* brown body is heavily spotted with buff; pale eye ring.

Size: *L* 22 cm.

Status: uncommon to common from April to October; occasionally overwinters.

Habitat: avalanche slopes and spruce, sub-alpine fir and lodgepole pine forests.

Nesting: on the ground, in a bank or in a hollow snag; cup nest is built with twigs, grass and conifer needles; incubates 4 eggs for up to 13 days; eggs are light blue, patterned with brown.

Feeding: flycatches and gleans vegetation and the ground for invertebrates and berries.

Voice: call is a harsh *piink. Male:* song is a long, bubbly warble.

Similar Species: *Gray Catbird* (p. 276): black cap; red undertail coverts. *Bluebirds* (pp. 265–67): females lack the peach-coloured wing and tail patches and the white outer tail feathers; female Mountain Bluebird has a faint rusty breast.

Best Sites: Bow Valley PP; Jasper NP; Banff NP; Kananaskis Country.

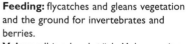

VEERY
Catharus fuscescens

The Veery's voice, like a musical waterfall, descends through liquid ripples. This reclusive forest bird's song is heard far more often than the bird is seen, because the Veery favours thick undergrowth. Don't let that fact deter you; like most thrushes, the Veery is a bird of music, not fashion, and it can be mightily appreciated by voice alone. • The Veery is the most terrestrial of the North American thrushes: it nests and forages on the ground among tangled vegetation. Unlike the American Robin, the Veery does not walk or run; rather, it travels in short springy hops. • When startled by an intruder, the Veery either flushes or faces the threat, exposing its whitish underparts in the hope of concealment. • 'Veery' is a feebly onomatopoeic version of this bird's airy song. The scientific name *fuscescens* is from the Latin word for 'dusky,' in reference to the bird's colour.

ID: *Sexes similar:* brownish back; thin, grey eye ring; moderately spotted throat; light underparts; grey flanks; pinkish legs.
Size: L 18 cm.
Status: uncommon to common from mid-May to September.
Habitat: deciduous forests with a dense, shrubby understorey.
Nesting: on the ground; bulky nest is made with leaves and moss; female incubates 3 or 4 eggs for up to 15 days.

Feeding: gleans the ground and lower vegetation for invertebrates and berries.
Voice: *Male:* song is a musical, descending *da-vee-ur, vee-ur, vee-ur, veer, veer, ver.*
Similar Species: *Swainson's Thrush* (p. 271): bold eye ring; golden face; olive brown upperparts. *Hermit Thrush* (p. 272): reddish rump and tail; brownish back; bold eye ring. *Gray-cheeked Thrush* (p. 270): olive brown upperparts with bold breast spots; typically a migrant.
Best Sites: parkland forests; Fish Creek PP; Weaslehead Natural Area, Calgary.

GRAY-CHEEKED THRUSH

Catharus minimus

Only in Alberta's coolest subartic forests, where stunted black spruce trees are anchored in frost, does the Gray-cheeked Thrush sing its liquid courtship song. This thrush breeds in Alberta's northern Rockies and foothills, and also in the Caribou Mountains. • The Gray-cheeked Thrush is probably the most difficult thrush to see in Alberta. Few people have had the fortune to rest on a bed of lichens and listen to this bird's song, whose musical beauty rivals that of its cousins. Most sightings of this bird come during migration, when Gray-cheeks move through the province in loosely collected flocks. The Gray-cheeked Thrush travels primarily at night, so a morning walk through a park or backyard during their passing often reveals the thrushes hopping about under the cover of shrubs. Like other members of its family, the Gray-cheek will give little opportunity for a clear view, and it will never utter more than a simple warning note during migration.

ID: *Sexes similar:* olive brown upperparts; lightly streaked breast; light underparts; grey face; no eye ring; no wing bars; light-coloured legs.

Size: *L* 16–20 cm.

Status: locally uncommon from May to September; rare in migration.

Habitat: *Breeding:* dwarf black spruce and willow in subarctic environments. *In migration:* forested areas, parks and backyards.

Nesting: usually quite low to the ground in a tree in subarctic forests; nest is woven from twigs, moss and grass; female incubates 4 pale blue eggs for 12–14 days.

Feeding: hops along the ground, picking up insects and other invertebrates; might also feed on berries in trees during migration.

Voice: typically thrush-like in tone: *wee-a, wee-o, wee-a, titi wheeee.*

Similar Species: *Swainson's Thrush* (p. 271): prominent eye ring; golden cheek. *Hermit Thrush* (p. 272): reddish upperparts; lacks the grey cheek. *Veery* (p. 269): reddish upperparts; very light breast spotting.

Best Sites: Caribou Mountains; Jasper NP; Taber PP (spring).

SWAINSON'S THRUSH
Catharus ustulatus

The upward spiral of the Swainson's Thrush's song lifts the soul with each rising echo. This inspiring song can be heard late on spring evenings, because the Swainson's Thrush is routinely the last of the forest songsters to be silenced by nightfall. This thrush is also an integral part of the morning chorus that invites campers back into the waking world, sometimes long before the campers really wish to be awoken. • The Swainson's Thrush is most often seen on its breeding ground, perched high in a treetop and cast in silhouette by the light of dusk. In migration, Swainson's Thrushes skulk about low in the shrubs and even find themselves in the backyards of many wooded neighbourhoods. • This thrush often gives its sharp warning call at some distance—a wary bird, it does not give much opportunity to be seen. • William Swainson was an English zoologist and illustrator. His name also graces the Swainson's Hawk. This bird was formerly known as the Olive-backed Thrush.

ID: *Sexes similar:* olive brown upperparts; bold, white eye ring; golden cheek; moderately spotted throat and breast; white belly and undertail coverts; brownish-grey flanks.
Size: *L* 18 cm.
Status: common from May to September.
Habitat: coniferous and mixed-wood forests and steep ravines.
Nesting: usually in a shrub or small tree; small cup nest is built with grass, moss, leaves, roots and lichens; female incubates 3 or 4 eggs for 12–13 days.
Feeding: gleans vegetation and

forages on the ground for invertebrates; also eats berries.
Voice: song is a slow, rolling, rising spiral: *Oh, Aurelia will-ya, will-ya will-yeee;* call is a sharp *wick.*
Similar Species: *Hermit Thrush* (p. 272): greyish head and back; grey face; heavily spotted breast; lacks the bold eye ring. *Veery* (p. 269): lacks the bold eye ring, the golden face and the olive brown back.
Best Sites: Sir Winston Churchill PP; shrubby river valleys in migration (Bow River in Calgary; Red Deer River in Drumheller).

HERMIT THRUSH
Catharus guttatus

Beauty in forest birds is often gauged by sound and not appearance. Given this criterion, the Hermit Thrush is certainly one of the most beautiful birds in Alberta. The exquisite song of the Hermit Thrush has inspired many writers, including the great naturalist John Burroughs: 'Listening to this strain on the lone mountain, with the full moon just rounded on the horizon, the pomp of your cities and the pride of your civilization seemed trivial and cheap.' • Many of the Hermit Thrush's features can be remembered by association with its name: its memorable song always begins with a single, lone (hermit) note; its rump and tail are red, like a lonely old hermit wearing nothing but a pair of red long underwear. • The scientific name *guttatus* is Latin for 'spotted' or 'speckled,' in reference to this bird's breast.

ID: *Sexes similar:* reddish-brown tail and rump; grey-brown head and back; brown wings; black-spotted breast; light undertail coverts; grey flanks; pale eye ring.
Size: *L* 18 cm.
Status: common from May to September.
Habitat: spruce-fir forests, avalanche slopes and pine forests
Nesting: occasionally on the ground, but usually in a small tree or shrub; cup nest is built with grass, twigs and mud; female incubates 4 eggs for up to 13 days.

Feeding: forages on the ground and gleans vegetation for insects and other invertebrates; also eats berries.
Voice: call is *chuck;* song is a warbling, upward spiral, always preceded by a lone, thin note.
Similar Species: *Swainson's Thrush* (p. 271): golden cheek; olive brown back and tail. *Veery* (p. 269): lightly streaked upper breast. *Fox Sparrow* (p. 325): stockier build; conical bill; brown breast spots.
Best Sites: Kananaskis Country; shrubby river valleys in migration (Bow River in Calgary; Red Deer River in Drumheller).

AMERICAN ROBIN

Turdus migratorius

Valued as a harbinger of spring, the American Robin is one of our most familiar birds. The ubiquitous robin's close association with urban areas makes this species a predictable part of the suburban landscape. Its cheery songs, spotted young and vulnerability to house cats are all familiar themes throughout Alberta. • Although it might look like robins listen for worms beneath a lawn, they are actually searching visually for movements of the soil—they tilt their heads because their eyes face to the side. • The American Robin was named by English colonists after the robin of their native land. Both birds look and behave similarly, even though they are only distantly related. • Each year, more and more robins are overwintering in Alberta. They usually eat berries and stay close to open springs. • The rude-sounding scientific name *Turdus* means 'a thrush.'

ID: *Sexes similar:* grey-brown back; darker head; white throat streaked with black; white undertail coverts; incomplete, white eye ring; yellow, black-tipped bill. *Female:* dark grey head; light red-orange breast. *Male:* deeper, brick red breast; black head. *Juvenile:* heavily spotted breast.

Size: *L* 25 cm.

Status: abundant from March to October; a few birds overwinter.

Habitat: townsites, forests, ranchlands, forest edges and roadsides.

Nesting: in a coniferous or deciduous tree or shrub; cup nest is well built of grass, moss and loose bark and cemented with mud; female incubates 4 baby blue eggs for 11–16 days.

Feeding: forages on the ground and among vegetation for larval and adult insects, other invertebrates and berries.

Voice: song is an evenly spaced warble: *cheerily cheer-up cheerio;* call is a rapid *tut-tut-tut.*

Similar Species: *Varied Thrush* (p. 274): adult has a black breast band and 2 orange wing bars; juvenile has wing bars and a white belly.

Best Sites: suburban lawns and gardens.

VARIED THRUSH

Ixoreus naevius

The haunting courtship song of the Varied Thrush is unlike any other sound in nature. In single notes—first at one pitch; then higher or lower—it consists simultaneously of a hum and a whistle. This lovely sound wafts from the shadows of misty conifers; it penetrates well through the dense forest foliage. • The Varied Thrush is typically a bird of damp coastal coniferous forests, but it extends its range into Alberta in appropriate habitat. • Varied Thrushes arrive early to Alberta; they can be seen hopping under feeders and along open shorelines in mountain townsites by the end of March. Many Varied Thrushes (as well as other songbirds) can perish during harsh spring storms. In fall, most Varied Thrushes have left the mountains by the end of September. Every year, a few birds seem to become disoriented and head east instead of west, appearing during winter in Calgary and less frequently in other urban areas.

ID: *General:* dark upperparts; orange eyebrow; 2 orange wing bars; orange throat and belly. *Male:* black breast band; black-blue upperparts. *Female:* brown upperparts; faint breast band.
Size: *L* 24 cm.
Status: uncommon to common from April to October; a few overwinter.
Habitat: coniferous forests, especially Engelmann spruce and lodgepole pine.

Nesting: often against the trunk of a conifer; bulky cup nest is made of twigs, leaves, moss and grass; female incubates 3 or 4 eggs for 14 days.
Feeding: forages on the ground and among vegetation for insects, seeds and berries.
Voice: *Male:* long, steam whistle–like notes, always delivered at different pitches.
Similar Species: *American Robin* (p. 273): adult lacks the black breast and the orange wing bars.
Best Sites: Banff NP; Kananaskis Country; Waterton Lakes NP.

EUROPEAN STARLING
Sturnus vulgaris

Although most naturalists aren't about to praise the activities of introduced species, European Starlings have at least one admirable quality: long before other songbirds even think about returning to Alberta, a few of these birds appear suddenly one cold February morning. We know that these birds have just returned from warmer climes, because they treat us to imitations of their winter neighbours: the Killdeer, the Red-tailed Hawk and the Sora. • The European Starling was introduced to North America in 1890 and 1891, when about 100 of the birds were released in New York's Central Park as part of the local Shakespearean society's plan to introduce to the city all the birds mentioned in their favourite author's play. The starling spread quickly across the continent, often at the expense of many native cavity-nesting birds that are unable to withstand the aggression of the introduced invaders. The European Starling is now one of the most abundant urban birds throughout much of North America. Starlings first appeared in Alberta in 1934, and they have been a regular feature ever since.

breeding

Habitat: forest edges, townsites, agricultural areas, landfills and roadsides

Nesting: in an abandoned woodpecker cavity, natural cavity, nest box or almost any other cavity; nest is made of grass, twigs and straw; female incubates 4–6 bluish eggs for 12–14 days.

Feeding: very diverse diet, including many invertebrates, berries, seeds and garbage, taken from the ground and vegetation.

Voice: rambling whistles, squeaks and gurgles; imitates other birds throughout the year.

Similar Species: *Brewer's Blackbird* (p. 349): longer tail; black bill. *Brown-headed Cowbird* (p. 351): adult male has a longer tail and a shorter bill; juvenile has streaked underparts, a stout bill and a longer tail.

Best Sites: cites and towns.

ID: *Sexes similar:* short, squared tail; pointed, triangular wings in flight. *Breeding:* blackish, iridescent plumage; yellow bill. *Fall adult:* brown plumage overall; white spotting on the underparts; dark bill. *Juvenile:* grey-brown plumage; brown bill.

Size: *L* 22 cm.

Status: common from February to October; individuals often overwinter.

GRAY CATBIRD

Dumetella carolinensis

True to its name, the Gray Catbird has a call that sounds like a mewing cat—but it spoils the effect by adding phrases that sound like a rusty gate hinge and by mimicking other birds. This bird is often far easier to hear than to see, because it prefers to remain in the underbrush and in dense riparian shrubs. • The Gray Catbird's courtship activities involve an unusual 'mooning' display in which the male raises his long, slender tail to show off his red undertail coverts. As if proud of his red posterior, the male often looks back over his shoulder in mid-performance. • Gray Catbirds vigorously defend their nesting territories. They are so thorough in chasing away intruders that the nesting success of neighbouring warblers and sparrows increases as a result of the catbird's vigilance. Even if a cowbird sneaks past the watchful female catbird, the foreign egg is often recognized and ejected by the mother catbird. • *Dumetella* is Latin for 'small thicket'; it is an appropriate genus name for a bird that inhabits dense tangles.

ID: *Sexes similar:* dark grey overall; black cap and tail; red undertail coverts; black eyes, bill and legs; long tail.
Size: *L* 22 cm.
Status: uncommon to common from mid-May to September.
Habitat: dense thickets and shrublands, often near water.
Nesting: in a dense shrub or thicket;
bulky cup nest is loosely built with twigs, leaves and grass and lined with fine material; female incubates 4 eggs for up to 15 days.
Feeding: forages on the ground and in vegetation for a wide variety of ants, beetles, grasshoppers, caterpillars, moths and spiders; also eats berries and visits feeders.
Voice: call is a cat-like *meoow;* song is of variable warbles, usually in pairs.
Similar Species: *Gray Jay* (p. 235): lacks the black cap and the red undertail coverts.
Best Sites: Dinosaur PP; Writing-on-Stone PP; Red Deer River valley downstream from Drumheller.

NORTHERN MOCKINGBIRD

Mimus polyglottos

The Northern Mockingbird has yet to establish itself in great numbers in Alberta. Southern Alberta is at the northern limit of its range, and because the mockingbird tends to be non-migratory throughout most of its range, Alberta's winters might be an insurmountable barrier to its northward expansion. Elsewhere, mockingbirds are generally found in urban areas. They nest and perch in close association with berry bushes, into which they retreat when threatened. • The Northern Mockingbird is a delightful neighbour in many U.S. communities, thrilling people with its incomparable vocal repertoire and its springtime courtship dances. Northern Mockingbirds have been known to sing more than 400 different song types and to imitate other birds, barking dogs and even musical instruments. They can imitate other sounds so closely that a computerized auditory analysis is often unable to detect differences between the original source and the mockingbird. • Mockingbirds are irregular breeders in Alberta. One individual even tried to winter in Calgary—it survived until the end of January before disappearing.

ID: *Sexes similar. Adult:* grey upperparts; dark wings and tail; 2 white wing bars; white outer tail feathers; light grey underparts; long, black tail. *In flight:* large white patch at the base of the black primaries. *Juvenile:* paler overall; spotted breast.
Size: *L* 25 cm.
Status: very rare from May to August; might overwinter, but very few records.
Habitat: dense tangles, shrublands, thickets, agricultural areas and riparian forests.
Nesting: often in a small shrub or small tree; cup nest is built with twigs, grass, fur and leaves; female incubates 3–5 eggs for 12–13 days.

Feeding: gleans vegetation and forages on the ground for beetles, ants, wasps and grasshoppers; also eats berries; visits feeders for suet and raisins.
Voice: song is a variable musical medley, with the phrases often repeated 3 times or more; call is a harsh *chair*; habitually imitates other songs and noises.
Similar Species: *Shrikes* (pp. 228–29): hooked bill; adults have a black mask; juveniles are stockier and less vocal.
Best Sites: Bindloss and Oyen to Jenner.

277

SAGE THRASHER

Oreoscoptes montanus

In Alberta, the Sage Thrasher can be found in only a few southeastern coulees where the sagebrush flats extend across the valley floor. As a result of its scarcity, few naturalists have made the pilgrimage to see this bird on its Alberta breeding grounds. • Like all thrashers, the Sage is a skulker that hides deep in the bushes. In spite of your great efforts to see this bird, it stubbornly remains hidden and refuses to become airborne. • This species was formerly known as the Mountain Mockingbird or the Sage Mockingbird, because its mannerisms are similar to those of a Northern Mockingbird: while perched, the Sage Thrasher slowly raises and lowers its tail; while running along the ground, it holds its tail high. • 'Thrasher' is derived from 'thrush'—thrashers belong to the family Mimidae, the Mimic Thrushes. (These birds do not 'thrash,' whatever that might mean.) *Oreoscoptes* is Greek for 'mimic of the mountains'—really a misconception, because most of their range lies outside the Rockies.

Status: very rare during summer (migration dates unknown).
Habitat: sagebrush flats and shrublands.
Nesting: usually in sagebrush; bulky cup nest is made of grass, twigs and leaves and lined with fine vegetation; pair incubates 3–5 eggs for up to 17 days.
Feeding: forages on the ground and among vegetation for adult and larval invertebrates; also eats berries.
Voice: *Male:* song is sustained, lasting up to 2 minutes, with the phrases usually repeated without a pause.
Similar Species: *Brown Thrasher* (p. 279): long, reddish tail; reddish back; heavily streaked underparts. *Northern Mockingbird* (p. 277): juvenile has less heavily streaked underparts and large, white wing patches.
Best Site: Manyberries.

ID: *Sexes similar:* grey-brown upperparts; heavily streaked underparts; yellow eyes.
In flight: 2 white wing bars; white-tipped tail; short, straight bill.
Size: *L* 22 cm.

BROWN THRASHER

Toxostoma rufum

Among the vocal clamour that rises from shrubs along our prairie rivers, the song of the Brown Thrasher stands alone. Male Brown Thrashers have the largest vocal repertoire of any Alberta bird: more than 3000 song variations. They frequently repeat phrases twice, often combining them into complex choruses. • The Brown Thrasher, in spite of its size, can easily remain hidden in its shrubby sanctuary, and it stares out from the shadows with its gleaming yellow eyes. A typical sighting of this thrasher consists of nothing more than a flash of rufous colour as the bird flies from one tangle to another. • Brown Thrashers are among the most aggressive and vigilant defenders of their nests, and pairs have been known to attack nest robbers to the point of drawing blood. Because the Brown Thrasher nests on or close to the ground, its unguarded eggs and nestlings are particularly vulnerable to predation by bullsnakes, weasels, skunks, raccoons, foxes and other animals.

ID: *Sexes similar:* reddish-brown upperparts; white underparts with heavy, brown streaking; long, downcurved bill; orange-yellow eyes; long, rufous tail; white wing bars.
Size: *L* 29 cm.
Status: uncommon to common from mid-May to early September.
Habitat: dense shrubs and thickets in prairie river valleys.
Nesting: usually in a low shrub; cup nest is made of grass, twigs and leaves and lined with fine vegetation; pair incubates 4 or 5 eggs for up to 14 days.

Feeding: gleans the ground and vegetation for larval and adult invertebrates; occasionally tosses leaves aside; also eats seeds and berries.
Voice: repeats a variety of phrases, typically resembling *dig-it dig-it, hoe-it hoe-it, pull-it-up, pull-it-up*; pauses between phrases.
Similar Species: *Hermit Thrush* (p. 272): shorter tail; grey-brown back and crown; dark brown eyes. *Sage Thrasher* (p. 278): grey back; shorter bill and tail.
Best Sites: Dinosaur PP; Writing-on-Stone PP; Red Deer River valley downstream from Dry Island Buffalo Jump PP.

AMERICAN PIPIT
Anthus rubescens

American Pipits nimbly walk across the damp spring landscape, fueling their flight muscles with meals of waste grain and newly emerged insects. The pipits blend well into the dull browns of the landscape, with only their smooth movements and continuous tail bobs alerting attentive eyes to their presence. • The American Pipit is a bird of open areas. This resilient bird breeds on alpine and Arctic tundra, and it does not allow the presence of snow to interrupt its life cycle. Most American Pipits are seen in Alberta during their spring migration to the Arctic, but hardy mountaineers can also encounter nesting birds during summer in Alberta's treeless alpine areas. • Like the Sprague's Pipit of the grasslands, the American Pipit performs marvellous courtship flights. Many American Pipits arrive on their breeding territories already paired up— courtship and pair formation often occur at lower elevations—which is thought to save valuable time in a place with a very brief summer.

breeding

ID: *Sexes similar:* faintly streaked, grey-brown upperparts; lightly streaked 'necklace' on the upper breast; streaked breast and flanks; black legs; black tail with white outer tail feathers; buff-coloured underparts; slim body.
Size: *L* 15–18 cm.
Status: common migrant in May and in August and September; common on its on breeding grounds from June to August.
Habitat: *Breeding:* alpine tundra and wet alpine meadows.
In migration: agricultural fields, pastures and the shores of wetlands and rivers.
Nesting: in a shallow depression;

small cup nest is made with coarse grass and sedges and is sometimes lined with fur; frequently has an overhanging canopy; female incubates 4 or 5 eggs for 13–15 days.
Feeding: gleans the ground and vegetation for terrestrial and freshwater invertebrates and seeds.
Voice: familiar flight call is *pip-it pip-it.*
Male: harsh, sharp *tsip-tsip* or *chiwee.*
Similar Species: *Horned Lark* (p. 242): black 'horns' and facial markings. *Brewer's Sparrow* (p. 315) and *Timberline Sparrow* (p. 316): unstreaked breast; conical bill; stout body.
Best Sites: Kinbrook Island PP; Jasper NP; Ptarmigan Cirque, Kananaskis Country; Beaverhill Lake (migration)

SPRAGUE'S PIPIT
Anthus spragueii

The music of this prairie songster is delivered from high above the ground, and its uplifting melody carries across the open landscape. The male delivers his courtship song while he flies a continuous circle, sometimes for more than an hour at a time. • Although the Sprague's Pipit is becoming less common, it seems that every patch of healthy prairie rangeland still has at least one bird singing overhead. • The Sprague's Pipit has few musical rivals, but it seems to have been cheated out of a matching plumage. Instead, it wears a pattern common to many prairie passerines: camouflaged browns with white outer tail feathers that only show in flight. • Unlike most of the world's pipits, this species does not habitually wag its tail. • Isaac Sprague was a talented illustrator who accompanied John J. Audubon across the Great Plains. He later became one of America's foremost botanical artists.

ID: *Sexes similar:* white outer tail feathers; thin bill; light-coloured legs; greyish-brown upperparts streaked with buff; lighter underparts; faint breast streaks.
Size: *L* 16–17 cm.
Status: uncommon from May to September.
Habitat: native shortgrass prairie.
Nesting: in a depression in the ground, often with overarching grasses; well-built cup nest is made of woven grasses; female incubates 4 or 5 heavily spotted, white eggs.

Feeding: walks along the ground picking grasshoppers, beetles, moths and other invertebrates from vegetation and the ground; might also eat seeds.
Voice: swirling and descending, bell-like *choodly choodly choodly choodly chooodly.*
Similar Species: *American Pipit* (p. 280): darker plumage; darker legs; wags its tail. *Vesper Sparrow* (p. 317): heavier bill; chestnut shoulder patch. *Baird's Sparrow* (p. 321): lacks the white outer tail feathers.
Best Sites: Brooks to Medicine Hat; stop along any quiet prairie road to listen during the breeding season, but don't expect them in croplands.

BOHEMIAN WAXWING
Bombycilla garrulus

Looking like a great, flying amoeba, a flock of waxwings is an impressive sight over a suburban neighbourhood in winter. The faint, quavering whistles of these birds attract the ears of attentive naturalists, who take pleasure in watching the birds descend on berry-filled trees. Bohemian Waxwings are very closely linked to mountain ash berries during our cold winters, and they can often be closely approached when they are feeding. They usually arrive just in time to be included in reasonable numbers in Christmas bird counts. During summer, these waxwings retreat into boreal woods, where they are infrequently encountered. • Waxwings get their name from the colourful spots on their secondary feathers. These 'waxy' spots are actually colourful enlargements of the feathers' shafts, whose pigments are derived from the birds' berry-filled diet. • Bohemia is allegedly the ancestral home of the gypsies—it is an appropriate name for this northern wanderer.

ID: *Sexes similar. Adult:* cinnamon crest; black mask; black throat; soft grey-brown body; yellow terminal tail band; red undertail coverts; white, red and yellow spots on the wings. *Juvenile:* brown-grey above; streaked underparts; light throat; no mask; white wing patches.

Size: *L* 20 cm.

Status: uncommon to common year-round; common winter visitor.

Habitat: *Summer:* open conif-erous forests, frequently near water. *Winter:* townsites.

Nesting: in a conifer; cup nest is made with twigs, grass, moss and lichens and sometimes lined with fur; female incubates 4–6 eggs for 12–16 days.

Feeding: gleans vegetation or catches flying insects on the wing; depends on berries and fruit in winter.

Voice: faint, high-pitched, quavering whistle.

Similar Species: *Cedar Waxwing* (p. 283): smaller; slight yellow wash on the belly; lacks the red undertail coverts and the white in the wings.

Best Sites: cities and large towns in winter.

CEDAR WAXWING
Bombycilla cedrorum

The Cedar Waxwing is Alberta's summer waxwing: it commonly nests throughout the province in close proximity to houses and campgrounds. In winter, you might see the occasional Cedar Waxwing in a flock of Bohemians. • Flocks of handsome Cedar Waxwings gorge on berries during late summer and fall. If a bird's crop is full and it is unable to eat any more, it will continue to pluck fruit and pass it down the line like a bucket brigade, until it is gulped down by a still-hungry bird. If the fruits have fermented, the waxwings will show definite signs of tipsiness—they might fly erratically or flop around on the ground. • Cedar Waxwings are among of the last birds to nest in Alberta. Because they delay nesting, the berry crop is well developed when their nestlings are growing quickly and need lots of food. • Waxwings often are the most numerous birds at fruit trees, but they are easily 'bullied' by robins and starlings, forcing the beautiful waxwings to whistle patiently from nearby trees.

ID: *Sexes similar. Adult:* cinnamon crest; brown upperparts; black mask; yellow wash on the belly; grey rump; yellow terminal tail band; white undertail coverts; red spots on the wings. *Juvenile:* no mask; streaked underparts; grey-brown body.
Size: *L* 18 cm.
Status: uncommon to common from May to October; a few overwinter.
Habitat: forest edges, deciduous forests, shrublands and riparian woodlands.

Nesting: in a coniferous or deciduous tree or shrub; cup nest is made with twigs, grass, moss and lichens and often lined with fine grass; female incubates 3–5 eggs for 12–16 days.
Feeding: gleans vegetation or catches flying insects on the wing; also eats berries and fruit, especially during fall and winter.
Voice: faint, high-pitched whistle: *tseee-tseee-tseee*.
Similar Species: *Bohemian Waxwing* (p. 282): adult is larger, has red undertail coverts and has yellow and white wing spots; juvenile has red undertail coverts and white wing patches.
Best Sites: Red Deer River valley east from Dry Island Buffalo Jump PP.

TENNESSEE WARBLER

Vermivora peregrina

This plain-clothed warbler is a common bird: in migration it passes through most of Alberta in large numbers, and about the same numbers are encountered on its Alberta breeding grounds. Territorial males offer up one of the north's most characteristic voices. In August and September, Alberta's river valleys and woodlots are once again bustling with these small migrants, which occasionally produce an abbreviated but recognizable extract of their spring song. • Tennessee Warblers sing their songs and forage for insects in the upper parts of trees, but they return to ground level for nesting. • Alexander Wilson discovered this species along the Cumberland River in Tennessee, and he named it after that state. This warbler is only a migrant in Tennessee, however, and it breeds almost exclusively in Canada. • *Vermivora* means 'worm-eater'; *peregrina* is Latin for 'wandering.'

♀

♂

breeding

Status: uncommon from May to September.
Habitat: coniferous or mixed mature forests and occasionally spruce bogs.
Nesting: on the ground or on a raised hummock; female builds a small cup nest of grass, moss and roots and lines it with fur; female incubates 5 or 6 eggs for 12 days.
Feeding: gleans foliage and buds for small insects, caterpillars and other invertebrates; also eats berries; visits suet feeders.
Voice: *Male:* accelerating, loud, sharp *ticka-ticka-ticka swit-swit-swit-swit chew-chew-chew-chew-chew.*
Similar Species: *Warbling Vireo* (p. 232): stouter bill; lacks the blue-grey cap. *Orange-crowned Warbler* (p. 285): lacks the eye line and the blue-grey head.
Best Sites: Lesser Slave Lake PP; Sir Winston Churchill PP; Cold Lake PP; Kananaskis Country.

ID: *Breeding male:* grey crown; olive green back, wings and tail; white eyebrow; black eye line; white underparts; thin bill. *Breeding female:* yellow breast; olive-grey head; yellowish eyebrow.
Non-breeding: yellow underparts; dark green head; yellow eyebrow; white underparts.
Size: *L* 12 cm.

284

ORANGE-CROWNED WARBLER

Vermivora celata

Don't bother to look for the Orange-crowned Warbler's hidden orange crown, because this warbler's most distinguishing characteristic is a lack of obvious field marks—wing bars, eye rings and colour patches are all conspicuously absent. Only the closely-related Tennessee Warbler rivals this species for dullness of plumage. • The Orange-crowned Warbler is one of the top five warbler species most regularly seen or heard in Alberta. It is frequently encountered low in shrubs and bushes, whether in migration or on its breeding grounds, as an olive bundle flitting nervously while picking insects from leaves, buds and branches. • Wood warblers are strictly confined to the New World. All 109 species (56 of them occur in North America) originated in South America, where they have the highest diversity. • The scientific name *celata* comes from the Latin for 'hidden,' a reference to this bird's inconspicuous crown.

ID: *Sexes similar:* olive-grey body; lighter undertail coverts; dark eye line; yellowish eyebrow; faintly streaked underparts; thin bill; faint orange crown patch.
Size: *L* 13 cm.
Status: common from May to September.
Habitat: deciduous or mixed forests, shrubby avalanche slopes, woodlands and riparian thickets.
Nesting: on the ground or in a low shrub; well-hidden, small cup nest is made of coarse grass; incubates 4 or 5 eggs for 12–14 days.

Feeding: gleans foliage for invertebrates, berries, nectar and sap.
Voice: *Male:* faint trill that breaks downward halfway through.
Similar Species: *Tennessee Warbler* (p. 284): blue-grey head; olive back; dark eye line. *Ruby-crowned Kinglet* (p. 264): broken eye ring; wing bars. *Wilson's Warbler* (p. 307): female has no eyebrow, yellower underparts and light-coloured legs.
Best Sites: Canmore; Cold Lake PP; Sir Winston Churchill PP.

NASHVILLE WARBLER
Vermivora ruficapilla

The Nashville Warbler makes rare appearances in the Alberta during its spring and fall migrations, usually flitting about in deciduous forests. In spring, the males can be heard singing, as if intending to breed, but very few nesting records exist for Alberta. • This warbler has an unusual distribution, with two distinct summer populations: one eastern and the other western. Most of the Nashville Warblers that filter through our area seem to be western birds that overshot their usual range in B.C. A few eastern Nashvilles have been recorded in the Cold Lake area, in the aspen parkland–boreal forest transition zone. • The Nashville Warbler was first described from Tennessee, but it does not breed in that state. Such a misnomer is not an isolated incident: the Tennessee, Palm, Cape May, Magnolia, Connecticut and Prairie warblers all bear names that misrepresent their breeding distributions.

ID: *Male:* blue-grey head; white eye ring; yellow-green upperparts; yellow underparts; small red crown. *Female* and *Immature:* light eye ring; olive-grey head; yellow underparts; yellow-green upperparts. *Western race:* brighter yellow rump; more noticeable white patch between the belly and the undertail.
Size: *L* 12 cm.
Status: very rare from mid-May to August.

Habitat: open deciduous forests and 2nd-growth woodlands, especially aspen and birch forests with low shrubs.
Nesting: on the ground; female constructs a cup nest of grass, bark strips, moss, conifer needles and fur; female incubates 4 or 5 eggs for 11–12 days.
Feeding: gleans foliage for insects, such as caterpillars, flies and aphids.
Voice: *Male:* 1st part of the song is a high-pitched, thin *see-it see-it see-it see-it, ti-ti-ti-ti-ti.*
Similar Species: *MacGillivray's Warbler* (p. 305): male has a slate grey hood and lacks the yellow throat. *Common Yellowthroat* (p. 306): female lacks the grey head.
Best Sites: Cold Lake PP; Grande Prairie area.

286

YELLOW WARBLER
Dendroica petechia

The Yellow Warbler is one of Alberta's most common wood warblers; as a result, it is usually the first warbler that birdwatchers identify—sometime after they realize that there is no such thing as a 'wild canary' in Alberta. • Yellow Warblers are among the most frequent victims of cowbird parasitism. Unlike many bird species of the forest interior, however, Yellow Warblers can recognize the foreign eggs, and they will either abandon their nest or build another nest overtop the old eggs. One persistent warbler was found on a nest five layers high! • Yellow Warblers often leave their nesting grounds before the end of July, just after their young have fledged. • During their fall migration, plain-looking young Yellow Warblers can cause almost no end of confusion for birdwatchers who have been lulled into a false sense of familiarity with this species. • The scientific name *petechia* is Latin for 'red spots on the skin.'

breeding

ID: *Sexes similar:* canary yellow body; black bill and eyes; dark green wings and tail. *Breeding male:* red breast streaks. *Breeding female:* faint red breast streaks.
Size: *L* 13 cm.
Status: very common from mid-May to September.
Habitat: wet, shrubby meadows, willow tangles and shrubby avalanche slopes, usually near water.
Nesting: in a fork in a deciduous tree or small shrub; female builds a compact cup nest of grass, plant down, lichens and

spider silk; female incubates 4 or 5 eggs for 11–12 days.
Feeding: gleans foliage and vegetation for invertebrates, especially caterpillars, inchworms, beetles, aphids and cankerworms.
Voice: *Male:* song is a fast, frequently repeated *sweet-sweet-sweet shredded wheat.*
Similar Species: *Orange-crowned Warbler* (p. 285): lacks the beady, black eyes; male has red streaks and yellower plumage. *American Goldfinch* (p. 364): black wings and tail; male often has a black forehead. *Wilson's Warbler* (p. 307): female has a shorter, darker tail and yellower underparts.
Best Sites: almost any poplar forest.

CHESTNUT-SIDED WARBLER
Dendroica pensylvanica

Chestnut-sided Warblers are typically inquisitive and energetic, and a boldly patterned male might very well hop within an arm's length of a curious onlooker.
• Alberta lies at the western edge of the Chestnut-sided Warbler's range, but it is likely that the breeding population of these birds in our province will increase over time. The Chestnut-sided Warbler tends to favour early-succession forests, and elsewhere its numbers have increased dramatically and its range has expanded in response to increases in young aspen stands. A good indicator of this species's success is the fact that a naturalist in Alberta today can see more Chestnut-sided Warblers in one day than John J. Audubon saw in his entire life—he saw only one! • To spell the species name correctly one must leave out one *n* from 'Pennsylvania.' The rules of zoological nomenclature insist that original misspellings be perpetuated—the names are, after all, only arbitrary labels for the species they represent and not a genuine attempt to communicate in Latin.

breeding

ID: *General:* chestnut sides; white underparts; yellow cap; black legs; yellow wing bars; black and white facial markings. *Breeding male:* intense colours. *Female:* washed out markings.
Size: *L* 11.5–13 cm.
Status: rare from late May to September.
Habitat: aspen woods with dense undergrowth.
Nesting: low in bushes, shrubs or trees; small cup nest is made of bark strips and grass and

lined with finer materials; female incubates 4 eggs for up to 12 days.
Feeding: picks insects from leaves and branches at the mid-level of trees and shrubs.
Voice: loud, clear song: *so pleased, pleased, pleased to meet-cha!*
Similar Species: *Bay-breasted Warbler* (p. 297): dark crown; dark cheek. *American Redstart* (p. 300): never has yellow on the crown or chestnut on the flanks.
Best Sites: Cold Lake PP; Long Lake PP.

MAGNOLIA WARBLER

Dendroica magnolia

The Magnolia Warbler is widely regarded as one of the most beautiful wood warblers. Like a customized Cadillac, the Magnolia has all the luxury options—eyebrows, wing bars, a 'necklace,' a yellow rump and breast, tail patches and a dark cheek. As if aware of its beauty, the Magnolia Warbler seems to flaunt its colours by 'posing' for birders. This beautiful warbler forages on lower branches, and it often closely approaches patient birdwatchers. • Magnolia Warblers tend to migrate at night. When spring cold fronts cross Alberta, thousands of these birds can be grounded. At such times, forests can be literally crawling with Magnolias gently hopping around in the dark. • There is a debate over the origin of this bird's name: some people say it bears the name of French botanist Pierre Magnol (in which case it should be spelled *magnoli*); others say it was named after being collected from a magnolia tree.

breeding

ID: *Male:* yellow underparts with black streaks; black mask; white eyebrow; blue-grey crown; dark upperparts; white wing bars. *Female:* lacks the black mask; duller overall. *In flight:* yellow rump; white tail patches.
Size: L 13 cm.
Status: uncommon from mid-May to early September.
Habitat: open coniferous and mixed forests, often near water.
Nesting: on a horizontal limb in a conifer; loose cup nest is made with grass, twigs and rootlets;

female incubates 4 eggs for 11–13 days.
Feeding: gleans vegetation and buds, and occasionally flycatches, for beetles, flies, wasps and caterpillars; sometimes eats berries.
Voice: *Male:* song is a quick, rising *pretty pretty lady* or *wheata wheata wheet-zu.*
Similar Species: *Yellow-rumped Warbler* (p. 292): male 'Audubon's' has a yellow crown and lacks the yellow belly and the white eyebrow.
Best Sites: Cold Lake PP; Sir Winston Churchill PP.

CAPE MAY WARBLER
Dendroica tigrina

In ancient northern Alberta spruce groves, when the morning sun strikes the swaying branches it stirs insect life from dormancy. The rising sun is the Cape May Warbler's alarm clock, and this energetic bird rushes to take advantage of the breakfast bounty. The Cape May holds the feeding rights to the very tops of the spruce, and, through binoculars, foraging birds can look like flickering stars atop a Christmas tree. • Throughout most of its almost exclusively Canadian breeding range, this small bird seems to be a spruce budworm specialist—in years of budworm outbreaks, Cape Mays can successfully fledge more young. The use of pesticides to control budworms might adversely affect populations of this warbler. Short logging rotations might also contribute to declines in the Cape May Warbler, because this species is linked to old white spruce stands in Alberta. • The Cape May's tubular tongue is unique among wood warblers. It uses its specialized tongue to feed on nectar and fruit juices in winter.

breeding

ID: *General:* dark stripes on yellow underparts; yellow collar; dark green upperparts. *Breeding male:* yellow underparts; chestnut cheek; large white wing patch; yellow rump. *Female:* greyer overall; 2 thin white wing bars.
Size: L 12–14 cm.
Status: uncommon from late May to September.
Habitat: mature white spruce–fir forests.

Nesting: near the top of a mature white spruce, often near the trunk; cup nest is made of moss, grass and fur; female incubates 6 or 7 eggs.
Feeding: forages on the topmost branches, gleaning budworms, flies, beetles and other invertebrates; occasionally hover-gleans
Voice: very high-pitched, weak whistle: *see see see see.*
Similar Species: *Bay-breasted Warbler* (p. 297): chestnut throat; lacks the yellow in the face. *Black-throated Green Warbler* (p. 294): black throat; lacks the chestnut cheek.
Best Sites: Cold Lake PP; Sir Winston Churchill PP.

BLACK-THROATED BLUE WARBLER
Dendroica caerulescens

The Black-throated Blue Warbler's closest breeding population appears to occur in Manitoba, but this small wood warbler tends to wander, and a number of records exist for Alberta, usually of lone individuals. Although most Black-throated Blues are seen in Alberta during September and October, there have been several sightings of singing males in June. These males are attempting to establish territories, but no females answer their courting notes, so they typically give up after a few weeks and disappear from prominence. • Fortunately for birdwatchers in Alberta, the Black-throated Blue retains its strikingly distinctive plumage throughout the year. Although it is not an expected member of the fall movement of warblers through our province, it is not easily overlooked if it is present. • All sightings of this species should be reported to Alberta's rare bird committee or your local rare bird hotline.

breeding

ID: *Male:* black throat, mask and sides; deep blue upperparts; white underparts and wing patch; pinkish legs. *Female:* olive brown upperparts; buff underparts; white eyebrow; black legs; small white wing patch.
Size: L 12–14 cm.
Status: very rare in summer; most records are from September and October.
Habitat: deciduous and mixed-wood forests.

vagrant

Nesting: does not nest in Alberta.
Feeding: less energetic than other wood warblers; thoroughly gleans the understorey for caterpillars and other insects; occasionally eats berries and seeds.
Voice: slow wheezy *I am soo lay-zeee.*
Similar Species: male is distinctive. *Tennessee Warbler* (p. 284): lighter cheek; green back; lacks the white wing patch.
Best Sites: check bird hotlines for recent sightings.

YELLOW-RUMPED WARBLER
Dendroica coronata

The Yellow-rumped Warbler is the most abundant and most widespread wood warbler in North America. It tends to favour the lower branches of trees, which helps the birdwatcher get a good look at the bird's boldly contrasting colours without getting a kinked 'warbler neck'. • Both races of the Yellow-rumped Warbler occur in Alberta: the 'Audubon's Warbler,' which has a yellow throat, and the 'Myrtle Warbler,' which has a white throat. Myrtles are more prevalent in the boreal forest; Audubons dominate in the Rockies, the foothills and the Cypress Hills. These two races of the Yellow-rumped Warbler were once considered separate species. • The scientific name *coronata* is Latin for 'crowned,' referring to this bird's yellow crown.

'Myrtle Warbler'
breeding

'Audubon's Warbler'
breeding

ID: *General:* yellow rump; white tail patches; yellow side patch; white belly; white undertail coverts; dark cheek; yellow crown. *Male:* blue-black upperparts. *Female:* grey-brown upperparts. *'Audubon's Warbler':* yellow throat; large, white wing patches; yellow crown extends to the nape. *'Myrtle Warbler':* white throat; thin, white wing bars.
Size: *L* 14 cm.
Status: common from late April to September.
Habitat: all forested areas, especially conifer forests.
Nesting: in a crotch or on a horizontal limb in a conifer; female builds a compact cup nest with grass, bark strips, moss, lichens and spider silk; female

incubates 4 or 5 eggs for up to 13 days.
Feeding: hawks, hovers or gleans vegetation for beetles, flies, wasps, plant lice and caterpillars; sometimes eats berries.
Voice: call is a sharp *chip. Male:* song is a tinkling trill that rises or falls at the end; much variation between races and individuals.
Similar Species: *Magnolia Warbler* (p. 289): male has a yellow belly and a white eyebrow but lacks the yellow crown.
Best Sites: Sir Winston Churchill PP; Cold Lake PP.

TOWNSEND'S WARBLER

Dendroica townsendi

Easy to hear but hard to find, the Townsend's Warbler forages near the tops of large coniferous trees in Alberta's Rocky Mountains. Behaving for all the world like a Black-throated Green Warbler, the Townsend's Warbler flashes only glimpses of its yellow breast. If not for their constant flitting and characteristic song, most Townsend's Warblers would escape detection. • Pishing and squeaking can sometimes draw these birds down for a closer look. Although these activities are currently widely accepted among birders, this sort of disruption of the birds' normal activities should be avoided in heavily birded locations. • Most wood warblers spend the winter months in the New World tropics, but the Townsend's Warbler commonly overwinters in western California. • This western warbler bears the name of one of the West's pioneering ornithologists, John Kirk Townsend. John Kirk Townsend.

breeding

ID: *General:* yellow underparts streaked with black; black cheek; olive green upperparts; 2 wing bars; white undertail coverts.
Male: black throat, crown and cheek patch.
Female: yellow throat; white belly; dusky cheek.
Size: L 13 cm.
Status: uncommon to common from late May to early September.
Habitat: mature coniferous forests, usually not far from water.

Nesting: in a crotch or on a horizontal limb in a conifer; compact cup nest is built with grass, moss, lichens and spider silk; female incubates 4 or 5 eggs for 12 days.
Feeding: gleans vegetation and buds and flycatches for beetles, flies, wasps and caterpillars.
Voice: *Male:* 2 songs: *dzeer dzeer dzeer dzeer, tseetsee* and *weazy weazy seesee*.
Similar Species: *Black-throated Green Warbler* (p. 294): yellow cheek; lacks the yellow breast.
Best Site: Banff NP.

293

BLACK-THROATED GREEN WARBLER

Dendroica virens

High up in coniferous spires lives the Black-throated Green Warbler. Conifer crowns can be penthouses for neotropical warblers, and many species choose to nest and forage exclusively at these great heights. Because so many warbler species occur in the heights of our conifer forests, the food supply in these areas can come under pressure. Fortunately, many species of warblers can coexist because they partition the food supplies by foraging exclusively in certain areas. Black-throated Greens feed just below the crowns on the outer branches. • If it weren't for the Black-throated Green's flitting habits and its unmistakable *see-see-see SU-ZY* song, it would often escape detection. The song of this small warbler is a distinctive voice of Alberta's mature boreal forests.

breeding

ID: *General:* yellow face; black throat; olive back; dark wings and tail; white wing bars. *Male:* black bib.
Size: *L* 12–14 cm.
Status: uncommon from mid-May to mid-September.
Habitat: mixed woods and mature coniferous forests.
Nesting: in a crotch or on a horizontal limb in a conifer; compact cup nest is made with grass, moss, lichens, spider silk and fur; female incubates 4 or 5 eggs for 12 days.

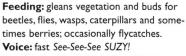

Feeding: gleans vegetation and buds for beetles, flies, wasps, caterpillars and sometimes berries; occasionally flycatches.
Voice: fast *See-See-See SUZY!*
Similar Species: *Bay-breasted Warbler* (p. 297): chestnut throat; lacks the yellow face. *Cape May Warbler* (p. 290): chestnut cheek; yellow underparts. *Townsend's Warbler* (p. 293): black cheek; found in the foothills and mountains.
Best Sites: Cold Lake PP; Sir Winston Churchill PP.

BLACKBURNIAN WARBLER
Dendroica fusca

Male Blackburnian Warblers are ablaze in spring with a fiery orange throat—they rival orioles for sheer colour saturation. Blackburnians are widely regarded as Alberta's most beautiful warblers, and they are regularly looked upon with awe.
• Increased pressure from forestry on the mature spruce stands in which Blackburnians breed might cause declines in their already poorly understood breeding populations. • These awesomely coloured birds charge up from their tropical wintering grounds through central North America. They arrive in Alberta near the Victoria Day long weekend in May. • This bird's name is thought to honour the Blackburne family of England. Ashton Blackburne is thought to have collected the type specimen, and Anna Blackburne managed the museum in which it was housed. • The scientific name *fusca* is Latin for 'dusky,' an odd reference to the unspectacular winter plumage of this bird.

♂

breeding

♀

ID: *Breeding male:* fiery orange throat, face and crown stripe; black cheek, back and flank streaks; large white wing patch; white outer tail. *Female* and *Non-breeding male:* yellow-orange throat; yellow stripes on the head; white belly.
Size: *L* 11–14 cm.
Status: rare to uncommon from mid-May to September.
Habitat: mature coniferous and mixed-wood forests.
Nesting: high in a mature white spruce, often near a branch tip; cup nest is made of conifer needles, bark, twigs and grass; female incubates 3–5 eggs for up to 13 days.
Feeding: forages on the uppermost branches, gleaning budworms,

flies, beetles and other invertebrates; occasionally hover-gleans.
Voice: soft, faint high-pitched *see-me see-me see-me* or *come-see, come-see, come-see.*
Similar Species: *Townsend's Warbler* (p. 293): yellow throat; found in western Alberta. *American Redstart* (p. 300): lacks the orange throat.
Best Sites: Cold Lake PP; Sir Winston Churchill PP.

295

PALM WARBLER
Dendroica palmarum

What the heck is a Palm Warbler doing in Alberta, you might ask? The answer to that question is on this warbler's wintering grounds—it is just as much at home in the subtropics as it is in a black spruce stand (although even in winter it has no special preference for palms). 'Bog Warbler' would have been a more appropriate, though less charismatic, name for this species. • The Palm Warbler is easily recognized by its tail-wagging habit: its posterior pumps whether the bird is hopping on the ground or momentarily perched on a convenient limb. In fall, this tail wag is as good a field mark as any, but in breeding plumage the male has a handsome, if understated, appearance. • The song of the Palm Warbler is be one of the most distinctive sounds of Alberta's black spruce bogs—not counting the buzzing of mosquitoes. This bird sings proudly from the stunted trees, adding life to a fascinating environment.

breeding

ID: *Sexes similar:* chestnut cap; light yellow throat and undertail coverts; white underparts streaked with brown; yellow eyebrow; olive brown upperparts.
Size: *L* 14 cm.
Status: uncommon from mid-May to early October.
Habitat: semi-open habitats, including bogs, fields and wetlands bordered by woodlands.
Nesting: on the ground or in a short shrub; small cup nest is made with grass, weeds and feathers; incubates 4 or 5 eggs for 12 days.

Feeding: gleans the ground and short vegetation for grasshoppers, beetles, moths and flies.
Voice: *Male:* song is a weak trill with a quick finish.
Similar Species: *Yellow-rumped Warbler* (p. 292): yellow rump; darker upperparts; white wing bars. *Orange-crowned Warbler* (p. 285): lacks the rufous crown and the streaked underparts. *Chipping Sparrow* (p. 313): stouter body; unstreaked underparts; no yellow in the plumage.
Best Sites: bogs around Fort McMurray and High Level; Cold Lake PP (migration).

BAY-BREASTED WARBLER
Dendroica castanea

We have never met a warbler we didn't like, and the Bay-breasted is no exception. In fine warbler fashion, it moves about continuously in its treetop spruce neighbourhood, dancing between half-hidden perches. The Bay-breasted Warbler is among the most difficult of all wood warblers to see in Alberta, and most birdwatchers consider themselves lucky if they count even one in a year. • Like most wood warblers, the Bay-breasted is a neotropical migrant that winters in the New World tropics. Deforestation in both its summer and winter habitats, environmental contaminants and migration hazards have all contributed to its decline over the past few decades. This bird is truly an international resident, so its conservation requires the efforts of several nations. • Although 'bay-breasted' is simply a reference to the colour of this bird's breast, when viewed from below, the chestnut colour also seems to form an embayment.

♀

♂

breeding

ID: *Breeding male:* chestnut crown, throat and flanks; black mask; creamy belly and undertail coverts; cream patch behind the ear; 2 white wing bars. *Female:* pale face, throat and flanks; cream-coloured underparts; faint chestnut cap; 2 white wing bars.
Size: *L* 14 cm.
Status: rare to uncommon from late May to mid-September.
Habitat: mature riparian and coniferous forests.
Nesting: usually on a horizontal conifer branch; cup nest is loosely built of grass, twigs, moss and bark; female incubates 4 or 5 eggs for 13 days.

Feeding: gleans vegetation and terminal branches for caterpillars and adult invertebrates; usually forages at the mid-level of trees.
Voice: extremely high-pitched *seee-seese-seese-seee.*
Similar Species: *Cape May Warbler* (p. 290): red cheek; lacks the reddish flanks and crown.
Best Sites: Cold Lake PP; Sir Winston Churchill PP.

BLACKPOLL WARBLER
Dendroica striata

When aspen leaves unfold in mid-May, Blackpoll Warblers move through Alberta individually, usually avoiding the mixed-species flocks that typify other wood warblers. Blackpolls migrate with a business-like determination to reach their stunted-spruce breeding destinations. Once there, the males sing their characteristic but not particularly inspiring song—it is a weak melody that often goes unnoticed by birders in the volume of spring's orchestra. • The Blackpoll is the greatest warbler migrant: weighing less than a wet teabag, eastern migrants are known to fly south over the Atlantic, leaving land at Cape Cod and not resting again until they reach the coast of Venezuela. • The male Blackpoll Warbler is easily identified by his chickadee-like head. The resemblance between the species is an example of evolutionary convergence, although its cause is poorly understood. • The scientific name *striata* comes from the Latin word for 'striped.'

breeding

ID: *General:* 2 white wing bars; orange legs. *Breeding male:* black cap and upperparts; white cheek; black-streaked underparts. *Breeding female:* streaked, greenish upperparts; black-streaked or white underparts; dirty cheek. **Size:** *L* 14 cm. **Status:** uncommon to common from mid-May to September.

Habitat: black spruce forests, muskeg bogs, burns and occasionally mixed forests. **Nesting:** well-concealed in a stunted spruce tree; nest is made of twigs, bark shreds, grass, lichens and fur; female incubates 4 or 5 eggs for about 12 days. **Feeding:** gleans buds, leaves and branches for larval insects, aphids and scale insects; also flycatches for insects. **Voice:** high-pitched, uniform *tsit tsit tsit*. **Similar Species:** *Black-and-white Warbler* (p. 299): dark legs; striped, black-and-white crown. **Best Sites:** Caribou Mountains; Cold Lake PP.

BLACK-AND-WHITE WARBLER
Mniotilta varia

In a general sense, this is a normal-looking warbler, but the foraging behaviour of the Black-and-white Warbler stands in sharp contrast to most of its kin. Rather than hopping quickly between twig perches, Black-and-white Warblers behave like nuthatches—a very distantly related group of birds. As if possessed by nuthatch envy, Black-and-whites cling gingerly to tree trunks, searching up and down the bark for food. Even a novice birdwatcher can easily identify this two-toned warbler, which lives up to its name in both spring and fall. A keen ear also helps: the gentle oscillating song—like a wheel in need of greasing—is easily recognized and remembered. • The Black-and-white Warbler is the odd man out among Alberta's forest dwelling warblers. It is alone in its genus, *Mniotilta,* which means 'to pull out moss.'

breeding

ID: *General:* black-and-white-streaked crown and upperparts; 2 white wing bars; black legs; streaked flanks. *Breeding male:* black cheek and throat. *Breeding female:* grey cheek; white throat.
Size: *L* 13 cm.
Status: uncommon from mid-May to September.
Habitat: deciduous or mixed-wood forests, often near water, and alder and willow thickets bordering muskegs and pools.
Nesting: often on the ground; in a

shallow scrape lined with grass, leaves and fine plant materials; female incubates 5 eggs for 10 days.
Feeding: forages on tree trunks for insect eggs, larval insects, beetles, spiders and other invertebrates.
Voice: oscillates between 2 high notes: *wee-see wee-see wee-see* (like a squeaky wheelbarrow).
Similar Species: *Blackpoll Warbler* (p. 298): orange legs; solid black cap in breeding plumage.
Best Sites: Cold Lake PP; Sir Winston Churchill PP.

AMERICAN REDSTART
Setophaga ruticilla

American Redstarts are always in motion, rhythmically swaying their tails even when they are perched. Few birds can rival a mature male redstart for his contrasting black-and-orange plumage, which is continually displayed in an enthusiastic series of flutters, twists and spreadings of the feathers. American Redstarts behave in much the same way on their Central American wintering grounds, where they are locally known as *candelita* (little candle), obviously reflecting the energy and enthusiasm they display wherever their wings carry them. • Although American Redstarts are among the most common warblers to breed in the forested areas of northern Alberta, their songs are so wonderfully various that even after listening to them all spring, they can still be confusing. Every spring we must relearn their mysterious warbles and trills. • The genus name *Setophaga* comes from the Greek for 'insect-eater.'

ID: *Male:* black overall; salmon red shoulder, wing and tail patches; white belly and under-tail coverts. *Female:* olive green upperparts; grey-green head; yellow shoulder, wing and tail patches; white belly and undertail coverts. *Immature male:* resembles a female, but with breast streaks.
Size: L 13 cm.
Status: uncommon to common from mid-May to August.
Habitat: mature deciduous forests, shrubbery, avalanche slopes, willow patches and lowland forests, usually near water.

Nesting: in the fork of a shrub or short tree; tight cup nest is made of plant down, grass, roots and bark shreds and lined with feathers and soft materials; female incubates 4 eggs for 12 days.
Feeding: actively gleans foliage and hawks for insects and spiders on leaves, buds and branches.
Voice: *Male:* wonderfully variable (but confusing) series of *tseet* notes, often given at different pitches.
Similar Species: male is distinctive; female and immature can resemble other warblers, but they have yellow patches on their wings and tails.
Best Sites: Cold Lake PP; Sir Winston Churchill PP.

300

OVENBIRD
Seiurus aurocapillus

The loud, pulsing song of the Ovenbird has a ventriloqual quality that makes it difficult to locate. The Ovenbird, unlike most of the warbler clan, chooses to do much of its singing on the ground or in a low shrub. Its song is among the easiest to learn, and it is a familiar spring voice in May and June. • Even when they are threatened, Ovenbirds stubbornly refuse to become airborne. They prefer to escape on foot through dense tangles and shrubs. • Ovenbirds (and most other warblers) are most easily observed during migration. Their spring and fall movements carry these birds through suburban neighbourhoods, where almost any of our Alberta species might suddenly appear outside a kitchen window. • The scientific name *aurocapillus* is from the Latin for 'golden hair,' an allusion to the Ovenbird's infrequently seen crown. 'Oven' refers to the shape of its ground nest.

ID: *Sexes similar:* olive brown upperparts; white eye ring; heavily streaked breast and flanks; rufous crown bordered by black; pink legs; white undertail coverts; no wing bars.
Size: *L* 15 cm.
Status: uncommon to common from mid-May to September.
Habitat: riparian and deciduous forests and shrubbery; occasionally in mixed woods with semi-open undergrowth.
Nesting: on the ground; oven-shaped, domed nest is made of grass and weeds and lined with fine materials; female incubates 4 or 5 eggs for 11–13 days.

Feeding: gleans the ground for worms, snails, insects and occasionally seeds.
Voice: loud, distinctive *tea-cher tea-cher Tea-CHER Tea-CHER*, increasing in speed and volume; the emphasis is on the 2nd syllable of each doublet.
Similar Species: *Northern Waterthrush* (p. 302): light eyebrow; lacks the rufous crown; darker upperparts. *Swainson's Thrush* (p. 271) and *Hermit Thrush* (p. 272): larger; lack the rufous-and-black crown.
Best Sites: Cold Lake PP; Sir Winston Churchill PP; Lesser Slave Lake PP.

NORTHERN WATERTHRUSH

Seiurus noveboracensis

The Northern Waterthrush is in many ways a less colourful version of the Oven-bird. Its voice is loud and raucous for such a small bird, so it seems fitting that this bird was once known as the New York Warbler, after a city well known for its decibels. • Like so many other birds that tend to forage in damp areas, the Northern Waterthrush walks with a bit of a teetering motion. Although it does not do a full 'tipsy teapot' like the Spotted Sandpiper, its behaviour is still dissimilar to any other species of Alberta wood warbler. • Birders who are not satisfied by simply hearing a waterthrush must literally get their feet wet if they want much hope of seeing the bird on its nesting territory. If you don't mind seeing them in non-breeding plumage, your best chance is during their fall migration, when they appear in drier, upland forests from time to time. • The scientific name *noveboracensis* means 'of New York.'

ID: *Sexes similar:* pale yellow eyebrow; streaked breast; spotted throat; olive brown upperparts; pinkish legs; often teeters.
Size: *L* 13–15 cm.
Status: uncommon from mid-May to September.
Habitat: deciduous, riparian thickets, forests and streams.
Nesting: often on the ground, on a mossy mound or low on a broken stump or branch; usually near water; small, well-hidden cup nest is made of moss, leaves and fine bark shreds; female incubates 4 or 5 eggs for 13 days.

Feeding: gleans foliage and the ground for invertebrates, frequently tossing aside vegetation with its bill; also dips into shallow water for aquatic invertebrates and very occasionally for small fish.
Voice: loud, penetrating *chew chew chew chew where-where-where-where-where.*
Similar Species: *Ovenbird* (p. 301): russet crown; lacks the pale eyebrow.
Best Sites: Lesser Slave Lake PP; Sir Winston Churchill PP; Hinton area.

CONNECTICUT WARBLER

Oporornis agilis

Alberta is as good a place as any, and far better than most, to see a Connecticut Warbler. This uncommon species, sought after by many North American bird-watchers, sings its Ovenbird-like song from trees along forest openings. It occurs across Alberta, though it is generally spread very thinly. Along a few backroads in the Swan Hills area, however, Connecticut Warblers abound during the first few weeks of June. • The Connecticut Warbler is one of the top species on the must-see lists of visiting birdwatchers, and to a committed birder, the sight of this small warbler is as impressive as the snow-capped peaks of the Rockies. • The three look-alike species of *Oporornis* warblers can best be separated in the field by their eye rings: the Connecticut has a 'connect-ic-ed' eye ring; the MacGillivray's has an incomplete eye ring; and the Mourning has no eye ring. • This bird only visits Connecticut during its fall migration; its breeding range lies almost entirely in Canada.

breeding

ID: *General:* light eye ring; very short tail; pinkish legs; yellow underparts; greenish upperparts. *Breeding male:* blue-grey hood. *Female:* grey-brown hood; light grey throat.
Size: L 11–14 cm.
Status: uncommon to locally common from late May to September.
Habitat: open deciduous forests, mixed woods and occassionally bogs.
Nesting: on the ground or low in a shrub; messy nest is made of leaves, weeds and grasses; female incubates 3 or 4 eggs for about 12 days.
Feeding: forages in dense shrubs for caterpillars, beetles, spiders and other invertebrates.
Voice: husky, 2-part song that descends at the end: *cheery cheery cheery, chorry chorry.*
Similar Species: *Mourning Warbler* (p. 304): no eye ring; dark black breast patch. *MacGillvray's Warbler* (p. 305): incomplete eye ring; dark black breast patch.
Best Sites: southern Swan Hills; Sundre area.

MOURNING WARBLER
Oporornis philadelphia

Living in Alberta, the North American hotspot for *Oporornis* warblers, naturalists face the enviable challenge of sorting through these three similar birds. Of the three, the Mourning Warbler has the widest distribution in our province, but it is still seen far less frequently than one might expect. It is a bird that seldom leaves the undergrowth, and it sings only on its breeding territory. • The Mourning Warbler is the eastern counterpart of the MacGillivray's Warbler, and these species sometimes hybridize in a narrow region around Hinton. Hybridization in such a limited region does not necessarily mean that two species should be considered one—it does not seem to indicate that the two species are merging in an evolutionary sense. • This bird's black hood reminded Alexander Wilson of someone in mourning. We like to remember this bird's name by thinking that it is mourning the loss of its eye ring.

breeding

ID: *General:* very short tail; orange legs; yellow underparts; greenish upperparts. *Breeding male:* blue-grey hood; black upper breast patch. *Female:* lacks the dark hood.

Size: *L* 11–14 cm.

Status: uncommon from late May to early September.

Habitat: dense and shrubby thickets, often around deadfall, in deciduous forests.

Nesting: on the ground or low in a shrub; messy nest is made of leaves, weeds and grass; female incubates 3 or 4 eggs for about 12 days.

Feeding: forages in dense shrubs for caterpillars, beetles, spiders and other invertebrates.

Voice: husky, 2-part song that descends at the end: *cheery cheery cheery, chorry chorry.*

Similar Species: *Connecticut Warbler* (p. 303): complete eye ring; lacks the black breast patch. *MacGillivray's Warbler* (p. 305): incomplete eye ring; lacks the black breast patch.

Best Sites: Sir Winston Churchill PP; Lesser Slave Lake PP.

MacGILLIVRAY'S WARBLER
Oporornis tolmiei

Keeping to dense, impenetrable shrubs in the mountains, foothills and Cypress Hills, the MacGillivray's Warbler is a very difficult bird to get a clear view of—you must often crouch down, peer deep into the shadows and strain your neck in rapid response to this bird's faintly perceptible actions. All of this is worth while, however, because the male MacGillivray's Warbler is certainly one of the most beautiful warblers in Alberta. • The MacGillivray's Warbler, along with a number of other mountain species, has an isolated breeding population in the Cypress Hills, which are an oasis of boreal forest in the prairies. • John J. Audubon named this warbler in honour of William MacGillivray, who edited and reworked the manuscript of Audubon's classic work on birds, but who never set foot in North America. Another Scotsman, William Tolmie, is remembered in this bird's scientific name. Tolmie spent his adult life on the Pacific coast of North America, where he undoubtedly had several encounters with this endearing warbler.

breeding

♀

♂

ID: *General:* yellow underparts; olive green upperparts; broken, white eye ring; pinkish legs. *Male:* dark slate grey hood; black bib. *Female* and *Immature:* light grey-brown hood.
Size: L 13–15 cm.
Status: uncommon from late May to September.
Habitat: shrubby under-storeys and dense, deciduous, riparian thickets and forests.
Nesting: between vertical stems in a low tree or a shrub; small cup

nest is made with weeds and grasses; female incubates 4 eggs for up to 13 days.
Feeding: gleans low vegetation and the ground for beetles, bees, leafhoppers, insect larvae and other invertebrates.
Voice: clear, high-pitched, rolling *sweeter sweeter sweeter sugar sugar.*
Similar Species: *Nashville Warbler* (p. 286): yellow chin; complete eye ring. *Common Yellowthroat* (p. 306): female lacks the greyish throat and has no eye ring.
Best Site: Cypress Hills PP.

COMMON YELLOWTHROAT

Geothlypis trichas

The Common Yellowthroat shuns the forests so loved by most of its kin; instead it chooses to bound around in a world of cattails, bulrushes and willows. Yellowthroats are so characteristic of this habitat that their undulating song is one of the most distinguishing sounds of Alberta's sloughs. • The Common Yellowthroat is one of the most widespread warblers in Alberta. During summer, it is likely that every person in the province is within a half-hour drive of a nesting pair.
• Closely following their potential mates, the displaying males flick their wings, fan their tails and perform courtship flights. • Common Yellowthroat nests are often parasitized by Brown-headed Cowbirds, which are primarily birds of open country and commonly target nests in less-forested habitats.

ID: *General:* yellow throat; green upperparts; orange legs. *Male:* black mask with a pale border. *Female:* no mask.
Size: L 11–14 cm.
Status: common from May to September.
Habitat: cattail marshes, riparian willow and alder clumps, sedge wetlands and beaver ponds.
Nesting: low to the ground, usually in a small shrub or among emergent vegetation; large, compact nest is made of weeds, grass and dead leaves; female incubates 3–5 eggs for 12 days.
Feeding: gleans vegetation and hovers for adult and larval insects, including dragonflies, spiders and beetles; occasionally eats seeds.
Voice: oscillating, clear *witchety witchety witchety-witch.*
Similar Species: male is distinctive. *Nashville Warbler* (p. 286): similar to a female yellowthroat, but with a complete eye ring and darker upperparts.
Best Sites: all cattail wetlands throughout Alberta; Slack Slough.

WILSON'S WARBLER
Wilsonia pusilla

Even a lazy-eyed glance into willow shrubs will often catch the energetic activity of a Wilson's Warbler busily hopping around at eye level. This yellow bird flickers quickly through the leaves and branches, as if a motionless moment would break some unwritten law of warblerdom. Because of its continuous dance, the Wilson's Warbler is one of the most pleasing songbirds to see in Alberta. It is also eye opening the first time a beginning birder sees what might initially look to be a Yellow Warbler with a jet black crown. • The Wilson's Warbler is richly deserving of its name. Named after Alexander Wilson, this species epitomizes the energetic devotion that that pioneering ornithologist exhibited in the study of North American birds.

ID: *General:* yellow underparts; yellow-green upperparts; beady, black eyes; black bill; orange legs. *Male:* black cap. *Female:* cap is very faint or absent.
Size: *L* 11–13 cm.
Status: uncommon to common from mid-May to September.
Habitat: shrubby shorelines, willow and alder thickets, wet meadows, avalanche slopes, revegetated burns and krummholz areas.
Nesting: on the ground, sunken into soft substrate, or in a low shrub or thicket; neat cup

nest is made of moss, grass and leaves and occasionally lined with fine grass; female incubates 4–6 eggs for 10–13 days.
Feeding: gleans vegetation, hovers and catches insects on the wing; eats mostly adult and larval invertebrates.
Voice: during spring and summer, a chatty series that falls off at the end: *chi chi chi chi chet chet.*
Similar Species: male is distinctive. *Yellow Warbler* (p. 287): male is similar to a female Wilson's, but with red breast streaks, lighter upperparts and a shorter tail.
Best Sites: Jasper NP; Banff NP; Caribou Mountains.

307

CANADA WARBLER
Wilsonia canadensis

Male Canada Warblers, with their bold white eye rings, have a wide-eyed, alert appearance. They are fairly inquisitive birds, and they occasionally pop up from dense shrubs in response to passing hikers. • You will never tire of seeing a Canada Warbler, especially in Alberta, which lies at the western edge of its breeding range. Unfortunately, few of these energetic birds are encountered in our province, and they have the shortest stay of all our wood warblers. • Although there are several wood warblers that breed almost exclusively in Canada, the Canada Warbler isn't one of them. It breeds across Canada east of Alberta, but it can also be found nesting throughout the Appalachians as far south as Georgia. In a way, the Canada Warbler compensates for poorly named warblers, such as the Palm Warbler. • The Canada Warbler is one of the few wood warblers whose wardrobe is just as colourful in fall as it is in spring.

ID: *General:* pale yellow 'spectacles'; yellow underparts; dark upperparts; orange legs; white undertail coverts. *Male:* blue-black back; dark necklace. *Female:* blue-green back; faint necklace.

Size: *L* 13–14 cm.

Status: uncommon from late May to August.

Habitat: willow and alder thickets, riparian shrublands and dense understoreys.

Nesting: on a mossy hummock or an upturned root; bulky cup nest is made of leaves, grass, ferns and bark shreds and

lined with finer plant materials and fur; female (and possibly the male) incubates 4 eggs for about 10–14 days.

Feeding: gleans vegetation and the ground and occasionally hovers for beetles, flies, hairless caterpillars and mosquitoes.

Voice: lively and expressive *tea tea tea for-the-TEAcher.*

Similar Species: *Magnolia Warbler* (p. 289): white wing bars; yellow rump; black mask; white eye ring. *Yellow-rumped Warbler* (p. 292): yellow rump; white wing bars or patches; white belly.

Best Sites: Cold Lake PP; Sir Winston Churchill PP; Lesser Slave Lake PP.

YELLOW-BREASTED CHAT
Icteria virens

At nearly 20 cm, the Yellow-breasted Chat is quite literally a warbler and a half. It behaves like a typical wood warbler, with a curiosity and flitting habits that seem misplaced in so large a bird. • In Alberta, most wood warblers nest in the northern boreal forest, but these oddballs nest exclusively in the south, along prairie river valleys whose lush vegetation draws birds like a magnet in the otherwise sparsely vegetated landscape. • Chats are bizarre birds, and they often attract attention to themselves through strange vocalizations and noisy thrashing in dense under-growth, more like a catbird than a warbler. When they are present, they seem to do their best to ensure that they are not overlooked. • It was only in 1941 that the first Yellow-breasted Chat was recorded in Alberta; this species has certainly become increasingly more common since then. • 'Chat' is a wonderfully descriptive and imaginative name; anyone who encounters this bird will certainly leave with a 'chatty' impression of it.

ID: *General:* white 'spectacles'; white jaw line; heavy, black bill; yellow breast; white undertail coverts; olive green upperparts; long tail; grey-black legs. *Male:* black lore. *Female:* grey lore.
Size: L 19 cm.
Status: uncommon from late May to September.
Habitat: riparian shrublands and shrubby coulees.
Nesting: low in a shrub or small tree; well-concealed, bulky nest is made of leaves, straw and weeds, with a tight inner cup woven with bark and plant fibres; female incubates 3 or 4 eggs for about 11 days.
Feeding: gleans low vegetation for insects.
Voice: whistles, *kuks* and 'laughs,' together or alone in no obvious arrangement.
Similar Species: *Nashville Warbler* (p. 286): much smaller; white eye ring; thinner bill.
Best Sites: Writing-on-Stone PP; Medicine Hat; Red Deer River valley downstream from Dinosaur PP.

WESTERN TANAGER

Piranga ludoviciana

No other Alberta bird can match the tropical splendour of a male Western Tanager. His golden body, accentuated by black wings and a black tail, expresses the true character of this bird. Western Tanagers are tropical for most of the year—they fly to Alberta for only a few short months to raise a new generation on the seasonal explosion of food in our forests. Their exotic colours remind us of the ecological ties between Alberta's boreal forests and the Latin American rainforests. • The song of the male tanager can be difficult to learn, because it closely parallels the phrases of a robin's song. The tanager's phrases tend to be hoarser, however, as if the bird has a sore throat. Fortunately, the tanager's hiccup-like *pit-a-tik* call, which falls frequently from its treetop perches, is distinctive. • The tanager family's roots extend deeply into the rainforests of the New World, where this group reaches its maximum diversity. 'Tanager' is derived from *tangara*, the Tupi name for this group of birds in the Amazon basin.

♀

♂

breeding

ID: *Breeding male:* yellow underparts, wing bars and rump; black back, wings and tail; often has red on the forehead or the entire head (variable); light-coloured bill. *Breeding female:* olive green overall; lighter underparts; darker upperparts; faint wing bars.
Size: *L* 18 cm.
Status: common from May to September.
Habitat: mature coniferous or mixedwood forests and aspen woodlands.
Nesting: on a horizontal branch or fork in a conifer, well out from the trunk; cup nest is loosely built of twigs, grass and other plant materials and

lined with fine vegetation; female incubates 4 eggs for 13–14 days.
Feeding: gleans vegetation and catches flying insects on the wing; eats wasps, beetles, flies and other insects, including caterpillars; also eats fruit.
Voice: call is a hiccup-like *pit-a-tik*. *Male:* song is hoarse and robin-like: *hurry, scurry, scurry, hurry.*
Similar Species: male is distinctive. *Baltimore Oriole* (p. 352): female has a thinner bill and darker olive plumage.
Best Sites: Cold Lake PP; Sir Winston Churchill PP; Sheep River Wildlife Sanctuary; Fish Creek PP.

SPOTTED TOWHEE

Pipilo maculatus

Pipilo maculatus

Where dried leaves have accumulated on the ground under shrubs, you might easily encounter a Spotted Towhee. This large sparrow is a noisy forager that scratches at loose leaf litter with both feet. Sometimes these birds are so noisy that you expect an animal of deer-sized proportions to be the source of all the ruckus. • Spotted Towhees rarely leave their sub-arboreal world, except to proclaim their courtship song or to evaluate a threat in their territory. These cocky, spirited birds can often be enticed into view by 'squeaking' or 'pishing,' noises that alert curious birds to an intrusion. • Until recently, the Spotted Towhee was grouped together with the Eastern Towhee (a spotless, eastern bird) as a single species, known as the Rufous-sided Towhee. • Spotted Towhees are seen fairly regularly in the campgrounds of both Dinosaur Provincial Park and Writing-on-Stone Provincial Park, but they tend to make themselves scarce when the parks become crowded with campers.

ID: *Male:* black hood, back, wings and tail; rufous flanks; dark, conical bill; white spotting on the wings; white outer tail coverts; white belly and undertail. *Female:* somewhat paler overall.
Size: *L* 18–22 cm.
Status: uncommon to common from May to September.
Habitat: riparian shrublands and shrubby fields.
Nesting: low in a bush, on the ground under cover or in a brushy pile; cup nest is made with leaves, grass and bark shreds and lined with fine material; primarily the female incubates 3 or 4 eggs for 12–13 days.
Feeding: scratches the ground vigorously for insects and seeds, including caterpillars, moths, beetles,

ants and other common invertebrates; visits feeding stations periodically.
Voice: song is *here here here PLEASE*; call is a raspy or whining *chee*.
Similar Species: *Black-headed Grosbeak* (p. 341): much heavier bill; lacks the red eyes and rufous on the sides. *Dark-eyed Junco* (p. 333): smaller; 'Oregon' race has pale rufous on the back as well as the sides.
Best Sites: Dinosaur PP; Writing-on-Stone PP; Medicine Hat; Red Deer River valley downstream from Dry Island Buffalo Jump PP.

AMERICAN TREE SPARROW

Spizella arborea

If you wanted to let the yearly movements of birds guide your activities, there would be no better bird to follow than the American Tree Sparrow. With its unassuming, but doggedly regular, migratory habits, this species quietly announces the arrivals of both spring and fall. The gentle flow of American Tree Sparrows through Alberta usually precedes the emergence of willow leaves, and they are rarely seen perched atop anything but bare branches. • While there might be isolated instances of breeding American Tree Sparrows in the province, most of the individuals we see migrate through without nesting. • While both its common and scientific names (*arborea* means 'tree') might imply that this is a forest-dwelling bird, it is most often found in semi-open areas. As an Arctic nester that prefers bushes to trees, perhaps a more appropriate name would be 'Arctic Shrub Sparrow.'

ID: *Sexes similar:* pale rufous cap; unstreaked breast; dark, central breast spot; grey face; soft grey underparts; mottled brown upperparts; dark legs; dark upper mandible; light lower mandible.

Size: L 14–17 cm.

Status: common from March to April and from September to October; a few breed here and a few overwinter.

Habitat: brushy thickets, roadside shrubs, semi-open fields and agricultural areas.

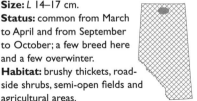

Nesting: usually on the ground; often on a raised tussock or other dry area; small cup nest is woven with grass, moss and bark shreds and lined with feathers and fur; female incubates 3–5 eggs for 12–13 days.

Feeding: scratches exposed soil or snow for native plant seeds and occasionally insects; occasionally visits feeding stations during migration and in winter.

Voice: sometimes practises its breeding song before departing for the Arctic: *tseet* notes followed by a warble or trill.

Similar Species: *Chipping Sparrow* (p. 313): clear black eye line; white eyebrow; lacks the central breast spot. *Swamp Sparrow* (p. 328): lacks the central breast spot and the white wing bars.

Best Sites: Beaverhill Lake; Helen Schuler Coulee Centre, Lethbridge (spring).

CHIPPING SPARROW

Spizella passerina

The Chipping Sparrow and the Dark-eyed Junco do not share the same tailor, but they must have attended the same voice classes, because the differences between these two birds' songs are down right difficult to learn. The classic, rapid trill of the Chipping Sparrow is slightly faster, but it often needs to be tracked to its source for confirmation. • Chipping Sparrows are found from the forest floor to the topmost spires of conifers. These birds can be very common in migration, when loose flocks of them can dominate the birding theater. • This sparrow commonly nests at eye level, so you can easily have the good fortune to watch their breeding and nest-building rituals close-up. Chipping Sparrows are well known for their preference for hair as a nesting material. By offering your pet's, or even your own, hair in backyard baskets in spring, you could contribute to the nesting success of these delightful little birds. • 'Chipping' refers to this bird's call; *passerina* is Latin for 'little sparrow.'

ID: *Sexes similar:* prominent rufous cap; white eyebrow; black eye line; light grey, unstreaked underparts; mottled brown upperparts; all-dark bill; 2 faint wing bars; light-coloured legs.
Size: L 13–15 cm.
Status: very common from April to September.
Habitat: dry coniferous forests, mixed forests, pure deciduous forests and forest edges.

Nesting: usually low to mid-level in a coniferous tree; compact cup nest is woven with grass, rootlets and fine weeds and lined with fur (often uses black horsehair if it is available); female incubates 3 or 4 eggs for 11–14 days.
Feeding: hops along the ground and outer branches gleaning seeds, especially from grasses, dandelions and clovers; also eats adult and larval invertebrates; occasionally visits feeding stations.
Voice: simple, long, frequently heard trill; call is a high-pitched *chip*.
Similar Species: *American Tree Sparrow* (p. 312): central breast spot; lacks the bold white eyebrow and the black eye line. *Swamp Sparrow* (p. 328): lacks the white eyebrow, black eye line and wing bars.
Best Sites: Cold Lake PP or any other forested park.

313

CLAY-COLORED SPARROW

Spizella pallida

Despite their insect-like qualities, many of the buzzing sounds we hear in open fields and aspen edges are actually produced by this small, subdued sparrow. The Clay-colored Sparrow is often overlooked because its plumage, habit and voice all contribute to a cryptic lifestyle. It can be spotted, however, if a little time and patience are used to find the source of its odd song. This sparrow often perches motionlessly on an exposed branch, as if it knows that its drab characteristics provide adequate concealment and protection. • The subtlety of the Clay-colored Sparrow's plumage contributes to its unassuming beauty. By having to study the bird closely to assure its identification, the observer unknowingly gains an appreciation of the delicate shading, texture and form so often overlooked in birds with more colourful plumages. • Clay-colored Sparrows are quite common throughout Alberta, and visiting birders from the East often have a great desire to view this western specialty.

ID: *Sexes similar:* light brown cheek edged with darker brown; light brown, unstreaked breast; white eyebrow; light jaw stripe; dark crown with a pale stripe through the centre; pale bill; light-coloured legs.
Size: *L* 13–14 cm.
Status: common from May to September.
Habitat: forest edges, open deciduous forests, birch and willow shrubs, patches of rose bushes.
Nesting: very low in a grassy tuft or small bush; cup nest is woven with grass and small roots and lined with fine materials, including fur; pair incubates 3 or 4 bluish-green, speckled eggs for 10–12 days.
Feeding: forages on the ground and gleans low vegetation for seeds; also eats grasshoppers and other insects.
Voice: call is a soft *chip*; song is an insect-like, repeated, flat buzz that usually skips between 2–3 pitches.
Similar Species: *Brewer's Sparrow* (p. 315): less contrast in the face markings; faint eye ring; faint (if present) crown stripe.
Best Sites: Beaverhill Lake; Clifford E. Lee Nature Sanctuary.

BREWER'S SPARROW
Spizella breweri

Strip away all the breast streaks, caps, crown stripes and facial markings that adorn most other sparrows, and you're left with the Brewer's Sparrow. This sparrow does not oblige binocular-toting birders, because it infrequently perches in the open. Rather, its identity is often determined from its buzzy call and its characteristic, quick getaway flights. • In Alberta, Brewer's Sparrows are most frequently encountered in sagebrush habitats, which, like this sparrow, are in decline in our province. Brewer's Sparrows are remarkably well adapted to their dry environments; they can survive long periods of drought by getting sufficient water from their diet of seeds. • Dr. Thomas Mayo Brewer made significant contributions to the understanding of the breeding behaviour of North American birds. Unfortunately, he is best remembered as leading the 'winning side' of the House Sparrow war, which resulted in the introduction of that species to North America.

ID: *Sexes similar:* light brown, unstreaked underparts; brown cheek patch; faint eye ring; finely streaked, brown upperparts; pale bill; light throat; pale eyebrow and jaw stripes; light-coloured legs.
Size: *L* 13–14 cm.
Status: uncommon from early May to September.
Habitat: sagebrush flats and grasslands.
Nesting: in a low, dense shrub; small, compact cup nest is woven with grass and roots and lined with fine materials and

fur; pair incubates 3–5 eggs for 11–13 days.
Feeding: forages on the ground and gleans low vegetation for adult and larval invertebrates and seeds.
Voice: extremely variable, canary-like song with buzzes and trills, up to 10 seconds long; often includes trills of different speeds and pitches in the same song.
Similar Species: *Clay-colored Sparrow* (p. 314): more pronounced facial markings and crown stripe; no eye ring.
Best Sites: Brooks, Taber and Pakowki Lake areas; Dinosaur PP.

TIMBERLINE SPARROW

Spizella breweri taverneri

The Timberline Sparrow is apparently the high-altitude counterpart of the resolutely low-elevation Brewer's Sparrow. We say 'apparently,' because at the time of this writing it is not officially recognized as a distinct species, although word has it that it soon will be. So hold onto this book for a few years, check the authoritative references, and then write either a confirmatory or derogatory note in the margin of this page. • As its name suggests, this sparrow lives near the peaks of mountains, where vegetation only grows 1 m or so above the ground. It is most frequently encountered in Alberta during spring, along high-elevation passes in our mountain parks. Timberline Sparrows seem satisfied with this lack of cover, and when they are disturbed they seem to be able to find the thickest bush in the landscape in which to hide. • In open areas, buzzy bird songs have an advantage over the simple whistles of forest-dwelling birds. The buzzing sounds are very complex auditory signals that do not distort over great distances, temperature gradients or air turbulence.

ID: *Sexes similar:* light brown, unstreaked underparts; brown cheek patch; faint eye ring; finely streaked, brown upperparts; pale bill; light throat; pale eyebrow and jaw stripes; light-coloured legs.
Size: *L* 13–14 cm.
Status: uncommon to common from June to August.
Habitat: willow and birch shrubbery, krummholz and avalanche slopes.
Nesting: in a low, dense shrub; small, compact cup nest is woven with grass and roots and lined with fine plant materials and fur; pair incubates 3–5 eggs for 11–13 days.
Feeding: forages on the ground and gleans low vegetation for adult and larval invertebrates and seeds.
Voice: extremely variable, canary-like song with buzzes and trills, up to 10 seconds long; often includes trills of different speeds and pitches in the same song.
Similar Species: *Clay-colored Sparrow* (p. 314): more pronounced facial markings and crown stripe; no eye ring.
Best Sites: The Whistlers and Columbia Icefield, Jasper NP; Bow Pass, Banff NP; Highwood Pass, Kananaskis Country.

VESPER SPARROW
Pooecetes gramineus

For birdwatchers who live on the flat prairies, with multitudes of confusing sparrows, the Vesper Sparrow offers a welcome relief—a chestnut patch tucked neatly on this bird's shoulder announces its identity in flight. When the Vesper Sparrow is perched, its dress is off-the-rack sparrow drab, but its song is simple and customized. This grass-loving bird is one of the lead singers of the prairie chorus, backed up by a multitude of prairie bells. • The Vesper Sparrow is not as fussy about habitat as many other grassland birds, and a simple ditch seems to meet its needs. It is one of the most common small roadside birds, but it is too often overlooked as we drive through Alberta's grasslands. Its song is harder to pass up as the delicious notes drift endlessly across a calm prairie landscape during long spring evenings. • 'Vesper' is from the Latin for 'evening.' The scientific name refers to this species's preferred habitat: *Pooecetes* is Greek for 'grass dweller'; *gramineus* is Latin for 'grass loving.'

ID: *Sexes similar:* chestnut shoulder patch; white outer tail feathers; pale yellow lore; weak flank streaking; white eye ring; dark upper mandible; lighter lower mandible; light-coloured legs.

Size: *L* 14–17 cm.

Status: common from April to September.

Habitat: grasslands, semi-open shrublands and agricultural areas.

Nesting: in a scrape on the ground, often under a canopy of grass; small cup nest is woven with grass and lined with finer materials; primarily the female incubates 4 or 5 eggs for 11–13 days.

Feeding: walks and runs along the ground, picking up grasshoppers, beetles, cutworms and seeds.

Voice: 4 characteristic, preliminary notes followed by an aimless melody: *here-here there-there, everybody-down-the-hill.*

Similar Species: *Savannah Sparrow* (p. 320): lacks the white outer tail feathers and the chestnut shoulder patch. *Baird's Sparrow* (p. 321): well-defined 'necklace'; lacks the white outer tail feathers. *Lincoln's Sparrow* (p. 327): buff wash on the breast; lacks the white outer tail feathers.

Best Sites: any piece of native prairie or pasture in Alberta's grasslands.

LARK SPARROW
Chondestes grammacus

Good habitat for the Lark Sparrow is easy to spot: the air and landscape are dry, and the sweet smell of sagebrush hangs in the air. In Alberta, such areas are largely restricted to our badlands, where Lark Sparrows sing atop short sagebrush plants or on rocky ledges. If you drive down into the badlands chasm of Dinosaur Provincial Park, the road-side sagebrush often yields close-ups of this large sparrow, whose presence makes this bizarre region even more interesting. • Although the Lark Sparrow's head pattern is distinctively bold, most sparrows share the same basic pattern in a mixture of not-so-contrasting browns and greys. • Male Lark Sparrows fluff their chestnut feathers, spread their tails, droop their wings and bubble with song in the presence of potential mates. Their beautiful arias reminded early naturalists of the famed Sky Lark of Europe.

ID: *Sexes similar:* distinctive 'helmet' made up of a white throat, eyebrow and crown stripe and a few black lines breaking up an otherwise chestnut red head; unstreaked, pale, breast with a central spot; black tail with white outer feathers; soft brown, mottled back and wings; light-coloured legs.
Size: L 15 cm.
Status: uncommon to common from May to August.
Habitat: semi-open shrub-lands, sandhills, sagebrush and occasionally pastures.

Nesting: on the ground or in a low bush; bulky cup nest is made of grass and twigs and lined with finer material; occasionally reuses abandoned thrasher nests; female incubates 4 or 5 eggs for 11–12 days.
Feeding: walks or hops on the ground, gleaning seeds; also eats grasshoppers and other invertebrates.
Voice: melodious and variable song that consists of short trills, buzzes, pauses and clear notes.
Similar Species: no other sparrow has the distinctive head pattern.
Best Sites: Dinosaur PP.

LARK BUNTING
Calamospiza melanocorys

Where the grasslands of Alberta stretch without evidence of cultivation, you might be lucky to witness the annual courtship of the Lark Bunting. Like a large dark butterfly, the male flutters and rises high above the flat prairie, beating his wings slowly and deeply. His bell-like, tinkling song spreads over the flat landscape, until he folds in his wings and floats to the ground like a falling leaf. • The Lark Bunting's courtship behaviour evolved before the arrival of fenceposts and power poles. Because there were no high points on which to perch on the prairies, Lark Buntings delivered their songs on the wing. • Because of the male Lark Bunting's distinctive, dark breeding plumage, he appears to be unrelated to his drab sparrow neighbours. The appearance of the female, however, reassures us that the Lark Bunting is a sparrow after all. • The scientific name *melanocorys* is Greek for 'black lark'—although the Lark Bunting is not related to the Sky Lark, its manner of singing in flight reminded pioneering naturalists of that European bird.

♂

breeding

ID: *General:* dark, conical bill; large, white wing patch. *Breeding male:* all-black plumage; white patch at the tip of the tail. *Female:* mottled brown upperparts; lightly streaked underparts; pale eyebrow.
Size: *L* 18 cm.
Status: rare to uncommon from late May to August.
Habitat: shortgrass prairie and sagebrush.
Nesting: on the ground; sheltered by a canopy of grass or by a small bush; cup nest is loosely built with grass, roots and

other plant materials and lined with plant down and fur; primarily the female incubates 4 or 5 pale blue eggs for 11–12 days.
Feeding: walks or hops along the ground gleaning insects, including grasshoppers, beetles and ants, seeds and waste grain.
Voice: rich and warbling, with clear notes.
Similar Species: all other sparrows lack the white wing patch. *Bobolink* (p. 344): male has a creamy nape, a white rump and white back patches.
Best Sites: roadsides between Bindloss and Patricia; Pakowki Lake–Manyberries area.

319

SAVANNAH SPARROW

Passerculus sandwichensis

The Savannah Sparrow is one of Alberta's most common open-country birds. Its dull brown plumage and streaked breast conceal it perfectly in the long grasses of its preferred habitat. It is most often seen darting across roads, highways and open fields in front of an advancing intruder. Fleeing Savannah Sparrows take flight only as a last resort—they prefer to run swiftly and inconspicuously through the grass, like feathered voles. • The Savannah Sparrow is likely to be the first of the confusing grassland sparrows that novice birdwatchers will identify. Although it shares many similarities with its cousins, its yellow lore spot and easy-to-remember song make it a respectable ambassador for its clan. • The common and scientific names of this bird reflect its broad North American distribution: 'Savannah' refers to the city in Georgia; *sandwichensis* is derived from Sandwich Bay in the Aleutian Islands off Alaska.

ID: *Sexes similar:* finely streaked breast; light-coloured, streaked underparts; mottled brown upperparts; yellow lore; light jaw line; light-coloured legs and bill.
Size: L 13–17 cm.
Status: very common from late April to October.
Habitat: moist meadows, marshy edges and weedy fields.
Nesting: on the ground; in a scrape sheltered by a canopy of grass or by a small bush; cup nest is woven with grass and lined with finer materials; pair incubates 3 or 4 eggs for 12–13 days.
Feeding: walks or runs on the ground, occasionally scratching for seeds and insects.
Voice: clear, distinct *tea tea tea teeeeea Today!*
Similar Species: *Vesper Sparrow* (p. 317): white outer tail feathers; chestnut shoulder patches. *Lincoln's Sparrow* (p. 327): buff jaw line; buff wash across the breast; greyer face. *Baird's Sparrow* (p. 321): buff head and nape. *Grasshopper Sparrow* (p. 322): unstreaked breast.
Best Sites: any natural open areas.

BAIRD'S SPARROW
Ammodramus bairdii

Baird's Sparrows are frustrating grassland denizens. Just when the form of the sparrow drifts into focus through your binoculars, the bird dives out of view from its perch. Baird's Sparrows sing atop grass stems and low shrubs, but when they stop singing they are almost impossible to find. • The Baird's Sparrow is a bird of native grasslands: it favours lush areas as opposed to grazed, short-grass plains. The variety of birdlife on Alberta's grasslands demonstrates the rich diversity of this landscape, the complexity of which goes largely unrecognized. • Spencer Fullerton Baird was forced to decline an invitation to join John J. Audubon's expedition on which this bird was collected. If you think this species is difficult to find and recognize now, consider that it took 30 years for a second ornithologist to 'rediscover' the Baird's Sparrow after it was first described.

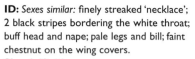

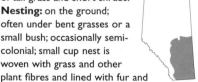

ID: *Sexes similar:* finely streaked 'necklace'; 2 black stripes bordering the white throat; buff head and nape; pale legs and bill; faint chestnut on the wing covers.
Size: *L* 13–14 cm.
Status: uncommon from May to September.
Habitat: native grasslands and lightly grazed pastures with clumps of tall grass and short shrubs.
Nesting: on the ground; often under bent grasses or a small bush; occasionally semi-colonial; small cup nest is woven with grass and other plant fibres and lined with fur and

other fine materials; female incubates 4 or 5 eggs for 11–12 days.
Feeding: gleans the ground, pecking and running through tall grass; eats mainly grass seeds; also eats other plant seeds and occasionally insects.
Voice: tinkling, musical trill: *zip-zip-zip-zrrr-r-r-r*; call is a harsh *chip*.
Similar Species: *Savannah Sparrow* (p. 320): lacks the buff head and nape; often has a yellow lore. *Vesper Sparrow* (p. 317): white outer tail feathers; lacks the delicate 'necklace' streaking. *Grasshopper Sparrow* (p. 322): breast is unstreaked.
Best Sites: Pakowki Lake area; Kinbrook Island PP; Jenner to Bindloss.

GRASSHOPPER SPARROW
Ammodramus savannarum

If you find yourself in prime Grasshopper Sparrow habitat, odds are you are either a birdwatcher or a rancher—or your car has experienced a mechanical break-down. Few people stop to enjoy Alberta's native grasslands, and, as a result, this region and its exceptional birdlife are generally underappreciated by the public. • The Grasshopper Sparrow is an open-country bird that is named not for its diet but rather for one of its buzzy, insect-like songs. The males sing two completely different, squeaky courtship songs, one short and the other more sustained. During the courtship flight, the male chases the female through the air, buzzing at a frequency that is inaudible to our ears. • If a nesting female Grasshopper Sparrow is flushed from her nest, she will run quietly away, instead of flying, to swiftly separate herself from the danger. • *Ammodramus* is Greek for 'sand runner'; *savannarum* is Latin for 'of the savanna,' the typical habitat of this species.

ID: *Sexes similar:* unstreaked breast; unmarked face; buff cheek; flat head; pale legs; mottled, brown upperparts; beady, black eyes; sharp tail; pale crown stripe.
Size: *L* 11–13 cm.
Status: uncommon from mid-May to September.
Habitat: grasslands, native prairies and sandhills.
Nesting: occasionally semi-colonial; in a shallow depression on the ground, usually under a dome of bent grass; small cup nest is woven with grass and lined with plant fibres, fur and small roots; female incubates 4 or 5 eggs for 12–13 days.
Feeding: gleans the ground and low plants, pecking and scurrying through the grass; eats mainly grasshoppers; also eats other invertebrates and seeds.
Voice: song is an insect-like buzz: *pit-tuck zee-ee-e-e-e-e-e-e.*
Similar Species: *Baird's Sparrow* (p. 321): faint 'necklace'; 2 stripes bordering a white chin. *Le Conte's Sparrow* (p. 323): buff-orange face markings. *Nelson's Sharp-tailed Sparrow* (p. 324): orangish face; grey cheek and shoulders.
Best Sites: sandhills south of Bindloss.

LE CONTE'S SPARROW

Ammodramus leconteii

With sputtering wingbeats, a flushed Le Conte's Sparrow flies weakly over its marshy home before it noses down and seemingly crashes into a mass of grasses. The Le Conte's Sparrow is a secretive bird that is usually difficult to observe; even a singing male chooses a low perch from which to offer his love ballad. His song is very similar to that of a Grasshopper Sparrow, but it is even weaker, briefer and more buzzy. When a male is singing he is fairly easy to approach, but when you get too close, he will dive into the vegetation and disappear from view.
• John Le Conte is best remembered as one of the pre-eminent American entomologists of the 19th century, but he was interested in all areas of natural history—he is an inspiration to us all.

ID: *Sexes similar:* buff-orange face markings; grey cheek; orange breast; lightly streaked breast; light crown stripe; mottled brown upperparts; light legs.
Size: *L* 11–13 cm.
Status: uncommon to common from late April to September.
Habitat: flooded sedge and grass meadows and willow flats.
Nesting: on the ground or very low in a shrub, in a dry area of marshland; well-concealed cup nest is woven with grass; female incubates 3–5 eggs for 12–13 days.

Feeding: forages on the ground and gleans low vegetation for insects, spiders and seeds.
Voice: *Male:* quick, insect-like buzz: *take-it ea-zeee!*
Similar Species: *Nelson's Sharp-tailed Sparrow* (p. 324): grey nape with white streaks on the back. *Grasshopper Sparrow* (p. 322): lacks the dark streaking on the breast. *Baird's Sparrow* (p. 321): lacks the buff-orange in the face.
Best Sites: Beaverhill Lake; Big Hill Springs PP.

NELSON'S SHARP-TAILED SPARROW
Ammodramus nelsoni

It's hard to find a Nelson's Sharp-tailed Sparrow without getting your feet wet. This relatively colourful sparrow lives in marshy areas, and it will unexpectedly pop out of a soggy hiding place to perch completely exposed at a close distance. The best way to identify a Nelson's Sharp-tail is by sound—the same way most sparrows are identified. This sparrow produces a single sharp note followed by a buzzy trill, which is a unique combination among Alberta birds. • The Nelson's Sharp-tailed Sparrow has a very unusual breeding strategy: the males rove around the marsh mating with all the available females, which are also promiscuous, and this sparrow does not establish pair bonds or territories. • Edward William Nelson was the chief of the U.S. Biological Survey and president of the American Ornithologists' Union. His greatest contribution was the creation of the Migratory Bird Treaty, which is still in effect today. • This species was formerly grouped with the Saltmarsh Sharp-tailed Sparrow as a single species, known as the Sharp-tailed Sparrow.

ID: *Sexes similar:* orangish face; grey cheek; grey nape; lightly streaked breast; white stripes on the back; light bill.
Size: L 13–15 cm.
Status: common from late May to September.
Habitat: marshlands with tall emergent vegetation and shoreline vegetation.
Nesting: on the ground or low in upright grass or sedge stems; bulky cup nest is woven with dry grass and sedges and lined with fine

materials; female incubates 3–5 eggs for 11 days.
Feeding: runs or walks along the ground gleaning ants, beetles, grasshoppers and often invertebrates; also eats seeds.
Voice: raspy *ts tse-sheeeee*.
Similar Species: *Le Conte's Sparrow* (p. 323): lacks the grey nape and the white stripes on the back. *Grasshopper Sparrow* (p. 322): lacks the streaking on the breast. *Savannah Sparrow* (p. 320): yellow colour on the head is restricted to the lore.
Best Sites: Big Hill Springs PP; Whitford Lake; Beaverhill Lake.

FOX SPARROW
Passerella iliaca

Fox Sparrows literally scratch out a living: they scuffle around beneath shrubs and bushes, using an energetic double-kick to stir up the leaves and dig into moist soil. The noise Fox Sparrows make as they shift the dry leaf litter often betrays their presence in the understorey. Their loud songs are equally revealing, and to the attentive listener they are as moving as the bugles of elk and the howls of wolves. • Three slightly different-looking subspecies of the Fox Sparrow occur in Alberta: one nests in the boreal forest; the second nests in the Rockies from Jasper National Park to Kananaskis Country; the third (and least common) nests in Waterton Lakes National Park. Go to the mountains if you want to spend time with these birds in summer; during migration, birds from the boreal forest are fairly common backyard visitors. • It is the Fox Sparrow's rufous-red lower back and tail that give it its name.

Jasper to Kananaskis

Southwestern Alberta

ID: *Sexes similar:* heavily streaked underparts; greyish upperparts; reddish tail and flight feathers; breast streaking often merges to a central spot; light grey bill; light legs.
Size: *L* 17–19 cm.
Status: uncommon to common from mid-April to October.
Habitat: willow flats and meadows, dense woodland thickets, avalanche slopes, open forests and forest edges.
Nesting: on the ground or low in a shrub or small tree; cup nest is woven with twigs, grass, moss and bark shreds and

often lined with the hair of large mammals; female incubates 3 or 4 eggs for 12–14 days.
Feeding: scratches the ground to uncover seeds, berries and invertebrates; visits backyard feeding stations in migration, foraging on seeds that have dropped to the ground.
Voice: variable; long, warbling *All I have is what's here dear, won't you won't you take it?*
Similar Species: *Song Sparrow* (p. 326): generally has an eye line and an eyebrow; lighter breast streaks. *Hermit Thrush* (p. 272): lighter breast streaks; thin bill. *Swainson's Thrush* (p. 271): olive tail; light breast streaks; prominent eye ring.
Best Sites: Banff NP; Waterton Lakes NP.

SONG SPARROW
Melospiza melodia

The Song Sparrow's heavily streaked, low-keyed plumage doesn't prepare you for its symphonic song. This bird produces wondrous melodic surprises, usually beginning with a sharp *hip-hip-hip,* and then ending with a prolonged warble. Many beginner birdwatchers hesitate at the song, because the tune conjures up images of a far more exotic species. This well-named sparrow stands among the great Alberta songsters for its song's complexity, rhythm and emotion.

• Song Sparrows (and many other songbirds) learn to sing by eavesdropping on their fathers or on rival males. By the time a young male is a few months old, he will have the basis for his song. • When these birds stop over in backyards during their migration, they appear equally faithful to the birdseed as to messy piles of leafy branches. • The scientific name *melodia* means 'melody' in Greek.

ID: *Sexes similar:* heavy breast streaking often converges into a central spot; grey face with a dark eye line; white jaw line (as if milk has dribbled from the bill); red-brown crown (often erect) with a grey stripe; mottled back; white throat; plumage is variable throughout its range.

Size: L 14–18 cm.

Status: very common from mid-April to October; a few might overwinter.

Habitat: willow shrublands and shrubby riparian areas.

Nesting: usually on the ground, occasionally in a shrub or small

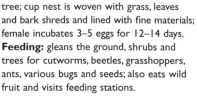

tree; cup nest is woven with grass, leaves and bark shreds and lined with fine materials; female incubates 3–5 eggs for 12–14 days.

Feeding: gleans the ground, shrubs and trees for cutworms, beetles, grasshoppers, ants, various bugs and seeds; also eats wild fruit and visits feeding stations.

Voice: 1–3 distinctive introductory notes, followed by a pleasant melody: *Hip Hip Hip Hooray Boys, the spring is here again* or *Maids Maids Maids, hang up your tea kettle kettle kettle.*

Similar Species: *Fox Sparrow* (p. 325): heavier breast streaking; generally has a plain face. *Lincoln's Sparrow* (p. 327): lightly streaked breast with a buff wash; buff jaw line. *Savannah Sparrow* (p. 320): lightly streaked breast; yellow lore; lacks the grey face.

Best Site: Edmonton river valley.

LINCOLN'S SPARROW

Melospiza lincolnii

There is a certain beauty in the plumage of a Lincoln's Sparrow that is greater than the sum of its feathers. Sightings of this bird, linked with the sounds and smells of it's natural habitat, create an aura of their own. • The Lincoln's Sparrow seems to be more fearful than many other sparrows in Alberta. It sits openly on exposed vegetation and look-out perches when it is singing its bubbly, wren-like courtship song, but otherwise it always seems within a split-second flight into dense cover. During the breeding season, Lincoln's Sparrows are vigilant defenders of their young, uncharacteristically exposing themselves to intruders and chirping noisily. • The nesting territories of Lincoln's Sparrows are frequently flooded by snow melt and swollen streams in spring and early summer. • This sparrow bears the name of Thomas Lincoln, a young companion to John J. Audubon on his voyage to Labrador.

ID: *Sexes similar:* lightly streaked breast with a buff wash; buff jaw line; grey eyebrow; brown cheek; dark cap; white belly; grey 'collar'; brown-grey, mottled upperparts; very faint, white eye ring.

Size: *L* 15 cm.

Status: uncommon to common from late April to October.

Habitat: shrubby meadows, shoreline forests, roadsides, bog edges and wetlands with emergent sedges and tall shoreline vegetation.

Nesting: on the ground, often sunk into soft moss or concealed beneath shrubs; well-hidden cup

nest is woven with dry grass and lined with fine materials; female incubates 4 or 5 eggs for 11–14 days.

Feeding: scratches at the ground, exposing invertebrates and seeds; occasionally visits feeding stations.

Voice: very wren-like warble—*kee kee kee, see see seedle seedle seedle see-see-see-see*—with a trill in the middle.

Similar Species: *Song Sparrow* (p. 326): heavier breast streaking; white jaw line. *Savannah Sparrow* (p. 320): yellow lore; white eyebrow and jaw line.

Best Sites: roadsides around Rocky Mountain House and Fort McMurray.

SWAMP SPARROW
Melospiza georgiana

Although Swamp Sparrows can be fairly common in Alberta wetlands, they are far less visible than their neighbours, the blackbirds and yellowthroats—except, that is, when a male Swamp Sparrow pounces atop a bulrush or willow branch to sing his sweet, loose trill. • Of the sparrows in our area, the Swamp Sparrow is the best adapted to life around water. Like all other sparrows, it is unable to swim, but that is no deterrent to this rufous-crowned wetland skulker—it gleans much of its insectivorous diet directly from the surface of wetlands. Because the Swamp Sparrow eats a smaller proportion of hard seeds in its diet, its bill and jaw muscles are comparatively smaller than those of other sparrows. • Swamp Sparrows can be readily enticed to pop up to a cattail head in response to a birder's urging squeaks. • Winter records of Swamp Sparrows in Alberta are rare, but not unheard of.

breeding

ID: *Sexes similar:* grey face; rufous upperparts and wings; streaked back. *Breeding:* red cap; white throat and jaw line; grey underparts. *Non-breeding:* streaked brown cap.
Size: L 13.5–15 cm.
Status: uncommon from mid-May to October; a few might overwinter.
Habitat: wet shrublands, often near lakes or streams, and marshes.
Nesting: in emergent vegetation or shoreline bushes; cup nest, woven with coarse marsh vegetation and lined with fine materials, has a side entrance; female incubates 4 or 5 eggs for 12–15 days.

Feeding: picks food primarily from the ground, but also from vegetation and the water's surface; much of its summer diet includes beetles, grasshoppers and caterpillars; eats seeds in late summer and fall.
Voice: sharp, metallic *Weet-Weet-Weet-Weet.*
Similar Species: *Chipping Sparrow* (p. 313): clean white eyebrow; black eye line; uniform grey underparts. *American Tree Sparrow* (p. 312): central, dark breast spot; 2-toned bill. *Song Sparrow* (p. 326): lacks the grey 'collar'; fine breast streaks.
Best Sites: extremely local in the foothills; brushy areas along the Bow River (fall).

WHITE-THROATED SPARROW
Zonotrichia albicollis

While the White-throated Sparrow might lack the physical stature of many of Alberta's most renowned vocalists, its song rings memorably in the ears of all who have visited the northern woods in summer. This handsome sparrow's simple song is freely offered throughout the spring months, and while many weekend cottagers might not know the bird, most know its song. The song's purposeful phrases are occasionally delivered late into the night. • The White-throated Sparrow is easily identified by its white, bib-like throat. Two colour morphs are common throughout Alberta: one has black and white stripes on the head; the other has brown and tan stripes. • *Zonotrichia* means 'hair-like,' in reference to the striped heads of birds of this genus; *albicollis* is Latin for 'white neck.'

ID: *Sexes similar:* black-and-white (or brown-and-tan) striped head; white throat; grey cheek; yellow lore; black eye line; grey, unstreaked underparts; mottled, brown upperparts.
Size: *L* 17–18 cm.
Status: common to very common from late April to October; a few might overwinter.
Habitat: willow shrublands, mixed forest edges, mixed deciduous forests, river floodplains and brushy areas.
Nesting: usually concealed under a fallen log; occasionally in a low shrub; cup nest is woven with grass, twigs and conifer needles and lined with fur and fine materials; female incubates 4–6 eggs for 11–14 days.

Feeding: scratches the ground to expose invertebrates, seeds and fruit; gleans vegetation and catches invertebrates in flight; visits feeding stations in winter.
Voice: clear and distinct: *dear sweet Canada Canada Canada*; variable, but always recognizable.
Similar Species: *White-crowned Sparrow* (p. 331): lacks the white throat and the yellow lore. *Swamp Sparrow* (p. 328): rusty cap; slightly streaked breast.
Best Sites: Elk Island NP; Miquelon Lake PP; Cold Lake PP; Sir Winston Churchill PP; Long Lake PP; Thunder Lake PP; Crimson Lake PP.

HARRIS'S SPARROW
Zonotrichia querula

There are never uneventful days in the natural calendar of Alberta. During the spring and fall migrations, for example, there looms the possibility, however slim, of seeing a Harris's Sparrow almost anywhere in Alberta. An unassuming migrant, the Harris's Sparrow passes through Alberta not in spectacular waves, but in isolated trickles, frequently mixing with flocks of White-throated Sparrows and White-crowned Sparrows. These robust Arctic breeders are known to visit backyard feeders, but they are most commonly encountered in rural areas, perched in leafless shrubs. • The Harris's Sparrow is among the last of the migrant songbirds to leave the province in fall. Although most have passed through Alberta by the time November's first wintry blast arrives, a few Harris's Sparrows successfully winter in southern communities. • John J. Audubon named this bird after an amateur naturalist and friend, Edward Harris, with whom he travelled up the Missouri River in 1843.

non-breeding

ID: *Sexes similar. Breeding:* black crown, throat and bib; grey face; white underparts; pink-orange bill; black streaks on the flanks; mottled upperparts. *Non-breeding:* brown face; buff flanks.
Size: L 18–20 cm.
Status: uncommon from April to May and from September to early November; a few might overwinter.
Habitat: roadsides, shrubby vegetation, forest edges and thickets.

Nesting: does not nest in Alberta.
Feeding: gleans the ground for plant seeds and vegetation for buds, invertebrates and berries; occasionally visits feeding stations.
Voice: alarm call is *zheenk;* occasionally gives a rolling *chug-up chug-up* in flight.
Similar Species: *White-throated Sparrow* (p. 329): dark bill; yellow lore. *White-crowned Sparrow* (p. 331): grey collar; striped head.
Best Sites: birdfeeders in very late fall; check bird hotlines.

WHITE-CROWNED SPARROW
Zonotrichia leucophrys

While most of Alberta's sparrows can quite honestly be described as LBJs (little brown jobs) the White-crowned Sparrow is smart-looking—it always gives the impression of being freshly turned out. Aside from its good looks, this large, bold sparrow is one of our finest singers. There are several different races of the White-crowned Sparrow in Alberta, so not all birds sound alike, but they all give a slight variation of *I-I-I-got-to-go-wee-wee now!* These birds are tireless singers in spring, and they even burst into song under the light of the moon. • The White-crowned Sparrow is widespread through Alberta—it is equally at home in a lakeshore willow in the Cypress Hills, an avalanche slope in the mountains or atop a black spruce in a northern bog. • This species is the most studied sparrow in North America. It has given science tremendous insight on physiology and geographic variation in song dialects. • The scientific name *leucophrys* is Greek for 'white eyebrow.'

ID: *Sexes similar:* large white crown bordered by black; white eyebrow; black eye line; orange-pink bill; grey face; grey, unstreaked underparts; brown, streaked back.
Size: *L* 14–18 cm.
Status: common from mid-April to October; a few might overwinter.
Habitat: open environments with shrubby meadows, krummholz, bogs, alpine and riparian willow shrubs.
Nesting: usually in a shrub or small coniferous tree, or on the ground; neat cup nest is woven with twigs, grass, leaves and

bark shreds and lined with fine materials; female incubates 3–5 eggs for 11–14 days.
Feeding: scratches the ground to expose insects and seeds; also eats berries, buds and moss caps; visits feeding stations.
Voice: variable; frequently *I-I-I gotta go wee-wee now!*
Similar Species: *White-throated Sparrow* (p. 329): clearly defined, white throat; darker bill; yellow lore. *Golden-crowned Sparrow* (p. 332): golden-yellow fore crown; dark bill.
Best Sites: Cypress Hills PP; Fortress Mountain, Kananaskis Country; Jasper NP; Banff NP.

GOLDEN-CROWNED SPARROW
Zonotrichia atricapilla

Aside from the spectacular scenery, one of the rewards of climbing Alberta's peaks is to walk through the world of the Golden-crowned Sparrow. Breeding in the open scrubby areas near treeline, the Golden-crowned Sparrow offers its sad, flat song to the rugged landscape. • Birdwatchers are not the only ones to attribute words to bird songs—Alaskan prospectors thought that this bird's descending three-note song, *oh dear me*, sounded as tired as they felt. Ironically, the only gold most of the prospectors were to encounter was on the crown of this mountain songbird. • The Golden-crowned Sparrow is not often encountered in Alberta, because its breeding grounds are fairly remote. Along high mountain passes, bird-watchers might choose to pull over and walk among the bushes to see if any of these large sparrows appear. • The scientific name *atricapilla* is Latin for 'black hair,' in reference to the broad outline to the golden crown.

ID: *Sexes similar:* heavy black eyebrows that converge on the nape; golden-yellow fore crown; grey hind crown; grey face; dark bill; long tail; grey-brown, unstreaked underparts; streaked upperparts; faint, white wing bars.
Size: *L* 15–18 cm.
Status: locally uncommon to common from mid-May to September.
Habitat: high-elevation meadows, mountain tundra and stunted fir and spruce forests near treeline.
Nesting: usually in a scrape or depression on the ground, near the base of a shrub or small tree; bulky cup nest is woven with grass, twigs, leaves and bark shreds and lined with fine materials; incubates 4 or 5 eggs.
Feeding: gleans the ground for invertebrates, buds, seeds and occasionally fruit.
Voice: 3–5 notes: *Oh dear me* or *three blind mice.*
Similar Species: *White-crowned Sparrow* (p. 331): lacks the golden-yellow crown. *Harris's Sparrow* (p. 330): black bib; orange-pink bill.
Best Sites: The Whistlers, Jasper NP; Sunwapta Pass, Jasper-Banff boundary; Highwood Pass, Kananaskis Country.

DARK-EYED JUNCO
Junco hyemalis

The Dark-eyed Junco passes through virtually every moderately sized woodlot in Alberta at some point in the year, and it is one of the our most familiar forest species. No less than four distinct races are found in Alberta, so it is always interesting to study junco flocks to figure out their nesting destinations: the 'Slate-colored Junco' nests in the boreal forest; the 'Oregon' nests in the Rockies south of Jasper; the 'Northern Rockies' nests in Jasper National Park; the 'Pink-sided' nests in the Cypress Hills. • Juncos are ground dwellers that flush readily from wooded trails and backyard feeders. Their distinctive, white outer tail feathers flash as they fly away before diving into a thicket. • Although juncos stick around feeders past the first snowfall, most of them seem to leave the province before the Christmas bird counts. You can still find a few here and there, and small numbers tend to congregate near springs in mid-winter.

'Oregon Junco'

'Slate-colored Junco'

ID: *General:* white outer tail feathers; pink bill. *'Slate-colored Junco':* white belly; otherwise grey or brown-grey. *'Oregon Junco':* reddish-brown back and flanks; white belly; male has a black hood and a grey rump; female has a dark brown hood and a brown rump. *'Pink-sided Junco':* grey head; pink flanks; white belly; light brown back. *'Northern Rockies Junco':* black hood; brownish back; light brown sides.
Size: *L* 13–17 cm.
Status: very common from late March to November.

Habitat: coniferous and mixed forests, shrublands, roadsides, wooded urban areas, forest edges and avalanche slopes.
Nesting: usually on the ground, often with an overhanging canopy, or low in a shrub or small tree; deep cup nest is woven with grass, bark strips and roots and lined with fine materials and fur; female incubates 3–5 eggs for 12–13 days.
Feeding: scratches the ground for invertebrates; also eats berries and seeds; commonly visits feeding stations.
Voice: long, dry trill; call is a 'smacking' note.
Similar Species: none.
Best Sites: all forested and mountain parks.

McCOWN'S LONGSPUR
Calcarius mccownii

If you are in the deep south of Alberta, do yourself a favour and pull off onto a gravel road that steaks across the grasslands. If you've entered a good piece of native Alberta prairie, you might see a McCown's Longspur retreating from a fencepost. As with so many other grassland species, the range of the McCown's Longspur has been shrinking—a condition that is directly linked to the cultivation of native grasslands. • The McCown's Longspur delivers its love song on the wing, tinkling as it sails to the ground with its tail fanned and its wings held high. Its soft voice does not dominate the morning chorus of prairie birds; rather it is a complementary song that adds dimension to the musical feast. • Female McCown's Longspurs are persistent incubators: they abandon their nests only when they are practically stepped upon. • John McCown was an American military officer posted in southern Texas, where he collected several birds, including the species that now carries his name.

breeding

ID: *Breeding male:* black cap and bib; rufous shoulder; black whisker; light grey face and underparts; black bill; white outer tail feathers; black tail tip and central stripe (like an inverted T). *Breeding female:* similar to the male in patterning, but not as bold; grey plumage.
Size: *L* 14–16 cm.
Status: uncommon from late April to September.
Habitat: shortgrass prairie, native grasslands, pastures and agricultural areas.
Nesting: on the ground, at the base of a clump of vegetation; cup nest is woven with coarse grass and lined with finer materials; female incubates 3 or 4 eggs for up to 12 days.
Feeding: walks on the ground gleaning seeds and invertebrates, especially grasshoppers, beetles and moths; occasionally drinks at shallow ponds.
Voice: a fast twittering warble delivered on the wing; call is *poik*.
Similar Species: *Chestnut-collared Longspur* (p. 337): breeding male has black underparts. *Lapland Longspur* (p. 335): greater number of black central tail feathers. *Vesper Sparrow* (p. 317): chestnut wing patch; more white in the face. *Savannah Sparrow* (p. 320): lacks the white outer tail feathers.
Best Site: Tilley area.

LAPLAND LONGSPUR

Calcarius lapponicus

Lapland Longspurs wheel about in uncountable masses over frozen Alberta fields in late fall and early spring. In fall, the birds have left their beautiful breeding plumage behind in the Arctic, but they continue to show communal grace in their flocking synchrony. Before farmers get a chance to work their fields in spring, the Lapland Longspurs are back, this time clothed in the wonderfully surprising colours they wear through summer in the Arctic. • Large flocks of Lapland Longspurs are normally quite easy to find during migration, but it's another matter to get a rewarding glimpse of individual birds. Lapland Longspurs scurry imperceptibly along the ground, and they might allow a naturalist to approach closely, but memories of this bird are usually associated with the flocks, not individuals.
• These winter residents of farmlands (typically south of Alberta) feed themselves by scraping away the ice and snow to reach the leftover grain that the combines could not catch. • The Lapland Longspur breeds in northern polar regions, including the area of northern Europe known as Lapland.

non-breeding

ID: *Non-breeding:* white outer tail feathers; often has rufous in the wings; light underparts; mottled upperparts; lightly streaked flanks; dark bill; male has pale chestnut on the nape; female lacks the chestnut nape. *Breeding male:* black crown, face and upper breast; chestnut nape; light bill.
Size: *L* 16 cm.
Status: common from late March to May and from September to October; a few might overwinter in southern Alberta.

Habitat: grasslands and stubble fields.
Nesting: does not nest in Alberta.
Feeding: *Winter:* gleans the ground and snow for seeds and waste grain. *Summer:* eats insects and seeds.
Voice: flight song is a rapid warbling; musical calls; also a dry rattle in flight.
Similar Species: *Snow Bunting* (p. 338): shows black-and-white patterning in flight; lacks the brown mottling on the back.
Best Site: Beaverhill Lake.

SMITH'S LONGSPUR
Calcarius pictus

When birdwatchers start taking more notice of the Smith's Longspur in Alberta, they will likely be surprised at the numbers of these birds over frozen fields in spring. The Smith's Longspur is an uncommon species during its spring and fall migrations—its passing is framed among the much larger movements of Lapland Longspurs. Although it takes patience, large flocks of Laplands should be checked thoroughly in spring for the presence of boldly coloured male Smith's Longspurs. In fall, the two species look so similar that the exercise might prove too daunting for anyone who hopes to maintain their sanity. • Smith's Longspurs often remain very still on the ground, and they can effectively disappear from view from one moment to the next. • John J. Audubon named this bird in honour of his friend and subscriber, Gideon Smith. The scientific name was given to this species 12 years previously, when a specimen was taken on the banks of the Saskatchewan River (*pictus* means 'painted').

breeding

ID: *General:* white outer and black inner tail feathers; white shoulder (often concealed). *Breeding male:* black crown and face with a white eyebrow and cheek patch; buff underparts and collar.
Non-breeding male, Female and *Immature:* dark crown and facial markings.
Size: L 15–16 cm.
Status: uncommon migrant from early April to May and in August and September.

Nesting: does not nest in Alberta.
Feeding: forages on the ground for waste grain and seeds; might also eat insects.
Voice: alarm call is a slow *tick tick tick*, like a watch; song is a warbling *switoo-whideedee-dew, whee-tew.*
Similar Species: *Lapland Longspur* (p. 335): less white in the tail; black on the neck; male has white underparts.
Best Sites: Beaverhill Lake; Hanna area.

CHESTNUT-COLLARED LONGSPUR

Calcarius ornatus

In spring, in areas where the dry, flavourless smell of stale prairie dust hangs in the breeze, cock your ear for the tinkling song of the Chestnut-collared Longspur. The colourful males can occasionally be seen in flight or atop boulders, shrubs or fenceposts that rise out of the dancing waves of grass. The Chestnut-collared Longspur is the most colourful of the grassland sparrows—it is gaudily marked in comparison to the dull plumage typical of its neighbours. • The Chestnut-collared Longspur was one of the most abundant birds in southern Alberta before the plough arrived and altered the landscape. Now it is only found in areas that have escaped cultivation, or where the natural forces of the grasslands have restored once-ploughed fields. • Longspurs are so named because they have an extremely long hind claw. It is thought that this elongated appendage is beneficial to a bird that spends so much of its life on the ground.

♂

breeding

ID: *Breeding male:* chestnut nape; black underparts; yellow throat; black cap; white eyebrow; mottled brown upperparts; white outer tail feathers; black central and terminal tail feathers; white undertail coverts. *Breeding female:* might show a chestnut nape; mottled brown overall; light breast streaks.
Size: *L* 14–16 cm.
Status: uncommon to common from April to September.
Habitat: shortgrass prairie; tall grass is not usually tolerated.
Nesting: well concealed by grass in a depression or scrape; small cup nest is woven with grass and lined with feathers and fur; female incubates 3–5 eggs for 10–13 days.
Feeding: gleans the ground for plant seeds and invertebrates.
Similar Species: breeding male is distinctive. *McCown's Longspur* (p. 334): female has a hint of chestnut in the wing. *Vesper Sparrow* (p. 317): chestnut wing patch; more white in the face. *Savannah Sparrow* (p. 320): lacks the white outer tail feathers.
Best Sites: Hwy. 36 south of Hanna; Brooks area; Pakowki Lake; Medicine Hat–Suffield area.

SNOW BUNTING
Plectrophenax nivalis

When autumn frosts settle on the farmlands of Alberta, Snow Buntings are surely close behind. Unlike most migrant songbirds in Alberta, Snow Buntings arrive in fall and endure the winter here in tight flocks. They prefer expansive open areas, where they scratch and peck at exposed seeds and grains. • As flocks of Snow Buntings lift in unison, their startling black-and-white plumage flashes in contrast with the clean white snow-covered backdrop. In Alberta, Snow Bunting flocks typically contain several hundred birds, but prior to their northward migration, certain flocks might boast more than half a million! • The northern wanderings of summer Snow Buntings are not exceeded by any other songbird. A single individual, likely misguided and lost, was recorded not far from the North Pole.

♂

♀

non-breeding

ID: *Non-breeding:* white underparts; light golden-brown crown and back (male has a paler back); pale bill. *In flight:* black wing tips and tail contrast with the light body plumage and white wing patches.
Size: *L* 15–19 cm.
Status: common from October to early May.
Habitat: grasslands, frozen marshes, roadsides and railways.

Nesting: does not nest in Alberta.
Feeding: gleans the ground and snow for seeds and waste grain.
Voice: spring song is a musical, high-pitched *chi-chi-churee*; call is a whistled *tew.*
Similar Species: *Lapland Longspur* (p. 335): brown, mottled back; lacks the black-and-white contrast in flight.
Best Sites: Beaverhill Lake; Frank Lake.

NORTHERN CARDINAL

Cardinalis cardinalis

If you are the gambling type, there might well be a wager out there about the first breeding location of cardinals in Alberta. You might have to wait a few more years to collect, however, because all Alberta records so far have been of pioneering birds well outside their natural range. That cardinals are on their way west into our province is undisputed—sightings of cardinals in Alberta are increasing in frequency, and the western edge of their breeding range continually approaches our province. The proliferation of backyard feeders and ornamental shrub plantings has helped in the expansion of their range. • The Northern Cardinal was originally a bird of the American South, and it doesn't do very well in cold weather, relying on other birds to remove the snow from covered seeds. • The Northern Cardinal forms one of the bird world's most faithful pair bonds. Never far from one another year-round, male and female cardinals softly vocalize back and forth, as if sharing sweet nothings. • The cardinal owes its name to the vivid red plumage of the male, which matches the robes of Roman Catholic cardinals.

ID: *Male:* unmistakable; red overall; black mask and throat; pointed crest; red, conical bill; *Female:* similar to the male, except the plumage is quite a bit duller.
Size: *L* 20–23 cm.
Status: rare year-round; most records are from winter.
Habitat: backyards, city parks, thickets and woodlands.

Nesting: does not nest in Alberta.
Feeding: hops on the ground or in low bushes, picking seeds, insects and berries.
Voice: distinctive, bubbly *What cheer! What cheer! birdie-birdie-birdie What cheer.*
Similar Species: none.
Best Sites: check local bird hotlines for recent sightings.

vagrant

ROSE-BREASTED GROSBEAK
Pheucticus ludovicianus

With a range that gently curves overtop the northern Great Plains, the Rose-breasted Grosbeak, near its western limit, embraces the forests of northern Alberta. The delicious songs of these birds can be heard cascading among the quivering leaves of aspens. The Rose-breasted Grosbeak's songs are quite similar to those of robins, but this grosbeak runs its phrases together without pausing to take a breath. • Rose-breasted Grosbeaks will only rarely leave the green treetop canopy when they descend cautiously to drink at water puddles. • The Rose-breasted Grosbeak migrates primarily at night. It is known to stray widely during its spring and fall trips, and it often pleasantly appears one morning in unsuspecting yards and parks. • The species name *ludovicianus,* Latin for 'from Louisiana,' is misleading, because this bird is only a migrant through that and other southern states.

ID: *General:* large, light-coloured, conical bill. *Male:* black hood, back, tail and wings; red breast and inner underwings; white underparts, rump and wing patches. *Female:* light eyebrow and crown stripe; brown upperparts; light underparts; streaked breast; white wing bars.

Size: *L* 18–22 cm.

Status: uncommon to common from May to September.

Habitat: deciduous, mixed and riparian woodlands and wooded urban parks.

Nesting: in a tree or tall shrub, often near water; cup nest is

loosely built of twigs, bark strips and grass; pair incubates 3–5 eggs for 9–12 days.

Feeding: gleans vegetation; occasionally hovers and catches flying insects on the wing; primarily eats seeds, buds, blossoms and invertebrates; eats fruit in season; periodically visits feeding stations.

Voice: long, continuous series of robin-like notes; usually contains a 'wolf whistle.'

Similar Species: male is distinctive. *Black-headed Grosbeak* (p. 341): female has a dark bill and faint flank streaking. *Purple Finch* (p. 356): female is much smaller and has heavy streaking on the underparts.

Best Sites: Elk Island NP; Miquelon Lake PP; Sundre area.

BLACK-HEADED GROSBEAK
Pheucticus melanocephalus

Regardless of whether the nest is tended by the male or the female, young Black-headed Grosbeaks are continually enveloped in a world of song. The Black-headed Grosbeak is a brilliant singer that flaunts its voice in performances from treetops and from atop its nest. It breeds very locally in Alberta, so its unusual nest chorus is made even more interesting by the scarcity of this bird. • Although this grosbeak's bill looks like it can crush any seed imaginable, during its stay in Alberta, the Black-headed Grosbeak also eats many insects. Strangely, this bird regularly dines on Monarch Butterflies, which are distasteful and even toxic to most birds. The distribution of Black-headed Grosbeaks and Monarch Butterflies in Alberta is nearly identical. • Male and female Black-headed Grosbeaks look so dissimilar that they can be mistaken for different species. • The scientific name *melanocephalus* is Greek for 'black-headed.'

ID: *General:* large, dark, conical bill. *Male:* orange-brown underparts and rump; black head, back, wings and tail; white wing bars and undertail coverts. *Female:* dark brown upperparts; buff underparts; lightly streaked flanks; pale eyebrow and crown stripe.
Size: L 18–22 cm.
Status: rare from late May to August.
Habitat: lowland forests and shrubby coulees.
Nesting: in a tall shrub or deciduous tree, often near water; cup nest is loosely woven of twigs and lined with fine grass; female builds the nest in 3–4 days; pair incubates 3–5 eggs for 12–14 days.

Feeding: forages the upper canopy for invertebrates and plant foods; occasionally visits feeding stations.
Voice: long series of robin-like phrases, without any breaks.
Similar Species: male is distinctive. *Rose-breasted Grosbeak* (p. 340): female has a pale bill and a streaked breast. *Purple Finch* (p. 356): female is much smaller and has heavily streaked underparts.
Best Sites: Writing-on-Stone PP; Waterton Lakes NP.

LAZULI BUNTING

Passerina amoena

Alberta is not richly populated by the charming Lazuli Bunting, but where this species does occur, the males set up obvious territorial districts. Neighbouring males copy and learn their songs from one another, producing 'song territories.' Each male within a song territory sings with slight differences in the song sylla- bles, producing his own acoustic fingerprint. • Lazuli Buntings nest in isolated pockets in the southern quarter of Alberta. Whether they are found in an arid coulee bottom or on an east-slope meadow, the buntings confine their activities to shrubs and bushes. • Before leaving our province in fall, Lazuli Buntings undergo an incomplete molt—they fly to the American Southwest to complete their change of wardrobe. • This bird is named after the colourful gemstone lapis lazuli. The generally accepted pronunciation of the name is 'LAZZ-you- lie,' but personal variations are plentiful. • The scientific name *amoena* is from the Latin for 'charming,' 'delightful' or 'dressy,' all of which this bird certainly is.

ID: *General:* stout, conical bill. *Male:* tur- quoise blue hood and rump; chestnut breast; white belly; dark wings and tail; 2 white wing bars. *Female:* soft brown overall; hints of blue on the rump.
Size: L 13–15 cm.
Status: rare to uncommon from late May to August.
Habitat: brushy areas, forest edges and willow and alder shrublands.
Nesting: in an upright crotch low in a shrubby tangle; small cup nest is woven with grass and lined

with finer grass and hair; female incubates 3–5 eggs for 12 days.
Feeding: gleans the ground and low shrubs for grasshoppers, beetles, other insects and native seeds; visits feeding stations.
Voice: *Male:* song is a fast *swip-swip-swip zu zu ee, see see sip see see.*
Similar Species: *Indigo Bunting* (p. 343): no wing bars; male lacks the chestnut breast. *Western Bluebird* (p. 266): male is larger, has a slimmer bill and has no wing bars.
Best Sites: Medicine Hat; Highwood River valley, Kananaskis Country; Waterton Lakes NP.

INDIGO BUNTING
Passerina cyanea

In poor light, a male Indigo Bunting can look almost black. If this happens during your first encounter with this finch-like bird, reposition yourself quickly so that the sun strikes and enlivens this bunting's incomparable indigo colour. • The Indigo Bunting is quite rare in Alberta, but our province is one of the few places in North America where the Indigo Bunting nests practically alongside the closely related Lazuli Bunting. A double-bunting day, with an opportunity to learn the differences in their vocalizations and behaviours, is an experience that is shared by very few naturalists. Indigo Buntings in Alberta might show some degree of hybridization with Lazuli Buntings. • The Indigo Bunting undertakes a clever and comical foraging strategy to reach the grass and weed seeds upon which it feeds: the bird lands midway on a stem and then shuffles slowly towards the seed head, which eventually bends under the bird's weight and gives the bunting easier access to the seeds.

ID: *General:* dark, stout, conical bill; beady, black eyes; black legs; no wing bars. *Male:* royal blue overall. *Female:* soft brown overall; faint flank streaks.

Size: *L* 14 cm.

Status: rare from late May to August.

Habitat: forest edges, shrubby fields, orchards, overgrown pastures and hedgerows.

Nesting: usually in an upright fork in a small tree or shrub; well-built cup nest is woven with grass, leaves and bark strips and lined with fine materials; female incubates 3 or 4 eggs for 12–13 days.

Feeding: gleans low vegetation and the ground for insects, especially grasshoppers, beetles, weevils, flies and larvae; also eats the seeds of thistles, dandelions, goldenrods and other native plants.

Voice: paired warbling couplets: *fire-fire, where-where, here-here, see-it see-it.*

Similar Species: *Lazuli Bunting* (p. 342): 2 pale wing bars; male has a chestnut breast. *Mountain Bluebird* (p. 267); larger; slimmer bill; lacks the darker wings and tail.

Best Sites: Medicine Hat; Cypress Hills PP; Turner Valley.

vagrant

343

BOBOLINK

Dolichonyx oryzivorus

The female Bobolink is dressed in sparrow drab, but the male, with his dark belly and light-and-dark upperparts, is coloured like no other bird in Alberta. Roger Tory Peterson was inspired to describe the male Bobolink as wearing a backward tuxedo. • Bobolinks are not commonly seen in Alberta, and only the occasional male is spotted singing atop a swaying roadside bush. • Male Bobolinks execute their promiscuous breeding strategies with a certain zest. Their enthusiasm is short-lived, however, because their plumage and attitude soon fade when summer wanes and the fields turn gold. • The paraphrase of the Bobolink's song given below is from the poem 'Robert of Lincoln,' by American William Cullen Bryant. Some people think that the name of this bird is an abbreviation of 'Robert O. Lincoln,' but others think it is a reference to the bird's song.

♂

♀

breeding

Nesting: on the ground, among tall grass; well-concealed cup nest is loosely woven with coarse grass, plant stems and fine materials; female incubates 5 or 6 eggs for 10–13 days.

Feeding: gleans the ground and low vegetation for adult and larval invertebrates; also eats many seeds.

Voice: banjo-like twangs: *bobolink bobolink spink spank spink.*

Similar Species: *Lark Bunting* (p. 319): male lacks the yellow nape and white rump; females are very similar. *Savannah Sparrow* (p. 320): faint breast streaks; yellow lore. *Vesper Sparrow* (p. 317): faint breast streaks; white outer tail feathers. *Grasshopper Sparrow* (p. 322): white belly; golden orange in the face.

Best Sites: Pincher Creek; Beaverhill Lake; very localized—ask experienced birders for tips.

ID: *Breeding male:* black bill, head, wings, tail and underparts; buff nape; white rump and wing patch. *Breeding female:* mottled brown overall; streaked back, flank and rump; pale eyebrow; dark eye line; light central crown stripe bordered by brown stripes.
Non-breeding male: similar to breeding female, but darker above and golden-buff below.
Size: *L* 15–20 cm.
Status: uncommon from late May to August.
Habitat: tall, grassy meadows, prairies, hayfields and croplands.

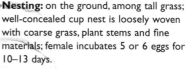

RED-WINGED BLACKBIRD

Agelaius phoeniceus

No cattail marsh in Alberta is free from the classic calls and bossy, aggressive nature of the Red-winged Blackbird. The male's bright red shoulders and short, raspy song are his most important tools in the often intricate strategy he uses to defend his territory from rivals. In experiments, males whose red shoulders were painted black soon lost their territories to rivals that they had previously defeated. • Male Red-winged Blackbirds arrive at the marshes and wetlands of Alberta a week or so before the females. In the females' absence, the males stake out territories through song and visual displays. A flashy and richly voiced male who has managed to establish a large and productive territory can attract several mates to his cattail estate. After been courted so glamorously, the females do all the work, weaving a nest amidst the cattails. Her cryptic colouration enables her to sit like a camouflaged cork on the nest, blending perfectly with the surroundings.

♂

♀

ID: *Male:* all-black, except for the large, red shoulder patch edged in yellow (occasionally concealed). *Female:* heavily streaked underparts; mottled brown upperparts; faint red shoulder patch; light eyebrow.
Size: L 19–24 cm.
Status: very common from mid-April to October.
Habitat: cattail marshes, wet meadows, croplands and shoreline shrubs.
Nesting: colonial and polygynous; in cattails or shoreline bushes; nest is woven with dried cattail leaves and grass and lined with grass and soft materials; female incubates 3 or 4 eggs for 10–12 days.

Feeding: gleans the ground for seeds, waste grain and invertebrates; also gleans vegetation, catches insects in flight and eats berries; occasionally visits feeding stations during migration.
Voice: loud, raspy *konk-a-ree* or *eat my CHEEzies*.
Similar Species: male is distinctive (when shoulder patch shows). *Brewer's Blackbird* (p. 349) and *Rusty Blackbird* (p. 348): females lack the streaked underparts.
Best Sites: any cattail marsh.

WESTERN MEADOWLARK
Sturnella neglecta

A meadowlark's song is like a stream of music being poured from a pitcher. The Western Meadowlark's trademark tune is the voice of Alberta's grasslands, ringing from fenceposts and powerlines across the flat landscape in spring. • The meadowlark's yellow breast, with its black V, and its white outer tail feathers serve to attract mates. Potential partners face one another, raise their bills high and perform a grassland ballet. • Oddly, the colourful breast and white tail feathers are also used to attract the attention of potential predators. Foxes, hawks and falcons focus on these bold features in pursuit, so the meadowlark can mysteriously disappear into the grass whenever it chooses to turn its back or fold away its white tail flags. • The Western Meadowlark was overlooked by the Lewis and Clark expedition, which mistakenly thought it was the same species as the Eastern Meadowlark. This oversight is represented in the scientific name *neglecta*.

breeding

ID: *Sexes similar:* yellow underparts; broad, black bib; mottled brown upperparts; short tail; long, pinkish legs; yellow lore; brown crown stripes and eye line; white outer tail feathers; black spotting on the white flanks; slender bill.

Size: L 20–25 cm.

Status: common from late March to October.

Habitat: croplands, agricultural areas, grasslands and roadsides.

Nesting: in a dry depression or scrape on the ground; domed nest, with a side entrance, is woven

into the surrounding vegetation with grass and plant stems; female incubates 3–7 eggs for 13–15 days.

Feeding: walks or runs along the ground, gleaning grasshoppers, crickets and spiders off the grass and the ground; also eats seeds.

Voice: rich series of flute-like warbles.

Similar Species: none.

Best Sites: roadsides throughout the grassland region.

YELLOW-HEADED BLACKBIRD
Xanthocephalus xanthocephalus

In a perfect world, the Yellow-headed Blackbird would have a song to match its splendid plumage. Unfortunately, when the male arches his golden head backward, he struggles to produce a painful pathetic grinding noise. Although the song of the Yellow-headed Blackbird might be the worst in North America, its quality soon becomes an appreciated aspect of its marshy home—together with the smell, the insects and the overall sogginess. • Where Yellow-headed Blackbirds occur with Red-winged Blackbirds, the larger Yellow-head dominates, commandeering the centre of the wetland and pushing the Red-wings to the periphery. • A large cattail marsh is often highlighted by the well-spaced presence of male Yellow-headed Blackbirds perched high atop the plants like candle flames. They might fly aggressively at intruders, but if a male enters a neighbour's territory, he will be pursued in turn. • *Xanthocephalus* means 'yellow-headed.'

ID: *Male:* yellow head and breast; otherwise black; white wing patches; black lore; long tail; black bill. *Female:* dusky brown overall; yellow breast, throat and eyebrow; hints of yellow in the face.

Size: *L* 20–28 cm.

Status: common from mid-April to September.

Habitat: cattail marshes, croplands, shoreline vegetation and ranchlands.

Nesting: loosely colonial; in cattail marshes and shoreline shrubs; bulky, deep basket nest, usually woven into emergent plants

over water, is made with wet vegetation, which tightens when dry; female incubates 3–5 eggs for 11–13 days.

Feeding: gleans the ground for seeds, beetles, snails, waterbugs and dragonflies; also probes into cattail heads for larval invertebrates.

Voice: strained, metallic grating that seems prolonged by the bird's unmusical efforts.

Similar Species: male is distinctive. *Rusty Blackbird* (p. 348) and *Brewer's Blackbird* (p. 349): females lack the yellow throat and face.

Best Sites: Kinbrook Island PP; Clifford E. Lee Nature Sanctuary.

RUSTY BLACKBIRD
Euphagus carolinus

The Rusty Blackbird owes its name to the colour of its fall plumage, but its name could just as well reflect this bird's grating, squeaky song, which sounds very much like a rusty hinge. • Unlike other blackbirds, the Rusty Blackbird is not a significant 'nuisance' bird, because it tends to avoid human-altered environments. Overshadowed by all other typical blackbirds in Alberta in both abundance and aggressiveness, the Rusty Blackbird is the subdued member of the group. • When Rusty Blackbirds are migrating, they use a wide variety of habitats, but they typically roost in marshy or swampy areas. • *Euphagus* means 'good eater,' which is a rather puzzling name. It might reflect the habit of early ornithologists to eat their specimens. (They saved the skins, of course.)

♀

♂

breeding

ID: *General:* yellow eyes; dark legs and bill. *Breeding:* dark plumage; male is darker and has a subtle green gloss. *Non-breeding:* rusty wings, back and crown; male is darker; female has buffy underparts.
Size: *L* 23 cm.
Status: uncommon from mid-April to October.
Habitat: beaver ponds, roadsides, landfills, wet meadows and shoreline shrubs.
Nesting: in a shrub or small tree, often near water; bulky nest

is woven with twigs and lichens, with an inner cup of mud and grass; female incubates 4 or 5 eggs for 14 days.
Feeding: walks along shorelines, gleaning waterbugs, beetles, dragonflies, snails, grasshoppers and small fish; also eats waste grain and seeds.
Voice: call is like a rusty door hinge.
Similar Species: *Brewer's Blackbird* (p. 349): male has 'whiter' eyes and glossier plumage; female has dark eyes. *Common Grackle* (p. 350): keeled tail; larger body and bill size.
Best Sites: Kinbrook Island PP; cattle feed lots.

BREWER'S BLACKBIRD
Euphagus cyanocephalus

The Brewer's Blackbird is the drier-land counterpart to its marsh-loving Rusty relative. It looks like a Red-winged Blackbird without the red shoulder patches, but the Brewer's feathers actually show an iridescent quality as reflected rainbows of sunlight move along the feather shafts. The Brewer's Blackbird jerks its head back and forth as it walks, which can help separate it from other blackbirds. • Brewer's Blackbirds are frequently seen throughout summer along roadside shoulders, confidently strutting in defiance of nearby, rapidly moving vehicles. These birds have taken advantage of a fairly recent feeding opportunity—roadkilled insects—and they have also invaded many of our city parks. Elsewhere, they spend winters at ski lodges, scavenging whatever leavings they can find. • John J. Audubon named this bird after his friend and prominent oologist (student of eggs) Thomas Mayo Brewer.

ID: *Male:* glossy black plumage; dark blue on the head; green body iridescence; yellow eyes. *Female:* flat brown plumage; black eyes.
Size: L 20–25 cm.
Status: common from mid-April to October.
Habitat: wet meadows, grasslands, roadsides, landfills, stockyards and shrublands.
Nesting: loosely colonial; on the ground or in a shrub or small tree; well-built cup nest is woven with twigs, grass, mud, roots

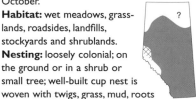

and fur; female incubates 4–6 eggs for 12–14 days.
Feeding: walks along shorelines and open areas, gleaning invertebrates and seeds.
Voice: song is a creaking, 2-noted *k-shee*.
Similar Species: *Rusty Blackbird* (p. 348): longer, more slender bill; lacks the blue and green gloss in the plumage; female has yellow eyes. *Common Grackle* (p. 350): much longer, keeled tail; heavier bill. *Brown-headed Cowbird* (p. 351): shorter tail; male has black eyes and a brown head.
Best Site: Drumheller area.

COMMON GRACKLE

Quiscalus quiscula

The Common Grackle is a poor but spirited, singer. Usually while perched in a shrub, a male grackle will slowly take a deep breath that inflates his breast and causes his feathers to rise; then he closes his eyes and gives out a loud, surprising *swaaaack*. Despite our perception of the Common Grackle's musical weakness, the male proudly poses with his bill held high after his 'song.' • In Alberta, Common Grackles are most frequently encountered in rural areas, where small flocks might band together to take over birdfeeders. Even the normally assertive jays yield feeding rights to these cocky and aggressive birds. • In September, many species of blackbirds flock together prior to their southward migration. The birds gather in croplands and marshy areas, where they gorge themselves on the fall harvest. • In flight, the grackle's long tail trails behind it like a hatchet blade. • *Quiscalus* means 'quail.' It is an odd name for a grackle, which does not resemble a quail in any way.

ID: *Sexes similar:* glossy black plumage; overall purple iridescence; long, keeled tail; yellow eyes; heavy bill; female is smaller and duller than the male. *In flight:* tail resembles a flattened, vertical rudder.

Size: *L* 28–34 cm.

Status: uncommon to common from April to September.

Habitat: fields, wet meadows, urban areas, shorelines and willow shrublands.

Nesting: semi-colonial; in a tree, often near water; bulky cup nest is made of twigs, grass, mud, feathers and occasionally human-made trash; female incubates 3–6 eggs for 12–14 days.

Feeding: slowly struts along the ground, gleaning, snatching and probing for insects, earthworms, seeds, grain and fruit; also catches insects in flight and eats small vertebrates, including bird eggs.

Voice: call is a quick, loud *swaaaack*.

Similar Species: *Rusty Blackbird* (p. 348) and *Brewer's Blackbird* (p. 349): smaller; lack the heavy bill and the keeled tail. *Red-winged Blackbird* (p. 345): shorter tail; male has a red shoulder patch. *European Starling* (p. 275): very short tail; long, thin bill.

Best Site: Kinbrook Island PP.

BROWN-HEADED COWBIRD
Molothrus ater

The Brown-headed Cowbird's song, a bubbling *glug-ah-whee*, might translate to other birds as 'here-comes trouble!' Historically, Brown-headed Cowbirds followed bison herds—now they follow cattle—and their nomadic lifestyle makes it impossible for them to tend a nest. Instead, cowbirds engage in 'nest parasitism,' laying their eggs in the nests of other songbirds. Many of the parasitized songbirds do not recognize the cowbird eggs and incubate them and raise the young cowbirds as their own. The rapidly growing cowbird chick frequently outsizes its foster parent, whose own offspring often get squeezed out of the nest or die from lack of food.
• The expansion of ranching and the fragmentation of forests has significantly increased the Brown-headed Cowbird's range, and it now parasitizes more than 140 bird species in North America, including species that probably had no contact with it 300 years ago.

ID: *Male:* glossy, green-black plumage; soft brown head; short, squared tail; dark eyes; conical bill. *Female:* grey-brown overall; slight streaking on the underparts; dark eyes.
Size: L 15–20 cm.
Status: common from late April to September.
Habitat: fields, shrublands, forest edges, roadsides, mountain meadows, landfills, campgrounds, day-use areas and near large mammals.
Nesting: does not build a nest; female lays up to 40 eggs a year in the nests of other birds, usually laying 1 egg per nest, but exceptionally up to 8 (probably from several different cowbirds); eggs hatch after 10–13 days.

Feeding: gleans the ground for seeds, waste grain and invertebrates, especially grasshoppers, beetles and true bugs.
Voice: call is a squeaky, high-pitched *wee-tse-tse*; song is a high, gurgling *bubble-bubble-zeee*.
Similar Species: *Rusty Blackbird* (p. 348) and *Brewer's Blackbird* (p. 349): lack the contrasting brown head and darker body; slimmer bills; longer tails. *Common Grackle* (p. 350): much longer tail; larger.
Best Sites: stockyards.

BALTIMORE ORIOLE
Icterus galbula

It is a wonderful thing when someone does a double-take at a Baltimore Oriole. Major League Baseball has made this bird surprisingly easily to identify: the male's vivid colours strike a distinctive pattern. • Scientists have gone around in circles for years trying to decide whether Alberta's orioles comprise one species or two. Currently, our orioles are separated into two species, but it is apparent that they can and do interbreed in more than a casual way. When the Baltimore Oriole and the Bullock's Oriole were grouped together, they were called the Northern Oriole. • Irishman George Calvert, the Baron of Baltimore, established a colony in Maryland. Mark Catesby, one of America's first naturalists, chose this bird's name because the male's plumage mirrored the colours of the baron's coat of arms. • 'Oriole' is derived from words meaning 'golden bird.'

ID: *Male:* black head, throat, back, wings and central tail feathers; brilliant orange underparts, wing patches, rump and outer tail feathers; small, white wing patches. *Female:* olive brown upperparts, darkest on the head; dull orange underparts.
Size: *L* 18–20 cm.
Status: uncommon to common from late May to August.
Habitat: deciduous, riparian and mixed forests.
Nesting: high in a deciduous tree, suspended from a branch; hanging pouch nest is woven with fine plant fibres, hair, string and fishing line and lined with fine grass and fur; female incubates 4–6 eggs for 12–14 days.
Feeding: gleans canopy vegetation and shrubs for caterpillars, beetles, wasps and other invertebrates; also eats fruit and nectar; visits hummingbird feeders and feeding stations that offer orange halves.
Voice: song consists of slow, clear, purposeful whistles: *peter peter here here peter.*
Similar Species: *Bullock's Oriole* (p. 353): orange cheek; large, white wing patch. *Black-headed Grosbeak* (p. 341): heavy, conical bill; darker orange plumage; broad, white wing patches. *Western Tanager* (p. 310): yellow body plumage; lacks the black head.
Best Sites: Miquelon Lake PP; Dinosaur PP.

BULLOCK'S ORIOLE
Icterus bullockii

The male Bullock's Oriole has a striking, Halloween-style, black-and-orange plumage that flashes like embers amidst the treetops while his sibilant whistles drip to the ground. In early spring, female Bullock's Orioles sing also—a rare phenomenon among birds. • Bullock's Orioles are far less common in Alberta than their Baltimore brethren, but they can be sighted with some regularity in the lower reaches of prairie river valleys, among the cottonwoods and tangled bushes. • Alberta lies at a crossroads for many birds with closely related eastern and western forms. For this reason, Alberta birdwatchers are among those most affected when taxonomists change bird species names (such as when the Northern Oriole was reclassified as two species, the Baltimore Oriole and the Bullock's Oriole). Of course, the birds themselves are oblivious to their status and concern themselves only with habitat, food, reproduction and predators. • In naming this bird, William Swainson honoured a Mexican father-and-son team of amateur naturalists, both of whom were named William Bullock.

ID: *Male:* bright orange eyebrow, cheek, underparts, rump and outer tail feathers; black throat, eye line, cap, back and central tail feathers; large, white wing patch. *Female:* dusky yellow face, throat and upper breast; grey underparts; olive-grey upperparts and tail; small, white wing patches.
Size: *L* 18–22 cm.
Status: rare to uncommon from late May to August.
Habitat: deciduous riparian forests, willow shrublands and urban areas.
Nesting: high in a deciduous tree, suspended from a branch; hanging pouch nest is woven with fine plant fibres, hair, string and fishing line and lined with horsehair, plant down, fur and moss; female incubates 4 or 5 eggs for 12–14 days.

Feeding: gleans canopy vegetation and shrubs for caterpillars, beetles, wasps and other invertebrates; also eats fruit and nectar; occasionally visits feeding stations that offer hummingbird feeders and orange halves.
Voice: accented series of 6–8 whistled, rich and guttural notes.
Similar Species: *Baltimore Oriole* (p. 352): lacks the orange cheek and the large, white wing patch. *Black-headed Grosbeak* (p. 341): heavy, conical bill; black cheek; darker underparts. *Western Tanager* (p. 310): yellow body plumage; lacks the black cap and throat.
Best Sites: Milk River valley; South Saskatchewan River valley; Waterton Lakes NP.

353

GRAY-CROWNED ROSY-FINCH
Leucosticte tephrocotis

The breeding grounds of the Gray-crowned Rosy-Finch lie high in the Rockies, where the air is thin and the wind is frigid. There, these alpine breeders nest on isolated islands of tundra that are sprinkled with fragile flowers. • The Gray-crowned Rosy-Finch is the most widely distributed of the three rosy-finches. Until recently, these birds were classified as a single species, the Rosy Finch, but geographic breeding isolation is thought to contribute to the unique features of the three forms. The other two rosy-finches are the Brown-capped Rosy-Finch of the southern U.S. Rockies and the Black Rosy-Finch of the Great Basin and the northern U.S. Rockies. • During summer, rosy-finches develop rodent-style cheek pouches that allow them to carry larger amounts of insects to their rapidly developing young. • When the bite of fall weather becomes too much for them, these finches spill out of the attics of the Rockies to flock together at lower elevations. A few of these birds spend winter in Alberta on chinook-warmed slopes and at feeding stations in the foothills, but most leave the province for better climes to the south.

ID: *Sexes similar:* dark bill; black forehead; grey crown; rosy shoulder, rump and belly; brown cheek, back and breast; black legs; dark tail and flight feathers.

Size: L 14–17 cm.

Status: locally common from mid-March to October; a few might overwinter.

Habitat: mountain meadows, alpine tundra, avalanche slopes, roadsides and occasionally towns.

Nesting: on the ground, among rocks or in a crevice; bulky nest is made of moss, grass, fur and feathers; female incubates 4 or 5 eggs for 12–14 days.

Feeding: gleans small seeds from the ground or snow; occasionally visits feeders.

Voice: calls are high, chirping notes and a constant chattering; song is a long, goldfinch-like warble.

Similar Species: none.

Best Sites: Sunshine Meadows and Lake Louise area, Banff NP; Crowsnest Pass (migration).

PINE GROSBEAK

Pinicola enucleator

It is a great moment in a typical Alberta winter when the Pine Grosbeaks emerge from the wilds to settle on your backyard feeder. They might hang around for the entire winter or, in typical irruptive fashion, disappear suddenly. • When birders are out 'pining' for grosbeaks, the prize is the sight of a mature male. Search the tops of spruce and pine trees—the spires are favourite perching sites for this grosbeak. The male's splendid red plumage strikes a vivid contrast against the snow and spruce bows. • Cold pedestrians can be warmed somewhat by the soft warbles these birds sing during the coldest days. Many a mistaken Albertan has seen the red breast, heard the lovely song and announced: 'The robins have come back early this year!' • Pine Grosbeaks breed in Alberta, but their nesting territories are so remote that most observations of them are made against a snowy backdrop. • *Pinicola* is Latin for 'pine dweller'; *enucleator* is Latin for 'one who takes off shells.'

ID: *General:* stout, conical, dark bill; white wing bars; black wings and tail. *Male:* rosy red head, underparts and back. *Female* and *Immature:* rusty crown, face and rump; ashy grey back and underparts.

Size: *L* 20–25 cm.

Status: uncommon to common year-round.

Habitat: spruce-fir forests; townsites from fall to spring.

Nesting: in a conifer or tall shrub; bulky cup nest is loosely made of twigs, moss, grass, lichens and fur; female incubates 4 eggs for 13–15 days.

Feeding: gleans buds, berries and seeds from trees; also forages on the ground; visits feeding stations in winter.

Voice: song is a short, musical warble.

Similar Species: *White-winged Crossbill* (p. 360): much smaller; lacks the stubby bill. *Evening Grosbeak* (p. 365): female has a light-coloured bill and broad, white wing patches.

Best Sites: Banff NP; backyard feeders in winter; highly variable from year to year.

PURPLE FINCH
Carpodacus purpureus

The courtship of Purple Finches is a gentle and appealing ritual. The liquid warbling song of the male bubbles through conifer boughs, announcing his intentions to receptive mates. When a female approaches, the colourful male dances lightly around her, quickly beating his wings until he softly lifts into the air. • The Purple Finch's gentle nature and simple but stunning plumage endears it to bird-watchers. It occasionally visits city backyard feeders in migration, but it can be found around rural feeders throughout summer. • Purple Finches prefer to nest in conifers, but they tend to forage in deciduous forests. • Purple (*purpureus*) is an overstated description of this bird's delicate colour. Roger Tory Peterson said it best when he described the Purple Finch as a sparrow dipped in raspberry juice.

ID: *Male:* light bill; raspberry red head, throat, breast and nape; brown-and-red-streaked back and flanks; reddish-brown cheek; red rump; notched tail; light, unstreaked belly and undertail coverts. *Female:* dark brown cheek and jaw line; white eyebrow and 'drool'; heavily streaked underparts; unstreaked under-tail coverts.
Size: *L* 13–15 cm.
Status: uncommon to common from late April to October; a few overwinter.
Habitat: pine, spruce and mixed forests and townsites.

Nesting: in a conifer, far from the trunk; tight cup nest is woven with twigs, grass, moss, lichens and fur; female incubates 4 or 5 eggs for 13 days.
Feeding: gleans the ground and vegetation for seeds, buds, berries and insects; readily visits feeding stations.
Voice: song is a bubbly, continuous warble; call is a single metallic *cheep* or *weet.*
Similar Species: *House Finch* (p. 358): squared tail; male lacks the reddish cap; female lacks the distinct cheek patch. *Cassin's Finch* (p. 357): male has a brown nape and lightly streaked, brown flanks; female lacks the distinct cheek patch and has streaked undertail coverts.
Best Sites: Fish Creek PP; Beaverhill Lake.

CASSIN'S FINCH
Carpodacus cassinii

In Waterton, the Cassin's Finch is the townsite's most common bird—but only for a few short days. This bird moves through the park in spring, and its mass migrations often find it in town for a short time. On those days, it seems that scarcely a tree, not to mention a feeder, is free of this near look-alike to the Purple Finch. (The Purple Finch does not regularly occur in Alberta's southern Rockies, so if you think you've seen one, double-check to make sure it's not a Cassin's.) Once the Cassin's Finch has moved off to the high country to breed, it is more difficult to find, but it bubbling courtship song serves as a pleasant reminder of its time in the lowlands. • The Cassin's Finch is not a terribly energetic bird—individuals might perch in place for minutes at a time. • John Cassin was a leading bird taxonomist in the 19th century; his name graces five species of birds. Coincidentally, the Cassin's Vireo shares much of the same range in Alberta as the Cassin's Finch.

ID: *Male:* reddish crown, throat and rump; brown nape; white underparts; streaked undertail coverts and flanks; deeply notched tail; mottled brown upperparts. *Female:* indistinct facial patterning; streaked undertail coverts; finely streaked underparts.
Size: *L* 15–16 cm.
Status: locally uncommon from late May to October; a few might overwinter.
Habitat: *Summer:* spruce-fir forests. *Migration:* townsites.
Nesting: on an outer limb in a conifer; cup nest is woven with grass, moss, bark shreds, fur and small roots; female incubates 4 or 5 eggs for 12–14 days.
Feeding: eats mostly seeds, but also eats insects and buds in spring and berries in winter; often visits birdfeeders.
Voice: call is a 2-syllable *kee-up*; song is a long, varied warble.
Similar Species: *Purple Finch* (p. 356): male has a reddish nape and flanks; female has a distinct cheek patch and unstreaked undertail coverts. *House Finch* (p. 358): squared tail; male has a brown cap; female has heavily streaked underparts.
Best Sites: Waterton Lakes NP; Crowsnest Pass.

357

HOUSE FINCH
Carpodacus mexicanus

Before cities began to dot North America's soil, the House Finch was restricted to the American Southwest. Then, during the 1920s and 1930s, it became a popular cage bird and was sold across the continent as the 'Hollywood Finch.' Releases of cage birds in the East and expansion of the House Finch from its historic range into farmlands and cities in the West have resulted in two separate distributions that are converging like a zipper along the Rocky Mountains. The birds seen in Alberta come from both populations, and they are being encountered with increasing frequency. It is likely that the increasing abundance of this finch will be met warmly by Albertans, because these colourful birds will add character and song to our neighbourhoods. • The expansion of the House Finch's range illustrates both the intentional and indirect results of human influence on wildlife communities.

ID: *General:* streaked undertail coverts; square tail. *Male:* brown cap; red eyebrow, forecrown, throat and breast; heavily streaked flanks. *Female:* indistinct facial patterning; heavily streaked underparts.
Size: L 13–15 cm.
Status: increasingly common year-round.
Habitat: cities, towns and agricultural areas.
Nesting: in a cavity, building, dense foliage or abandoned bird nest; cup nest is woven with grass, twigs, leaves, fur and string; female incubates 4 or 5 eggs for 12–14 days.
Feeding: gleans vegetation and the ground for seeds; visits feeding stations.
Voice: song is a warble lasting about 3 seconds, with the last note usually rising.
Similar Species: *Cassin's Finch* (p. 357): notched tail; male has a reddish cap and finely streaked flanks; female has finely streaked underparts. *Purple Finch* (p. 356): notched tail; male has a reddish upper back and flanks; female has a distinct cheek patch.
Best Sites: birdfeeders in Calgary, Lethbridge and Medicine Hat.

RED CROSSBILL
Loxia curvirostra

Red Crossbills are the great gypsies of the bird world, coming and going in response to food availability. These nomads scour Alberta's forests for pine cones, and if they discover a bumper crop they might breed regardless of the season—it is not unusual to hear them singing in mid-winter. Look for this species in pine forests, near sources of mineralized water, to which they will descend from the trees for a drink. • The strangely shaped bills of crossbills are clearly an adaptation for prying open conifer cones to get at the seeds tucked under each scale. There are few other birds in Alberta that are as closely tied to a single food source. • The two species of crossbill that occur in Alberta have different habitat preferences, so they rarely flock with one another. • The scientific name *curvirostra* is Latin for 'curve-billed.'

♂

ID: *General:* crossed bill tips. *Male:* dull orange-red to brick red plumage; dark wings and tail; always has colour on the throat. *Female:* olive-grey to dusky yellow plumage; plain, dark wings. *Immature:* streaked underparts; otherwise resembles the female.

Size: *L* 14–17 cm.

Status: uncommon to common year-round.

Habitat: coniferous forests, especially lodgepole pine, but also spruce-fir forests.

Nesting: on an outer branch in a conifer; cup nest is loosely woven with twigs, grass, moss, fur

and bark strips; female incubates 3 or 4 eggs for 12–18 days; can breed at any time of the year.

Feeding: primarily conifer seeds (especially pine); also eats buds, deciduous tree seeds and occasionally insects; often licks road salt or minerals in soil; rarely visits feeders.

Voice: distinctive call note: *jip-jip;* song is a varied warble (similar to other finches).

Similar Species: *White-winged Crossbill* (p. 360): 2 broad, white wing bars. *Pine Siskin* (p. 363): similar to immature Red Crossbill, but lacks the crossed bill and is smaller.

Best Sites: mostly seen in the mountains; Sibbald Flats, Kananaskis Country.

WHITE-WINGED CROSSBILL
Loxia leucoptera

Birdwatchers frequently measure the 'exoticity' of a bird by its bill. The bills of toucans, hornbills and cassowaries are elaborate, but they are not as odd as those of the crossbills. White-winged Crossbills primarily eat spruce seeds, and their bills are perfectly designed to pry open the cones. • Crossbills overwinter in flocks. The presence of a foraging group high in a spruce tree creates an unforgettable shower of spruce cone scales and crackling chatter. Like many finches, they can be abundant one winter and nearly absent the next. • When not foraging in spruce spires, White-winged Crossbills are frequently seen licking salt from winter roads. This dangerous habit results in many birds dying from vehicle collisions. • Crossbills can either be right-billed or left-billed; there seems to be no advantage either way in their cone prying ways. • The scientific name *leucoptera* means 'white wing.'

ID: *General:* crossed bill tips; 2 bold, white wing bars. *Male:* reddish-pink overall; black wings and tail. *Female:* dusky yellow overall; slightly streaked underparts; dark wings and tail. *Immature:* like the female, but more heavily streaked.
Size: L 15–17 cm.
Status: uncommon to common year-round.
Habitat: coniferous forests, primarily spruce-fir, and occasionally townsites and deciduous forests.

Nesting: on an outer branch in a conifer; cup nest is loosely woven with twigs, grass, moss, fur, cocoons and bark strips; female incubates 4 eggs for 12–14 days.
Feeding: prefers conifer seeds (mostly spruce and fir); also eats deciduous tree seeds and occasionally insects; occasionally licks salt and minerals from roads.
Voice: call is composed of harsh *chet* notes; song is a high-pitched series of trills.
Similar Species: *Red Crossbill* (p. 359): lacks the white wing bars; male is paler. *Pine Grosbeak* (p. 355): much larger; lacks the crossed bill tips.
Best Sites: Sir Winston Churchill PP; Edmonton (winter); mountain parks (year-round); highly irruptive.

COMMON REDPOLL

Carduelis flammea

A predictably unpredictable winter visitor, the Common Redpoll is seen in Alberta in varying numbers. It might appear in flocks of hundreds or in groups of a dozen or less, depending on the year. Redpolls might seem to have good winter survival skills, but they are in constant danger of running out of fuel and dying from hypothermia, so they are almost always eating, gleaning waste grain from bare fields or stocking up at winter feeders. Because of their focus on food, wintering redpolls are remarkably fearless of humans, as long as you move slowly and unthreateningly. • The Common Redpoll's light, fluffy body allows it to 'float' on the softest snowbanks without sinking beyond its belly. • Common Redpolls sometimes breed in Alberta, but most of the birds that appear during winter nest far to the north. • The scientific name *flammea,* Latin for 'flame,' refers to this bird's red cap.

ID: *Sexes similar:* red forecrown (cap); black chin; pale bill; streaked rump; lightly streaked flanks. *Male:* breast is often pinkish. *Female:* light grey breast.

Size: *L* 13–14 cm.

Status: common from October to April.

Habitat: open fields, meadows, roadsides, townsites, railways and forest edges.

Nesting: on a platform of twigs in a shrub or among rocks; cup nest is woven with small roots, grass, lichens and moss and thickly lined with feathers; female incubates 4 or 5 eggs for 10–11 days.

Feeding: gleans the ground, snow and vegetation in large flocks for seeds, especially birch; visits feeding stations.

Voice: song is a twittering series of trills; calls are a soft *chit-chit-chit-chit* and a faint *swe-eet*; indistinguishable from the Hoary Redpoll.

Similar Species: *Hoary Redpoll* (p. 362): unstreaked rump; very faintly streaked flanks; generally paler. *Pine Siskin* (p. 363): heavily streaked overall; yellow flashes in the wings and tail.

Best Sites: Elk Island NP; summer cottage villages (winter); irruptive.

HOARY REDPOLL

Carduelis hornemanni

During winter, great flocks of redpolls descend into birch trees or onto feeders along forest edges in Alberta. Mixed in with the abundant Common Redpolls, you will often see a more lightly coloured bird with an unstreaked rump. The Great Redpoll Debate predictably ensues as birdwatchers compare notes on the ambiguous field marks of these two species. Things were simpler when the two redpolls were considered a single species. • The Hoary Redpoll is one of the most northerly wintering songbirds. It survives the cold only by replenishing its energy reserves daily. Redpolls are so well insulated, however, that a dead bird found frozen outside can take several days to thaw at room temperature. (At least, that's what we've been told.) • Jens Wilken Hornemann was one of Denmark's leading botanists, and he helped organize an expedition to Greenland, where the first scientific specimen of this bird was taken.

ID: *Sexes similar:* red forecrown (cap); black chin; yellow bill; pale plumage overall; lightly streaked flanks; unstreaked rump. *Male:* pinkish-tinged breast. *Female:* light grey breast.
Size: L 13–14 cm.
Status: rare to uncommon from October to April.
Habitat: meadows, open fields, roadsides, townsites, railways and forest edges.
Nesting: does not nest in Alberta.
Feeding: gleans the ground, snow and vegetation in flocks for seeds and buds; occasionally visits feeding stations.
Voice: song is a twittering series of trills; calls are a soft *chit-chit-chit-chit* and a faint *swe-eet*; indistinguishable from the Common Redpoll.
Similar Species: *Common Redpoll* (p. 361): streaked rump; more heavily streaked flanks; red cap is often less defined. *Pine Siskin* (p. 363): very heavily streaked; yellow flashes in the wings and tail.
Best Sites: summer cottage villages (winter); irruptive.

PINE SISKIN
Carduelis pinus

You can spend days, weeks and months in pursuit of Pine Siskins, or you can set up a finch feeder filled with niger seed and wait for them to appear. Pine Siskins will visit feeders at just about any time of year, but they will disappear just as suddenly as they appeared. • Tight flocks of these gregarious birds are frequently heard before they are seen. Their characteristic *zzweeeet* call starts off slowly and then climbs to a high-pitched climax. Once you recognize this distinctive call, you can confirm the presence of these finches by looking for a flurry of activity in the treetops that shows occasional flashes of yellow. • The Pine Siskin's wardrobe might be sparrow-like, but its behaviour reveals the soul of a goldfinch. After the first hard-won identification, you will encounter Pine Siskins surprisingly frequently in coniferous woodlands, forest edges and other areas that previously seemed not to have these birds. • Prior to recent taxonomic changes, the Pine Siskin had the coolest scientific name of all: *Spinus pinus*.

ID: *Sexes similar:* heavily streaked underparts; yellow at the base of the tail feathers and in the wings (easily seen in flight); dull wing bars; darker, heavily streaked upperparts; slightly forked tail; indistinct facial pattern. *Immature:* dull white in the wings and tail.
Size: *L* 11–13 cm.
Status: uncommon to common year-round.
Habitat: coniferous and aspen forests, forest edges, meadows, townsites, roadsides, agricultural areas and grasslands.
Nesting: occasionally loosely communal; often on an outer branch in a conifer; flat nest is woven with grass and small roots and lined with fur and feathers; female incubates 3 or 4 eggs for 13 days.

Feeding: gleans the ground and vegetation for seeds, buds, thistle seeds and some insects; attracted to road salts, mineral licks and ashes; regularly visits feeding stations.
Voice: song is a coarse but bubbling expression; call is a prolonged, accelerating, rising *zzweeeet.*
Similar Species: *Common Redpoll* (p. 361) and *Hoary Redpoll* (p. 362): red cap; no yellow in the wings. *Purple* (p. 356), *Cassin's* (p. 357) and *House* (p. 358) *finches:* females have a thicker bill and no yellow in the wings or tail.
Best Sites: irruptive in the foothills and mountains.

AMERICAN GOLDFINCH
Carduelis tristis

The American Goldfinch is a bright, cheery songbird that is commonly seen in weedy fields, roadsides and backyards in summer. It often feeds on thistle seeds and flutters over fields in a distinctive, undulating flight style, filling the air with its jubilant *po-ta-to-chip* call. • The American Goldfinch delays nesting until June to ensure a dependable source of thistles and dandelion seeds to feed to its young. It is enjoyable to watch a flock of goldfinches rain down to ground level and poke at the heads of dandelions. The birds often have to step down on the flowerheads so that they can reach the seeds with their bills. A dandelion-filled lawn seems less weedy with a flock of yellow goldfinches hopping among the similarly coloured flowers. • The male's black cap and wings distinguish him from the other yellow birds that are also mistakenly called 'wild canaries.' • The scientific name *tristis,* Latin for 'sad,' refers to the goldfinch's voice. It is an unfair tribute to this pleasing and playful bird.

breeding

ID: *Breeding male:* black forehead, wings and tail; bright yellow body; white wing bars, undertail coverts and tail base; orange bill and legs. *Non-breeding male:* olive brown back; yellow-tinged head; grey underparts. *Female:* yellow-green upperparts and belly; yellow throat and breast.
Size: *L* 11–14 cm.
Status: common from late May to September; a few might overwinter.
Habitat: open forests, fields, meadows, roadsides and townsites.

Nesting: in a fork in a shrub or dense bush; cup nest is tightly woven with plant fibres, grass and spider silk and lined with fur; female incubates 4–6 eggs for 10–12 days.
Feeding: gleans vegetation for seeds, primarily thistle, birch and alder, as well as for insects and berries; commonly visits feeding stations.
Voice: calls are *po-ta-to-chip* (often delivered in flight) and *dear-me, see-me*; song is varied and long, with trills, twitters and sibilant notes.
Similar Species: *Evening Grosbeak* (p. 365): much larger; massive bill. *Wilson's Warbler* (p. 307): greenish wings without wing bars; thin bill.
Best Sites: Dinosaur PP; Elk Island NP; Gooseberry Lake PP.

EVENING GROSBEAK

Coccothraustes vespertinus

Unannounced, a flock of Evening Grosbeaks descends one chilly December day on a rural birdfeeder filled with sunflower seeds. For the proprietor of the feeder, the gold-and-black grosbeaks are both an aesthetic blessing and a financial curse. The birds will eat an incredible amount of birdseed and then suddenly disappear in late winter, in an expression of their wild and independent spirit. • The Evening Grosbeak nests in northern Alberta, and it sometimes visits feeders in August, but it is during winter that these glorious snow birds are most often encountered. Large irruptions of Evening Grosbeaks occur every two to three years, but some long-time naturalists moan that we haven't had a really big year for a few decades now. • The Evening Grosbeak's bill can exert an incredible force per unit area—it might be the most powerful of any North American bird. • It was once thought that the Evening Grosbeak sang only in the evening, a fact that is reflected in both its common and scientific names *(vespertinus* is Latin for 'of the evening').

ID: *General:* massive, light-coloured, conical bill; black wings and tail; broad, white wing patches. *Male:* black crown; yellow eyebrow; dark brown head gradually fades into the golden-yellow belly and lower back. *Female:* grey head and upper back; yellow-tinged underparts; white undertail coverts.

Size: L 18–22 cm.

Status: uncommon, but erratic, year-round.

Habitat: *Summer:* open coniferous forests. *Winter:* townsites, cottages and deciduous forests.

Nesting: on an outer limb in a conifer; flimsy cup nest is loosely woven with twigs, small roots, plant

fibres and grass; female incubates 3 or 4 eggs for 11–14 days.

Feeding: gleans the ground and vegetation for seeds, buds and berries; also eats insects and licks mineral-rich soil; visits feeding stations for sunflower seeds.

Voice: song is a wandering warble; call is a loud, sharp *clee-ip.*

Similar Species: *American Goldfinch* (p. 364): much smaller; small bill; smaller wing bars. *Pine Grosbeak* (p. 355): female has a black bill and smaller wing bars.

Best Sites: Fort Vermillion (summer); Turner Valley and Athabasca areas (winter); irruptive.

HOUSE SPARROW

Passer domesticus

Since its introduction to North America in the 1850s, the House Sparrow has managed to colonize most human-altered environments on the continent. This rowdy and raucous bird first began making inroads into Alberta in 1898, and since that time it has become one of our most abundant and conspicuous backyard species. People with a dislike for this introduced 'avian mouse' go to amazing lengths to combat the species, but House Sparrows are here to stay. • The House Sparrow was introduced around Brooklyn, New York, as part of a plan to control the numbers of insects that were damaging grain and cereal crops. Contrary to popular opinion at the time, the diet of these Eurasian sparrows is largely vegetarian, and their impact on crop pests has been minimal. • House Sparrows are not closely related to the other North American sparrows; they belong to the family of Old World sparrows (Passeridae).

ID: *Breeding male:* grey crown; black bib and bill; chestnut nape; light grey cheek; white wing bar; dark, mottled upperparts; grey underparts. *Non-breeding male:* smaller black bib; light-coloured bill. *Female:* plain grey-brown overall; buffy eyebrow; streaked upperparts; indistinct facial patterns; greyish, unstreaked underparts.
Size: *L* 14–17 cm.
Status: abundant year-round.
Habitat: townsites, agricultural areas, railyards and developed areas; absent from undeveloped areas.

Nesting: often communal; in a nest box, natural cavity or building; when not in a cavity, a large, dome-shaped nest is woven with grass and other plant fibres; female incubates 4–6 eggs for 10–13 days.
Feeding: gleans the ground and vegetation for seeds, insects and fruit; frequently visits feeding stations.
Voice: familiar, plain *cheep-cheep-cheep-cheep.*
Similar Species: male is distinctive; female is distinctively drab.
Best Site: your backyard.

ACCIDENTAL BIRD SPECIES

All these birds have been recorded in Alberta fewer than 10 times. The reports are documented by photographs or specimens or are sightings accepted by the Alberta Rare Bird Committee.

LITTLE BLUE HERON (*Egretta caerulea*): The closest breeding locales are in Texas and Oklahoma. There are very few records for Alberta, including one photo record.

TRICOLORED HERON (*Egretta tricolor*): Typically a year-round resident of the southern Atlantic and Gulf Coast states. There is only one photo record for Alberta. (Formerly know as the Louisiana Heron.)

GREEN HERON (*Butorides virescens*): There are several possible occurrences from the southern half of Alberta, including Calgary and Banff National Park, which might represent wandering individuals from breeding populations in Washington State or the Dakotas.

MUTE SWAN (*Cygnus olor*): A few city parks in Alberta (such as Calgary and Camrose) have 'domesticated' Mute Swans, and the few occurrences of birds in the wild might represent escapees from these or out-of-province sites. Mute Swans are native to Europe.

GARGANEY (*Anas querquedula*): This Eurasian species of waterfowl occasionally occurs in North America, particularly in Alaska. A few spring reports in Alberta seem to represent wild birds and not escapees. Most reports are from the southern half of the province.

TUFTED DUCK (*Aythya fuligula*): This duck is a Eurasian relative of our scaups. The Tufted Duck occurs regularly in Alaska, and it has reached Alberta at least once—it was recorded east of Calgary in early May.

KING EIDER (*Somateria spectabilis*): An immature male from the Calgary area, collected in 1894, is the only evidence of this bird's occurrence in Alberta. Reportedly, a possible mature male was seen with that individual.

COMMON EIDER (*Somateria mollissima*): This species of sea duck nests in the Arctic and winters on both coasts. It typically migrates at sea, but a single bird has been reported from Alberta during the fall migration.

COMMON CRANE (*Grus grus*): A single individual of this Eurasian species was seen in 1957 and 1958. The sightings were from Lethbridge to Athabasca, but it was likely the same individual bird, thought to be migrating to Alaska. No Common Cranes have been recorded since then.

PACIFIC GOLDEN-PLOVER (*Pluvialis fulva*): One confirmed Alberta specimen exists of this Alaska-breeding species, which typically migrates over the Pacific Ocean to the Hawaiian Islands and beyond. This species very closely resembles the American Golden-Plover, especially in fall plumage.

MONGOLIAN PLOVER (*Charadrius mongolus*): This species was photographed only once in Alberta, north of Fort McMurray. The Mongolian Plover is a Eurasian shorebird that occasionally wanders to Alaska and along the Pacific coast.

WANDERING TATTLER (*Heteroscelus incanus*): This species nests along gravelly streams in northern B.C., the Yukon and Alaska, and it winters off the coasts of California and Mexico. There are one specimen, one photo record and several sightings from Alberta.

SURFBIRD (*Aphriza virgata*): Surfbirds generally migrate between the Pacific coast and the mountains of Alaska and the Yukon. One was photographed in Alberta at Beaverhill Lake.

CURLEW SANDPIPER (*Calidris ferruginea*): A Eurasian species that very rarely breeds in northern Alaska, the Curlew Sandpiper has been recorded throughout much of North America, including just a few times in Alberta.

POMARINE JAEGER (*Stercorarius pomarinus*): For a number of years in Alberta, there have been probable records for this species by individuals very familiar with jaegers. The first documented evidence of a Pomarine Jaeger came in November 1996, when an individual was accidentally shot.

LITTLE GULL (*Larus minutus*): This primarily Old World species breeds in the Great Lakes area and is locally common on the East Coast during winter. There are a small number of reports from Alberta, including at least one photograph.

ICELAND GULL (*Larus glaucoides*): This species from the eastern Arctic is thought to freely hybridize with the Thayer's Gull, and it very closely resembles the Thayer's Gull and the Glaucous Gull. There are very few records from Alberta, including at least one photograph.

LESSER BLACK-BACKED GULL (*Larus fuscus*): This Eurasian species regularly occurs as a non-breeder on the East Coast. There are several reports of this bird from Alberta, including a photo record.

GREAT BLACK-BACKED GULL (*Larus marinus*): The great gull of the East Coast has been reported from Cold Lake on two occasions and photographed once. It regularly occurs as far west as Niagara Falls.

BLACK-LEGGED KITTIWAKE (*Rissa tridactyla*): This gull, which typically lives on open oceans, was first confirmed in Alberta in 1976 from Calgary. Several other records include ones from Jasper National Park and Wabamun Lake. Most records have been during fall.

IVORY GULL (*Pagophila eburnea*): The Ivory Gull is a small Arctic bird that typically does not venture very far inland. There is some evidence of it from Alberta, including one photograph of an immature individual.

BLACK GUILLEMOT (*Cepphus grylle*): A single Black Guillemot was found dead in Alberta. This seabird is restricted to salt water, and even inland records on the West Coast are highly unusual.

LONG-BILLED MURRELET (*Brachyramphus perdix*): The Long-billed Murrelet is a seabird of the Asian Pacific. The single specimen that has been found in Alberta was in the early stages of decomposition.

ANCIENT MURRELET (*Synthliboramphus antiquus*): The Ancient Murrelet holds the title as the most frequently seen alcid in Alberta. Two specimens and a few photographs have documented the occurrence of this bird in the province. Most observations have occurred during fall.

WHITE-WINGED DOVE (*Zenaida asiatica*): A single White-winged Dove regularly came to a feeder in the town of Slave Lake, and it was photographed several times. The White-winged Dove is typically found at its northern limit in southern New Mexico, Arizona and California.

YELLOW-BILLED CUCKOO (*Coccyzus americanus*): A few records exist for this species in Alberta, including photographs of one in Elk Island National Park and one specimen record. This bird, which reaches the northwestern limit of its breeding range in the Dakotas and eastern Montana, very closely resembles the Black-billed Cuckoo in appearance and habits.

WESTERN SCREECH-OWL (*Otus kennicottii*): The Western Screech-Owl reaches the eastern limit of its range to the southwest of Alberta. A breeding record from Banff National Park in 1897 might refer to this species rather than to the Eastern Screech-Owl. These two screech-owls were only recently split into separate species, and any screech-owls encountered in Alberta should be well documented.

WHITE-THROATED SWIFT (*Aeronautes saxatalis*): This swift is common in mountains and rocky canyons, and its typical range ends just south of Alberta. There is one verified sight record of this species from Alberta.

GREEN VIOLET-EAR (*Colibri thalassinus*): This species is probably the most unexpected bird so far documented in Alberta. The Green Violet-ear is a tropical hummingbird that only rarely crosses the Mexican border into the United States. The Alberta records are of a bird photographed in Peter Lougheed Provincial Park. It apparently remained there from August to December, 1993.

ANNA'S HUMMINGBIRD (*Calypte anna*): There have been several reports of this hummingbird in Alberta, mostly from the mountains southwest of Calgary. There is a photo record from the Turner Valley. The Anna's Hummingbird is a year-round resident along the southern coast of B.C.

COSTA'S HUMMINGBIRD (*Calypte costae*): The only record for this bird from Alberta was documented with a photograph. The Costa's Hummingbird typically inhabits dry desert-scrub habitats in southern Arizona and California.

RED-BREASTED SAPSUCKER (*Sphyrapicus ruber*): This West Coast species has only been seen a few times in Alberta, and it was officially recorded only once, from Lethbridge. This colourful woodpecker breeds through central B.C. and winters along the Pacific coast.

WILLIAMSON'S SAPSUCKER (*Sphyrapicus thyroideus*): The nearest breeding populations of the Williamson's Sapsucker are in northwestern Montana. It has been recorded a few times in Alberta, usually in spring and from the southwestern parts of the province. There is one specimen from Calgary.

PACIFIC-SLOPE FLYCATCHER (*Empidonax difficilis*): There is little information about the status of the Pacific-slope Flycatcher in Alberta, because, only a short time ago, it and the Cordilleran Flycatcher were considered one species—the Western Flycatcher. Song dialects might be the best was to determine whether or not some of the Cordilleran Flycatchers in Alberta are actually Pacific-slope Flycatchers.

SCISSOR-TAILED FLYCATCHER (*Tyrannus forficatus*): This species is the most spectacular North American flycatcher. It has been reported from Alberta from as far back as 1943. A photograph of one was taken in 1986, thereby offering some support to the rumors of this distinctive species's occasional presence.

PLUMBEOUS VIREO (*Vireo plumbeus*): With the recent splitting of the Solitary Vireo complex into the Blue-headed, Plumbeous and Cassin's vireos, it is not known for certain whether or not the Plumbeous Vireo is part of our provincial fauna. Birds fitting its field characteristics have been sighted from the Rockies in southern Alberta, but it is unclear whether these are Plumbeous Vireos, intergrades or variants of the Blue-headed or Cassin's vireos.

CANYON WREN (*Catherpes mexicanus*): This inconspicuous wren of steep, shady canyons and cliffs typically reaches its northern limit in southwestern Montana. There is at least one confirmed sight record from Alberta.

CAROLINA WREN (*Thryothorus ludovicianus*): The only report from Alberta of this small songbird, which typically breeds as far west as the American Midwest, was of a singing individual near Medicine Hat.

BLUE-GRAY GNATCATCHER (*Polioptila caerulea*): This bird was recorded in two consecutive years from Inglewood Bird Sanctuary in Calgary. Typically, Blue-gray Gnatcatchers breed as close as Minnesota or Wyoming. Reports of them in Alberta are usually from fall.

NORTHERN WHEATEAR (*Oenanthe oenanthe*): This thrush breeds in Alaska and the Yukon and winters in Eurasia. A single Northern Wheatear was photographed near Calgary in 1989.

WOOD THRUSH (*Hylocichla mustelina*): Typically ranging as far west as Manitoba and Minnesota, the Wood Thrush is the voice of eastern hardwood forests. A single individual, recorded in Lethbridge during the fall of 1980, was the first record from Alberta. A single bird was caught in a mist net in October 1997, in Edmonton.

BENDIRE'S THRASHER (*Toxostoma bendirei*): A Bendire's Thrasher was photographed in Jasper National Park in 1988. No other reports of this bird exist from Alberta.

NORTHERN PARULA (*Parula americana*): This eastern warbler has been seen in Alberta by several experienced birdwatchers. A specimen has existed since 1958, and birds have been observed periodically from the southern half of the province.

BLACK-THROATED GRAY WARBLER (*Dendroica nigrescens*): Black-throated Gray Warblers breed from the West Coast to the interior of B.C. There have been numerous sight reports and one tape recording of this bird from Alberta, but there have been no photo or specimen records to date.

PINE WARBLER (*Dendroica pinus*): There is one specimen and several sight records of the Pine Warbler from Alberta, primarily during fall. This bird typically ranges as far west as Manitoba.

KENTUCKY WARBLER (*Oporornis formosus*): Typically ranging only as far west as the American Midwest, only one Kentucky Warbler has been recorded from Alberta. That individual was seen and photographed in Calgary by a number of observers.

HOODED WARBLER (*Wilsonia citrina*): This beautiful eastern wood warbler was photographed in the Cypress Hills in 1991. The Hooded Warbler typically does not range west of the American Midwest.

SUMMER TANAGER (*Piranga rubra*): There is one specimen of a male Summer Tanager in a museum in the St. Paul area. This species typically breeds no closer to Alberta than southern Utah.

SCARLET TANAGER (*Piranga olivacea*): Almost 10 sight records of the Scarlet Tanager exist from Alberta, and there is a specimen dating back to 1964. Most of the records are from southern Alberta, but they might also have been seen in the mountains.

GREEN-TAILED TOWHEE (*Pipilo chlorurus*): This bird typically lives in the arid American Southwest. There is one record from Calgary in 1996 and one other confirmed sighting in southern Alberta.

EASTERN TOWHEE (*Pipilo erythropthalmus*): The eastern version of the Spotted Towhee, this species was seen and photographed at a birdfeeder west of Edmonton in December 1994. The Eastern Towhee and the Spotted Towhee used to be grouped together as the Rufous-sided Towhee, so unusual observations of these birds should be carefully documented to help determine the status of Eastern Towhee in Alberta.

CASSIN'S SPARROW (*Aimophila cassinii*): This grassland sparrow typically breeds in the southern Great Plains, but it has been seen in Alberta at least once, near Empress. Also, there is a tape recording of the Cassin's Sparrow's distinctive song from Alberta.

BLACK-THROATED SPARROW (*Amphispiza bilineata*): This sparrow typically inhabits the arid American Southwest. There are two confirmed photo records and one sighting of the Black-throated Sparrow from Alberta.

DICKCISSEL (*Spiza americana*): One specimen of this grassland bird exists from Alberta. There have been very few sight records since the 1960s. The Dickcissel breeds as far west as southeastern Saskatchewan.

EASTERN MEADOWLARK (*Sturnella magna*): This species has been reported several times in Alberta, but because it looks extremely similar to the Western Meadowlark, many of these observations might not be valid. Based on vocalizations and careful identification, an Eastern Meadowlark was recorded near Rocky Mountain House in 1989. Any further sightings of this typically eastern bird will require photographic or sonographic documentation to confirm its status.

BRAMBLING (*Fringilla montifringilla*): This species has been documented photographically at least twice from Alberta. Both instances involved a bird visiting a feeder in winter. The Brambling is a Eurasian finch that is an irregular migrant in Alaska.

GLOSSARY

accipiter: a forest hawk (genus *Accipiter*); characterized by a long tail and short, rounded wings; feeds mostly on birds.

brood: *n.* a family of young from one hatching; *v.* sit on eggs so as to hatch them.

corvid: a member of the crow family (Corvidae); includes crows, jays, magpies and ravens.

covey: a brood or flock of partridges, quails or grouse.

crop: an enlargement of the esophagus; serves as a storage structure and (in pigeons) has glands that produce secretions.

dabbling: a foraging technique used by some ducks, in which the head and neck are submerged but the body and tail remain on the water's surface; dabbling ducks can usually walk easily on land, can take off without running and have brightly coloured speculums.

dimorphism: the existence of two distinct forms of a species, such as between the sexes.

eclipse: the dull, female-like plumage that male ducks briefly acquire after molting from their breeding plumage.

elbow patch: a dark spot at the bend of the outstretched wing, seen from below.

flycatching: a feeding behaviour where a bird leaves a perch, snatches an insect in mid-air and returns to the same perch; also known as 'hawking' or 'sallying.'

fledgling: a young chick that has just acquired its permanent flight feathers but is still dependent on its parents.

flushing: a behaviour where frightened birds explode into flight in response to a disturbance.

gape: the size of the mouth opening.

irruption: a sporadic mass migration of birds into a non-breeding area.

leading edge: the front edge of the wing as viewed from below.

litter: fallen plant material, such as twigs, leaves and needles, that forms a distinct layer above the soil, especially in forests.

lore: the small patch between the eye and bill.

molting: the periodic replacement of worn out feathers (often twice a year).

morphology: the science of form and shape.

nape: the back of the neck.

neotropical migrant: a bird that nests in North America but overwinters in the New World tropics.

niche: an ecological role filled by a species.

open country: a landscape that is primarily not forested.

parasitism: a relationship between two species in which one benefits at the expense of the other.

phylogenetics: a method of classifying animals that puts the oldest ancestral groups before those that have arisen more recently.

pishing: making a sound to attract birds by saying *pishhh* as loudly and wetly as possible.

polygynous: having a mating strategy where one male breeds with several females.

polyandrous: having a mating strategy where one female breeds with several males.

plucking post: a perch habitually used by an accipiter for plucking feathers from its prey.

raptor: a carnivorous (meat-eating) bird; includes eagles, hawks, falcons and owls.

rufous: rusty red in colour.

speculum: a brightly coloured patch in the wings of many dabbling ducks.

squeaking: making a sound to attract birds by loudly kissing the back of the hand, or by using a specially design squeaky bird call.

talons: the claws of birds of prey.

understorey: the shrub or thicket layer beneath a canopy of trees.

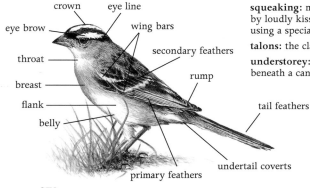

crown   eye line

eye brow   wing bars

throat   secondary feathers

breast   rump

flank

belly

tail feathers

undertail coverts

primary feathers

BIBLIOGRAPHY

American Ornithologists' Union. 1983. *Check-list of North American Birds*. 6th ed. (and its supplements). American Ornithologists' Union, Washington, D.C.

Bent, A. C. 1921–68. Life Histories of North American Birds Series. *U.S. National Museum Bulletin*. Washington, D.C.

Butler, J. 1989. *Alberta Wildlife Viewing Guide*. Lone Pine Publishing, Edmonton.

Campbell, R. W., N. K. Dawe, I. McTaggart-Cowan, J. M. Cooper, G. W. Kaiser and M. C. E. McNall. 1990. *The Birds of British Columbia: Volumes 1 & 2—Nonpasserines*. Royal British Columbia Museum, Victoria.

Chapman, F. M. 1968. *The Warblers of North America*. Dover Publishing, New York.

Dekker, D. 1991. *Prairie Water*. BST Publications, Edmonton.

Dunne, P., D. Sibley and C. Sutton. 1988. *Hawks in Flight*. Houghton Mifflin Co., Boston.

Ehrlich, R. R., D. S. Dobkin and D. Wheye. 1988. *The Birder's Handbook*. Fireside, New York.

Elphinstone, D. 1990. *Inglewood Bird Sanctuary: A place for all seasons*. Rocky Mountain Press, Calgary.

Evans, H. E. 1993. *Pioneering Naturalists: The Discovery and Naming of North American Plants and Animals*. Henry Holt and Co., New York.

Farrand, J., ed. 1983. *The Audubon Society Master Guide to Birding*. Vols. 1–3. Alfred A. Knopf, New York.

Godfry, W. E. 1986. *The Birds of Canada*. 2nd ed. National Museum of Natural Sciences, Ottawa.

Gotch, A. F. 1981. *Birds:Their Latin Names Explained*. Blandford Press, Dorset, England.

Gruson, E. S. 1972. *Words for Birds*. Quadrangle Books, New York.

Griscom, L., and A. Sprunt, Jr., eds. 1957. *The Warblers of America*. Doubleday and Co., Garden City, N.Y.

Holroyd, G. L., and H. Coneybeare. 1990. *The Compact Guide to Birds of the Rockies*. Lone Pine Publishing, Edmonton.

Holroyd, G. L., and K. J. Van Tighem 1983. *The Ecological (Biophysical) Land Classification of Banff and Jasper National Parks: Volume 3—The Wildlife Inventory*. Canadian Wildlife Service, Edmonton.

Kaufman, K. 1996. *Lives of North American Birds*. Houghton Mifflin Co., Boston.

Leahy, C. 1982. *The Birdwatcher's Companion*. Hill and Wand, New York.

Mearns, B., and R. Mearns. 1992. *Audubon to Xantus: The lives of those Commenmorated in North American Bird Names*. Academic Press, San Diego.

Peterson, R. T. 1990. *A Field Guide to the Western Birds*. 3rd ed. Houghton Mifflin Co., Boston.

Pinel, H. W., W. W. Smith and C. R. Wershler. 1991. *Alberta Birds, 1971-1980*. 2 vols. Provincial Museum of Alberta Natural History Occasional Paper No. 20. Edmonton.

Reader's Digest Association. 1990. *Book of North American Birds*. The Reader's Digest Association, Pleasantville, N.Y.

Richards, A. 1988. *Shorebirds of the Northern Hemisphere*. Dragon's World, Surrey, England.

Salt, W. R. 1973. *Alberta Vireos and Wood Warblers*. Provincial Museum and Archives of Alberta. Publication No. 3. Edmonton.

Salt, W. R., and J. R. Salt 1976. *The Birds of Alberta*. Hurtig Publishers, Edmonton.

Semenchuck, G. P., ed. 1992. *The Atlas of Breeding Birds of Alberta*. Federation of Alberta Naturalists, Edmonton.

Scott, S. S. 1987. *Field Guide to the Birds of North America*. National Geographic Society, Washington, D.C.

Slinger, J. 1996. *Down and Dirty Birding*. Fireside, New York.

Stokes, D., and L. Stokes. 1996. *Stokes Field Guide to Birds: Western Region*. Little, Brown and Co., Boston.

Terres, J. K. 1995. *The Audubon Society Encyclopedia of North American Birds*. Wings Books, New York.

Van Tighem, K. 1988. *Birding Jasper National Park*. Parks and People, Jasper, Alberta.

CHECKLIST

The following checklist will help you keep track of your birdwatching experiences in Alberta. Species with fewer than 10 confirmed records in our province are listed in italics.

Loons (Gaviidae)

- ❏ Red-throated Loon
- ❏ Pacific Loon
- ❏ Common Loon
- ❏ Yellow-billed Loon

Grebes (Podicipedidae)

- ❏ Pied-billed Grebe
- ❏ Horned Grebe
- ❏ Red-necked Grebe
- ❏ Eared Grebe
- ❏ Western Grebe
- ❏ Clark's Grebe

Pelicans (Pelecanidae)

- ❏ American White Pelican

Cormorants (Phalacrocoracidae)

- ❏ Double-crested Cormorant

Herons (Ardeidae)

- ❏ American Bittern
- ❏ Great Blue Heron
- ❏ Great Egret
- ❏ Snowy Egret
- ❏ *Little Blue Heron*
- ❏ *Tricolored Heron*
- ❏ Cattle Egret
- ❏ *Green Heron*
- ❏ Black-crowned Night-Heron

Ibises (Threskiornithidae)

- ❏ White-faced Ibis

Vultures (Cathartidae)

- ❏ Turkey Vulture

Waterfowl (Anatidae)

- ❏ Greater White-fronted Goose
- ❏ Snow Goose
- ❏ Ross's Goose
- ❏ Canada Goose
- ❏ Brant
- ❏ *Mute Swan*
- ❏ Trumpeter Swan
- ❏ Tundra Swan
- ❏ Wood Duck
- ❏ Gadwall
- ❏ Eurasian Wigeon
- ❏ American Wigeon
- ❏ American Black Duck
- ❏ Mallard
- ❏ Blue-winged Teal
- ❏ Cinnamon Teal
- ❏ Northern Shoveler
- ❏ Northern Pintail
- ❏ *Garganey*
- ❏ Green-winged Teal
- ❏ Canvasback
- ❏ Redhead
- ❏ Ring-necked Duck
- ❏ *Tufted Duck*
- ❏ Greater Scaup
- ❏ Lesser Scaup
- ❏ *King Eider*
- ❏ *Common Eider*
- ❏ Harlequin Duck
- ❏ Surf Scoter
- ❏ White-winged Scoter
- ❏ Black Scoter
- ❏ Oldsquaw
- ❏ Bufflehead
- ❏ Common Goldeneye
- ❏ Barrow's Goldeneye
- ❏ Hooded Merganser
- ❏ Red-breasted Merganser
- ❏ Common Merganser
- ❏ Ruddy Duck

Hawks & Eagles (Accipitridae)

- ❏ Osprey
- ❏ Bald Eagle
- ❏ Northern Harrier
- ❏ Sharp-shinned Hawk
- ❏ Cooper's Hawk
- ❏ Northern Goshawk
- ❏ Broad-winged Hawk
- ❏ Swainson's Hawk
- ❏ Red-tailed Hawk
- ❏ Ferruginous Hawk
- ❏ Rough-legged Hawk
- ❏ Golden Eagle

Falcons (Falconidae)

- ❏ American Kestrel
- ❏ Merlin
- ❏ Prairie Falcon
- ❏ Peregrine Falcon
- ❏ Gyrfalcon

Grouse & Allies (Phasianidae)

- ❏ Gray Partridge
- ❏ Ring-necked Pheasant
- ❏ Ruffed Grouse
- ❏ Sage Grouse
- ❏ Spruce Grouse
- ❏ Blue Grouse
- ❏ Willow Ptarmigan
- ❏ White-tailed Ptarmigan
- ❏ Sharp-tailed Grouse
- ❏ Wild Turkey

Rails & Coots (Rallidae)

- ❏ Yellow Rail
- ❏ Virginia Rail
- ❏ Sora
- ❏ American Coot

Cranes (Gruidae)

- ❏ Sandhill Crane
- ❏ *Common Crane*
- ❏ Whooping Crane

Plovers (Charadriidae)

- ❏ Black-bellied Plover
- ❏ *Pacific Golden-Plover*
- ❏ American Golden-Plover
- ❏ *Mongolian Plover*
- ❏ Semipalmated Plover
- ❏ Piping Plover
- ❏ Killdeer
- ❏ Mountain Plover

Stilts & Avocets (Recurvirostridae)

- ❏ Black-necked Stilt
- ❏ American Avocet

Sandpipers & Allies (Scolopacidae)

- ❏ Greater Yellowlegs
- ❏ Lesser Yellowlegs
- ❏ Solitary Sandpiper
- ❏ Willet
- ❏ *Wandering Tattler*
- ❏ Spotted Sandpiper
- ❏ Upland Sandpiper
- ❏ Eskimo Curlew
- ❏ Whimbrel
- ❏ Long-billed Curlew
- ❏ Hudsonian Godwit
- ❏ Marbled Godwit

❏ Ruddy Turnstone
❏ *Surfbird*
❏ Red Knot
❏ Sanderling
❏ Semipalmated Sandpiper
❏ Western Sandpiper
❏ Least Sandpiper
❏ White-rumped Sandpiper
❏ Baird's Sandpiper
❏ Pectoral Sandpiper
❏ Sharp-tailed Sandpiper
❏ Dunlin
❏ *Curlew Sandpiper*
❏ Stilt Sandpiper
❏ Buff-breasted Sandpiper
❏ Ruff/Reeve
❏ Short-billed Dowitcher
❏ Long-billed Dowitcher
❏ Common Snipe
❏ Wilson's Phalarope
❏ Red-necked Phalarope
❏ Red Phalarope

Gulls & Allies (Laridae)

❏ *Pomarine Jaeger*
❏ Parasitic Jaeger
❏ Long-tailed Jaeger
❏ Franklin's Gull
❏ *Little Gull*
❏ Bonaparte's Gull
❏ Mew Gull
❏ Ring-billed Gull
❏ California Gull
❏ Herring Gull
❏ Thayer's Gull
❏ *Iceland Gull*
❏ *Lesser Black-backed Gull*
❏ Glaucous-winged Gull
❏ Glaucous Gull
❏ *Great Black-backed Gull*
❏ *Black-legged Kittiwake*
❏ Sabine's Gull
❏ *Ivory Gull*
❏ Caspian Tern
❏ Common Tern
❏ Arctic Tern
❏ Forster's Tern
❏ Black Tern

Alcids (Alcidae)

❏ *Black Guillemot*
❏ *Long-billed Murrelet*
❏ *Ancient Murrelet*

Doves (Columbidae)

❏ Rock Dove
❏ Band-tailed Pigeon
❏ *White-winged Dove*
❏ Mourning Dove

Cuckoos (Cuculidae)

❏ Black-billed Cuckoo
❏ *Yellow-billed Cuckoo*

Owls (Strigidae)

❏ Eastern Screech-Owl
❏ *Western Screech-Owl*
❏ Great Horned Owl
❏ Snowy Owl
❏ Northern Hawk Owl
❏ Northern Pygmy-Owl
❏ Burrowing Owl
❏ Barred Owl
❏ Great Gray Owl
❏ Long-eared Owl
❏ Short-eared Owl
❏ Boreal Owl
❏ Northern Saw-whet Owl

Nightjars (Caprimulgidae)

❏ Common Nighthawk
❏ Common Poorwill

Swifts (Apodidae)

❏ Black Swift
❏ Vaux's Swift
❏ *White-throated Swift*

Hummingbirds (Trochilidae)

❏ *Green Violet-ear*
❏ Ruby-throated Hummingbird
❏ Black-chinned Hummingbird
❏ *Anna's Hummingbird*
❏ *Costa's Hummingbird*
❏ Calliope Hummingbird
❏ Rufous Hummingbird

Kingfishers (Alcedinidae)

❏ Belted Kingfisher

Woodpeckers (Picidae)

❏ Lewis's Woodpecker
❏ Red-headed Woodpecker
❏ Yellow-bellied Sapsucker
❏ Red-naped Sapsucker
❏ *Red-breasted Sapsucker*
❏ *Williamson's Sapsucker*
❏ Downy Woodpecker
❏ Hairy Woodpecker
❏ Three-toed Woodpecker
❏ Black-backed Woodpecker
❏ Northern Flicker
❏ Pileated Woodpecker

Flycatchers (Tyrannidae)

❏ Olive-sided Flycatcher
❏ Western Wood-Pewee
❏ Yellow-bellied Flycatcher
❏ Alder Flycatcher
❏ Willow Flycatcher
❏ Least Flycatcher
❏ Hammond's Flycatcher
❏ Dusky Flycatcher
❏ *Pacific-slope Flycatcher*
❏ Cordilleran Flycatcher
❏ Eastern Phoebe
❏ Say's Phoebe
❏ Great Crested Flycatcher
❏ Western Kingbird
❏ Eastern Kingbird
❏ *Scissor-tailed Flycatcher*

Shrikes (Laniidae)

❏ Northern Shrike
❏ Loggerhead Shrike

Vireos (Vireonidae)

❏ Blue-headed Vireo
❏ Cassin's Vireo
❏ *Plumbeous Vireo*
❏ Warbling Vireo
❏ Philadelphia Vireo
❏ Red-eyed Vireo

Jays & Crows (Corvidae)

❏ Gray Jay
❏ Steller's Jay
❏ Blue Jay
❏ Clark's Nutcracker
❏ Black-billed Magpie
❏ American Crow
❏ Common Raven

Larks (Alaudidae)

❏ Horned Lark

Swallows (Hirundidae)

❏ Purple Martin
❏ Tree Swallow
❏ Violet-green Swallow
❏ Northern Rough-winged Swallow
❏ Bank Swallow
❏ Barn Swallow
❏ Cliff Swallow

Chickadees (Paridae)

❏ Black-capped Chickadee
❏ Mountain Chickadee
❏ Chestnut-backed Chickadee
❏ Boreal Chickadee

Nuthatches (Sittidae)

- ❑ Red-breasted Nuthatch
- ❑ White-breasted Nuthatch

Creepers (Certhiidae)

- ❑ Brown Creeper

Wrens (Troglodytidae)

- ❑ Rock Wren
- ❑ *Canyon Wren*
- ❑ *Carolina Wren*
- ❑ House Wren
- ❑ Winter Wren
- ❑ Sedge Wren
- ❑ Marsh Wren

Dippers (Cinclidae)

- ❑ American Dipper

Kinglets (Regulidae)

- ❑ Golden-crowned Kinglet
- ❑ Ruby-crowned Kinglet

Gnatcatchers (Sylviidae)

- ❑ *Blue-gray Gnatcatcher*

Bluebirds & Thrushes (Turnidae)

- ❑ *Northern Wheatear*
- ❑ Eastern Bluebird
- ❑ Western Bluebird
- ❑ Mountain Bluebird
- ❑ Townsend's Solitaire
- ❑ Veery
- ❑ Gray-cheeked Thrush
- ❑ Swainson's Thrush
- ❑ Hermit Thrush
- ❑ *Wood Thrush*
- ❑ American Robin
- ❑ Varied Thrush

Starlings (Sturnidae)

- ❑ European Starling

Mimic Thrushes (Mimidae)

- ❑ Gray Catbird
- ❑ Northern Mockingbird
- ❑ Sage Thrasher
- ❑ Brown Thrasher
- ❑ *Bendire's Thrasher*

Pipits (Motacillidae)

- ❑ American Pipit
- ❑ Sprague's Pipit

Waxwings (Bombycillidae)

- ❑ Bohemian Waxwing
- ❑ Cedar Waxwing

Warblers (Parulidae)

- ❑ Tennessee Warbler
- ❑ Orange-crowned Warbler
- ❑ Nashville Warbler
- ❑ *Northern Parula*
- ❑ Yellow Warbler
- ❑ Chestnut-sided Warbler
- ❑ Magnolia Warbler
- ❑ Cape May Warbler
- ❑ Black-throated Blue Warbler
- ❑ Yellow-rumped Warbler
- ❑ *Black-throated Gray Warbler*
- ❑ Townsend's Warbler
- ❑ Black-throated Green Warbler
- ❑ Blackburnian Warbler
- ❑ *Pine Warbler*
- ❑ Palm Warbler
- ❑ Bay-breasted Warbler
- ❑ Blackpoll Warbler
- ❑ Black-and-white Warbler
- ❑ American Redstart
- ❑ Ovenbird
- ❑ Northern Waterthrush
- ❑ *Kentucky Warbler*
- ❑ Connecticut Warbler
- ❑ Mourning Warbler
- ❑ MacGillivray's Warbler
- ❑ Common Yellowthroat
- ❑ *Hooded Warbler*
- ❑ Wilson's Warbler
- ❑ Canada Warbler
- ❑ Yellow-breasted Chat

Tanagers (Thraupidae)

- ❑ *Summer Tanager*
- ❑ *Scarlet Tanager*
- ❑ Western Tanager

Sparrows & Allies (Emberizidae)

- ❑ *Green-tailed Towhee*
- ❑ *Eastern Towhee*
- ❑ Spotted Towhee
- ❑ *Cassin's Sparrow*
- ❑ American Tree Sparrow
- ❑ Chipping Sparrow
- ❑ Clay-colored Sparrow
- ❑ Brewer's Sparrow
- ❑ Timberline Sparrow
- ❑ Vesper Sparrow
- ❑ Lark Sparrow
- ❑ *Black-throated Sparrow*
- ❑ Lark Bunting
- ❑ Savannah Sparrow
- ❑ Baird's Sparrow
- ❑ Grasshopper Sparrow
- ❑ Le Conte's Sparrow
- ❑ Nelson's Sharp-tailed Sparrow

- ❑ Fox Sparrow
- ❑ Song Sparrow
- ❑ Lincoln's Sparrow
- ❑ Swamp Sparrow
- ❑ White-throated Sparrow
- ❑ Harris's Sparrow
- ❑ White-crowned Sparrow
- ❑ Golden-crowned Sparrow
- ❑ Dark-eyed Junco
- ❑ McCown's Longspur
- ❑ Lapland Longspur
- ❑ Smith's Longspur
- ❑ Chestnut-collared Longspur
- ❑ Snow Bunting

Grosbeaks & Buntings (Cardinalidae)

- ❑ Northern Cardinal
- ❑ Rose-breasted Grosbeak
- ❑ Black-headed Grosbeak
- ❑ Lazuli Bunting
- ❑ Indigo Bunting
- ❑ *Dickcissel*

Blackbirds & Allies (Icteridae)

- ❑ Bobolink
- ❑ Red-winged Blackbird
- ❑ *Eastern Meadowlark*
- ❑ Western Meadowlark
- ❑ Yellow-headed Blackbird
- ❑ Rusty Blackbird
- ❑ Brewer's Blackbird
- ❑ Common Grackle
- ❑ Brown-headed Cowbird
- ❑ Baltimore Oriole
- ❑ Bullock's Oriole

Finches (Fringillidae)

- ❑ *Brambling*
- ❑ Gray-crowned Rosy-Finch
- ❑ Pine Grosbeak
- ❑ Purple Finch
- ❑ Cassin's Finch
- ❑ House Finch
- ❑ Red Crossbill
- ❑ White-winged Crossbill
- ❑ Common Redpoll
- ❑ Hoary Redpoll
- ❑ Pine Siskin
- ❑ American Goldfinch
- ❑ Evening Grosbeak

Old World Sparrows (Passeridae)

- ❑ House Sparrow

INDEX OF SCIENTIFIC NAMES

This index references only the primary species accounts.

375

INDEX

INDEX OF COMMON NAMES

Page numbers in boldface type refer to the primary, illustrated species accounts.

ABOUT THE AUTHORS

Shelley Humphries

Portrait of the authors as young men. John Acorn (left); Chris Fisher (right).

Chris Fisher and John Acorn are both native Albertans, hailing from Lethbridge and Edmonton respectively. Both studied zoology at the University of Alberta, and both have done their graduate training there as well. Chris and John are keen naturalists, and they spend most of their spare time exploring the province in search of interesting birds, insects and other natural phenomena. Chris is perhaps best known for his books on bird identification, while John is host of the television series *Acorn, The Nature Nut* and *Twits and Pishers*. Together, they bring many decades of field experience to the making of this book, along with an understanding of how to teach birdwatching to beginners, based on innumerable field trips and classes. It is their hope that this book will serve you well as an introduction to the fascinating birds of Alberta.